Labanotation

Chapter 19. The following clarification in terminology has been established. The two main categories are called 'Flexion' and 'Extension'. 'Contraction' and 'Elongation' are movements on a straight path. 'Folding' (curving, arching) and 'Unfolding' are movements on a curved path. The term 'Bending' is often used for folding but is used too freely in general parlance to be a definitive term.

Chapters 24 and 25. Figure numbers 626-630 are duplicated on pages 410-413 and pages 415-419.

Page

69   The staple has been replaced by the caret meaning 'the same'. The direction symbols indicate whether position writing or movement writing is being used. Two examples are given here.

New 72d   New 74a

327   477d-f. Drawings are of the back of the hand.

332   In the current way of writing shifts the pre-sign is not modified; an equal sign (=) is placed within the direction symbol to indicate equal displacement.

New 488c

365   The preferred pins for floor plans are: ♂ = female, ♀ = male. At the 1989 ICKL conference it was agreed that ⊥ now means 'a person'.

391   595a. Hip signs are missing in the support columns.

404   614c. Add: or

431   649d. Wording should be: Face center (R side to L.O.D.)
      649e. Wording should be: Face wall (L side to L.O.D.)

451   679b. Unspecified sliding is usually written with ᴗ .

462   705b. Improved description:

New 795b

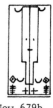

New 679b

Labanotation

or Kinetography Laban

**The System of Analyzing
and Recording Movement**

Third Edition, Revised

Ann Hutchinson

Illustrated by Doug Anderson

DANCE BOOKS
CECIL COURT, LONDON

Revised third edition published in 1977 by Theatre Arts Books

Reprinted in 1996
Dance Books Ltd
15 Cecil Court
London WC2N 4EZ

ISBN 0 903102 81 1

The principal centers of Labanotation (Kinetography Laban):

Dance Notation Bureau
31-33 West 21 Street, New York, NY

Dance Notation Bureau Extension
the Ohio State University

Language of Dance Centre
17 Holland Park, London W11 3TD

Laban Centre for Movement and Dance
Goldsmith College, University of London

Labanotation Institute
University of Surrey, Guildford, Surrey

Centre for Dance Studies
Les Bois St. Peter, Jersey Channel Islands, Great Britian

Centre Nationa d'Ecriture du Mouvement
Place St. Arnould, 6080000 Crepy-en-Valois, France

Table of Contents

Chapter

DEDICATION

This book is respectfully and affectionately dedicated to:

ALBRECHT KNUST

who has inspired us all by his example of
patience, logic and meticulous accuracy.
This book has drawn tremendously on his
knowledge and ideas.

LUCY VENABLE,
MURIEL TOPAZ, MIREILLE BACKER,
BILLIE MAHONEY and ALLAN MILES

who have each contributed immeasurably
to this book through their knowledge and
experience in using Labanotation as teach-
ers and notators and have helped to make
clear the needs this book must satisfy.

MARIA SZENTPAL
VALERIE PRESTON-DUNLOP and EDNA GEER

and other International Council of Kinetography
Laban colleagues who have helped in establishing
terminology and universal usage in the
"grammar" of Labanotation.

PHILIPPA HEALE

who helped so much with the organization
and coordination of this work.

Last, but not least, to the spirit of Fanny
Elssler who, keeping my husband Ivor
Guest engrossed, provided me much
needed time to work on this book!

ACKNOWLEDGEMENTS

This revised and expanded edition of LABANOTATION was made possible through the generosity of Marjorie and Irving Isaac and through a grant from the New York Foundation. In addition the author is grateful to the many members of the Dance Notation Bureau who contributed to the final funding of the work.

The preparation of the original edition of LABANOTATION was aided by a grant from the Rockefeller Foundation.

The author is particularly grateful to: Juli Nunlist, who went over the manuscript with a fresh eye and made many valuable suggestions; Terry Heard, who provided technical advice on mathematical terminology as well as proofreading and practical assistance; Maggie Burke, who drew the notation examples; Philippa Heale and Mary Ann Jones, who painstakingly "typeset" the manuscript, and who, together with my patient, understanding, and helpful husband, Ivor Guest, assisted continuously in countless ways.

The author is also pleased to acknowledge the aid she has had in referring to the following works: Handbook of Kinetography Laban by Albrecht Knust, Readers in Kinetography, Series B by Valerie Preston-Dunlop, and Marie Szentpal's correspondence course in the Laban system.

LABANOTATION (Kinetography Laban) conforms to the orthographic rules established by the Dance Notation Bureau, Inc. in conference with the International Council of Kinetography Laban (I.C.K.L.)

Author's Note to the Second Edition

In the fifteen years that have elapsed between publication of the original edition of the textbook "Labanotation" and the present publication, more has happened in the development of notation than during the previous three decades. The system itself has changed very little; rather, there has been a period of change in how notation is used and in approaches to movement analysis. Certain areas of transcription have required increased precision in recording detail, while other areas demanded broader over-all descriptions.

The intervening years have seen a tremendous advance in international exchange of ideas and experience in the whole field. The International Council of Kinetography Laban, founded in 1959, has brought together specialists in movement notation from many different countries who have benefited from each other's knowledge. Modifications in the system have resulted from a consensus of the most experienced research and field workers. Through the advent of Motif Writing, a specialized application of the system, the introduction of notation during the early stages in the study of dance and of dance composition is now possible. This provides the student with a greater insight into the nature of movement, as well as providing the tool of dance literacy from the start.

Because of the existence now of specialized Labanotation books and materials designed to fill the particular needs of different age levels, styles of dance, and areas of movement study, the aim of this book is to present the principles of the system in definitive terms with sufficient examples of its practical application to provide a firm foundation on which specialized skills may be built. Because each chapter progresses from a broad outline of the material at hand to specific detail in its application, the student may delve as lightly or as deeply as his needs demand. The teacher may modify the sequence of material to serve the interest of his students. Because so much separate reading material now exists only a few studies are given in this book. A second volume will deal with advanced material which is not presented in this book or is touched on only lightly. Albrecht Knust's dictionary of the system "A Handbook of Kinetography Laban," is a valuable companion book.

London, 1970   *Ann Hutchinson*

Preface by George Balanchine

The subject of dance notation has interested me since I first encountered it as a student at the Imperial Dancing Academy in Russia. At that time I studied the Stepanov method, a system based exclusively on the classic ballet vocabulary and unsuited for the recording of any other kind of dance. In spite of its limitations, knowledge of it made me aware of what was needed in a sound system of movement notation. Later, as a choreographer, I became more sharply aware of the need for an accurate and workable method for notating my works. To me, the prime requisite of such a notation system would be its ability to correlate faithfully the time values in the dance with the music, because my choreography either closely follows the line of the music or contrasts directly with it.

When I heard of Laban's system of notation it seemed the most completely developed method evolved to meet this need. After studying the system and watching Ann Hutchinson, America's leading notator and teacher, at work, I realized that this was indeed the answer and I decided to embark immediately on the long-range project of having my ballets recorded. "Symphony in C," "Orpheus," "Theme and Variations," "Symphonie Concertante," and "Bourrée Fantasque" are among those already completed. Thanks to these scores I am now assured that these ballets will be accurately performed in the future.

As the musician needs to record the precise and minute details of his composition to insure correct performance of his score, so the choreographer needs a notation capable of equal accuracy. While some people advocate the use of films to record ballet, I have found them useful only in indicating the style of the finished product and in suggesting the general over-all visual picture and staging. A film cannot reproduce a dance step by step, since the lens shoots from but one angle and there is a general confusion of blurred impressions which even constant re-showing can never eliminate. Labanotation records the structure of a dance, revealing with perfect clarity each of the specific movements of each performer.

Through Labanotation we can actually sit down and compare or analyze different styles of dance. Even the complicated techniques and studies take up little space and are easy to reconstruct intellectually through the notated patterns. There is no longer any need to wade through pages of verbal descriptions, which eventually become unintelligible.

In making the grant to Miss Hutchinson for the preparation of this book, the Rockefeller Foundation demonstrated its belief in the value of this system of notation and in the influence which its widespread use will have on the future development of dance. I am grateful for this belief and for the creative policy of this humanistic fund, for I am one of the choreographers who will benefit from the increased acceptance and use of Labanotation. I believe that it will soon be universally recognized as being as necessary to the dancer as musical notation is to the musician. Ann Hutchinson is the ideal person to have prepared this definitive text book, which will be of inestimable value to all persons working in the field of dance.

New York
April, 1954

Foreword by Rudolf Laban

Approximately two hundred years ago a writer on the manners and morals of the French court, J. P. Menetrier, complained that on the night tables of the ladies one could find many more choreographies than Bibles. It has to be surmised that these ladies were able to read the choreographies of dances written in the famous Beauchamps-Feuillet dance notation.* We assume that they could read them as fluently as music notation or ordinary writing, which were all subjects of their general education.

During the last fifty years an increasing number of people have had a nodding acquaintance with dance notation, and some are even convinced that written dance, or script-dance, is a cultural necessity of our time.

The author of this book, Ann Hutchinson, has for more than ten years contributed in a most efficient way to the spreading of script-dance in the United States. Miss Hutchinson and her numerous associates call this system of movement notation "Labanotation," in which title my own name is incorporated. I am most honoured, not only by this fact but also by her request that I write a few introductory words to her book.

In my early publications on this subject I have always stressed the point that the endeavour to describe the movements of a dance in special symbols has one main purpose. That is the creation of a literature of movement and dance. It is obvious that notation or

---

* Beauchamps was recognised in 1666 by a French Act of Parliament as the inventor of a system of dance notation. Feuillet published dances recorded in this notation a few decades later.

script facilitates the communication of movement ideas to other people. When, ages ago, mankind awoke to the idea of standardising pictures and signs in order to communicate certain ideas to one another, bodily actions and gestures were of course included from the very beginning. Early forms of writing are full of signs or symbols for action and movement. No form of writing could possibly omit the enormous number of verbs which, to a great extent, are always bodily actions involving movement. In my search for primary action signs, I found fascinating examples of movement description in the mantic symbols invented by ancient Tibetan monks and in the cuneiform characters of the Assyrians and Babylonians. In Egyptian and Chinese scripts I found a rich variety of movement symbols which are, in a sense, the archetypes of dance notation signs.

Noverre, the creator of the "Ballet d'Action," in which the rigid steps of his predecessors were liberated into a rich and all-round expression of the whole body, was a decided enemy of dance notation. He preferred to record the contents of his ballets in words. This is most regrettable for us because we have great difficulty in reconstructing his famous movement inventions from the contemporary drawings and illustrations of his productions. The dances written down by Feuillet do not need to be reconstructed, they can be simply read by anyone who takes the trouble to learn his system of notation.

In my newest book* on this subject I took the functional movement order on which Feuillet's notation is based as granted. His basic principles are universally valid and his system of notation is simple and rational - the egg of Columbus, as it were. One wonders that they were not discovered much earlier.

The first problem that faced modern notators of dance was to overcome the prejudice that a choreographic script is unable to describe all the subtle variations of movement in modern stage dancing and indeed in all other kinds of dance styles. Ballet, modern dance, folk and national dances, including all the historical and exotic forms of dancing which we study and perform today, cannot, it is true, be precisely fixed with Feuillet's restricted symbols, so the modern notator had to create a form of movement notation

---

* "Principles of Dance and Movement Notation " by Rudolf Laban (Macdonald & Evans, London, 1956).

which would be able to serve the purposes of industrial operations, of educational exercise and of psychological movement investigation.

So far as my own research is concerned, years of struggle were filled with the study of ancient movement symbols, with experiment and with controversial discussions. In the early twenties I decided to write two volumes containing the details of my investigations.* Only one volume appeared. Instead of the second volume, I compiled, a few years later, the first edition of the "Method and Orthography of Kinetography Laban."

Much has happened in the twenty-five years since the formulation of a contemporary dance-script became possible. The advent of a new generation of movement notators has made it possible to try out my ideas on a larger scale. My late friend and colleague, Dussia Bereska, who some forty years ago was the only supporter of my notation ideas and of my hope for a future script-dance literature, predicted the coming development with astonishing accuracy. To her are due my greatest thanks for the encouragement and advice which accompanied me on the thorny path of the first consolidation of the system.

In later years a number of enthusiastic supporters have helped to improve my first conception. A system of notation cannot arise from the solitary endeavour of one person only. The great merits of our senior dance notator, Albrecht Knust, are well-known, but people who have excelled chiefly in other fields of the dance as Kurt Jooss, Sigurd Leeder, Lisa Ullmann and others - have also contributed much to the early development of our system.

I have often been sceptical because I believed that it would be several generations before the creation of a dance literature could become a reality. However, we have moved on more quickly and here now, in 1954, is this book of Ann Hutchinson as a harbinger of things to come. Her activity as the founder and leader of the New York Dance Notation Bureau has everywhere awakened keen interest and appreciation. I can say that the gratitude of all people striving for the creation of a literature of dance and movement, with its own language and its own symbolic representation, is secured for this young author.

---

* "Choreographie" - First Volume, Publishers: Diedericks Jena, 1926

We must remember, too, that much has been collected and much is waiting to be published in the Dance Notation Bureau's desk and in many other places. A script-dance literature actually exists, if only in manuscript.

What do we expect to find in the script-dance libraries of the future? We surely need technical works on the orthography and proper use of the system. Training manuals are needed to develop capable notators. There must be books useful for spreading knowledge of movement and dance through the curricula of schools. Material on movement notations in industry and therapy, which younger notators have already begun to collect and record, will also have its place in future libraries and will indicate the possible ties for scientific· research in many fields, such as anthropology where the symbols of early times could be transcribed into the new idiom of modern dance notation.

The manifestation of human spirituality which has made dance a sister art of poetry and music can survive only if its products are written, printed and read by a large circle of laymen and performers. One could go on to describe what has to be done and what is partly already there, but unfortunately out of reach of the great public, such as a veritable encyclopaedia in many volumes by Albrecht Knust, in which all the possible variants of human movement are recorded. What the author of this present book, Ann Hutchinson, has already done in the field merits appreciation exceeding the limits of this foreword. I can only say that I heartily welcome this publication as an early flower in a fertile soil, where the productive spirit of our young dance creators and notators, I sincerely trust, will be able to plant solid roots.

Addlestone, Surrey
1954

Laban's death in 1958 has not diminished the constant growth of his influence as a major force in all movement research. The clarity and scope of his vision has inspired many others to carry on his work in a variety of fields. Though years ago Laban delegated responsibility for further development of the system of notation to Lisa Ullmann, Albrecht Knust, Sigurd Leeder and myself (the founding core members of the International Council of Kinetography Laban), this book, as its name suggests, stands as a tribute to this great man and an acknowledgement of our immeasurable debt to him. - Ann Hutchinson.

CHAPTER 1

A Brief History of Dance Notation

For at least five centuries attempts have been made to devise a system of movement notation. Some scholars believe that the ancient Egyptians made use of hieroglyphs to record their dances and that the Romans employed a method of notation for salutatory gestures. However, the earliest known attempt, recorded in two manuscripts preserved in the Municipal Archives of Cervera, Spain, dates from the second half of the fifteenth century. Since this time, many other systems have been devised. Some were published and achieved a measure of popularity for a while but all, until the present day, fell eventually into disuse.

It is significant that music notation, which opened the way for development in the art of music as we know it today, was first conceived in its modern form in the eleventh century, but was not established as a uniform system till the beginning of the eighteenth. Dance notation got off to a much later start and has undergone a long succession of false attempts.

That so many unsuccessful beginnings were made is not surprising. Dance is more complex than music because it exists in space as well as in time and because the body itself is capable of so many simultaneous modes of action. Consequently, the problems of formulating a movement notation that can be easily written and read are numerous.

Earlier methods were outgrowths of phases in the development of the dance itself, and, therefore, all of them ultimately failed because the continual expansion of the vocabulary made each system, in turn, outmoded. The three fundamental problems - recording complicated movement accurately, recording it in economical and legible form, and keeping up with continual innovations in move-ment - left dance notation in a state of flux, incapable of steady growth for centuries.

One of the first methods of notating dance - if it can be called a method - was the use of abbreviations for the names of steps, such as, R - reverencia, s - single, d - double, re - represa. This method presupposed a knowledge of the steps, and hence its limita-tions are obvious, but it flourished for about two hundred years.

The first book to define the many well known steps of the period was Thoinot Arbeau's "Orchesographie," published in 1588. Writ-ten descriptions of well-known positions and steps were accompa-nied by the name and by figure illustrations. His notation consist-ed of placing these names opposite the corresponding musical notes on which the given steps should be performed. Without Ar-beau's lengthy explanations of terms, the dances are unintelligible.

The development of professional dancing during the time of Louis XIV produced the first fully fledged system of notation. Based on an invention of Beauchamps, Raoul Feuillet first published the method "Chorégraphie, ou l'Art de décrire la Danse," in 1700. This was followed by several "Recueils des Danses" containing com-positions by Feuillet as well as by Louis Pécourt, a leading dancer and choreographer of the time. Thanks to Feuillet's notation, we can study the steps and dances which form the basis of the classi-cal ballet of today, but this system, although extremely well work-ed out, recorded little more than footwork and lacked a clear indi-cation of rhythm. It can be described as a "track drawing" method, the individual steps being represented on a drawing of the floor pattern made by the dancer. The book, however, obviously met the needs of the period, because translations appeared in England, Germany, Italy, and Spain and modifications of the system were well known throughout Europe until the end of the century.

The next device tried for a system of notation was based on the idea of stick figures depicting the various positions of the arms and legs. The dancer and choreographer Arthur Saint Léon pub-lished his book "Sténochorégraphie" in 1852. This placed the stick figures under the musical staff for clarification of timing. Another version of this system, published by Albert Zorn in 1887, was entitled "Grammatik der Tanzkunst." This attained a certain measure of success and was used as a textbook in dancing acade-mies in Europe. It was also published in English in the United

States in 1905. In spite of apparent immediate advantages, stick figure notation has three distinct drawbacks. It is usually drawn from the audience's point of view, so that right and left have to be reversed by the reader; the third dimension is not easily indicated and it gives a description of position rather than movement. Because timing must be indicated separately, only general indications of the timing of actions can be given.

The obvious need to indicate the accurate rhythm of movement led to the development of systems based on music notation. In the late nineteenth century, the most successful of these was that of Vladimir Stepanov, dancer and teacher at the Imperial Maryinsky Theatre in St. Petersburg. The title of his book, "Alphabet des Mouvements du Corps Humain," published in 1892, indicates his attempt to record the movements of the whole body in anatomical terms. The development of the system was limited by the early death of the inventor and the fact that it was used only as a ballet shorthand.

The idea of adapting music notes to meet the needs of describing movement has remained popular, but it has become ever more apparent that they are not sufficiently flexible in design to take care of the many needs in the field of movement notation.

Two systems concerned with universal aspects of movement appeared in 1928. Margaret Morris' book "Notation of Movement" is based on a sound anatomical analysis of movement, and illustrates the use of the system for many different forms of movement. The drawbacks in her system are its arbitrary choice of symbols, its asymmetrical indications of symmetrical positions and movements, and its need to indicate timing separately in a way that fails to show continuity and subtlety in the relative timing of actions.

"Schrifttanz" (written dance), the system by Rudolf von Laban, also first published in 1928, offers two innovations: the vertical staff to represent the body, which allows continuity as well as the correct representation of the right and left sides of the body, and elongated movement symbols, which, by their length, indicate the exact duration of any action. His analysis of movement, which is based on spatial, anatomical, and dynamic principles, is flexible and can be applied to all forms of movement.

During the decade between 1946 and 1956, two systems appeared based entirely on the mathematical description of movement in

terms of the degrees of a circle in a positive or negative direction.
The most complete of these, developed by Noa Eshkol and Abraham
Wachmann, published in 1958, deserves admiration for its accuracy in the form of movement description it employs. It is precise
in indicating timing, but it uses a cumbersome staff to represent
the body and does not allow movement to be described in terms familiar to dance, sports, or everyday life.

The desire for a quick means of recording ballet led to the development of the stick figure based system "Choreology," by Joan
and Rudolf Benesh, published in 1956. Adopted by the Royal Ballet
of England to fill its immediate needs in recording the repertoire,
the use of the system has spread to other ballet companies in different countries, notators being trained at the Institute of Choreology in London. Its analysis of movement is limited, because it
is based on the visual result of movement as seen by the outside
observer. While this method cleverly solved the problem of three-dimensional representation for general purposes, it did little to
improve timing problems inherent in a stick figure based notation.

Every few years a new system appears. Most fall back on one
or other of the devices already tried, and most favor one form of
dance. As modern technology develops, the emphasis is upon
mathematical systems which can be adapted to the computer. It is
essential, however, that the human aspect is not lost. The system
which can record objectively the changes in the angles of the limbs,
the paths in space, and the flow of energy and can also record the
movement motivation and the subtle expression and quality deserves special attention. Labanotation is such a system.

Because of his interest in movement in every phase of life - the
market place, the workshop, and the theatre - it was inevitable
that Laban should devise a system based not on any personal style
but on the universal laws of kinetics. His early interests had led
him to study all aspects of the theatre arts. At twenty-five, he
founded his own school in Munich where he developed his theories
of forms of movement in space (choreutics) and of the qualities of
movement (eukinetics). He later became director of movement at
the Berlin State Opera and thereafter held similar posts at other
state theatres. Laban spent his last years in England where, with
the businessman F. C. Lawrence, he examined the movements of
industrial workers and wrote the book "Effort." This study has
led to the present highly developed Effort-Shape analysis of move-

ment used for personnel assessment in business and also for medical and psychiatric purposes.

In the course of these varied activities, Laban formulated his
notation system, Kinetography Laban. Since the original text was
published tremendous strides have been made in the development of
the system, and it has been applied also to numerous other fields
of movement. Various individuals and dance centers both in
America and abroad have added their contributions. Acting as a
clearing house for ideas in the field, the Dance Notation Bureau Inc.
with headquarters in New York, is a non-profit, educational insti-
tution, founded in 1940, and dedicated to furthering the art of dance
through the use of a system of notation. The present day activities
of the Dance Notation Bureau have broadened to include acting as a
center for movement research and analysis as well as the practical
application of movement analysis, notation, and other recording devices in the performing arts and behavioural sciences. To this end
the Dance Notation Bureau has chosen to concentrate on the system
of analysing and recording movement which the members have determined to be the most effective and comprehensive - that originated by Laban. The Bureau works in cooperation with similar centers
in other countries and with the International Council of Kinetography
Laban (I.C.K.L.) for uniformity in usage and practice of the system.
Today Labanotation is comparable to music notation in its universal-
ity and application, and provides for movement a level of accuracy
and flexibility which music notation has yet to achieve.

CHAPTER 2

Introduction to Labanotation

Labanotation, or Kinetography Laban, is the system of recording movement originated by Rudolf Laban in the 1920's. By this scientific method all forms of movement, ranging from the simplest to the most complex, can be accurately written. Its usefulness to dancers is obvious. The system has also been successfully applied to every field in which there is the need to record motions of the human body - anthropology, athletics, and physiotherapy, to name just a few.

THE PRACTICAL APPLICATION OF LABANOTATION

A Means of International Communication

Labanotation is a triple-edged tool because it provides a means of recording movement on paper for future reference, a sound, fundamental analysis of movement and a carefully selected terminology which is universally applicable. It provides a universal understanding of movement and hence serves as a common "language" through which workers in all fields and in all countries can communicate. The system is, therefore, a "Rosetta stone" by which the kinetic content of all forms of movement and styles of dance can be understood. Common elements can be discerned and differences noted. Its nonverbal symbology poses no language barriers to international exchange and research.

A Dance Equivalent to Music Notation

Labanotation serves the art of dance much as music notation serves the art of music. The score plays an important part in the work of the composer, teacher, student, and, of course, performer. Because of the great wealth of printed music available, musicians have at their fingertips the works of great composers from previous eras and from other countries. The conductor or performer, wherever he may be, can obtain the score of Beethoven's piano sonatas or the latest work by Stravinsky. The student learns his instrument not only by practising exercises but also by playing the classics which are readily available in sheet music form. A parallel has now developed for the dance. Work in each comparable area - studying, teaching, rehearsing, and composing - is expedited through the use of notation.

A Means for the Preservation of Choreography

The use for movement notation which is immediately obvious is the preservation of choreography for future re-creation. This indeed was the purpose of each of the historical systems of dance notation. Because of the inadequacies of earlier methods of notation, we cannot be certain, even upon a careful reading of Feuillet for example, that eighteenth-century court dances are being reconstructed today precisely as they were originally performed. Details of style and execution were left unstated because knowledge of these was assumed. But generations to come will be able to dance choreographies of this period exactly as the choreographer would wish, for the professional notator of today works with the choreographer during the creative period, marking the directions as they are given to the dancers at the rehearsal, and adding as much or as little detail as the choreographer wishes. Every fine point of the correct performance is included to insure its proper re-creation in the future. Where only a general statement of movement is required in order to allow the performer freedom in interpretation, the notation can be handled accordingly, giving the reader the motive behind each movement without stating which specific form it should take.

An Adjunct to Films

A comparison between notation and film for the recording of movement is inevitable in any discussion of movement notation. Labanotation is a complement to film as a tool for movement analysis and choreographic preservation; neither can replace the other. A comparison with music makes the point for notation clear. Recorded music has not made the printed sheet unnecessary. A first impression of a musical work is best gained by hearing a performance of it, and, in the absence of a live performance, this will be a recording. But the study of the work itself for performance, for critical evaluation, or for educational purposes is still achieved through music notation. In dance, the film provides a similar record of a given performance of the work by a particular group under its director. The work itself is seen at second hand through the interpretation of that director and his company. All this quite apart from the practical advantage of paper and pencil in contrast to expensive photographic equipment, or the accessibility of a page of score which can be carried in a brief case and referred to on a train to film which requires a projector, a screen, and a darkened room. The pure concept of the work is best recorded in notation. The complete record of any choreographic work should include both a film and notation. Ideally, there should be several films, just as in music we have several recordings. In areas other than dance, such as in time-and-motion study and anthropology, films are particularly valuable because they can be studied in slow motion. Slowing down the film causes the movement elements of strength and weight to become distorted and timing to become less recognizable; therefore, a companion record in notation in which these elements are specifically stated is necessary.

A Tool for Movement Education

The Laban system has proved a valuable tool for movement education ranging from work with four- to five-year old children to post graduate and doctoral studies.

Visual Aids. New methods of teaching mathematics and several other subjects include the use of visual aids. Labanotation has provided a similar visual method for the dance and for physical education. Its symbols aid in clarifying the differences between the basic elements of movement as well as between variations in the structured forms. The method of learning movement through imitation does not guarantee the observer an understanding of what is occurring. Labanotation provides an additional channel through which knowledge can be imparted at every age and level of study.

Development of Movement Concepts. The raw material of the dance, indeed of all movement, should be studied at some point by every serious student. It is not enough just to learn the set structured patterns formed by variations and combinations of these basic actions. Recording the gist of an action, the idea or motivation behind it, its kinetic "sense," is called "Motif Writing." This has its place not only in certain types of choreography, but also in dance education where freedom for exploration and improvisation on a basic movement idea or theme is desired. By this method, the first broad statement of the action can gradually be defined in greater detail, producing an increasingly specific description until finally a very precise form has been achieved in which the exact use of the body, time, direction and energy have been stated. In training children, the teacher can work progressively from the simplest of disciplines in movement - concentrating on one aspect at a time while all else is left open to choice - toward a greater specificity of detail as the child's physical and mental abilities and coordination develop.

Training in Movement Observation. Careful observation is essential for everyone concerned with movement, from the small child to the professional performer. The untrained eye will catch only the broad outline of a movement. Only when the eye and the understanding have been trained to recognize differences can the viewer observe the specific details of a performance. Such recognition is greatly aided by codification of the elements of movement. By giving specific names and symbols to these elements, and by recognizing them in combined forms both in performance and in notated form, the viewer can grasp the many patterns which emerge. As in other fields, in movement a method for the rapid identification of similarities and differences is essential for good learning.

A Tool for Movement Research

The handing down of detailed knowledge in any field requires a system of notation for recording pertinent facts in an unambiguous way. Comparisons can then be made, differences evaluated, new ground broken. The scientist would be lost without his symbols by which he can communicate his ideas objectively to his colleagues everywhere. The student of movement requires a similar method of notation in order to compare variations of the same movement pattern and reach conclusions which would not otherwise be possible. His research may be for medical, psychiatric, anthropological, or scientific purposes. He may want to record motion during the weightless state or computerise the instructions for mechanical devices, such as robots. Or he may want to conduct research into the best way to analyse and teach a basic dance exercise. Only through a language can all forms of movement research be expressed in a way that is internationally understood. The Laban system provides such a language.

The Development of New Professions

The profession of Labanotator, or Kinetographer, has developed with the advent of the widespread use of the Laban system. The recorder of movement may specialize in many different fields, which range from medical research to classical choreography. The musicologist now has a counterpart in the Kinetologist, or specialist in the art or science of movement. The ethnomusicologist now has his counterpart in the ethnokinetologist, who may work with "Choreometrics," the movement analysis of work, play, and dance actions found in anthropology. The dance critic will, in future, be able not only to assess the dance composition on its own apart from a particular performance of it by reading the dance score, but also have an enlarged vocabulary for describing qualities and variations in performance.

A Means for the Establishment of Dance Libraries

Labanotation has given rise to the establishment of an authentic and unequivocal literature which will raise the level of knowledge in all areas. In dance it will mean raising this art out of the realm of the minor arts, a fact as yet recognized by few. All movement research, including that done in the art of dance, has until recently been hampered by the lack of a means of capturing the essential factors on paper, the absence of a common method of analyzing movement, a universal terminology, and the scarcity of the recorded knowledge of the past which would allow recent and future generations to build on what has been achieved rather than have to start again from the beginning. It is evident that Labanotation can fill the needs of the various fields of movement study in a way that no other system of the past or present can begin to approach.

CHAPTER 3

The Approach to Movement Notation

The process of recording movement on paper involves the conver-
sion of the elements of space, time, energy, and the parts of the
body involved into symbols which can be read and converted into
movement. When this process is understood, the logic behind the
Laban system and the reason for the range of choice in movement
description can be comprehended.

CHOICE OF MOVEMENT DESCRIPTION

The detailed description of every kind of movement which the
Laban system provides is not always required. According to his
field and his needs of the moment, the notator may select any one
of the three following kinds of description:

1. Motif Description (M)

2. Effort-Shape Description (E)

3. Structural Description (S)

MOTIF DESCRIPTION

Motif Writing provides a general statement concerning the
theme or most salient feature of a movement. It also pinpoints
the motivation of a movement, its idea, aim, or intention. The
Motif Description may be kept simple or may be made increasingly
detailed until eventually it becomes a fully structured description.
This method of progression is extremely valuable in teaching. It
also has a place in choreography when only the gist of the movement needs stating. In this book basic actions described by Motif
Writing are introduced with an indication of how they may become
more specific. Specialized books on Motif Writing are available.

EFFORT-SHAPE DESCRIPTION

"Effort Observation and Analysis" is the term applied to the investigation of movement according to its dynamic content. The word "Effort" refers to the use of energy. This method of observation and analysis and its symbols are concerned with the changing patterns which occur in the ebb and flow of energy within the body.

"Shape" refers specifically to the expressiveness inherent in the form which movement takes. The viewer must observe the relation of the path of a gesture to the performer or to the dimensional directions in order to assess its expressive or functional value.

Together, Effort-Shape provides a valuable description of movement in terms of its quality and expression, in contrast to the structural description which has been standard in Labanotation. The Effort-Shape approach is particularly valuable in the fields of physio- and psychotherapy, in personnel assessment, and in industry. It is also extremely valuable in anthropology and athletics as well as in all kinds of dance.

STRUCTURAL DESCRIPTION

The term "Structural" is given to the description of movement in clearly defined and measurable terms. Such description, the most commonly used, expresses movement in terms of:

the body - the specific parts that move;

space - the specific direction, level, distance, or degree of motion;

time - meter and duration, such as a whole note, a sixteenth;

dynamics - the quality or "texture" of the movement, whether it is strong, heavy, elastic, accented, emphasized, etc.

A very complete picture of the movement emerges if all these elements are described as they are used.

Such a complete method of description is needed for writing specifically structured exercises, whether these have been formulated for remedial, practical, or artistic reasons. It is essential for the preservation of folk and ethnic dances and choreographic works. Some fields require Structural Description together with Motif Description and Effort-Shape analysis. The various forms of notation may be freely combined to fill any need.

LONGHAND VERSUS SHORTHAND

Because notation uses symbols, it is often likened to shorthand. This analogy is, however, only correct for Motif Writing, for abbreviated versions of sequences written for students and memory aid scores for those already familiar with the work. Labanotators (Kinetographers) use shorthand devices for writing at speed. The standard system is, in fact, a longhand which scrupulously accounts for every detail necessary to the correct performance of each movement. The writer must always think in terms of the readers who must study his score in order to translate it back into movement. In preparing materials for publication the writer has no way of knowing the movement background or experience of his readers. Short cuts in writing are acceptable for personal use or among colleagues in the same field where certain knowledge can be taken for granted. But a score, research paper, or teaching manual for general circulation must contain all the details necessary for an accurate performance so that the result is completely unambiguous.

SIMPLE DESCRIPTION FOR SIMPLE MOVEMENT

The basic principle of structured Labanotation is that simple, natural movement should be written in the simplest and most direct way. The second premise is that everything that occurs must be recorded. These two statements may seem contradictory. Actually they are not, but one must know where to draw the line. For instance, walking is a simple, natural movement. Each person varies slightly in the manner in which he walks, but the basic process is essentially the same. It is such a familiar action that one forgets that it is a complicated process. In writing the movement of walking, we usually state only the direction into which the center of gravity moves by means of a step on the right or left foot. A detailed description is given only to denote a stylized walk or to explore the process in detail: how the leg is lifted to extend into the direction of each new step, how the foot contacts the floor, how the weight is transferred, and how the leg is freed of weight at the end of the step. Such description may include changes in level, changes in bending and stretching the legs, changes in the use of the different parts of the feet, use of rotations, deviations in the gestures, and changes in timing such as the use of accents, ritardando, etc. There should also be an accurate indication of when during the time taken for the whole transference of weight each such change occurs. From this breakdown we can see why Labanotation has adopted a convention for writing walking in a simple way. It is one of three such conventions devised to make familiar actions such as walking and jumping easy for even a five-year-old child to read. For the advanced student a more detailed analysis is always possible.

THE VISUALITY OF THE LABAN SYSTEM

Direct representation is impractical for converting movement into diagrams on paper. In any comprehensive system, information must be abstracted and put into symbols. In Labanotation the depiction of the elements of space, time, energy, and the parts of the body have been made as visual and pictorial as possible. This can be seen in the vertical staff representing the body with its pictorial division into right and left sides, the shape of the direction symbols which point into the required direction, and the length of the symbol to indicate timing. Reading is facilitated by having the block symbols state the basic form of the movement. Secondary symbols such as hooks, pins, and bows modify the basic form and indicate variations in style, and the strong, visual pattern provided by the block shapes enables groups of symbols to be read at a glance. The relative timing of the parts of the movement, the presence of simultaneous, sequential, overlapping, or separated actions can readily be seen from the lengths and placement of the block shapes.

PRINCIPLES OF MOVEMENT ANALYSIS

A complete method of movement analysis is required to record movement by means of symbols on paper. How movement is analyzed can vary widely according to the particular field of study. In the field of dance, the method of movement description is often based on a particular form of dance and therefore has no universal application or commonly understood terminology. While patterns which are the result of combined movements may be identified and given names, the content of these patterns, their basic structure, may not always be understood.

To the layman it might seem obvious that all movements should be described in anatomical terms, the contraction, extension, or rotation in the joints of the body. Because man is built the same the world over, such a description would seem to provide a universal basis for common understanding. As we shall see, there are sound reasons for providing other possibilities of movement description as well. These alternatives have arisen to meet specific needs.

THE NATURE OF MOVEMENT

Movement is the result of the release of energy through a muscular response to an inner or outer stimulus. This response produces a visual result in time and space. In transcribing movement, the notator does not record the initial stimulus. The muscular response itself is also not usually recorded, that is, not in terms of the use of specific muscles or groups of muscles. Rather, the observer must note the resulting changes which the muscular action produces. This will range from inner tensions in the body, which are felt by the performer and which vary the expression of his carriage, to the more obvious changes affecting the shape of the body and resulting in clearly visible changes in the placement of the limbs in time and space.

CATEGORIES OF MOVEMENT MOTIVATION AND ANALYSIS

The particular purpose of the choreographer or need of the researcher will dictate the form of description and the method of analysis he will select. Details of importance in one field of study may be of little value in another. Because it is a comprehensive system, Labanotation fills the various needs of movement study and research in the many fields in which movement is analyzed, codified, and recorded. There are eight basic categories of movement motivation, though seldom is any one used in isolation.

1. DIRECTIONAL DESTINATION. The common approach to movement description in dance and allied fields is in terms of the spatial directions into which the parts of the body move, that is, the directional destination (e.g. the right arm forward then up, the left arm side). The aim is to arrive at an established position or state. The way there is less important than the final position.

2. MOTION. Sometimes it is not the destination but the motion itself which needs to be stated. This may be movement away from a previous position or state or toward a focal point. This category also includes movement along a particular path for which no destination is stated. Such motion emphasizes change and allows freedom of interpretation and concentration on the act of moving rather than on the result of reaching a specific goal.

3. ANATOMICAL CHANGE. For some actions an anatomical description is more suitable. This is based on the changes occur-

ring in the various joints of the body, flexion, extension, or rotation (e.g. a flexion in the knee joint, a rotation of the thigh in the hip socket). The emphasis is centered on physical changes in the joints, taken singly or in unison.

4. <u>VISUAL DESIGN.</u> The visual design, the path in space created by the movements of the limbs or the whole body may be the basic idea to be conveyed. The shape or design produced may be a path across the floor, a design (trace form) made by the extremity of a limb (e.g. a circle, zigzag, or figure eight), or plastic shapes made by the limbs or the body as a whole.

5. <u>RELATIONSHIP.</u> The purpose of any action may be to relate to an object or person. This may be to approach it or move away from it, to be close to it, to touch, grasp, or carry it. The physical actions which must take place to produce these aims are often not important and not described.

6. <u>CENTER OF WEIGHT, BALANCE.</u> The focus of movement awareness and analysis may be concerned with the center of weight in the body and the use of, or loss of, balance for a particular purpose or effect. Such focus can range from placement and transference of weight in simple steps to complex acrobatics.

7. <u>DYNAMICS.</u> The quality of movement, patterns in the ebb and flow of energy, the expressive use of weight, space, force and time, may be of prime importance and actions may be described in these terms (e.g. a sudden thrusting action, or a freely flowing gliding movement). The kind of effort involved, the qualitative aspects of the component parts are more important than the specific quantitative use of space, force, and time.

8. <u>RHYTHMIC PATTERN.</u> Movement may occur as a direct response to a basic recurrent beat or to rhythmic patterns in music, the chief purpose being the translation of rhythms into physical action. Other aspects of movement are usually subservient to this; the part of the body or direction used may be unimportant.

This book will be concerned chiefly with the Directional Destination, this being the most commonly used category. The other types of description will be touched upon briefly where they apply and will be explored in greater detail in Book II.

SYSTEMS OF REFERENCE

In any spatial description of movement, the reader must know the frame of reference. When a forward direction is stated he must know whether the resulting movement should be toward the front of the room or stage or toward the front of the performer. These systems are the same only when he is standing facing the front of stage. If an upward movement is stated he must know whether this is a gesture toward the ceiling, or past his head. In the normal standing position these two systems are the same, but when the performer is lying down they are not. In describing directions there are three possible systems of reference:

1. The Constant Directions in the Room

2. The Standard System of Direction (the Constant Line of Gravity System)

3. The Constant Directions in the Body

Each of these systems is based on a cross of axes, that is, the cross of directions produced by the intersection at right angles of the lines extended in each of the three dimensions. For full details see Chapter 25.

THE GRAMMAR AND SYNTAX OF MOVEMENT

Dance is a "language" of expressive gestures through which nonverbal communication can be achieved. Like verbal language, it has basic "parts of speech." There is a clearly constructed grammar which defines the relationship of the movement "words" to each other and their given function in the movement "sentence" as a whole. The basic elements in this language of movement fall into the categories of nouns, verbs, and adverbs. Adjectives occur only rarely and are therefore not given in the following table.

Movement means change and to produce change an action of some sort must occur. In the grammar of movement, these actions are the verbs. The parts of the body that move are the nouns. How the action is done, the degree of change or the manner of performance, is described by the adverb. The following lists give some idea of the content of these three categories. These lists and the chart on page 19 are not intended to be complete.

NOUNS

- The individual parts of the body which move.
- A partner or other person to whom movement is related.
- Parts of the room to which the performer must proceed or toward which gestures are directed.
- Objects or properties which are carried or handled.

VERBS (numbers refer to the 13 root verbs)

- General statement of an action (1). Absence of action (2).
  The three basic anatomical possibilities:
- Contraction (3); Extension (4); Rotation (5).
  Movements produced by the three anatomical possibilities:
- Paths in space, of the body as a whole; of limbs (6).
- Direction, movement to defined points in space (7).
- Motion toward (8); Motion away (9); each in relation to points in space, a person, object or the performer himself.
  Mode of Progression, Change in the Support of the Body:
- Weight-bearing, transference of weight (10); Absence of support, jumping (11); Movement in balance, shift of weight (12); Loss of balance, falling (13).

Results of Basic Actions (statement of effect rather than cause):
- Relating to a person, object or part of the room.
- Visual design: the shape made by the body; linear trace forms.

ADVERBS

All the verbs mentioned above and their variants can be modified by the following adverbs:

- Timing: sudden or sustained, or any specific time value.
- Dynamics: use of energy, flow of movement, inner attitude.
- Degree of action: degree of rotation, distance covered, etc.
- Manner of performance: (i) physical modification: initiation of the action, part of the body leading, guidances, sequential actions, (ii) spatial modification: deviations in paths, variations in positions.

It is important to observe that while actions or retentions of a position always involve time, the use of time itself may be unimportant, unstressed, and therefore not specifically included in the description. The same is true of dynamics. All actions require some degree of energy, but only a greater or lesser amount than the functional level is stated.

MOVEMENT FAMILY TREE

The following condensed tree gives the basic elements involved in movement and their main subdivisions. The relationships of movement elements which can be seen from this tree help in understanding the progression from the broadest indication of movement to a specific description.

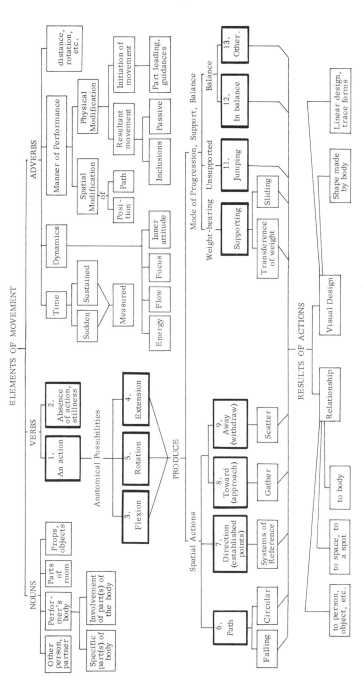

CHAPTER 4

Fundamentals of Labanotation

INDICATIONS OF ACTIVITY

In the study of transcription of movement, the broad general statement of an action will be followed by increasingly specific ones. Movement must often be indicated in broad terms. The first basic indication of any movement is simply the statement that "something happens," that one or more actions occur.

THE ACTION STROKE

A vertical stroke, called an "action stroke," represents the occurrence of movement of some kind. Its interpretation depends upon the performer. If the writer wishes to be more specific he must add the necessary details.

<u>Rule</u>: the reading direction in Labanotation is from the bottom of the page up, or, if the book is held horizontally, in the forward direction. A double horizontal line ═════ indicates the start, the beginning of movement.

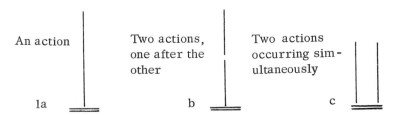

An action | Two actions, one after the other | Two actions occurring simultaneously

1a   b   c

Note that when two action strokes are written one after the other on the page, they occur one after the other in time. When they are written side by side, they occur at the same time.

THE CENTER LINE

The next step in a progression from general description to more specific is the indication of the use of right or left side of the body. An action may occur on one side of the body or the other. To show this, we draw a vertical line to represent the vertical center line in the body and place action strokes on either side of this center line. The vertical center line is centered on and connected to the double starting line.

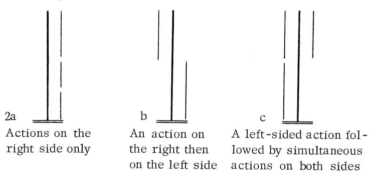

2a — Actions on the right side only

b — An action on the right then on the left side

c — A left-sided action followed by simultaneous actions on both sides

This vertical center line forms the basis of the vertical three-line staff on which structured description is written.

THE STAFF

Labanotation uses a vertical three-line staff.* This staff represents the body, the center line being the center line of the body, dividing right and left. Vertical columns on each side of the center line are used for the main parts of the body. Movements of the legs and feet are written within the three-line staff, and movements of

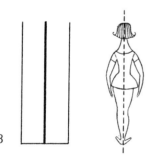

3

Left   Right   Left   Right

the torso, arms, and head are written outside. Within the staff there exist four major vertical columns (two on either side of the center line). Outside the three-line staff imaginary vertical lines, parallel to the main staff lines and comparable to ledger lines in music, provide additional vertical columns, as many as are needed.

* See Appendix B, note 1.

USE OF THE COLUMNS

By placing the movement indication in one of the vertical columns of the staff we state an action for one of the main parts of the body. Fig. 4 illustrates which part of the body each column represents.

1st Column: Supports. Immediately next to the center line are the support columns. The placement of the weight of the body is important, and is usually the factor we need to know first. Direction symbols placed in these columns indicate progressions of the whole body, that is, progressions of the center of gravity of the body by means of transference of weight, jumps, or falls. The weight of the body normally rests on the feet, but it can also be supported by the knees, hips, hands, and even the head. In such cases, a sign for the specific active part of the body is placed in one or other of the support columns.

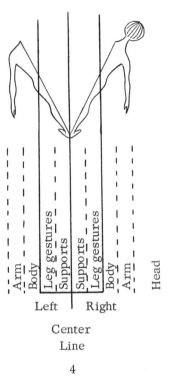

Left   Right

Center
Line

4

2nd Column: Leg Gestures. Adjacent to the support columns are columns for leg gestures. The term "gesture" is used for movement of a limb which does not carry weight. A direction symbol here describes a gesture of the whole leg moving in one piece. These columns are also used for the individual parts of the leg - thigh, lower leg, and foot - as indicated by specific signs for those parts.

3rd Column: Body. Columns immediately outside the three-line staff are used for the body. Direction symbols placed here without a specific pre-sign describe movements of the "upper part of the body," that is, superior spinal movements used freely as an accompaniment to arm gestures (see Appendix D). Movements of the whole torso, the chest, pelvis, shoulder girdle, etc. are written with the specific signs for those parts.

4th Column: Arms. Immediately beyond the body columns, to either side, are columns for the arms. A direction symbol in these columns describes a gesture of the whole arm moving in one piece. These columns are also used for individual parts of the arm, the upper and lower arm, as indicated by specific signs for those parts.

Columns beyond the fourth. Up to the fourth column no pre-sign for a main part of the body is needed. Beyond the fourth column the pre-sign for a specific part must be given. The fifth column may be used for the lower arm, but more frequently it is used for the hand. When complex hand gestures occur requiring a description for fingers and palm facing as well as for the hand itself, additional space outside the staff is used, and the appropriate pre-signs are given.

The Head Column. The head is written on the right side, slightly apart from the other columns. If a score is simple, head indications can be written closer to the staff in the sixth column from the center. Where complex hand movements require additional columns, the head is placed farther out. The specific sign for the head is always used to identify the column.

Additional Columns. Supplementary columns can be added as needed. These are placed outside the staff, as in the case of columns which indicate the handling of props, or within the staff if more room is needed for leg and body movements. Fig. 4 shows a simple staff, but this is often expanded as in Fig. 5. The additional columns allow room for symbols modifying the main movement. (Note: the additional columns between the support and leg gesture columns are called "a" subsidiary columns and those between the body and arm columns "b".)

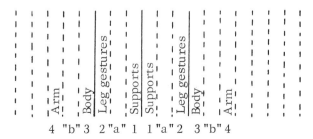

4 "b" 3 2 "a" 1 1 "a" 2 3 "b" 4

Left   Right

Indication of Action for the Main Parts of the Body

The occurence of movements for the main parts of the body is shown by placing action strokes on the three-line staff.

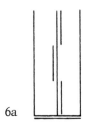  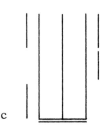

6a   b   c

Steps, supports   Two gestures   Gestures of the arms,
right, left, right   of the right leg   left, right, then both

SPACE

DIRECTION SYMBOLS

The directions in space emanate from a central point — the
spatial "center." This point is
called "place," and is represented by a rectangle. Directions
are judged from this point.

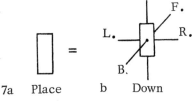

7a   Place   b   Down

Symbols for directions are
modifications of the shape of
this basic sign, and shapes
are pictorial in pointing to
the direction they describe.

7c   d

Forward   To the right

The Eight Main Directions

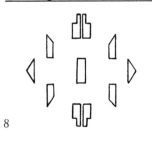

8

* See Appendix C, note 1.

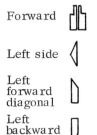

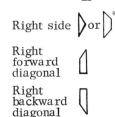

Forward	Backward
Left side	Right side
Left forward diagonal	Right forward diagonal
Left backward diagonal	Right backward diagonal

Note that there are two symbols for directions forward and backward, one for the right side of the staff and one for the left. The
indicator or "chimney" is placed on the inside, toward the center
of the staff. This is a convention in writing which does not, however, change the meaning of the symbol.

When this book is placed horizontally, forward symbols point
to the forward direction, a side right symbol points to the right,
and so on. Diagonal directions lie exactly between forward and
side directions (right forward and left forward diagonals), or between backward and side directions (right backward and left backward diagonals). The word "diagonal" is used in Labanotation as a
direction in space and not for a gesture which is slanting upward
or downward. Such oblique slanting is described in terms of level.

THE THREE LEVELS

The level of movement - upward, downward, or horizontal - is
indicated by the shading of a symbol. A movement into any direction can be horizontal, low, or high in level. Straight up is "high"
(place high). Straight down is "low" (place low). Down moves toward gravity, with the gravitational force; up, away from it. The
horizontal plane lies at right angles to both.

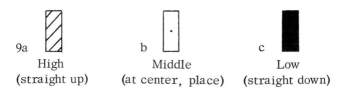

9a	b	c
High	Middle	Low
(straight up)	(at center, place)	(straight down)

Each of the main directions can be in any of the three levels.

Forward high (slant-ing up) 9d	Forward middle (horizontal) e	Forward low (slant-ing down) f
Right high (slant-ing up) 9g	Right middle (horizontal) h	Right low (slanting down) i
Right forward high 9j	Right forward middle k	Right forward low l

The Twenty-Seven Principal Directions

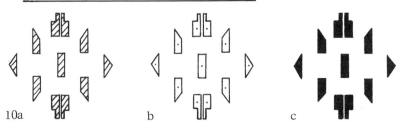

10a   b   c

For general purposes the twenty-seven main directions suffice. Intermediate (in between) directions are explained in Chapter 26. Note that for gestures place (center) is considered a direction.

GENERAL STATEMENT OF DIRECTIONAL MOVEMENT

By themselves, the direction symbols state only information concerning the element of direction. In order for us to know what part of the body moves in a stated direction, a symbol must either be placed in the appropriate column of the full vertical staff or be preceded by the symbol for that specific part of the body. The following progression from the broadest statement to the most specific (Figs. 11 and 12) illustrates the flexibility of the system.

Motif Writing

In Motif Writing (see page 11) a direction symbol by itself indicates an action whose principal feature is the use of that given direction in space. Exactly how this is performed may vary according to the interpreter. Fig. 11 (a) illustrates such a general description. Use of the vertical center line permits indication of movement for the right or left sides of the body as in (b) and (c).

 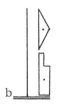 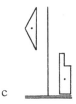

11a   b   c

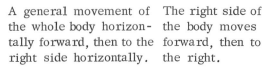

| A general movement of the whole body horizontally forward, then to the right side horizontally. | The right side of the body moves forward, then to the right. | The right side of the body moves forward, then the left side moves to the left. |

SPECIFIC STATEMENT OF DIRECTIONAL MOVEMENT

Placement of a direction symbol on the staff shows which part of the body moves in the stated direction. In the following example, which illustrates the highlight of a jump, only arm and leg gestures are given. There are no symbols in the support column.

Right arm forward high
Left leg forward low
Left arm backward low
Right leg backward low

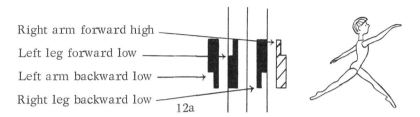

12a

For smaller parts of the body, the specific sign for the given part is placed in front of the direction symbol. Such indications can be used out of context, for example in Motif Writing, as in Figs. 12 (b) and (c), but usually appear in a structural description in which specific details of parts of the body, time, direction, and level are all stated, as in (d).

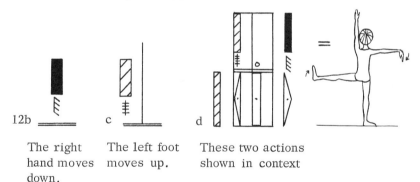

12b — The right hand moves down.

c — The left foot moves up.

d — These two actions shown in context

ANALYSIS OF DIRECTION AND LEVEL

In the analysis of direction and level, gestures and supports of the body differ basically from one another. Two entirely separate concepts are involved. Gestures are usually described in terms of movement toward a specific point, that is, a destination; steps are described as motion away from a previous point of support. We will consider these concepts first, then explore direction and level applied to them.

THE WRITING OF MOTION OR DESTINATION

Labanotation is a movement notation because the symbols represent change; absence of movement is shown by the absence of symbols. The basic premise of the system is that a position is a movement which has come to rest. In a description of movement a choice exists between one of the two following points of view:

1. Transition to an established point in space (destination);

2. Movement away from a starting point in a direction relative to that point (motion).

In the case of destination the description is in finite terms, movement toward a known destination. We use points in space as milestones. The path itself along which the movement travels is not described. In certain contexts a description in terms of a destination is called "position writing."

In the case of motion, the path of the movement is described as a movement away from a starting point. This might be a forward and upward movement in relation to the starting point. How far the movement progresses in that direction is not necessarily stated. Information on distance can be added if necessary. To differentiate clearly between destination and motion, we shall look at a geographical analogy.

Established Points - Destination

In traveling from Rome to London, one is moving between two fixed points in the world. The direction happens to be a northwesterly one, but the traveler need not be aware of this and will mark London as his destination and continue until London is reached.

Relative Direction of the Path

The relative direction from Rome to London is northwest. A traveler starting on a northwesterly path from Rome may not know what his goal is; he may only know his direction in relation to his starting point. If he continues for a short while, he will arrive in Milan. To reach London he must continue in the same direction for a measured distance. If he does not stop in time, he will go past London to an unknown destination.

From this analogy we can see that in writing movement, we may sometimes need to know the relative direction of the path, but in general it is more practical to state the destination.

Description in Terms of Established Points

In writing gestures we describe movement as the path of the extremity of a limb between established points in space. The actual
movement is the transition from one point to the next. To know
the exact path by which a point is reached, we must also know the
starting point.

In Fig. 13 (a) the starting
position for the arm is up.
The arm then takes a downward path to arrive at the
side middle destination. "x"
indicates the starting position,
"y" the path, and "z" the destination.

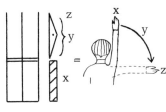

13a

In each of the following examples the destination is side middle,
but different starting positions result in different paths.

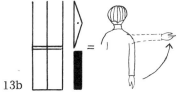

13b

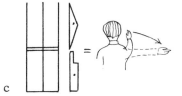

c

The arm moves from place
low upward to side middle

The arm moves horizontally
from forward to side middle.

Thus, the standard choice of description for gestures of the
limbs is in terms of the destination to be reached. Steps may be
described similarly: a performer can be instructed to make a path
the aim of which is to arrive in another part of the room.

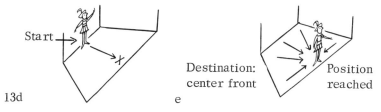

Start

Destination:
center front

Position
reached

13d

e

Fig. 13 (d) shows an actor starting at the center back of the
room. If told to move to a destination center front, his path will
lie between those two points. The same destination reached from
other starting points will result in other paths as in Fig. (e).

Description in Terms of Motion

For ordinary walking steps, jumps, leaps, etc., the direction of the path in which the center of gravity moves is described in terms of motion away from the starting point. This is the standard Labanotation description for steps; only occasionally is the description given in terms of destination. Fig. 14 (a) shows a step forward. From the starting position, the movement is a forward one. Once the step is finished (the forward motion ceases), the performer is standing with his center of weight over his point of support, in place. No evidence remains to indicate his forward movement. We can deduce this only if we know his starting point.

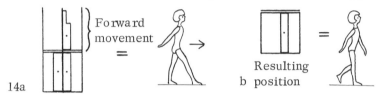

14a   In a forward step the direction symbol describes the movement.

b   Resulting position   At the end of the step only a support in place is evident.

For arm and leg gestures we seldom describe motion, but an example is given here for clarification to illustrate the method.

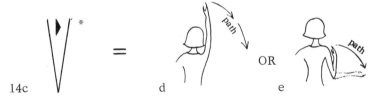

14c   d   OR   e

In Fig. 14 (d), from the starting position with the right arm up, the path of the gesture is side low. We may not know how far this sideward-downward motion progresses. It could end part way, as the first arrow suggests, or could continue until the side middle point is reached, as the second arrow indicates. Fig. 14 (e) shows another sideward-downward movement from another starting position. Spatially these actions all have something in common because they follow parallel paths, but in relation to the body each is different. To produce a specific action we need to know the starting position as well as the degree of "sideward and downward" motion.

* See Chapter 20, page 341.

POSITIONS: SUPPORTS ON THE FEET

The body is normally understood to be supported by the legs. We can show the exact flexion in ankle, knee, and hip used in standing or walking, and can also indicate the part of foot which contacts the floor. For general purposes, however, we have established a convention of three main levels: middle, low, and high.

In the following examples illustrating levels of support, the legs are shown as being together, in place, directly beneath the center of weight. The weight is divided equally between the feet. No statement is made concerning the rotation of the legs. The figure illustrations show the feet parallel and also with some degree of turnout to indicate that rotation of the legs does not change the basic direction and level of the position. Details on rotations of the legs are given in Chapter 17.

Middle Level Supports

In an ordinary stance the whole foot is on the ground. The knees are straight, but not taut. The level of this ordinary standing position is called middle level.

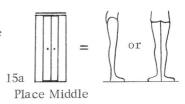

15a Place Middle

Low Level Supports

In a low support the center of gravity of the body is lowered by bending the legs. The weight is on the whole foot. This low support is called a "demi-plié" (half

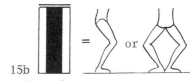

15b Place Low

bend) in ballet. Exactly how much the knees will bend in an ordinary low support will depend on the individual build of the performer, but in every case the whole foot should remain on the ground. The exact degrees of knee bend from the slightest to a full knee bend are shown with additional indications. (See page 175.)

High Level Supports

In a high support the raising of the center of gravity of the body produces an extension of the legs. The weight is on the ball of the foot, and the knees are straight.

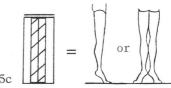

15c Place High (on demi-pointe)

POSITIONS FOR GESTURES

For gestures of the limbs, trunk, and head, direction and level are determined by the spatial relationship of the extremity (free end) to the base (point of attachment). A line drawn between the free end and the base indicates to which direction the limb has moved. This is true whether the limb is bent or stretched.

Place for Gestures

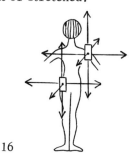

Place for gestures is the center point, the point from which all other directions and levels radiate. In Fig. 16 this center point is illustrated for the right arm and for the left leg. Place for the arm is at the shoulder. Place for the leg is at the hip joint.

16

Levels for Arm Gestures

The whole arm moves from the shoulder joint (point of attachment). The relation of the hand (free end) to the shoulder (base) determines direction and level for the arm as a whole. In the normal standing position the arm hangs straight down from the shoulder by the side of the body. As the hand is below the shoulder, the whole arm is place low. A middle level gesture is at shoulder level, horizontal, and parallel with the floor. A high level arm gesture slants upward, above shoulder level. A low arm gesture slants downward, below shoulder level.

17

Arms straight down, place low

forward low	forward middle	forward high	place high
18 side low	side middle	side high	place high

Levels for Leg Gestures

The whole leg moves from the hip joint, its point of attachment. Direction and level are determined by the relation of the foot (free end) to the hip (base). When in the air, as in Fig. 19, the legs are gesturing straight down, into the direction place low.

19 ___

Low leg gestures

In the following chart the extension of the legs shown in the figure illustration is not stated in the notation.

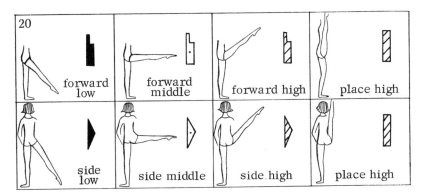

20			
forward low	forward middle	forward high	place high
side low	side middle	side high	place high

Place for the Arms and Legs

A limb is said to be at place when its extremity is close to its base. For the arms and legs this means being bent, drawn in close to the body. Place is directly between high (straight up) and low (straight down).

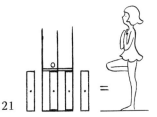

21

Starting Positions

Because indications placed before the double starting line mean positions, not motion, in writing a starting position for a sequence of movements we need not be concerned with timing. Fig. 22 indicates a starting position with the weight on the right leg, left leg gesturing backward low, right arm at side middle and left arm up.

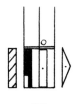

22

MOVEMENT

A Directional Support, a Step

The appropriate direction symbol is written in the support column to show the center of gravity of the body moving into a direction by means of a step. In moving away from a starting point, the whole body is transported by the action of the legs. In walking, each leg in turn takes over the weight of the body.

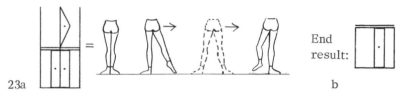

23a

In Fig. 23 (a) a step to the side is taken on the right leg in middle level. The action is basically one of the center of gravity moving to the right. The right leg must move out to the side to start the step, but this action is understood and is not written unless it is to be performed in a specific manner. The step itself may be defined as the movement of the center of gravity to the right by a transference of the weight to the right leg (foot). When the transference is completed the right support is in place, as in (b). Therefore the ending position, in which the center of gravity has come to rest, is different from the movement into that position.

A Directional Step with Change of Level

In changing the level of the support, we raise or lower the center of gravity by extending or contracting the legs. For this action we usually use the main levels: middle, low, and high.

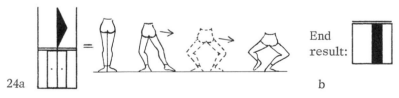

24a

The same process happens when we take a step with a change in level. Here the center of gravity simultaneously travels to the side (through the transference of weight) and lowers slightly (through bending the leg). Fig. 24 (a) illustrates this progression. When the transference of weight is completed, a support on the right leg in place low results, as in (b).

WHERE IS PLACE?

In Labanotation the concept of place must be kept clearly in mind; the word "place" has various connotations when used in other contexts. For example, in ballroom dancing the word "place" is used for the spot on the floor on which the performer was standing a moment ago. Thus the ballroom instruction: "Step side with the right foot, step in place with the left," may mean a step to the right side followed by a step to the left side, which would bring the performer back to the spot at which he started. In other forms of dance a performer may have his "place" in the formation or on stage, to which at certain times he is to return. In Labanotation the idea of place for supports follows the basic law that place is directly related to the center of gravity of the performer. This is true for the simplest steps as well as for complex acrobatic forms.

The following cartoon helps to illustrate this basic concept, particularly in relation to supports.

Have you been introduced to PLACE?

Do you know WHERE PLACE is?

PLACE is NOT WHERE YOU WERE

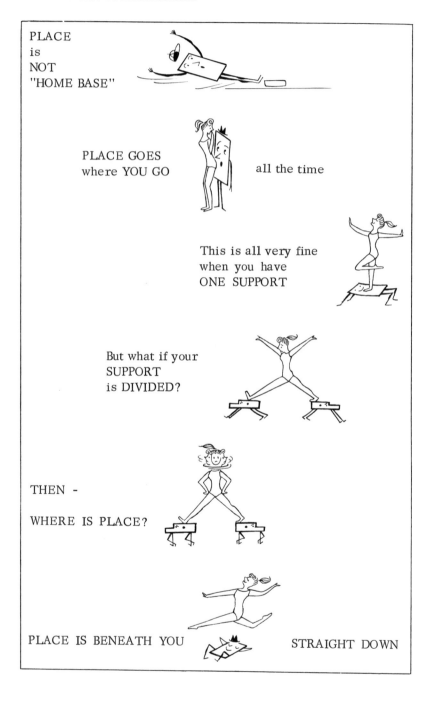

PLACE
is
NOT
"HOME BASE"

PLACE GOES
where YOU GO   all the time

This is all very fine
when you have
ONE SUPPORT

But what if your
SUPPORT
is DIVIDED?

THEN -

WHERE IS PLACE?

PLACE IS BENEATH YOU   STRAIGHT DOWN

PLACE
is
ALWAYS BENEATH YOU

PLACE is on the
PLUMB LINE
from your center of
WEIGHT

Your WEIGHT is
very IMPORTANT
and
PLACE
DEPENDS ON IT

INDEED -

No matter what
you may be
UP
TO

or
DOWN
TO

PLACE IS:

ABOVE,
AT,
or
BELOW
your
CENTER OF WEIGHT

TIMING

The center line of the staff is also the time line. When read from the bottom up, it indicates visually the flow of time.

GENERAL INDICATION OF TIMING

Movement indications placed side by side occur at the same moment in time and may be compared to the notes of a musical chord. Indications placed one after the other occur sequentially. We illustrate this first in a general way with action strokes. The sign o means hold.

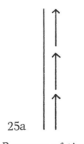

25a

Passage of time

Simultaneous actions of both arms, right support and left leg, before and after standing still

25b

Sequential actions of the right support, left leg, right arm, and left arm

c

The simultaneous actions shown in Fig. 25 (b) are described as being into specific directions in (d). In (e) the sequential actions indicated in (c) are now more specifically described by direction symbols.

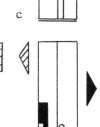

25d   e

Duration: General Statement

The longer the action stroke, the longer it takes to complete the given action, i.e. the slower the movement. The shorter the stroke, the sooner it is completed, i.e. the faster the movement. Fig. 26 (a) shows one slow sustained movement for the right arm. Fig. (b) shows three quick actions for the right arm.

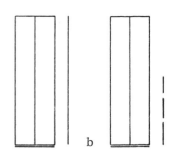

26a   b

FREE TIMING

The timing of actions may be free in that it is not measured. One action may have more duration, another less. One may start sooner or later than another. There may be a great deal or very little overlap in the occurrence of two or more actions. The relative duration of actions and when they start and finish with respect to one another may be clearly established but otherwise the timing is free; it is felt, sensed rather than measured or counted in any way. Even in choreographed theatre pieces timing may be based completely on a breath rhythm or a phrase rhythm which is felt and not counted. Labanotation provides

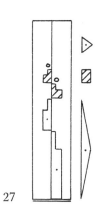

27

for such needs. In Fig. 27 action strokes have been replaced with specific direction symbols, but timing is still only general. A slow step leads into faster steps, and a slow right arm gesture is followed by two quick separated gestures.

PROPORTIONATE, MEASURED TIMING

To indicate metered (measured) time, the recurrence of a regular basic beat (pulse) and the grouping of such beats into measures (bars)* as in music, the center time line is marked off at regular intervals by small ticks.** Each tick marks the beginning of a new beat. The space between the ticks represents the duration of the beat. Because the amount of time occupied by each beat is regular, the distance allowed for each on paper must also be regular. A

one
beat

28

basic unit is taken for each beat. For the quarter note (crochet ♩) we usually allow four squares on graph paper or one half inch, (1.25 cm). More space may be needed for complex movements, in which case the basic unit can be increased to six or eight squares. The unit chosen must be kept uniform throughout the section or piece. A change in the unit must be indicated, see pages 42, 43.

* The term "measure" is technically correct, although the word "bar" is also commonly used. Strictly speaking the bar lines separate the measures.   **See Appendix A, note 1.

Length of Symbol

The relative length of each movement symbol indicates its time value. Once the basic unit, the length on the paper used for each beat, is established, the whole scale of values is accordingly determined. For instance, a whole note is

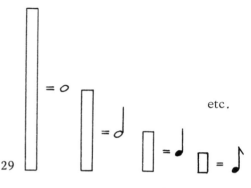

twice the length of a half note, and a half note twice the length of a quarter note. The music note is used to establish the value of the basic unit. Music notes are not otherwise needed in the dance score. Timing (the length of time used) is an integral part of each movement symbol; therefore the Labanotation score does not require the accompanying music to be written alongside its indication. The device of using different lengths of symbols to represent time values makes changes in rhythm visually easy to recognize. The flexibility of this device makes the system suitable for use with electronic scores and for scientific studies where time is measured in seconds.

Breakdown of a Count (Beat)

Just as a single count in music can be subdivided, so can the linear unit representing one count in Labanotation.

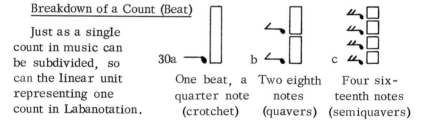

One beat, a quarter note (crotchet) Two eighth notes (quavers) Four sixteenth notes (semiquavers)

Verbal Subdivision of a Beat

In counting beats for dance and in writing word notes, we must use a common terminology which accurately states the subdivisions of a beat. The word "and" should be used only for subdivisions which fall on the half beat. The following terminology has been standardized in Labanotation and is presented as the best method available today.

The single count or beat is called "1, 2, 3," etc. according to its placement in the measure. When it is divided in half, the first part is still called by its appropriate number, and the second half

is called "&." Thus consecutive eighth notes would be counted:
"1, &, 2, &," etc. Divided into fours, that is, into sixteenth notes,
a beat is counted: "1, y, &, u, 2, y, &, u," etc. (The "y" is pronounced as in "any" and the "u" is pronounced as in "up".) In a triplet,
a beat is divided into three equal parts. A frequently met terminology for this, "1, &, a, 2, &, a," is not technically correct, as the
symbol "&" should be used only for a true half beat. A more accurate terminology for the triplet is: "1, a, da, 2, a, da," etc.

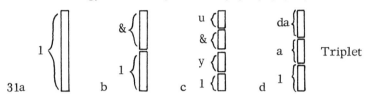

MARKING OFF THE MEASURES (BARS)

Simple Meters

Like music notation, Labanotation uses a staff which is marked
off in measures (bars) by horizontal bar lines. Fig. 32 shows examples of different meters: (a) the grouping of quarter note beats
into twos, 2/4 meter, or duple time; (b) into threes, 3/4 meter, or
triple time; (c) into groups of four, 4/4 meter or common time,
as it is called, and (d) into groups of five, 5/4 time. Remember to
read the dance staff from the bottom up.

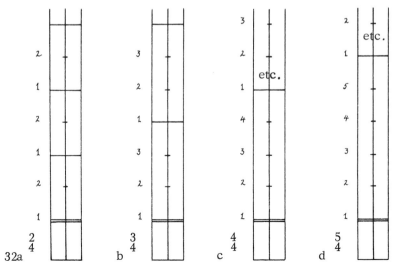

Compound Meters

In compound time in music each beat is divisible by three. Of the possible meters in this category, 6/8 is the most familiar, though 9/8 and 12/8 and also 6/4 and 9/4 are often met. Musically, 6/8 is to be compared with 2/4 in that there are two main beats in each measure. But in 6/8 each beat is divided into three eighth notes. This subdivision into three of each of the two main beats in the measure is always felt but not always counted. In studying dance and relating it to music, we may find it helpful to count all six beats of the measure in order to know on which one a certain action falls. But gen-

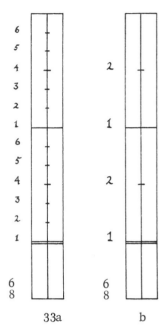

33a   b

erally speaking, in a measure of 6/8 we need count only the strong beats, "1,2." Fig. 33 (a) illustrates two measures of 6/8 meter with each of the six subdivisions (the eighth notes) marked. Note that the middle tick is made stronger to stress the main division into two. In (b) the same two measures of 6/8 are drafted with only the main subdivisions, but the possibility of triple subdivisions is still allowed for. 9/8 and 12/8 meter are handled in a similar way.

Statement of Basic Unit Used

It is common practice to establish the length of the basic unit being used for a given piece in the starting postion. In Fig. 34 (a) this unit is longer than in (b). Where the unit needs to be stated separately, it is written with the appropriate length and time value notes as in Figs. 34 (c) and (d).

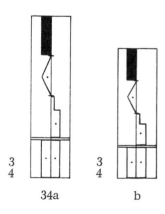

34a   b

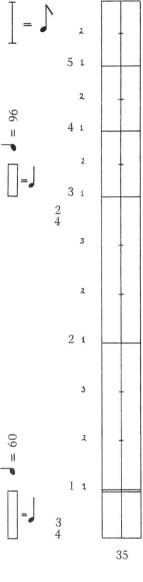

34c ⊔ = ♩.   **d** ⊔ = ♪   or   ⌐ = ♪ **e**

Fig. 34 (e) shows an alternate method of indicating length and time value. A basic unit statement can be written as a key under the staff or placed to the left near the starting position, as shown in Fig. 35. If during the course of the score we need to change this basic unit, the new length must be stated at this time. Such a statement appears outside the staff on the left as shown in the third measure of Fig. 35.

Statement of Change of Meter

The indication for a change of meter during a piece should appear just before the measure in which it takes place. This indication serves as a warning. In Fig. 35 a change from 3/4 to 2/4 occurs at the third measure, as well as a change in the basic length used.

SPECIFIC, FINITE TIME

Where exact tempi are required, the metronome indication is included. This indication is the same as that used in music — the number of beats per minute: ♩ = 60, ♩ = 112, etc. In a dance score this indication is placed at the beginning to the left of the staff as illustrated in Fig. 35. It is also placed on the left when a change occurs during the score as can be seen in measure 3 of this example. The indication of speed can be combined with that for the basic unit as shown in Fig. 36.

35

36   ⊔ = ♩ = 60

THE USE OF LINES IN DRAFTING A SCORE

The following principles of standardization in the use of lines have helped to make scores and kinetograms more uniform and hence easier to read.

<u>Beat Marks:</u>   The beats are separated by short horizontal strokes across the center line.*

<u>Bar Lines:</u>   The measures are marked off with horizontal lines extending across the three-line staff. While short bar lines, as in Fig. 37 (a), are standard, they may also be extended farther to facilitate reading, as in (b).

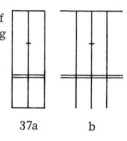

37a   b

<u>Base of Score:</u>   To give the staff a neat appearance, a line may be drawn across the three-line staff before the starting position, as illustrated in Fig. 37 (a).

<u>Start of Action:</u>   Double horizontal lines mark the beginning of action. In Fig. 37 (a) these fall on the bar lines. Indications before this double horizontal line signify a position; those following it signify movement.

The double starting line may come before the bar line. In Fig. 37 (c) the starting position is followed by an upbeat, a rising into the air on the "&" to land with feet apart on count 1 of the new measure. The double starting line often does not coincide with the bar line.

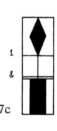

37c

<u>Ending Lines:</u>   At the end of a dance or exercise a double line is used. The upper one may be drawn thicker, as in (d). For extended lines, the drawing will be as in (e).

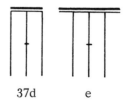

37d   e

Full details on use of lines in scoring will be given in Book II.

* See Appendix A, note 1.

USE OF NUMERALS

For easier reading of scores, the following standard use of numerals has been established. Note this practice in Figs. 33 and 35.

<u>Count Numbers.</u> Where counts for the beats are needed, they are indicated by small numerals placed outside the staff to the left, just after the mark separating the beats.

<u>Measure Numbers.</u>* The number for each measure is placed outside the count numbers to the left of the staff. These numbers are written larger than count numbers and are placed directly after the bar line. The measure numbers correlate with the numbered measures in the music score.

<u>Dancer's Counts.</u> The term "dancer's counts" applies to counting by the musical phrase, or to counting groups of individual movements in which the counts are established for the benefit of the dancers. When using relatively simple music, the dancer may need to count dance phrases of twelve or perhaps ten. When following the work of modern composers, the dancer may find it difficult, undesirable, or even impossible to count according to the written music. It is important that the relation of the dancer's counts to those stated in the music be noted in the dance score. Usually the counts which appear in the dance score are the musical counts; therefore, the dancer's counts are placed in parentheses. A typical example of counting by the phrase occurs with a 2/4 meter in which four measures are counted as a phrase of eight or eight measures are counted as a phrase of sixteen. Fig. 38 illustrates a phrase of 16 counts occurring in the middle of a dance score, beginning with musical measure no. 43. Any special usage of numbers should be explained at the start of a score.

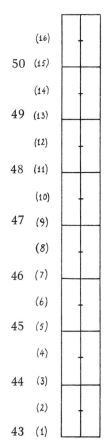

Fig. 38

* See Appendix A, note 2.

Variations in Steps

SUPPORTS AND STEPS WITH USE OF LEVELS

<u>IN PLACE</u>

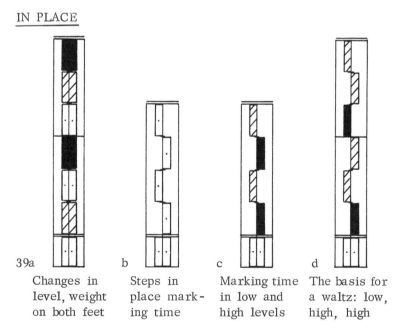

39a   b   c   d

| Changes in level, weight on both feet | Steps in place marking time | Marking time in low and high levels | The basis for a waltz: low, high, high |

Notes on reading. When the weight is on one foot, the other is free, just clear of the ground, as in ordinary walking. In performing Figs. 39 (b), (c) and (d), the right foot is lifted prior to the step on count one. The weight should be transferred completely from one foot to the other. In middle and high level the knees are not stiff; the natural pliancy in stepping is understood.

FORWARD AND BACKWARD STEPS

A direction symbol in the support column indicates that the center of gravity of the body has moved away from its previous standing position (stance) into the stated direction by means of a step on the right or left leg. Each step means a progression of the whole body in which the weight is transferred until it is vertically above the new point of support.

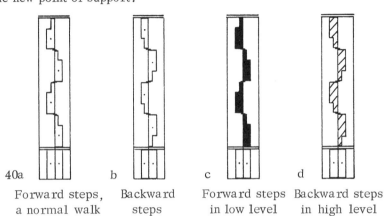

40a   b   c   d

Forward steps,   Backward   Forward steps   Backward steps
a normal walk   steps   in low level   in high level

Notes on reading. A step in any direction should be a normal-sized step, that is, the usual stride of the performer. Longer and shorter steps are discussed in Chapter 11. All directions relate to the front of the performer, that is, to the side or corner of the room which the performer is facing.

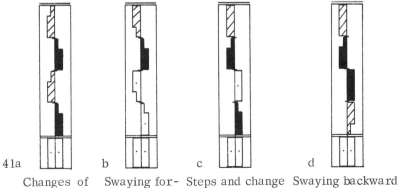

41a   b   c   d

Changes of   Swaying for-   Steps and change Swaying backward
level in for-   ward and   of level on the   and forward with
ward steps   backward   same leg   a change in level

STEPS TO THE SIDE

Step to the right
side with the
right foot, close
the left foot to
it in place, lift-
ing the right foot
just off the floor.
Repeat.

42a

Continuous
steps to the
right side,
the left leg
crossing in
front and
then behind

b

Steps to the side refer to the side direction from the body and not to the side of the room. In Fig. 42 (b) a black pin is used to show the relationship of the two legs as the step across is taken. The point of the pin is the indicator, as on a clock or compass.

In front: Behind (in back):

DIAGONAL STEPS

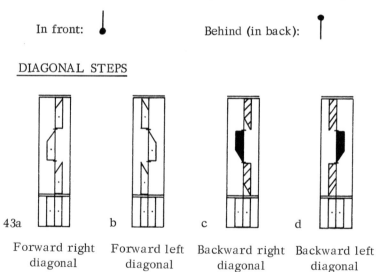

43a   b   c   d

Forward right   Forward left   Backward right   Backward left
  diagonal   diagonal   diagonal   diagonal

Notes on Reading. Be sure these steps are all taken diagonally from the body (the personal diagonal of the performer, not the diagonal of the room). Turning the body to face a new room direction will be discussed later. The diagonal direction from the body should be a clear cut line between the side (lateral) body directions and the forward-backward (sagittal) body directions.

THE RETENTION (HOLD) SIGN

The sign o when placed in a support column indicates that the weight on that foot is to be retained. This retention sign is usually called the "hold" sign, and when it appears in the support column, the "hold weight" sign. When both feet are to hold, the hold sign can be centered over both symbols, as in Fig. 44 (a) below, or a hold sign may be placed above each support as in (b).

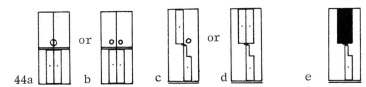

Hold on both feet.	Keep the weight on the right foot when the left closes.	The same as (c) and (d) with a change in level.	

Because the direction symbol represents movement and the simple act of holding the weight is not a movement, Fig. 44 (c) is a better description than (d). In stating the entire position, as in (d), we give the description in terms of the position reached, rather than of the movement (or absence of movement) which produced it. Where a change of level occurs, as in (e), the direction symbols must be written. Change of level is a movement and cannot be indicated by the hold sign.

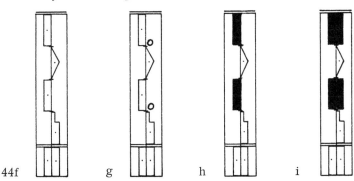

Step, close, ending with the weight on one foot.	Step, close, ending with the weight on both feet.	The same as (f) and (g) with a change in level. In (i) the hold sign cannot be used.	

STEPS IN DIFFERENT RHYTHMS

Rhythmical variations in steps are given here in different meters. Figs. 45 (a) and (b) are well-known ballroom steps using the timing "slow, slow, quick, quick, slow." Fig. (c) shows a limping "catch" step as found in folk dances. The term "catch step" is given to a fast step (change of weight) which occurs at the last moment before a main step. Note that it starts on the upbeat. In (d) the 5/4 meter is given with a "grapevine" step (crossing front and back).

Notes on Reading: The tempo chosen for the quarter note in Fig. 45 (a) should be kept for (b), (c) and (d) so that the faster and slower steps have a consistent relationship in time. Such consistency in tempo is understood for all comparable examples.

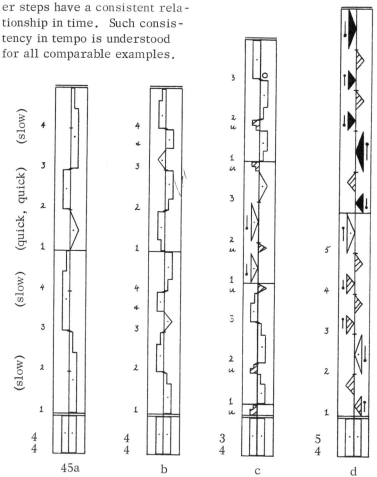

45a   b   c   d

DETAILS IN THE PERFORMANCE OF STEPS

A step is the total transference of the weight of the body from one foot to the other. The preparation for a step is the releasing of the active leg from the floor so that it can swing forward into the appropriate direction for the step. This preparation is not usually specified in the notation. The beginning of a step is understood to be the moment the stepping foot contacts the ground and the transference of weight begins. The beginning of the direction symbol represents this moment. A step ends when the weight is fully on the new support, centered on the supporting base.

Ordinary Walking

The direction symbol in the support column represents the simple, natural way of walking. The exact interpretation of "natural" is hard to define as people vary considerably in their movement; however, a "norm" can be observed and is distinct from stylized movement. When stylization is required we must add the specific details which produce the style in question. When these additions are constant throughout the piece, a key signature is given at the start to indicate such consistency.

Rotation of the Legs

Should these walking examples be performed with the legs turned out or with the feet parallel? Thus far no indication has been given for any rotation of the legs. Even though these patterns look and feel different when performed with outward rotation or with the legs parallel, the basic pattern remains unchanged. A step forward is still a step forward, and the feet together (in place) are still feet together whether turned out or not. To perform these steps in a simple, natural manner, the beginning reader should use the degree of rotation easiest for him; symbols for rotation will be discussed later.

Movement of the Center of Weight

In continuous walking in the same direction, the center of weight (center of gravity) of the body is set in motion and continues to move in the stated direction until it comes to rest on one or both supports A step in place or a pause between steps brings the center of weight to rest. When we change direction we must check the momentum of the center of weight so that we are ready to move fluently in the new direction. This anticipation of the new direction is not written, but is understood from what follows.

Center of weight comes to rest.

46a

Center of weight ceases to go forward and must prepare to go backward before the step backward.

b

Slow Steps

In a slow step, Fig. 47 (a), the transference of weight must be spread throughout the time allowed for the step, in this case three counts. Too often it is performed too quickly and then a pause ensues. A long step symbol indicates a sustained and continuous action in transferring the weight.

47a

Quick Steps

In a quick step, the action of contacting the floor with the foot and transferring the weight to the new support occurs almost simultaneously, as in Fig. 47 (b).

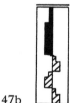

Legato Steps

47b

Legato means "tied together;" legato movements follow one another smoothly without a break. This type of movement is shown in the notation by one symbol following immediately after the other, as in the previous examples of walking and in Fig. 48 (a).

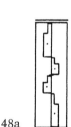

48a

Staccato Steps

Staccato means "separated", a break between movements. This break may be very slight as in Fig. 48 (b) where there is a slight pause, a hesitation or "breath" between the steps. In (c) there is a definite break, a pause of half a beat. Fig. (d) shows extremely staccato steps.

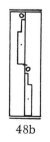

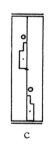

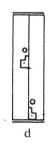

48b   c   d

Crossing Steps

To facilitate steps which cross the center line of the body, we tend to allow the hips to turn. Any such displacement returns to normal as soon as the step is over. If the hips should be specifically held still or should be specifically included in a crossing step, an additional indication must be written (see page 259).

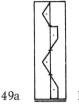 

49a   b

Middle Level Steps

Although in standing, middle level means that the knees are straight, in walking, normal pliancy is expected. This occurs as the leg is freed to prepare for the next step and also when the leg is released after it has relinquished the weight. This is also true of high steps.

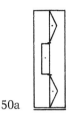 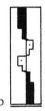

50a   b

CANCELLATION OF THE HOLD SIGN

A hold sign in the support column is valid until cancelled by:

(a) A step (on either foot), or
(b) An indication for a gesture of the leg previously held.

A step cancels a previous hold sign written for either foot or for both feet. A direction symbol in the support column indicates that all the weight is transferred to a given leg, therefore the hold sign will need to be repeated if a previous support is to be retained. An action stroke or a specific direction symbol written in the leg gesture column will cancel a previous held support on that leg. (See Fig. 103, page 90 and Fig. 200 (b), page 152.)

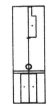      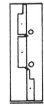

51a   b   c

| The step on the right foot cancels the previous hold on both feet. | The forward step on the left foot cancels the previous hold for the right foot. | The hold sign must be repeated to keep the weight on the right foot on count 3. |

Contrasts in the Use of Rhythms

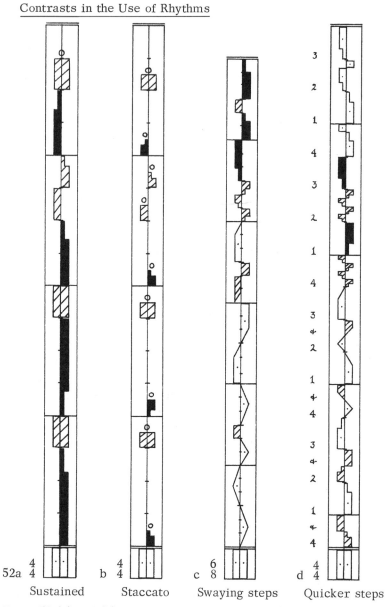

52a $\frac{4}{4}$	b $\frac{4}{4}$	c $\frac{6}{8}$	d $\frac{4}{4}$
Sustained	Staccato	Swaying steps	Quicker steps

Figs. 52 (a) and (b) are the same pattern but (a) is legato while (b) is staccato. In (d) two steps lead into the first measure, these form two upbeats on counts "4, &."

PATH OF THE CENTER OF GRAVITY IN STEPS

When the performer takes directional steps, his center of gravity moves into the direction stated. A rise and fall in the level of the center of gravity occurs with a change of level in the progression.

STRAIGHT PATHS

Horizontal Path

When a step follows in the same level as the previous step, the center of gravity will follow a horizontal path.

53a   b   c

In each of these examples the center of gravity moves horizontally, parallel with the floor, with no rise or fall.

Oblique Path

When a change of level occurs while the performer is progressing, his center of gravity rises or lowers on an oblique path. Both legs participate in effecting this change of level, though it is more noticeable in the leg actively becoming the new support.

In Fig. 54 (a) the center of gravity lowers on a direct line. The left knee begins to bend as the right foot steps out and both continue to bend during the transference of weight.

54a

Path of Center of Gravity:

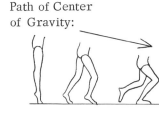

In Fig. 54 (b) the center of gravity rises on a direct line. The left knee begins to stretch as the right foot steps out and both legs continue to straighten and rise on half toe as the transference of weight continues.

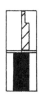

54b

Path of Center of Gravity:

ANGULAR PATH, CURVED PATH

A change of level which occurs during the process of transfer-ring weight produces a curved path for the center of gravity. These curves contrast with the angles produced when a change of level occurs after the progression (transference of weight) is finished. In the following examples the comparable angular movement will be given first.

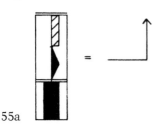

55a

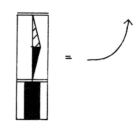

b

The sideward progression re-mains horizontal and is follow-ed by a vertical rising.

The sideward progression starts horizontally but begins to rise part way through.

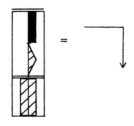

55c

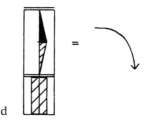

d

A horizontal sideward progres-sion followed by a vertical sinking. The transference of weight takes one count.

The sideward progression takes two counts and starts horizon-tally, but part way through it begins to sink.

It is important for the performer to note that (b) and (d) have transferences of weight which take two counts. This sustaining of the stepping action is physically difficult and requires control. Such changes in level within one step occur in all smooth flowing waltz steps. Fig. 55 (e) illustrates an un-dulating pattern which, starting in low level, if repeated, will move the center of gravity through the following path: ⌒⌒↘ .

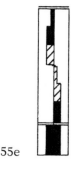

55e

READING MATERIAL

See next page for notes on reading.

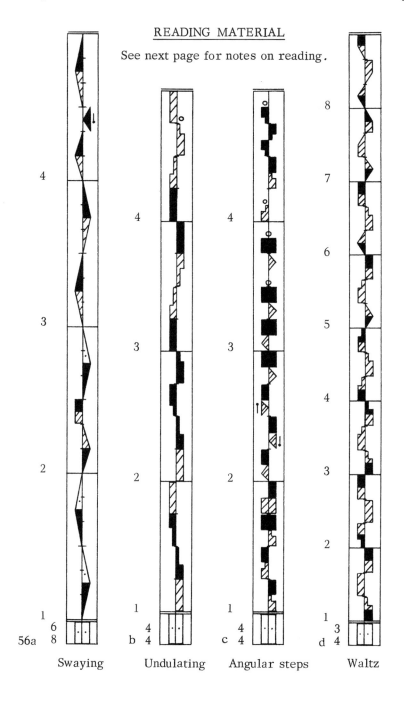

56a   6/8   b   4/4   c   4/4   d   3/4

Swaying   Undulating   Angular steps   Waltz

NOTES ON READING

Simple as walking patterns are, it is important to establish good reading habits from the start. Before physically performing the examples, glance over the whole exercise to get some idea of what is coming. Look for:

1. The meter used, and the tempo, if this is indicated.

2. The timing. Are the steps mainly slow, fast, at the same speed, or varying between all these?

3. Direction and level. What are the main directions used; is there constant change in direction? The sense of the spatial pattern often becomes clear when the rhythmic pattern has been worked out.

4. Familiar forms of movement. Are there known steps and patterns which can be called by name? Such recognition helps to speed up the memorizing process.

Our purpose in reading notation is not to become experts at deciphering symbols but to be able to translate into movement the information they contain as fast as possible. Because the dancer cannot perform with paper in hand, he must memorize the passages as soon as possible, teaching them to himself as though they were learned directly from a teacher. To be able to do this with ease, it is important to develop facility in recognizing the following:

5. Movement "words." The unit in movement which is comparable to a word in verbal language is any group of symbols forming a movement entity, an identifiable pattern. For example, a pas de basque is a dance word composed of three steps. This pattern may be performed simply or with much detail added but the unit remains the same. A dance word may coincide with a measure of music, it may be less, or more. The reader must discover this for himself; no rule can be stated.

6. Movement "phrases" and "sentences." A passage of two or more movement words forms a dance phrase or sentence. As in verbal language the phrase is incomplete, the sentence comes to a conclusion.

7. Major and minor words. Not all movement words are of equal importance in the dance sentence. Many words are conjunctions which serve as preparatory actions or as linking

movements for the main words. In western dance major
words usually begin and end on the strong musical beat, minor, linking or preparatory words falling on the weaker beats.

8. The kinetic sense. Look for the movement sense, or movement "meaning," as soon as possible. Do not memorize
long stretches in a superficial way; it is better to master
shorter sections more completely and find the kinetic meaning before moving on. The dance equivalent of musical
phrasing here comes into play: discovery of the natural unity
of thought, the long line of the movement, the correct placement of emphasis and the ebb and flow of energy. Attain-
ment of the kinetic sense includes awareness of how movement passages relate to the accompanying music. Even simple walking patterns provide leeway for subtle variations in
emphasis, dynamics, etc. underlying the movement pattern.

Once the piece has been memorized review it carefully, giving
attention to all important details, particularly the rhythms. Without a teacher on hand these are often inaccurately performed.

NOTES ON WRITING

In beginning to write we tend to take material in which we are
interested, without regard to its complexity. But for a first exercise it is better to choose something that can be done with simple steps, regarding as a challenge the making of an interesting
composition from such basic material. This chapter contains a
wealth of material with which can be written basic forms derived
from many styles of dance, particularly folk dance steps. Much
character and style can be indicated just by a change of direction,
and by the use of level, of rhythms, and of open and closed steps.

An experienced notator can record at once both sequence of steps
and timing, but the beginner should tackle one thing at a time. He
may first write the sequence and then adjust to the correct timing,
or indicate the timing by action strokes correctly placed on the
metered staff and then turn these into direction symbols.

Recording of Sequence First

For steps it is sufficient at first merely to draw the center line.
The following examples show a sequence first outlined simply, then
with counts added, and finally copied neatly. Fig. 57 (a) illustrates
the sequence of steps. In (b) the correct count numbers have been

placed next to the steps and the bar lines have been inserted. In (c) this information has been copied neatly onto graph paper with the step symbols correctly proportioned, some counts given as an indication, and the measure numbers added. For children, graph paper of 6 squares to the inch (or 2.5 cm) is usually used, for adults 8, for notators 10. Space is left for the starting position which is drawn the same length as the basic unit for the piece.

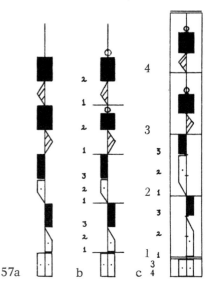

57a   b   c

Recording of Rhythm First

The notator may choose to pin down the rhythm of the steps by means of action strokes. He first marks off accurately the beat and measures so that the action strokes can be placed correctly. These then can be replaced by the appropriate direction and level symbols. Some notators prefer to write the rhythmic pattern this way, as in Fig. 58 (a), then give the spatial pattern separately, as in (b), finally combining the two as in (c).

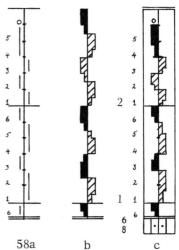

58a   b   c

Upbeats

Observe whether a piece begins with an upbeat. An upbeat occurs at the end of a measure and leads into the main movement which follows on the strong beat of the next measure. Allow room for an upbeat after the starting position and before the first bar line. Fig. 58 shows an upbeat step on count 6 of the previous measure prior to the main movement on count 1.

CHAPTER 6

Positions of the Feet

The five positions of the feet are part of the balletic heritage. The standard number is five, although some schools include a sixth. The best known terminology is given here as a guide. In these examples the positions are illustrated with the balletic turnout (90°), with a moderate turnout (45°), and with the feet parallel. The use of rotation of the legs is not stated in the notation of the position; this is given in Chapter 17.

THE CLOSED POSITIONS (Feet Together)

First Position

Normal standing position is understood to be with the feet together, side by side and touching, the center of weight being between the two feet, as shown in Fig. 59 (a). Any specific rotation of the legs (not written here, but necessary in stating balletic and other movement styles) does not change the basic relationship of the supports one to another or to the center of weight. The "false" first position referred to by Feuillet, in which the feet are turned in, as in (e), is written with the same place direction symbols but the toes are touching instead of the heels or inner edges of the feet. (See page 66, Fig. 68 (d) for the appropriate pins to show side by side relationship of the feet.)

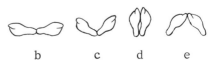

59   a   b   c   d   e

Third Positions

This position is basically the same as first in that the supports are directly beneath the center of weight, in place. The difference lies in the relation of the extremity of the legs, i.e. feet, one being diagonally in front of the other. A black pin is used to show this relationship, the point of the pin indicating the appropriate diagonal. The position can be described in terms of one foot being diagonally in front or the other foot being diagonally behind. The choice depends upon which foot is active. Both pins are used when both feet are active at the same time, as when the dancer is changing position in the air. The illustrations show third position with the right foot in front. Third position with the left foot in front is the same, but reversed laterally. In writing starting positions only one pin is needed, although both can be shown.

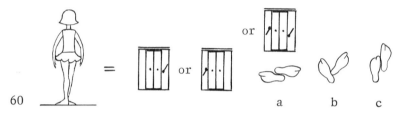

Fifth Position

Fifth position is basically the same as first position in that both supports are in place, but here one foot is directly in front of the other. To show this, the black pin points directly forward or backward. Fifth position can also be described as having one foot in front or as having the other behind, depending on which is active. When both feet are active, both pins are used. Only one pin need be used for a starting position. The choice of which pin to state is usually determined by which leg begins the next movement. The illustrations give fifth position with the right foot in front.

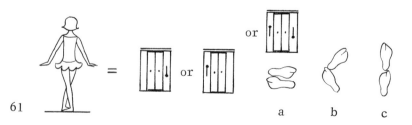

OPEN POSITIONS OF THE FEET (Feet Apart)

In the open positions the feet are apart and place (directly beneath the center of weight) lies exactly between the two feet. In the
diagrams here "X" marks place. The foot illustrations are drawn
with a comfortable degree of turnout. This has not been indicated
in the notation, which gives only the basic position.

Second Position

In second position, each support is
to the side of center, the right foot to
the right, the left foot to the left. The
symbols appear in the support columns
as for all weight-bearing indications.

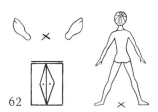

62

The Fourth Positions

The question of terminology arises here as differences exist in
what is termed "fourth" position, and some schools add a sixth position. In notation the ambiguity of terminology can be dispensed with
since the action itself is written. The following possibilities are
those most commonly met.

Fourth Position Opposite First.
Fig. 63 (a) shows the simple fourth
position taken as though opening out
from first position. The heels are
lined up on either side of the center
line of the body, just as they are in
first position. In ballet this position
is called fourth "ouverte" or open
fourth.   63a

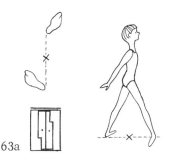

Fourth Position Opposite Third.
Fig. 63 (b) shows a fourth position
taken as though opening out from
third position.   63b

Fourth Position Opposite Fifth

Fig. 63 (c) shows a fourth position taken as though opening out from fifth position. The center line of the body extends through the center of each foot. In ballet this position is commonly called fourth "croisée" or crossed fourth.

63c

The Diagonal Positions

In certain forms of dance the diagonal positions are used.

The Open Diagonal Position

Fig. 64 (a) illustrates the open diagonal position (sometimes called an open fourth position). Each foot has a diagonal relationship to place.

64a

The Crossed Diagonal Position

Fig. 64 (b) shows the crossed diagonal position in which the right foot is in the left forward diagonal relation to place, and the left foot is in the right backward diagonal relation to place. To perform this correctly the body should not turn, otherwise the crossing effect is lost.

64b

The Crossed Second Position

In the crossed second position, familiar to us in folk dances and children's games, the black pin shows which leg is crossed in front or which behind. In Fig. 65 the left leg is in front. To show the feet on the lateral center line —• or •— must be added.

65

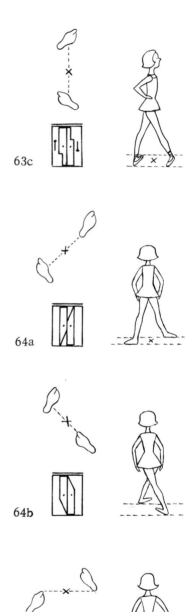

CHANGE OF LEVEL IN POSITIONS OF THE FEET

The position of the feet must be restated for each change of level. Low level is comparable to a half-knee bend (ballet demi-plié), and high level to a rise on the half toe (relevé). The full knee bend or deep knee bend (grand plié) is written with an additional indication, as explained on page 175.

66a   b   c

| Start in 2nd position on the half toe, knees straight; then lower the heels to a normal standing position. | Start in 4th position, left foot in front in low level; straighten the knees and rise to the half toe. | Start in 3rd, right foot front; bend knees, remaining in 3rd. |

In each of these examples, the feet do not move from the established position. Although in Figs. 66 (c) and (d) the feet do not move, we need to restate the pins for third and fifth positions. Without the pin, the position would become a first position. For a starting position only one pin is needed and to retain such a position only the same pin is needed.

66d

5th position, left foot front: start with bent knees, then straighten.

Mixed Levels in an Open Position

In an open position of the feet, a different level can occur on each support. When the levels are the same, the weight is placed equally on both feet. When one support is lower than the other, the center of weight will be closer to the lower support.

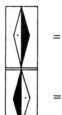 =     =

67a   b

INDICATION OF ACTIVE FOOT IN CLOSING

In closing into a third or fifth position, the pin is written for the foot which actively does the closing.

After the step forward, the left foot closes into 5th position.

68a

From 1st position while rising the right foot moves into 5th.

b

Where a change to first position occurs and it is not obvious from the context which foot should move, the pin which shows the sideward relationship of the feet must be added to show which foot makes the adjustment. Fig. 68 (c) shows first position as usually written, while (d) shows the fully stated lateral relationship of the legs.

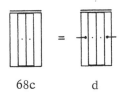

68c   d

Note the use of the sideward relationship pin in the following example where without it the meaning of the diagram is ambiguous.

A change from 5th position to 1st. No indication is given as to which foot is to move into 1st.

68e

The same change from 5th to 1st, with the right foot making the adjustment.

f

In a rise (relevé) in fifth position, it is usual for one foot to adjust so that the feet are neatly one in front of the other at the end of the rise. In lowering, an adjustment must also be made.

The right foot adjusts each time to form a neat 5th position.

68g

The left foot adjusts for each change of level (relevé and plié).

h

For a rise in fifth where neither foot adjusts, see page 69.

READING MATERIAL - Use of the Pins

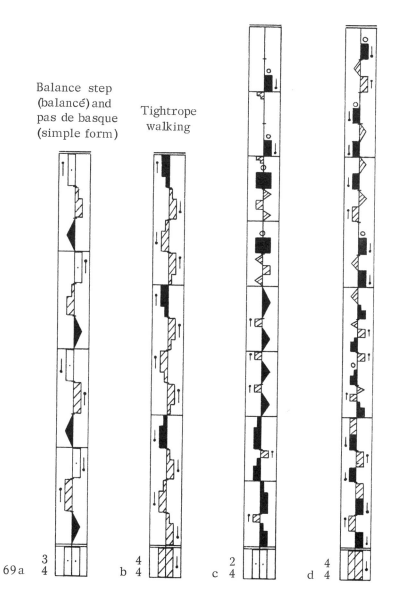

Balance step
(balancé) and
pas de basque
(simple form)

Tightrope
walking

69a 3/4   b 4/4   c 2/4   d 4/4

See page 58 for notes on reading.

TIGHTROPE WALKING

In normal walking each foot is placed on a path in line with its own hip. Walking on the center line, one foot in front of the other, as in tightrope walking, is shown by using black pins.

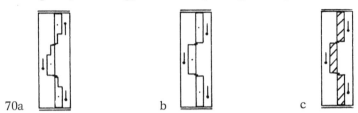

70a   b   c

Fig. 70 (a) shows tightrope walking, or walking on a center line. Each foot is placed in front of or behind the other. In (b) the steps are all in place, but each foot steps directly in front of the other foot. As a result, there will be a slight traveling motion forward. The amount of this traveling will depend on the rotation of the legs. If they are very turned out as in ballet, the distance covered will be only the width of the foot, but if the feet are parallel, it will be the length of the foot for each step. Fig. (c) shows the same pattern but performed in high level.

TRANSITIONS: OPEN AND CLOSED POSITIONS
RETENTION OF A PREVIOUS POINT OF SUPPORT

When there is no change of level a hold sign o is used to indicate that the foot remains on the ground carrying weight.

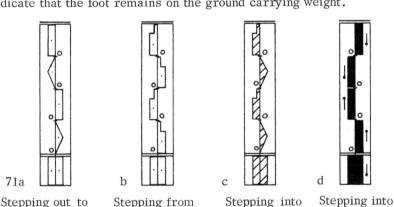

71a   b   c   d

Stepping out to   Stepping from   Stepping into   Stepping into
2nd position   one 4th position 2nd, then 4th   5th position
then back to 1st   into another

Where a change of level occurs, the hold sign cannot be used and a direction symbol must be written. Which direction symbol should be used depends on whether the action is described as: (a) Motion - the movement which produces the new position, or (b) Destination - the end result, the position to be reached.

MOVEMENT DESCRIPTION, POSITION DESCRIPTION

As explained in Chapter 4, the rule is to write steps (the path of the center of gravity) and changes in positions of the feet in terms of motion away from the previous point of support, and to write gestures in terms of destination, movement to established points. Finer descriptions of shift of weight from one position to another are written in terms of the movement of the center of gravity (movement description), but even advanced notators use position writing when it is more suitable to describe the end result.

The Staple - Position Writing

When choosing to write supports (transferences of weight) in terms of destination (the new position to be reached) this difference in description is expressed by the use of the staple [or] .

The staple makes the following statement: "Whatever the direction symbol states, the foot is to keep to the spot where it is at this moment (or where it was most recently)." A good example of a change in support best described through the use of the staple is a rise in fifth position in which neither foot is to be displaced. In writing such a rise, if no pin is written, the fifth position becomes a first position. If one pin is used, it indicates which foot actively adjusts to form a neat fifth position. If two pins are used they indicate that both feet adjust. (This can only be done with a slight spring.) Two staples are needed to anchor the feet to the ground when neither foot is to adjust.

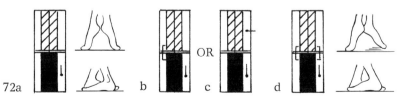

72a

b   OR   c   d

A rise changing to 1st position; either foot may adjust.

The right foot adjusts into 1st. (The left foot remains where it is.)

Neither foot adjusts; the balls of the feet remain where they are.

Stepping From Closed to Open Positions

Fig. 73 (a) states a simple opening out from first to second position by stepping with the right foot without any change in level. This basic action will be used in the following dis-   73a
cussions. Where a change of level occurs while stepping out into an open position, a direction symbol must be written instead of a hold sign, and a choice must be made between movement descrip-tion and position writing.

Movement Description. To finish in second position low level both legs must bend, the left staying where it is, the right taking a low step to the right. This action is correctly stated in Fig. 73 (b).

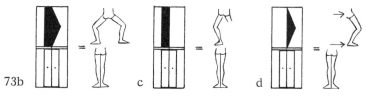

To understand the writing of Fig. 73 (b), which produces a second position with bent knees, we must first see that it is the combin-ation of (c) and (d) happening simultaneously. In (c) the weight is lowered while remaining over the left support. In (d) the weight is lowered while it is transferred completely to the right leg. When these two actions occur together, the center moves only half way to a point midway between the two feet.

Once the new position has been reached, any further change in the level of that position is written as usual (see Fig. 66).

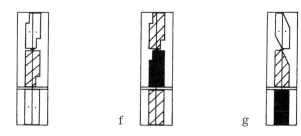

Step back with the   Step forward with   The right foot steps into
right leg into a high   the left leg into a a high crossed diagonal
4th position, then   low 4th position,   position, then lowers to
lower to middle level.   then rise.   middle level.

In all these examples it should be noted that the foot takes a normal-sized step in the stated direction but the center of gravity moves only half that distance.

With Change of Level: Position Description. In position writing, the destination to be reached is written and the staple is used to indicate how this destination was achieved, that is, which foot does not move.

Fig. 74 (a) shows a change into a low second position. The staple placed next to the side symbol for the left foot states that this is to be the end result (not the movement) and that the left foot is to remain where it is. Therefore, the right foot steps out to form the new position.   74a

Once the position is established, any further change of level in the same position does not require a staple, as illustrated in Figs. 74 (b), (c), and (d), which are the same as Figs. 73 (e), (f), and (g).

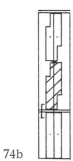

74b

c

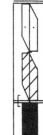

d

Stepping from One Open Position to Another: Position Description

Where no change of level occurs, the change in stepping from one open position into another can be written with the hold sign. In Fig. 75 (a) the right foot holds while the left steps forward into fourth, then the right holds while the left steps back into fourth. In (b) the same progression involves changes in level and so it is written as position writing with a staple.

75a

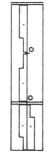

b

Stepping from Open into Closed Positions

The hold sign is used to show which foot remains where it is. The direction symbol shows which foot moves.

The right foot steps into place next to the left foot. The left foot steps into place next to the right foot.

76a   b

In the starting position of Fig. 76 (a), place is directly between the two feet. In the process of picking up the right foot to step, the center of weight automatically shifts to the left foot, and the direction place goes with it. This adjustment is understood and in simple examples need not be specifically written.

With Change of Level: Position Description. The transition from an open position into a closed position involving a change in level may need to be described as simply as possible. This is possible through position writing and the use of the staple.

77a   b   c

From a low 2nd position, close the right foot to the left in middle level.

From a high 4th position, close the right foot to the left bending the knees.

From an open diagonal position, close the left foot to the right while rising.

With Change of Level: Movement Description. In closing the feet together from an open position with a change of level, the movement description must show the center of weight shifting over to one support before the other closes in. Fig. 78 illustrates a low second position (a), followed by a shift of weight to the left foot coming up to middle level (b), then the right foot closing to the left (c). This two-part action of shifting and closing may involve specific timing for each part. Before exploring this timing basic shifts of weight will be discussed.

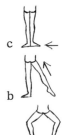

78

SHIFT OF WEIGHT

Unwritten Shifts of Weight

Fig. 79 (a) states simply that the weight is held on the left foot but not on the right, thus the shift over to the left foot is understood.

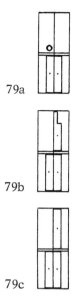

79a

The shift of weight which must occur prior to a step is often automatically understood and so need not be written. In (b) the feet start together with the weight equally on both feet. On count 1 there is a step forward on the right foot. The right foot must first be freed of weight in order to take this step. Therefore, just before count 1 the weight will shift completely over to the left foot. Spatially this is such a small shift that it is almost unnoticeable and it need not be written in the notation. The same shift occurs in (c), where the step on the right foot is in place.

79b

79c

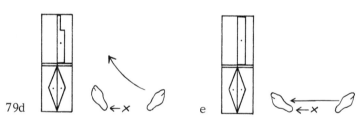

79d   e

In starting from an open position, the shift of weight before taking a step is larger, as in Fig. 79 (d). Here also the shift to the left foot is understood and need not be specifically written. The direction of the forward step will be judged from the new position of the center of gravity over the left foot. This same understood shift of weight occurs in a step in place, following an open position of the feet. In Fig. 79 (e) the right foot steps in place next to the left foot.

Fig. 79 (f) also shows the right foot stepping next to the left foot, in place, but in this example the weight ends on both feet, as indicated by the hold sign.

79f

Written Shifts of Weight

The following movement examples illustrate when the shift of
weight must be specifically indicated. Fig. 80 (a) shows a simple
step in place on the right foot in
low level. In (b) a sinking motion
on the right leg follows a start in

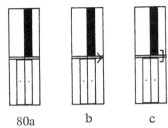

80a   b   c

first position. To show that this is a shift of weight, not a step in
place, the caret ⟨ or ⟩ must be used. This symbol is used in the
statement of the movement. The direction place low is also a statement of the position reached. The movement could also be written
with a staple, as in (c). In this instance both notations are correct.

A shift must also be written when the weight
is transferred to one foot after an open position
on both feet. In Fig. 80 (d) the weight is shifted from second position completely to the right
foot. The movement is one of the center of gravity moving to the side, lowering as it shifts.
The caret is used to indicate that this is not a
new step, because the foot is not lifted as it
would be prior to stepping.

80d

Movement
Description

In Fig. 80 (e) the same action has been written
as its final result. The position reached is a support on the right leg in place; therefore the place
symbol is used and the staple indicates that this is
position writing. The right foot does not move.

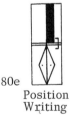

80e

Position
Writing

Meaning of the Caret. The symbol ⟨ or ⟩ , called the "caret,"
refers to a previous indication, stating that it is still in effect.
Basically the symbol means "the same." In shifts of weight it
shows that a previous partial support becomes a total support.

Timing and Change of Level in a Shift of Weight

Fig. 81 (a) is the notation of the action described in Fig. 78. Following a start in low second
position, the weight shifts to the left foot on count
1 while coming to middle level. On count 2 the
right foot closes to the left. Slight variations on
this same movement pattern will now be explored.

81a

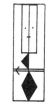

81b

c

d

Shift the weight
over to the left
foot in low level.
Straighten on the
closing.

The shift of weight
is slower and the
closing and straight-
ening are faster.

The shift of weight
is fast while the
straightening and
closing are slower.

Where a space occurs between this reference
and the previous support, the caret is not elongated but attached to the new indication where its
message is required. This is illustrated in Fig.
81 (e) in which there is a pause between the second position and the shift of weight to the left foot.   81e

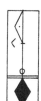

From these examples we see that a range of subtle variations
can be shown for such a movement. Illustrated below are some
of the possible variations which might occur if Fig. 81 (f), which
is written in position description, were written in movement description instead. Once the actual movement is described, questions concerning timing for the change of level as well as timing
for the shift of weight before the new fourth position must be answered specifically.

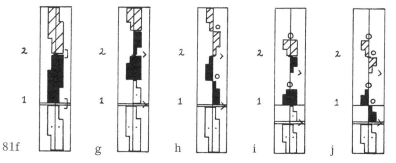

81f   g   h   i   j

Figs. 81 (g), (h), (i), and (j) each provide a subtle variation on the
step pattern simply described in Fig. (f). Such subtle description
is often not needed.

READING EXAMPLES

Stepping into Open Positions;   Shift of Weight.

Figs. 82 (a) and (c) are movement writing; (b) and (d) use position writing. Note that (a) and (b) are the same pattern.

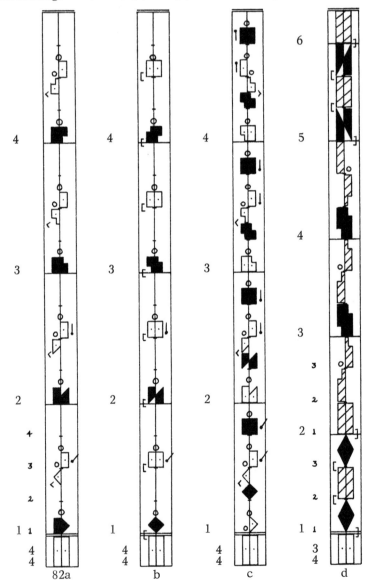

CHAPTER 7

Aerial Steps (Jumps)

SUPPORT AND ABSENCE OF SUPPORT

A gap between movement symbols means an absence of movement. In the support column, however, a gap between movement symbols means an absence of support.

 Continuous steps, the weight supported on the feet 83a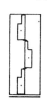

A run. The gap indicates no support; the weight leaves the ground. b

AERIAL STEPS, JUMPS

The term "jumps" is used here as a generic term referring to all modes of unsupported movement, i.e. aerial steps, steps of elevation which spring into the air. The term "a jump" is used for the specific form given in Fig. 85 (a) on page 79.

The Basic Rule Regarding Jumps

Springing into the air is written by leaving a space in both support columns. As long as the weight is shown to have a support, a jump does not occur. Where no movement symbol is written in the support column, the hold sign o is written to keep the weight on the ground.

The amount of space left between support symbols indicates how long the body is in the air. This may be momentary, or for one or more beats. The longer the space, the longer the time spent in the air. This time may be used to jump higher or travel farther.

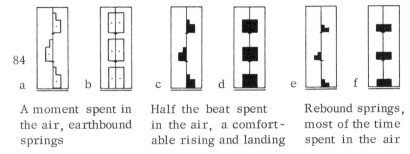

84					
a	b	c	d	e	f

A moment spent in the air, earthbound springs	Half the beat spent in the air, a comfortable rising and landing	Rebound springs, most of the time spent in the air

Fig. 84 (a) shows a simple run; (c) and (e) show leaps with (e) the more airborne.

THE WRITING CONVENTION

Through the convention of leaving the support column blank, the complex action of the legs required in rising off the ground and returning to it can be written simply. The level of the supports and the time spent in the air indicate the adjustments necessary for small springs, close to the ground, or for high jumps using the physical "springboard," without the need to write complex details.

TYPES OF JUMPS

For purposes of analysis, jumps fall into two general categories:

Minor Jumps

Simple unadorned steps such as those which occur in many folk dances need only be described by symbols in the support column. The free leg is used in a simple, unstressed way and so it need not be described.

Major Jumps

In larger jumps the use of the legs while in the air is often of particular importance. These include jumps in which the legs are spread or the knees pulled up. In such cases it is necessary to state what the legs do, and so leg gestures must be written.

Two leg gestures will cancel any previous support of the feet. A gesture of the supporting leg will send the body into the air. Only basic jumps will be dealt with in this chapter. For jumps with leg gestures, see Chapter 10.

The Five Basic Forms

Each aerial step, no matter how complicated, belongs to one of five basic forms. If these are recognized from the first, analysis of the more complex types met later on becomes easier.

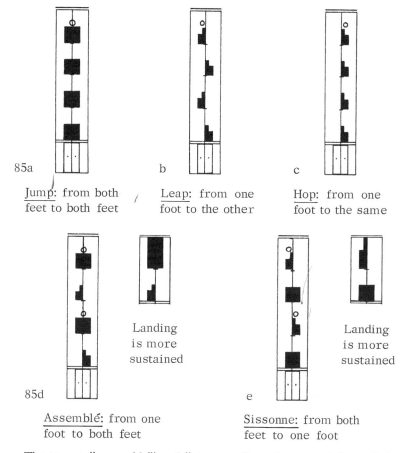

85a   Jump: from both   b   Leap: from one   c   Hop: from one
      feet to both feet   foot to the other   foot to the same

85d   Assemblé: from one   Landing
      foot to both feet   is more
                                  sustained

      e   Sissonne: from both   Landing
          feet to one foot   is more
                                  sustained

The terms "assemblé" and "sissonne" are borrowed from ballet, because there are no everyday terms for these two forms. However, they exist in all forms of dance, sports, etc.

JUMPS USING THE POSITIONS OF THE FEET

In jumping from one position of the feet to another, as in the examples below, the center of weight remains over the same spot, while the feet change their relation to the center, i.e. to place.

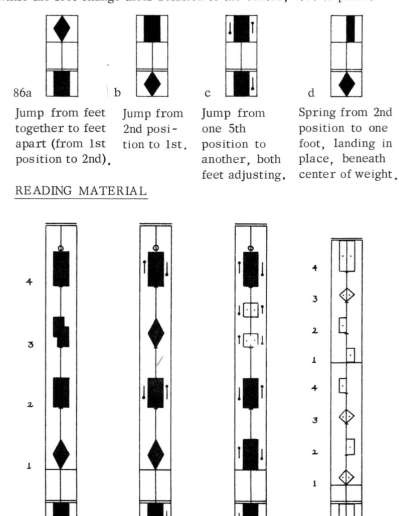

86a — Jump from feet together to feet apart (from 1st position to 2nd).

b — Jump from 2nd position to 1st.

c — Jump from one 5th position to another, both feet adjusting.

d — Spring from 2nd position to one foot, landing in place, beneath center of weight.

READING MATERIAL

87a   b   c   d

In all these examples the center of weight stays over the same spot, only the direction and placement of the supports change.

LEVELS OF JUMPS

The levels of supports used in steps are also used in jumps.

Middle Level

Jumps are written with middle level supports when there is very little vertical change (rise and fall), the body remaining in the same vertical area. The weight is supported on the whole foot or with the heel just slightly off the floor. The natural pliancy of the legs is understood because middle level does not imply stiff knees.

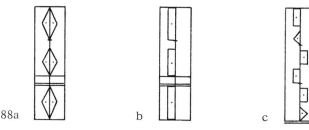

88a

Slight springs in
2nd position

b

Hops barely rising
off the floor

c

Tiny springs between
each support

High Level

Springs in high level also use the natural pliancy of the legs, but the weight is on the ball of the foot. Such jumps are basically high level supports with a moment in the air between each. The rise from the ground is achieved through use of the toes and by lifting the center of weight. Here knee flexion is slight. Only small springs can occur from high level supports. For a high jump the springboard produced by a low support (bending the legs) is needed.

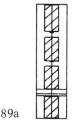
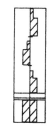
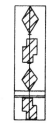

89a

Tiny springs in
1st position

b

A run in high level,
a tiny spring be-
tween each step

c

Tiny springs
from 4th to 2nd

Low Level

In jumps written with low level supports, the use of the legs depends on how high the jump is. If there is only a moment in the air, the legs do not have time to stretch and the feet will hardly leave the ground. Where a longer time is spent in the air, it is expected that the legs will extend as part of the springboard action.

Tiny springs in 1st position, the body hardly rising at all 90a	A normal-sized jump, half a beat spent in the air 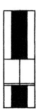 b	Transitions in level understood but not written in (b)  c

Lifting the Weight from the Feet

A change can be made from one position of the feet to another by lifting the weight off the feet enough for them to move to a new position without a real jump having occurred. This foot action is sometimes called "snatching"; in ballet it occurs in an "échappé" (escaping movement) and also in a spring from a low fifth into a high fifth in which both feet adjust. The feet are not usually clear of the floor but no marked sliding need occur. To show this lifting of the weight without lifting the feet clear of the floor at the moment of the unwritten preparation for the change, we indicate a partial support by writing action strokes in the gesture column next to the supports. Degrees of weight-bearing or part of the foot still contacting the floor can be shown when a detailed description is needed. Compare Fig. 91 (a) and (b) below. In (a) the tiny space between support symbols indicates a slight spring so that the échappé is performed with the feet just clear of the floor. In (b) no spring occurs but the weight is lifted so that the feet can shoot out simultaneously. In (c) the toes are drawn together in a high fifth by lifting the weight.*

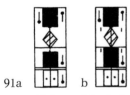

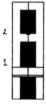

91a   b   c

Echappé in 2nd

Relevé in 5th

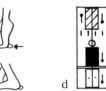

The same as (c), if a pause occurs

* See Appendix B, note 2.

TRAVELING JUMPS

A direction symbol in the support column indicates traveling of the center of weight. In stepping (transference of weight to a new point of support) the direction in which the center of gravity travels and the direction in which the foot steps are the same. This holds true for springing from foot to foot, and landing indicates the direction in which the center of gravity has traveled. In stepping the direction of the new support is judged from the previous point of support. In jumps direction of traveling is judged from the center of gravity.

Step to the side. Leap to the side.
The center of weight   The center of weight
moves to the side.   moves to the side.

92a   b

TRAVELING IN CLOSED POSITIONS OF THE FEET

In jumping with the feet together, the center of weight remains over both feet; in terms of direction the description can be the same as that for jumping on one leg.

93a | b | c

Hop on the right   Hop on the left   Jump on both legs,
leg, traveling to   leg, traveling   traveling to the right
the right.   to the right.   with the feet together.

It can readily be seen that Fig. 93 (c) is a combination of (a) and (b). Jumps in third and fifth position can also be written in this way, as can any spring which, though starting on one foot, or with the feet apart, ends with the feet together.

Jump in 5th 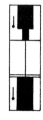 Jump from one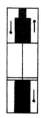
position, travel-   5th position to
ing backward.   the other, travel-
                                      ing forward.

93d   e

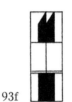 93f

 g

 h

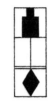 i

| Jump in 1st position travel-ing right for-ward diagonal. | Jump from 1st position into 5th, traveling left. | Jump from 2nd position into 1st, traveling right. | Jump from 2nd position into 1st, traveling forward. |

TRAVELING IN OPEN POSITIONS OF THE FEET

In jumping into an open position of the feet, the direction sym-bols in the support column state the relation of the two supports to the center (place) and do not state traveling of the center of weight as they do in a step or in a spring which lands on one foot.

 94a

 b

 c

| The support and center of weight move to the right. | The support and center of weight move to the left. | The supports move out but the center of weight remains over the same spot. |

In most cases traveling of the center in jumps in open positions must be shown by the addition of a path sign.

PATH SIGNS

A path sign to show the traveling of the center of weight is placed outside the staff on the right, adjacent to the jump it describes. Traveling on a straight path is shown by short horizontal lines connected by a vertical line as in Fig. 95 (a). The direction of the traveling motion is written inside the broken vertical line. The direction indicator is left blank unless one is specifically traveling up or down as in going up or downhill.

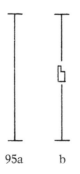 95a   b

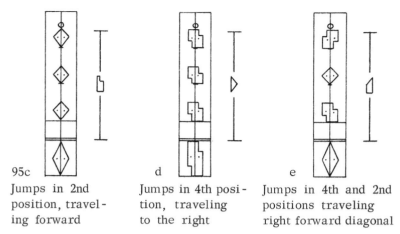

95c
Jumps in 2nd
position, travel-
ing forward

d
Jumps in 4th posi-
tion, traveling
to the right

e
Jumps in 4th and 2nd
positions traveling
right forward diagonal

Path for a Single Traveling Jump

Certain traveling jumps can be written either with direction
symbols in the support column or with a path sign. There is no
difference in meaning; it is just a choice of description.

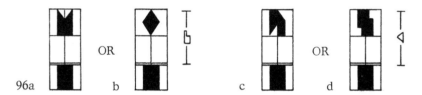

96a   OR   b   c   OR   d

In certain cases the most direct way to show traveling is with
a path sign, as in the following examples.

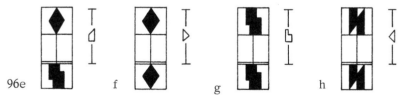

96e   f   g   h

The path signs are placed on the right side of the staff, outside
the column for the head. If there are no indications for the head
or for the arms, the path sign can be drawn closer to the staff as
in these examples. The path starts with the rising into the air
and finishes as the weight is centered (ceases to travel) over the
new support. This is usually after the foot touches the ground on
landing (after the start of the landing direction symbol).

Landing on the Same Spot

Sometimes in jumping from open to closed positions one foot should land on the same spot as that on which it was placed in the previous position. This can be shown by the use of a staple. The action is comparable to that of stepping into or out of an open position of the feet, but in this case it is sprung rather than stepped. The staple indicates the retention of the same spot for that foot.

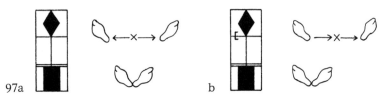

97a

| In a plain jump, both feet spring apart. The center of weight remains over the same spot. | The left foot lands where it was before. The right foot lands to the side while the center travels half that distance. |

As we can see, Fig. 97 (b) can be compared to stepping into second position, because the result is the same both for the placement of the feet and for the traveling of the center of weight.

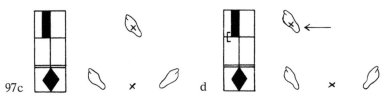

97c

| In a plain jump, the landing in place will be on the spot between the two feet. | Place is designated as being where the left foot was. Therefore, the foot will come down on that spot and the center will move left to end over that support. |

When a staple is written in consecutive stepping, the foot remains on the floor. In jumping the foot must release because of the spring, but it will return to the same spot. In Fig. 97 (d) the landing is written as place, being described as the final position reached. Fig. (e) shows the movement description of a similar action but does not specify that the foot lands on exactly the same spot.

97e

READING STUDY IN TRAVELING JUMPS

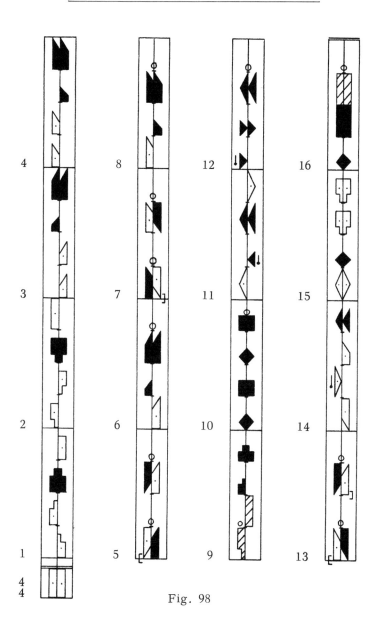

Fig. 98

THE TIMING OF JUMPS

Take-Off and Landing

The end of the support symbol before a jump shows the moment when the leg leaves the ground, and a prior push-off preparation is understood. In Fig. 99 (a) this is shown by "w." During the space that follows, a rise into the air is understood to take place and also a falling toward the ground again. This is shown by "x." The moment of contact with the ground, the start of a new support (landing) is shown at "y." The landing "z" can be abrupt, as in (a), where the duration of the shock absorbing action is short and the position reached is held, or it can be sustained as in (b), where the length of the landing symbol shows the cushioning effect, the control of landing softly. If this landing is followed by another jump, part of the symbol will be understood to include the preparation for the following jump. Thus as in representations of steps, the exact meaning of the support depends on what follows (see Appendix C for exact timing).

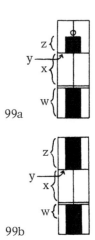

99a

99b

On Beat, Off Beat Jumps

Most forms of jumps land on the beat. The dancer's return to the ground, the landing, occurs on a relatively strong beat in the music. Off beat jumps in which the performer is in the air on the strong musical beat create a different expression and quality. If a jump is to land on the beat, the moment in the air must precede the beat. The space to show this moment in the air must be written before the landing support symbol, which is placed on the beat. In off beat jumps, the moment in the air will be on the beat.

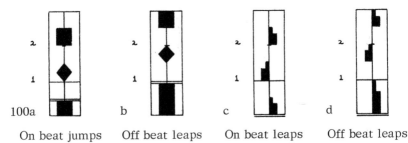

100a   b   c   d

On beat jumps   Off beat leaps   On beat leaps   Off beat leaps

SKIPS, GALLOPS

A skip can be analyzed as a step followed by a hop, as in Figs. 101 (b) and (c), or as a hop followed by a step, as in Fig. 101 (d), depending on where in the two-part action one starts. But a step-hop is not necessarily a skip. A skip always has an uneven rhythem. A step-hop may have even timing.

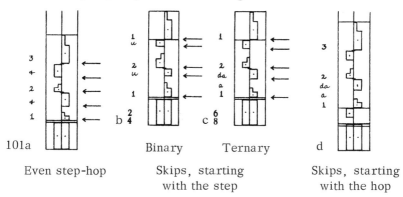

101a

Even step-hop   Skips, starting   Skips, starting
                     with the step   with the hop
                   Binary   Ternary
                     b 2/4   c 6/8   d

In Fig. 101 (a) the step occurs on count 1, and the hop lands on the "&." The arrow pointing to the start of each symbol (which gives the rhythm) shows the steps are evenly spaced. If each support were stamped, the regular division could be heard clearly. In (b) an uneven rhythm, as is illustrated by the arrows, is produced in 2/4 meter. This is termed a binary division; the step takes half the count, the moment in the air and the hop landing take the other half (one quarter each). In contrast, (c) shows the same skip pattern written in 6/8 meter with a ternary (three-part) subdivision. The latter is more comfortable to perform and hence more usual for skips. Note the slight difference in the spacing of the arrows between Figs. (b) and (c). In (d) the ternary skip starts with an upbeat hop.

The gallop is similar in rhythmic pattern to the skip but the footwork is a step-leap form. The same foot takes the step each time and the landing after the moment in the air is always on the other foot. Fig. 101 (e) shows a step-close pattern, and (f) the same pattern with the moment in the air after the step which turns it into a gallop.

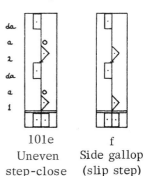

101e   f
Uneven   Side gallop
step-close   (slip step)

The gallops shown in Fig. 101 (f) in a ternary subdivision can also be performed in a binary rhythm and all gallops and skips can be done in different directions.

In another form of gal-
lop the moment in the air
occurs before the travel-
ing step, which is followed
immediately by the closing
step as in Fig. 101 (h).
The character of the step
is altered by this different
placement of the rising into
the air. Figs. (g) and (h)
are placed side by side for
comparison.

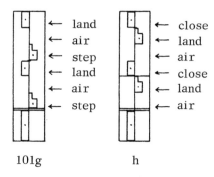

101g   h

Two forms of gallop

LOCOMOTOR PATTERNS

The term "locomotor" is given to all movements of the body which progress in space. These consist mainly of walking, run-ning, leaping, jumping, galloping, and skipping, and their many variations. In reading and writing
these, it is important to observe
where the moment in the air (the
"air space") occurs, as this may
change the basic form of the movement. Note that Fig. 102 (a) is a
step, hop and (b) a leap, hop, the
difference being shown by the gap
between the starting support and
the first forward symbol.

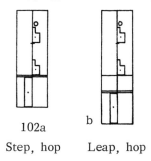

102a   b

Step, hop   Leap, hop

JUMPS FOLLOWING HELD SUPPORTS

When a spring into the air follows a held support,
an action stroke written in the appropriate leg gesture column indicates that the leg is free of weight,
thus cancelling the previous hold sign. In Fig. 103
an action stroke is needed for the right leg to show
springing into second position, then for each leg to
show springing into first. When specific leg gestures occur, appropriate direction symbols replace
the action strokes.

103

READING STUDY IN GALLOPS AND SKIPS

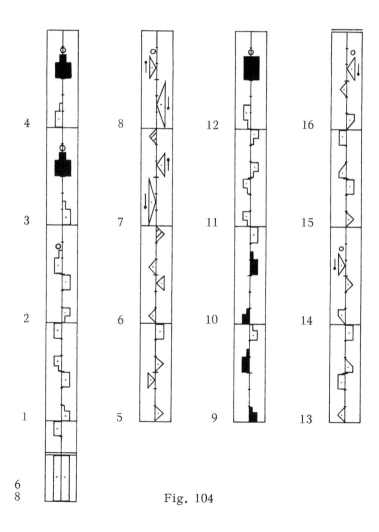

Fig. 104

CHAPTER 3

Turns

PIVOT TURNS

Turning (rotating) is one of the basic forms of movement. It can be performed by individual parts of the body, or by the body as a whole, revolving as a unit, as in a pivot turn. A pivot turn is a revolution around one's own vertical axis. Pivot turns are performed to the right (clockwise) or to the left (counterclockwise or anticlockwise). The symbol for turning is a parallelogram whose slanting lines indicate the direction of the turn.

DIRECTION OF TURN

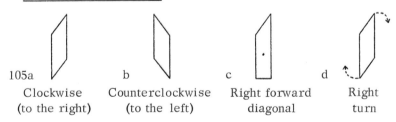

105a	b	c	d
Clockwise (to the right)	Counterclockwise (to the left)	Right forward diagonal	Right turn

Note in Fig. 105 (c) the difference between the drawing of a diagonal direction symbol in which there is one slanting line indicating the desired direction, and the turn sign which has two parallel slanting lines, thus indicating the revolving action.

The Composite Turn Sign

The composite turn sign, the two turn signs drawn on top of one another as in Fig. 106, serves certain purposes. It can state "turn either right or left," leaving the choice to the performer; it can be used as 106 a statement of focal point for a starting position (see Fig. 140 this chapter), or it can mean "rotated neither in nor out" when applied to gestures of the limbs (see Chapter 17).

GENERAL STATEMENT OF TURNING

In Motif Writing the turn sign by itself makes the general statement that such a revolution of the whole body is to be performed. The amount of turning is not stated, but is left open to the performer. Fig. 107 (a) illustrates a motif consisting of turning to the right followed by turning to the left. Fig. (b) states a general movement forward followed by a turn either to the right or to the left.

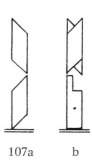

107a   b

SPECIFIC STATEMENT: PLACEMENT ON THE STAFF

The turn symbol is used for turns of the body as a whole as well as for rotations or twists of the individual parts of the body.

By placing a turn sign in the appropriate column of the staff, the part of the body that is to turn can be indicated. Fig. 108 (a) shows:

(1) the support column - turns of the body as a whole;
(2) the leg gesture column - rotations (twists) of the leg;
(3) the third (body) column - rotations (twists) of the torso;
(4) the arm column - rotations (twists) of the arm.

Rotations can also be shown for specific parts of the body by placing the specific sign for that part in front of the turn sign, as illustrated in Figs. 108 (b) and (c).

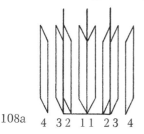

108a   4 3 2 1 1 2 3 4

b   C

c

| Placement of the turn sign on the staff | Rotations right and then left of the head | Outward and inward twists of the right lower arm |

The following discussion will center around pivot turns. Rotations of the arms and legs are dealt with in Chapter 17, rotations of the torso and its parts in Chapter 18.

In the Support Columns

A turn sign placed in the support column indicates a turn of the whole body on its support, usually one foot or both feet. During such turns the foot swivels on the floor. To show turning on both feet the symbol is drawn across both support columns. Note the meaning of the following:

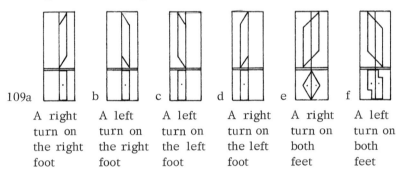

109a	b	c	d	e	f
A right turn on the right foot	A left turn on the right foot	A left turn on the left foot	A right turn on the left foot	A right turn on both feet	A left turn on both feet

DEGREE OF TURN

The amount of turn accomplished is stated within the turn sign. Black pins are used to indicate the degree of turn, that is, the relation of the new front to the front established just before the turn. This previous front is like the number 12 on a clock, and the black pins can be likened to the hands of the clock moving clockwise or counterclockwise through the possible degrees of rotation of $\frac{1}{8}$, $\frac{1}{4}$, $\frac{3}{8}$, $\frac{1}{2}$, etc. Note that these degrees are relative, the destination reached by $\frac{1}{4}$ turn right would require $\frac{3}{4}$ of a turn left.

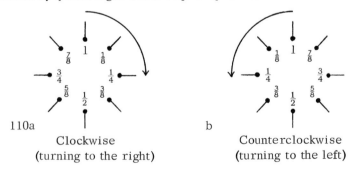

110a	b
Clockwise (turning to the right)	Counterclockwise (turning to the left)

Once a turn has been performed, a new front is established from which the amount of a subsequent turn will be judged. If, before starting a turn, the performer points into the direction indicated by the pin, this direction will become the new front. Thus it can be seen that in each case the black pin shows the relation of the new front to the old.

111a $\frac{1}{4}$ turn to the right   b $\frac{1}{2}$ turn to the right

For both half and full turns the destination is the same whether one turns clockwise or counterclockwise.

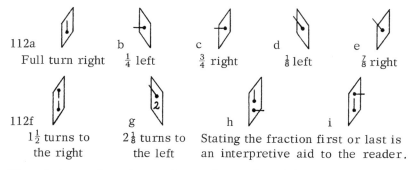

112a   b   c   d   e
Full turn right $\frac{1}{4}$ left $\frac{3}{4}$ right $\frac{1}{8}$ left $\frac{7}{8}$ right

112f   g   h   i
$1\frac{1}{2}$ turns to $2\frac{1}{8}$ turns to   Stating the fraction first or last is
the right   the left   an interpretive aid to the reader.

The pin is preferred as a sign to the number 1 because the latter is not always distinguishable from other symbols. However, for multiple turns of two or more the number is used, as in (g).

COMBINATION OF STEPPING AND TURNING

A turn can occur before a step, after a step, or during a step.

The Turn as a Preparation for a Step

A quick turn, often of only a small degree, frequently occurs just before a step, usually on the musical upbeat. The purpose of such a turn is to face into a new room direction. In performance it is given no importance and occurs without being stressed. 113a

Step as a Preparation for a Turn

Where the turning action is important the preceding step is usually fast, the weight being transferred quickly so that the allotted time can be
spent turning. Thus the step is not of particular
importance, even though it usually occurs on an
important beat in the measure.

113b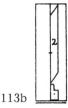

Blended Step-Turn

When one symbol (movement indication) follows another without a
break, it is understood that there is
no break in the continuity of movement. Fig. 113 (c) shows a turn following a step immediately. There is
no stop between the two actions; however, they are still clearly separate.
To blend the two, that is, to have the
one action overlap the other, the symbols must be tied by a vertical bow,
as explained below.

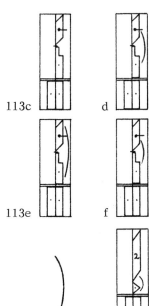

113c

d

113e

f

The Simultaneous Action Bow

The simultaneous action bow (a
round vertical bow, Fig. 113g) states
that two movements of a different nature, written one after the other on
paper, should occur simultaneously.

113g

h

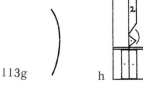

As applied here, the length of this bow indicates the duration of
the overlap of the two actions of stepping and turning. The longer
the bow, the more overlap, as in (d) and (e). A short bow indicates
only a slight overlap as in (f). In most such blended step-turn actions, the foot is placed on the floor in preparation for the step before the turning action begins, so that the direction of the step is
clear. To show this, the bow is not started until after the start
of the step. Where a fast step leads into a turn, the body tends
naturally to perform some overlap even when none is written. To
stress such overlap and the resulting smoothness, the bow can be
written as in (h). Other possibilities in combining turns with steps
are given on pages 102 and 113.

READING STUDY IN STEPS WITH PIVOT TURNS

This study presents some basic rumba patterns found in ball-room dancing. No style for exact performance is given, only the outline of the pattern of the steps.

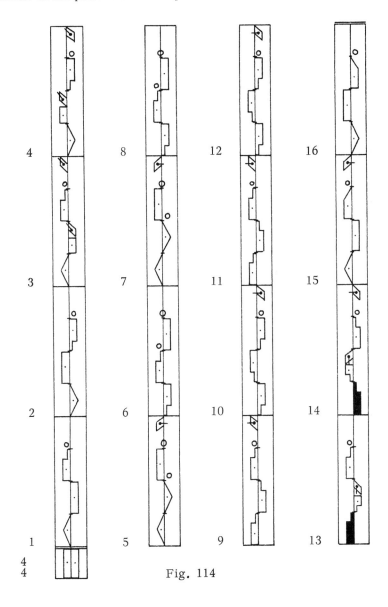

Fig. 114

LEVEL OF PIVOT TURNS

A turn is performed in the same level as the previous step or support. In low and middle level the heel is raised enough to avoid undue friction, this weight on the ball is understood and not written.

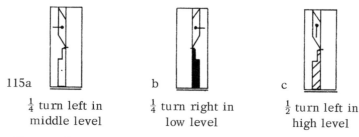

115a $\frac{1}{4}$ turn left in middle level

b $\frac{1}{4}$ turn right in low level

c $\frac{1}{2}$ turn left in high level

Change of Level During a Turn

If there is a change of level during a turn it can be shown by shading the turn sign. The shape of the parallelogram is kept intact. When a change of level occurs at the start of a turn, the beginning of the turn sign is shaded; when it occurs at the end, the end is shaded; when it occurs throughout the turning action, the whole sign is shaded, but a segment in the middle must be left blank for the pin showing the degree of turn. It is also possible to write the change of level as a support sign in place and to tie this indication to the turn sign with the simultaneous bow to indicate that the two happen at the same time.

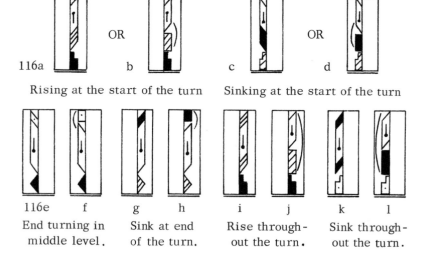

116a   OR   b   Rising at the start of the turn

c   OR   d   Sinking at the start of the turn

116e   f   End turning in middle level.

g   h   Sink at end of the turn.

i   j   Rise through-out the turn.

k   l   Sink through-out the turn.

There may be more than one
change of level during a turn,
as in Fig. 116 (m). Space
must be left for the pin.

Note the correct drawing of
the slanting lines and the

116m   n   o   p

method of indicating middle level as in Figs. 116 (n), (o), and (p).

PIVOT TURNS ON ONE FOOT

A complete pivot turn on one foot, called a "pirouette" in classical ballet, can start from any of the positions of the feet. In the
typical examples given below no indications have been stated for
the free leg, which may be in any direction, though it is usually
placed with the foot close to the supporting leg. For such pivots
the terms "outside turn" and "inside turn" are used. An "inside
turn" is a turn on the right foot to the right, or on the left foot to
the left. An "outside turn" is a turn on the right foot to the left or
on the left foot to the right.

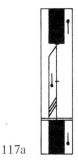 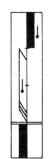 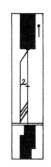 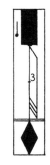

117a   b   c   d

| "Outside" turn (outward, en dehors) from 5th position | "Inside" turn (inward, en dedans) start- ing on one leg | Two "outside" turns from 4th position ending in 5th | Triple "out- side" turn starting from 2nd position |

Pivot Between Two Points

A combination of step turns can,
on being repeated, produce pivoting
around two points, as in Figs. 118
(a) and (b). Note the space patterns
produced by steps combined with
half turns in Figs. 118 (c) and (d).

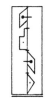

118a   b

Forward steps fol-
lowed by half turns
produce pivoting
around two points,
but no progression
in space.

118c

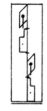

Alternating the di-
rection of the turn
does not change the
space pattern estab-
lished in Fig. 118 (c).

d

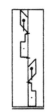

Chain of Turns

A continuous progression in space occurs when steps taken in opposite directions are combined with turning, as in the examples below. A common form of this movement (known in ballet as "petits tours," "enchainé" or "déboulé" turns) uses steps to the side with a half pivot turn between each step, turning always into the same direction. Such turns are usually composed of steps in high level as in Fig. 119 (b).

119a 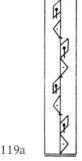 b 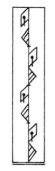 c 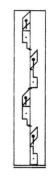 d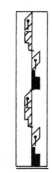

A chain of turns
traveling on a
straight path

A series of
enchainé
turns

A progression
on a straight
path with turns
to the right

The same se-
quence with a
change of level

Step-Close Turns

In step-close turns, called "posé" or "piqué" turns in ballet, a full turn appears to be performed on the foot which steps out, with the closing action occurring afterward, as is written in Fig. 120 (a). In practice, however, part of the turn is taken on the foot which closes to prepare for the following turn and to produce an unbroken flow of turning action. Fig. 120 (b) shows a single posé turn, and (c) a double. No position is given here for the free leg, which can be in any direction but is usually held close to the supporting leg.

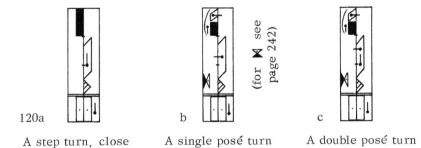

120a — A step turn, close   b — A single posé turn   c — A double posé turn

SLOW TURNS ON ONE FOOT

In a slow turn on one foot, called a "promenade" turn in ballet, the turning action is never interrupted. During the turn the heel is raised and lowered momentarily several times to assist the turning action, but this raising and lowering is not usually written.

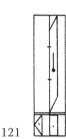

121

PIVOT TURNS ON TWO FEET

A pivot turn on two feet is like a swivel in which both feet remain where they are. The swiveling action normally occurs on the balls of the feet, rather than the heels. The turn sign is written across both support columns. For clarity in explaining these examples, the end position resulting from the turn has been written.

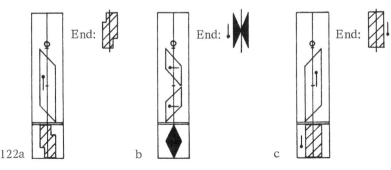

122a — A swivel from 4th to 4th in high level   b — Swivels starting in 2nd and finishing with the legs crossed   c — A swivel from one 5th position to the other

INTERWOVEN TURNS

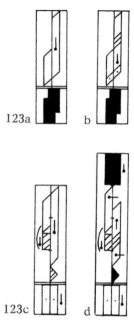

An interwoven turn can start on two feet and finish on one, or it can start on one foot and finish on two. In Fig. 123 (a) a low level swivel turn starts from fourth position and ends turning only on the right foot. Altogether one full turn is performed. In (b) the same turn occurs with a change in level. Here the swivel starts in middle level and then rises as the weight goes over the right foot. When the turn starts on one foot and continues on two, the second foot must be placed on the floor. Just when and where this support takes place must be indicated. In (c) a side step is followed immediately by a pivot turn on that foot. Then, while continuing to turn, the left foot is placed in front of the right and the turn continues on two feet. One full turn results. In (d) this same kind of turn is written with more precise detail. Starting in low level, the turn rises as the second foot takes on weight. The turn then continues on both feet until toward the end of the action, when all the weight is taken over by the left foot so that the right is free to be closed neatly into fifth position. In this example the amount of turn has been broken down for each part of the action, $\frac{1}{4}$, $\frac{1}{2}$, $\frac{1}{4}$, but there is no break in the flow of turning and a single full turn is thus achieved. (See page 142 for leg gestures.)

123a b

123c d

Soutenu turn
(Assemblé soutenu turn)

CONTINUOUS TURNING

Where continuous turning is combined with a change of level, it is better to place the turning action outside the staff. Fig. 124 (a) illustrates the placement of the turn sign in the support column as usual. The step forward is followed by a continuous rising and lowering while turning on that support. Although the continuity of turning is clear, the amount of turning must be divided. Such detailed analysis is often not required. 124a

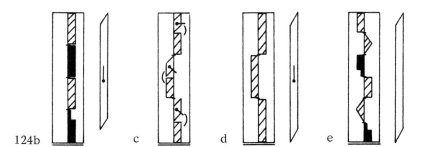

124b   c   d   e

In Fig. 124 (b) the turning action has been written outside the staff
(beyond indications of arm and head actions where these exist)
alongside the rising and lowering action in the support column. It
is understood that sliding friction occurs between the foot and the
floor. Fig. (c) shows steps in place constantly turning, the amount
of turn for each step being stated. When such a breakdown is unnecessary and all that is required is an over-all statement of how
much turning is achieved in all, the action of constant pivoting can
be written outside the staff as in (d). In (e), a box waltz pattern is
shown with continuous turning to the right. The performer will
pivot on each step. In this example no degree of turning is shown;
this is left open to the reader.

TURNS IN THE AIR

A turn in the air involves turning the whole body in an unsupported
state. To indicate a turn in the air, the turn sign is written across
both support columns and is accompanied by action strokes in the
leg gesture columns to indicate that both legs are in the air, as in
Fig. 125 (c). If special gestures are required, the appropriate
direction symbols take the place of the action strokes, as in Fig.
125 (d). (See Chapter 10 for jumps with leg gestures.)

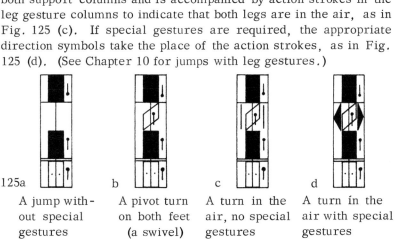

125a   b   c   d

A jump with-   A pivot turn   A turn in the   A turn in the
out special   on both feet   air, no special air with special
gestures   (a swivel)   gestures   gestures

Each of the five basic forms of aerial steps can be performed with turns. In performing aerial turns which travel, the direction of traveling is judged according to the front <u>after</u> the turn is completed, just as the direction of a step following a pivot turn is judged after the turn has been completed. The following examples show hop, leap, assemblé, and sissonne turns as well as a turning skip.

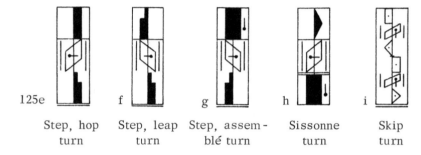

125e	f	g	h	i
Step, hop turn	Step, leap turn	Step, assemblé turn	Sissonne turn	Skip turn

INTERWOVEN AERIAL TURNS

The actions of turning on the floor and in the air can be interwoven. It is possible to start turning on one foot and then to rise into the air continuing to turn. It is also possible to start with a turn in the air and to continue to turn after landing.

An assemblé turn.
The turn starts on the
right foot and then
continues in the air
without any break.
126a

A sissonne turn
traveling to the
right which con-
tinues to turn
after landing on
the right foot.   b

Note the use of the simultaneous action bow in Fig. 126 (b) to show that the turning action does not stop.

FRONT SIGNS

Where movements are performed in a defined area, such as a room or stage, at some point there is a need to relate to that area, to state toward which direction in the room the performer's own personal front is facing. The defined area may also be a field in which nearby trees or buildings make it possible to establish which direction shall be designated as the front, which the back, and so on, of the effective stage.

A DEFINED AREA

The sign for a defined area is □ . Only rarely is a room, a stage, or work area completely square, but regardless of its shape, in relating to the directions in a defined area, one treats it as though it were square, using directions that are parallel with those of an imaginary square set at its center.

Once the area has been defined, one side is specified as the front, and the other main directions fall into place: the back, the right side, the left side, and the four diagonal directions in between - the right-front, the left-front, the right-back, the left-back.

The Constant Directions in the Defined Area

When a group of performers is spaced over the room and all face one of these room directions, they face a direction parallel to one arm of the central cross of directions in the room. As most rooms are oblong, in the following illustrations the area representing the room has purposely been so drawn. The white pin ♀ represents a girl performer (see page 365). The point of the pin indicates where she is facing. The dotted arrow in the diagrams indicates the central room direction to which all performers relate. The cross of directions emanating from the defined area is indicated by the sign ⊞ .

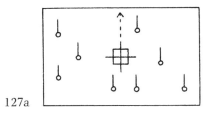

127a

All face the front
of the room.

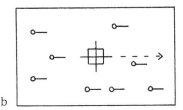

b

All face the right
side of the room.

The same principle applies if the dancers face a diagonal direction. Here each faces downstage right, parallel to the right front direction of the central cross of axes.

127c

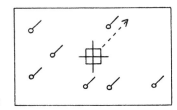

In orientating himself to this cross of
directions, the performer must imagine
that he has a duplicate cross centered in
his own body. This cross of directions
travels with him wherever he goes, but it
does not turn when he turns. The front
direction always points to the front of the
room. Thus it functions as a compass
in which the direction north is constant.
The person holding the compass may turn,
but its arrow remains pointing in the same
direction in the room. Fig. 128 (a) shows
a performer centered in such a square
compass, with the directions set. In (b) a
performer has turned, but his frame of reference has not changed.

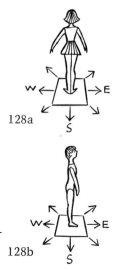

128a

128b

This idea of room directions is familiar
to students of ballet who are often told to imagine that they are
standing in the center of a perfect square (comparable to Fig. 128)
and are asked to relate their movements to the sides and corners
of that square. In various schools of dance these directions in the
room have been given numbers, but because different systems of
numbering exist, for clarity Labanotation uses special symbols.

THE CONSTANT CROSS OF AXES

The system of directions in a defined area is called the Constant Cross of Axes, or the Constant Directions in the Room. For
short it is called the Constant Cross. The word "constant" refers
to the fact that this cross of directions neither turns nor tilts. It
is the most fixed of the systems of reference used (see Chapter 25).

The symbol for this system of reference,
Fig. 129, is based on a square for a defined
area ☐ combined with a cross. When this
system of reference needs specifically to be
stated, this symbol serves as a key. From
it are derived the signs for the established
directions in the room, which are called the
"front signs," the "stage direction signs,"
or the "facing pins."

129

Key for the
Constant Room
Directions

The Front Signs*

▷   ⊥   ◁

⊣   ⊢

130   ◺   ⊤   ◸

The eight established
directions in the room

⊥ = the front of the room,
    the audience, downstage

⊢ = the right side of the
    room, stage right

◁ = the right-front
    direction, downstage
    right

etc.

General Use of the Front Signs

In Motif Writing where the destination for a change of front (the
new direction to be faced) is more important than the exact movement which produced this change of front, a simple statement for
the movement can be made by means of an action stroke. The performer is free to find his own way of achieving the stated result.

In Fig. 131 (a) the starting front is given.
This states "face the back of the room."
The performer is then told to perform an
action which will result in his facing the
front of the room at its conclusion. A
turn of some kind must take place. Note
that the final direction to be faced is tied
to the end of the action stroke, indicating
that this is the aim or result of the action.
In (b) the change from facing left front to
facing right is more sudden.

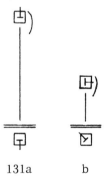

131a   b

Statement of Front in the Score

In Structural Description it is important to
tell the reader at once toward which direction
of the room he is facing. Thus a front sign
usually appears at the start of a score as part
of the starting position. The indication is
placed to the left, outside any indication for
the left arm or hand.** In the course of a
score, the front sign is given after each change

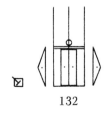

132

of front and also at the start of each new staff so that the reader
can pick up the action at any point and know where he is facing.

* See Appendix B, note 3.   ** See Appendix A, note 3.

Change of Front - Destination Description

Every change of front involves a turn to some degree, but if the turning action is less important than the new front, we indicate the change of direction by placing the new front sign at the point in the score where the new front is reached. It is understood that the performer will take the shortest route to the new front. In the case of changes that involve $\frac{1}{8}$, $\frac{1}{4}$, or $\frac{3}{8}$ of a turn there is no question as to which way the performer should turn, but for a $\frac{1}{2}$ turn such indication leaves the choice of direction open to the performer.

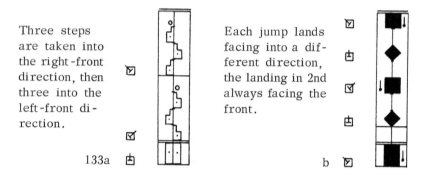

Three steps are taken into the right-front direction, then three into the left-front direction.

133a

Each jump lands facing into a different direction, the landing in 2nd always facing the front.

b

In Fig. 133 (a) unobtrusive turns occur just before the step into the new room direction, and in (b) the adjustment occurs while in the air. This description of facing is ordinarily used for abbreviated indications.

Change of Front - Movement Description

Where the details of a performance are important or when a full description for turning to face into a different stage direction is required, both the turn sign with the degree of turn as well as the front sign should be given. The manner of performing pivot turns, variations in the timing, or changes of level often need to be stressed and the full details for turning must be carefully recorded. Fig. 134 shows a possible variation of Fig. 133 (a), in which the turns indicate specific timing and changes of level.

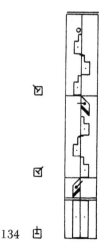

134

Front Signs within Turn Signs

When the new front to be faced in turning is of primary importance and no particular attention need be paid to the degree of rotation, the destination of the turn can be stated directly. The new
front sign is placed within the turn sign, taking the place of the
black pin. It is not necessary to include the box in stating the appropriate front sign; only the straight pin, known as a "tack," need
be written. The directions in which this tack points represent the
directions of the Constant Cross.

A stepping pattern
in which the first
step is toward
stage right, the
next to stage left,
and the last again
to stage right

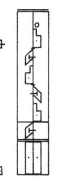

135a

A sissonne
pattern travel-
ing toward one
diagonal room
direction after
another

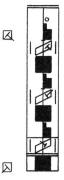

b

In these examples the degree of turning is not stated because it
need not be stressed. Although the pin in the turn sign states the
new front, we write the front signs outside the staff on the left as
usual to help the reader find his place. Here the outside front indication is stated at the conclusion of the movement phrase.

Multiple Turns Indicated with Front Signs. Where there is
more than one turn, it is necessary to state both how many turns
occur and the resulting change of front. The manner of performance is influenced by whether the focus on the new front takes
place at the start or at the end of the turn.

Start facing right-
front, perform
two turns, then
turn to face stage
left (a total of
$2\frac{3}{8}$ turns).

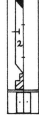

136a

Start facing left-
front. Turn to
face right-front
and then turn
twice more to
that direction (a
total of $2\frac{1}{4}$ turns).

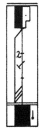

b

READING STUDY IN AERIAL STEPS WITH TURNS

This study gives only basic patterns and so lends itself to adaptation in style. It could be a gay, comic character, such as a jester.

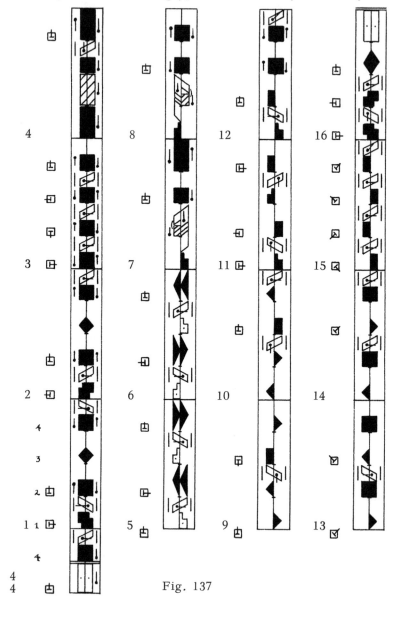

Fig. 137

FOCAL POINTS

In certain circumstances the directions to be faced do not relate to the directions in the room but to a focal point. This may be
the center of a circle or another person, such as one's partner in
a couple dance. In performing exercises, the focal point to which
the performer relates may be an apparatus, as for instance a
barre. The reader must know whether he is facing this focal
point, has his back to it or his right side to it, and so on.

For group dances, the center of the group is understood to be
the focal point; in a circle dance it is the center of the circle.
Any person, object, or fixed point in the room can be designated
as the focal point. When the focal point is not automatically obvious, it should be stated.

The indication for a focal point is ● . The statement identifying the focal point should be written as a key at the start of the
score. It may also appear during the score wherever needed.

138a   ● = P   b   ● = 🕊 or ● = Barre   c   ● = ⺄

Focal point is   Focal point is the barre. This   Focal point is
your partner.   can be indicated either way.   the chair.

Relation to Focal Point as the Destination of a Turn

By placing the black circle for the focal point on the appropriate
side or corner of the turn sign, the following instructions can be
given:

139a   b   c   d

Turn right until   Turn left until   Turn right until   Turn left until
the focal point is the focal point   the focal point   the focal point
in front of you.   is to your left. is behind you.   is at your left
                                                        back diagonal.

Focal Point as a Front Sign

The usual front signs (room direction indications) are not applicable to scores in which the descriptions must be given in terms
of facing a focal point, and so the turn sign, with the correct relation to the focal point, is used to replace the front sign. These
marks are placed outside the score to the left. The left-turn sign

is used after a turn to the left and the right-turn after a turn to the right, to show the kind of turn that has produced the new front. For a starting position the composite sign, made of the two turn signs, is used.

Starting Position Indications for Focusing

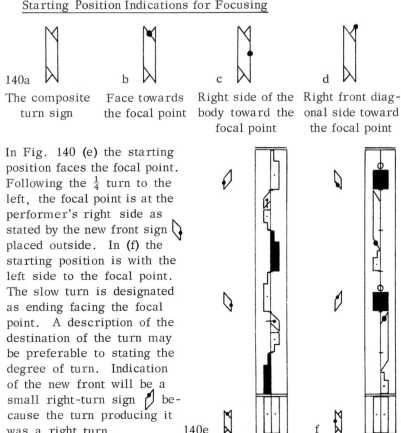

140a	b	c	d
The composite turn sign	Face towards the focal point	Right side of the body toward the focal point	Right front diagonal side toward the focal point

In Fig. 140 (e) the starting position faces the focal point. Following the $\frac{1}{4}$ turn to the left, the focal point is at the performer's right side as stated by the new front sign placed outside. In (f) the starting position is with the left side to the focal point. The slow turn is designated as ending facing the focal point. A description of the destination of the turn may be preferable to stating the degree of turn. Indication of the new front will be a small right-turn sign be-cause the turn producing it was a right turn.   140e   f

AMALGAMATED STEP AND TURN

The action of stepping and the action of turning can happen simultaneously. While the weight is being transferred the body is gradually changing front. The body direction into which the weight is transferred changes as the body turns. Where a forward step is combined with a half turn, the step begins in the forward direction but ends as a backward transference of weight. What has not changed is the spatial direction into which the weight is being transferred. To indicate this retention of the same spatial direction, the indication for a space hold ◊ (retention in space) is written within the step symbol.

The turning action can be written in the support column, tied to the step symbol with the simultaneous action bow as in Fig. 141(a), or it can be written outside alongside the step as in (b).

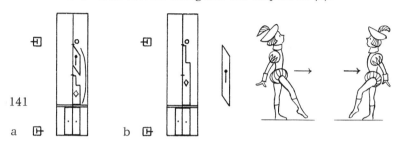

141

a   b

In Fig. 141 (a) the performer starts facing the right side of the room. He steps forward, turning constantly during the transference of weight, to end facing the left side of the room. Fig. (b) describes the same action. In each case there is sliding friction on the floor, the foot swiveling as the weight is transferred.

NON-SWIVEL (FIXED-BASE) TURNS

In a step followed by a pivot turn, the foot is first placed on the floor, then it takes the weight and, as the turn occurs, swivels on the floor. In writing pivot turns sliding friction on the floor is understood. Where the change of front is very slight, this sliding friction may be negligible.

For turns up to a half, swiveling can be avoided by the appropriate use of rotation in placing the foot on the step that precedes the turn. The whole body can then rotate above the supporting foot without any sliding friction occurring. The foot on the ground has a space hold, remaining pointed in the same spatial direction. In Figs. 142 an outward rotation of 45° of the legs is assumed.

In Fig. 142 (a) a step forward is followed by $\frac{1}{8}$ pivot turn to the right. There will be swiveling on the foot as the turning action occurs, and the foot will end turned out on count 3. The footprints illustrate the placement of the foot for the step and after the pivot turn.   142a

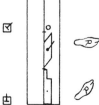

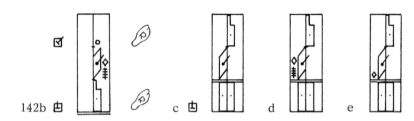

142b

c

d

e

In Fig. 142 (b) the right foot (indicated by the foot sign ‡ placed in the right leg gesture column) is shown to have a space hold (retention in space) during the turn and therefore the turning action will occur in the body above the ankle. Because the foot has not moved, the leg will end in the untwisted state, rotated neither in nor out. Such a non-swivel (fixed-base) turn previously had the nickname "blind turn." In (c) a pivot turn precedes a step. In (d) this action is specified as a non-swivel turn. Because the space hold is understood to refer to the foot, the indication is usually abbreviated to (e).

SPECIAL INDICATIONS FOR TURN SIGNS

Turning Right or Left

In a group situation where the performers face into different directions, the instruction may be given for all to turn to face a common focal point or room direction. Each will turn left or right according to which is most suitable (the shortest distance). For this the composite turn sign is used. Fig. 143 (a) states a turn right or left to face the focal point, while (b) states a turn right or left to face the front of the room.

143a   b

Optional Degree of Turn

The ad libitum sign ∤ (see analogy signs, p. 354) placed within the turn sign indicates freedom in the degree of turning to be performed. Fig. 144 shows such freedom in a turn in the air (tour en l'air).   144

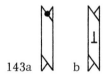

As Many Turns as Possible

Turning as many times as possible in the given time, that is, turning as fast as possible, is indicated by doubling the top and bottom lines of the turn sign or by using the infinity sign ∞. It is assumed that the performer will return to the previously established front.

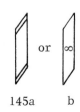

145a   b

CHAPTER 9

Arm Gestures

THE RANGE OF MOVEMENT FOR ARM GESTURES

Arm movements can be simple or extremely complex. Each form of dance employs a particular carriage of the arms and a characteristic way of moving them. The stylistic differences result from the use of the following, in isolation or in combinations: flexion, extension, rotation, deviation, intermediate directions, sequential movement, movement led by a particular part of the hand, etc. All these possibilities will be explored later. For the present we will be specifically concerned with natural, unstylized gestures.

THE PRINCIPAL DIRECTIONS FOR GESTURES

The arm has tremendous spatial freedom; it is restricted only by the presence of the rest of the body and by a natural physical limitation in the backward directions. In moving from the shoulder joint, there are hundreds of points in space to which or through which the extremity can move. Generally speaking, dance makes use of the principal directions for clarity in movement. These are the twenty-seven directions given on page 26. Certain styles of dance use subtle variations of these principal directions; for example, in classical ballet the arms are not held out in the true side horizontal direction but at a point slightly below and slightly forward. These variations may become the standard and take the place of the cardinal directions. Part of the training of a dancer is to strike the true direction or any designated point in-between, just as a violinist must produce each tone by the careful placement of his fingers on his instrument. The following discussion of arm movements deals with the principal points; intermediate directions are given in Chapter 26.

GESTURES - DESCRIPTION IN TERMS OF DESTINATION

Movements for the arms are usually described in terms of the extremity of the limb passing from one point in space (the starting point) to another (the finishing point). The direction symbol written in the arm gesture column states the finishing point or destination. Thus movement for arm gestures is expressed as the path to an established destination. This is in direct contrast to the writing of steps in which the description is given in terms of movement away from the starting point. It is important to recognize the different concepts behind the analysis of gestures and of supports.

Continuous movement for gestures is shown by one direction symbol following another without a break. A position results when a limb comes to rest after reaching a point in space. Where no movement indication is given in a gesture column, the limb stays still. An empty space implies no change, an absence of action.

MOVEMENTS OF THE WHOLE ARM

The whole arm (the upper arm to the hand taken as a unit) moves from the shoulder. Gestures of the whole arm may or may not include bending and stretching. The individual parts of the arm, the lower arm and hand in particular, may perform separate gestures. These will be discussed after simple gestures and spatial patterns of the whole arm have been considered.

CARRIAGE OF THE ARM

In the Laban system, we consider that the normal carriage is relaxed with an easy elbow and wrist. It is neither bent nor stretched and can best be observed when the arm is down at the side of the body while the performer is standing. The direction in which the palm faces is important because it influences the expressive character of the gesture. The direction in which the palm ordinarily faces and the method of writing specific indications for palm facing are given on pages 129 and 130.

DETERMINING DIRECTION FOR ARM GESTURES

Direction and level of arm gestures were analyzed in Chapter 4. Remember that direction and level are determined by the line between the hand and the shoulder. Therefore shoulder level is horizontal, middle level; above shoulder level is high, and below shoulder level is low.

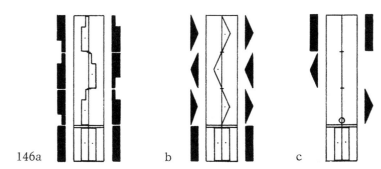

146a Natural oppositional arm
movement accompanying
an ordinary walk

b Steps with parallel
arm movements

c One arm moving
after the other, then
both arms moving

When no direction is indicated in the starting position for the
arms, as in Fig. 146 (c), we assume that for the upright standing
position they are hanging naturally by the side of the body.

Crossing Arm Gesture

When the right arm moves to the left or the left arm moves to
the right, it must cross the body. Where no additional indication
is given, as in Fig. 146 (b), it is understood to cross in front of
the body. If the arm crosses behind the body, the backward pointing black pin must be added. This is the same relationship pin
which is used for the positions of the feet. When both arms cross
in front, the forward pointing pin is added to show which arm is in
front of the other. When both arms cross behind the body, an additional pin is added to show which arm is behind the other.

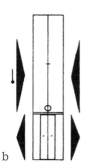
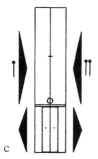

147a The right arm
crosses behind
the body.

b The left arm crosses in
front of the right (both
in front of the body).

c The right arm crosses
behind the left (both
behind the body).

PATH IN SPACE

In moving from one point to the next, the natural tendency for an arm is to move in a curve (on part of an arc) because it is attached at one end to the shoulder joint. When the points are some distance apart, the intention of a movement may be either for the extremity still to perform a curve, or for it to take the shortest route, i.e. to follow a straight line. To indicate such a straight path, we must add a straight path sign as explained on page 446.

Direct Path

Unless a deviation of some kind is shown, the extremity of the arm takes a <u>direct path</u> in moving from one direction to another. (Note that a direct path is not the same as a straight path, shortest route; the former is the natural route involving an arc or curve.) Where the points in space are close together, there is no change in the carriage of the arm. Where the points are far apart, the direct path involves some degree of bending. The following exploration of possible paths in space for the arms will illustrate what is understood by "direct path."

Degree of Distance between Points

In using the twenty six principal directions around the body (place being omitted), adjacent points are considered to be at a first degree distance from one another; and diametrically opposite points are considered to be at a fourth degree distance, with second and third degrees lying in between, as illustrated in Fig. 148.

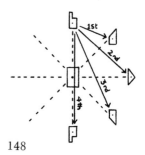

148

<u>First Degree Distance</u>. In Fig. 149 (a) the arm moves from forward middle to the adjacent right front diagonal point, a first-degree distance. The extremity of the arm, the hand, describes a slight arc, a part of a circle of which the shoulder is the center. This is a <u>peripheral</u> movement, one which moves along the external boundary (as on the periphery of a circle). All movements between first degree points will produce this kind of result.

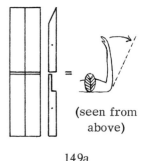

(seen from above)

149a

Second Degree Distance. Fig. 149 (b) shows a quarter circle arc in which the arm moves from forward middle to side middle, a second degree distance. This movement also produces a peripheral path.

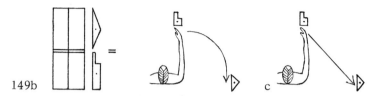

149b

In Labanotation it is understood that movement between second degree points are to be performed without special flexion of the arm so that a peripheral curve results. If the arm is to bend and the hand to follow a straight path, as in (c), the movement follows a transversal path (one running or lying across) which must be written with the addition of the straight path sign.

Third Degree Distance. In Fig. 149 (d) a third degree distance is shown. The points are too far apart for a circular path to occur automatically. The hand will take the direct route, a transversal path, which means that the elbow and the wrist will bend in passing as the arm moves diagonally backward. This flexion of the arm should be natural and unstressed. To produce the peripheral path of (e) an extra direction symbol must be written as in (f) or (g).

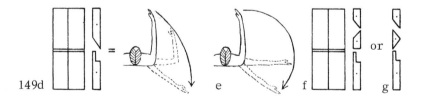

149d   e   f   g

Fourth Degree Distance. In Fig. 149 (h) the arm moves from forward middle to the extreme opposite direction, backward middle. The hand passes near the shoulder (the base of the limb). The elbow flexes, leading the arm backward. Later the wrist bends to keep the hand on the direct path. Neither of these actions should be at all stressed.

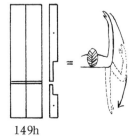

149h

Central Paths

The term "central path" refers to arm movements in which the hand passes close to the base of the limb, the shoulder.

Central Paths between Opposite Points. The direct path produced by moving from one point in space to its opposite results in a central gesture, as in Fig. 149 (h). Other examples of such paths appear below. In each the hand will pass somewhere near the shoulder, though this proximity should not be stressed.

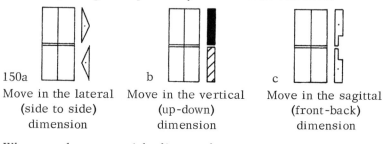

150a
Move in the lateral (side to side) dimension

b
Move in the vertical (up-down) dimension

c
Move in the sagittal (front-back) dimension

When a path on a straight line needs to be stressed in moving between fourth degree points, a place symbol is added. In (d) the hand should pass as closely as possible to the shoulder without actually touching it. This description stresses the use of the center point of direction i.e. place, making the reader aware of its importance in the movement.

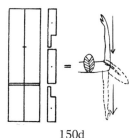

150d

Central Paths between Adjacent Points. Place can also be used to produce central paths in movements between other points, as the following examples illustrate. Such a use of place results in straight line paths.

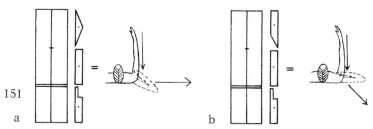

151
a

b

The hand passes through place on its way to side middle.

The hand passes through place on its way to right diagonal back.

Peripheral Paths

Semicircular Arm Movements.   Often an opposite point is
reached via another direction.   This other direction must be
stated.   A few examples are given here.

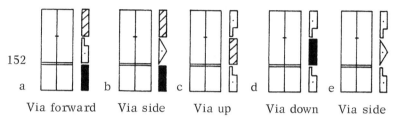

152

a   b   c   d   e

Via forward   Via side   Via up   Via down   Via side

Circular Arm Movements.   For the standard description of
movement in terms of directional destination, a complete circle
requires at least four direction symbols in addition to the starting position to be sure that no corners are cut.   We shall deal
with the special movement analysis and use of path signs for
writing circular paths for gestures in Book II.

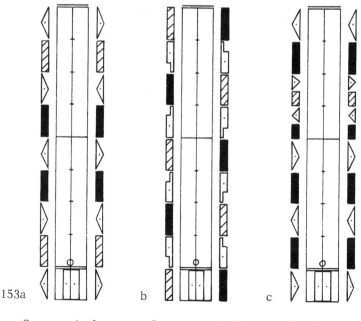

153a   b   c

Symmetrical arm   Large windmill   Parallel arm
patterns, circles   style movements   movements

TIMING OF ARM MOVEMENTS

The length of a direction symbol describes the amount of time required to
reach the stated destination. In Fig.
154 (a) the arm takes four counts to
lower to forward middle. Its sustained action is spread over these four
counts. This notation should not be
mistakenly performed as (b) in which
the arm reaches forward middle on
count one and then holds its position
for the three remaining counts.

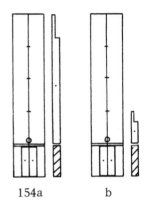

154a   b

LEGATO MOVEMENTS

In gestures described by several direction symbols, the reader may mistakenly see these as separate movements, pausing in each direction before
going on to the next. When there is no separation
between direction symbols, there is no interruption
in the continuity of movement. Thus Fig. 155 shows
one continuous arm gesture ending on count 4.

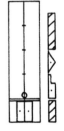

155

STACCATO MOVEMENTS

Staccato means separated, and the separation between movements is visually obvious in Labanotation. The following examples
show the progression from a slight hesitation between directions
to a definite pause and finally to an extremely staccato movement.

156

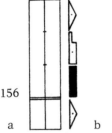
a

b

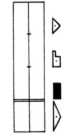
c

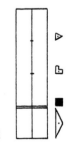
d

Legato, a con-   Demi-legato,   Staccato, an   Staccatissimo, a
stantly flowing   a slight hesi-   equal division   very fast, clipped
movement (no   tation between   between moving   action with long
separation)   movements   and pausing   pauses between

READING STUDY IN ARM MOVEMENTS

Only the outline is given here; style and expression may be added.

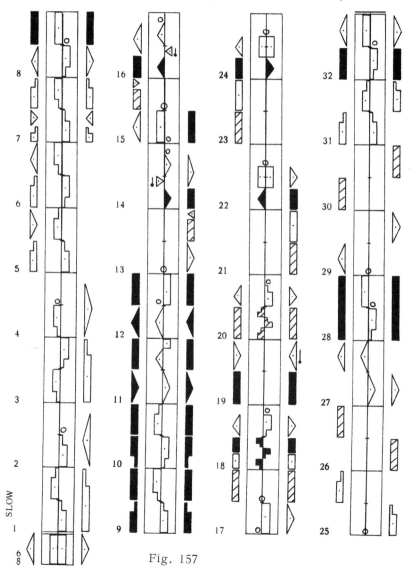

Fig. 157

CHANGE OF LEVEL WITHIN ONE SYMBOL

Identical Timing

The same movement may be written in several different ways, the choice of notation simply directing the reader's attention to one or another part of the action. Figs. 158 (a), (b), and (c) are three ways of notating the raising of the arm from down to up via side. The first is the simplest; all produce the same result.

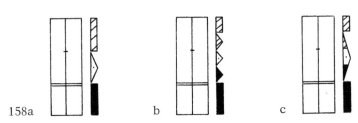

158a   b   c

In Fig. 158 (b) the intermediate side low and side high directions have been added to the description. In (c) these three side direction symbols have been combined into one longer side symbol showing within it the three levels equally spaced in time. The choice of one description or another depends largely upon whether the performer should be aware of each side level as a separate entity, or whether the continuity of the action should be stressed. Because one symbol follows another without a break, there is actually no difference between (a), (b), and (c). Fig. (b) should be performed without interruption, as there is no space between the symbols. The writer must choose the description which best suits the intention of the movement. For general purposes the simplest version, (a), is preferable.

Variation in Timing

A change of level within a direction symbol can indicate variation in the timing of the transition from one level to the next. Note the difference between the following examples. Fig. 159 (a) shows an arm gesture which takes two counts to move to forward middle. In (b) one count is used to move to forward low and one count to go from there to forward middle.

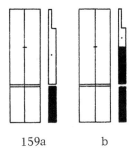

159a   b

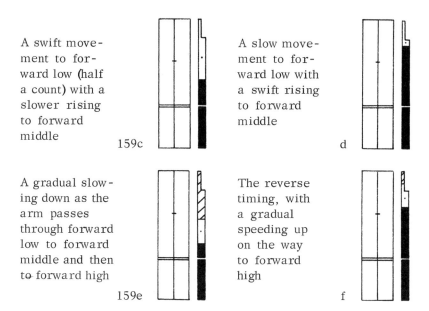

A swift move-
ment to for-
ward low (half
a count) with a
slower rising
to forward
middle   159c

A slow move-
ment to for-
ward low with
a swift rising
to forward
middle   d

A gradual slow-
ing down as the
arm passes
through forward
low to forward
middle and then
to forward high   159e

The reverse
timing, with
a gradual
speeding up
on the way
to forward
high   f

This use of level within one symbol allows for flexibility in showing such variations in timing.

Note the difference between two symbols following one another closely and
one symbol containing a change of level.
In the case of two symbols, (g), the separation is large enough to be clearly
visible but not so large as to cause a
rhythmic change. In drawing one symbol, (h), there is no break at all and
the relative length of the directional
indicator is usually greater.

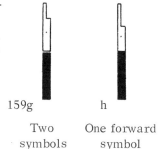

159g   h

Two   One forward
symbols   symbol

THE TIMING OF PASSING THROUGH DIRECTIONAL POINTS

Frequently in arm movements the path of a gesture may pass
several points in space during a given period of time. Where this
passage between points is evenly spaced in time, the symbols will
be of even length. Where the action is slowed down, the symbols
will become longer; where it is quickened, they will become shorter. In such gestures it is important to observe the over-all pattern and the relative lengths of these symbols. Each of the following examples takes three full counts.

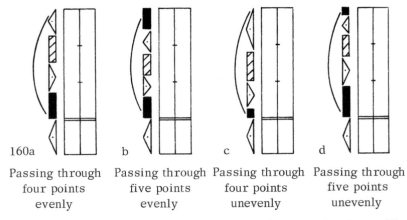

160a	b	c	d
Passing through four points evenly	Passing through five points evenly	Passing through four points unevenly	Passing through five points unevenly

In Fig. 160 (c) the timing is ritardando (slowing down), in (d), accelerando (speeding up).

The Phrasing Bow

Note the use of a vertical phrasing bow in Figs. 160 (a)-(d). This bow is used to show the unity in thought, in the movement sense, of several successive direction symbols. Such phrasing is often shown by a break between symbols at the conclusion of continuous movement. In Fig. 161 where no significant break occurs, the bow informs the reader how the movement is to be phrased.

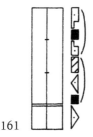

161

SWINGING MOVEMENT

A swinging action can vary between a regular pendulous swing, comparable to that of the pendulum of a clock, and an irregular swing, which starts with a greater momentum and then dissipates.

Pendulous Swing

In all swinging arm movements, the limb makes some use of the force of gravity. In a natural walk such as that in Fig. 162 (a), the arms "swing" in natural opposition, changing direction on each step or beat. Tempo has an important part to play in a swinging action. A comfortable tempo produces a natural swinging pattern with little or no effort on the part of the walker. Too slow a tempo involves an effort to hold back the arm swing; too fast a tempo involves an effort to move the arms fast enough.

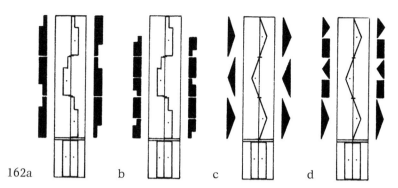

162a   b   c   d

The simple pattern shown in Fig. 162 (a) is described more exactly in (b). The action of passing through place low (down, toward
gravity) in between each change emphasizes this direction. There
is no noticeable pause at the end of each arm movement. The simple pattern of (c) is described more exactly in (d) for the same reason. Observe the difference between (b) and (d). It will be found
that in natural walking the arm reaches its forward or backward
destination as the foot contacts the floor and starts to take on
weight. While the weight is being centered over the new support
and the back leg is being freed of weight, the arms pass through
place low. In contrast to this movement in (d) we see that the arms
follow the path of the center of gravity. They are down when the
step starts and do not reach their side destination until the center
of gravity reaches its destination.

Impulse Swing

A swing which is uneven in its use of time and space, as in Fig.
160 (c), may start with an impulse using dynamic flow and ebb of
energy. The arm relaxes suddenly, giving in to the pull of gravity,
the downward path increases in speed, the upward path becomes
slower as momentum gradually lessens, and the limb, having become increasingly controlled, finally comes to rest. A noticeable
pause between the end of one swing and the start of the next is usual.

For a full description of such swings, dynamic indications
should be included. An accurate description of the correct timing
in the use of directions, however, will satisfactorily indicate the
swinging pattern. The following examples make use of 3/4 meter
which, with its ternary division, is suitable for swings when play-
ed at the right tempo, as is also 6/8 meter (a two-part time with
ternary subdivisions).

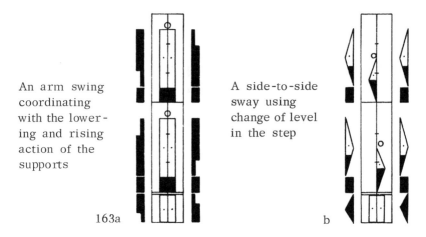

An arm swing coordinating with the lower- ing and rising action of the supports

163a

A side-to-side sway using change of level in the step

b

When reading swings, we must note the over-all pattern - where the swing starts, where it finishes in the measure, and how the di- rections are to be passed through. A characteristic feature of an impulsive swing is the increasing length of each symbol after the place low symbols as the momentum diminishes.

Note the following development of an evenly spaced arm circle into a swing and the variations in the timing of this swing, includ- ing the moment it ends.

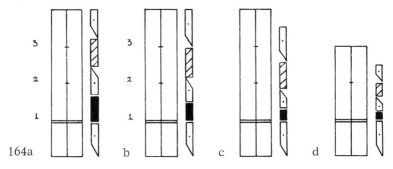

164a   b   c   d

Fig. 164 (a) shows a continuous circular arm movement per- formed in three counts; the proportioning is perfectly even. In (b) the movement to place low has become more rapid and each succeeding symbol slightly longer than the previous one to indicate slowing as the points are passed. If this movement were repeated, there would be no pause between circles as the movement fills all of count 3. In (c) the movement is slightly faster, so that there is time for a pause during the last half of count 3. Fig. (d) shows

the same swing performed in 2/4 meter. It is important to observe that even with the change of meter the relative proportioning of the symbols is the same.

DETAILS IN PERFORMANCE OF ARM GESTURES

Because of variations in the human build, we cannot consider any
one way of moving or of holding the arm as the only natural one.
For purposes of notation, however, a normal performance for various basic movements must be established so that the reader can
know what is to be taken for granted, and therefore is not indicated
in the notation, and what must be specified. The carriage of the
arms considered normal in Labanotation was described on page
116. Further details which we need to consider are the facing of
the palm, the occurrence of rotations which are not written, the
understood use of bending the arm, and the understood inclusion
of the shoulder area in certain gestures.

FACING DIRECTIONS FOR THE PALMS

To simplify reading and writing, a standard has been established
for the directions in which the palm most commonly faces when the
arm is held in the cardinal directions, and all other usages must
be specifically described.

The Unwritten Facing Directions for the Palm

When the arms hang down by the side of the body, the palms
face in, toward the body. The palms also face in toward each
other when the arms are raised forward or backward or are
straight up. In moving up or down in the sagittal (forward-backward) plane, there is no change in the direction the palms face.

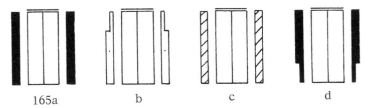

165a	b	c	d
Palms face in.	Palms face in.	Palms face in.	Palms face in.

When the arms are out to the side, the palms are understood to
face forward, no matter whether the side direction was reached via
forward, as in Fig. 165 (e); via down, as in (f); or via up, as in (g).

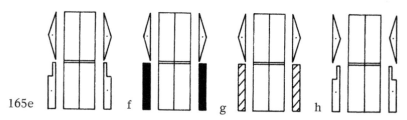

165e   f   g   h

When the arms cross to the opposite side, as in Fig. 165 (h), the palms face backward. For positions between these main directions, the palms face the logical intermediate direction. For instance, in forward diagonal gestures as in Fig. (i), the palms will face the opposite forward diagonal directions, the right palm facing ⬠ and the left palm facing ⬠ .

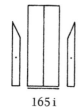

165 i

Specific Indication for Palm Facing

The sign for the palm (inner surface of the hand) is ⊓ . Note that it is drawn long and thin, not square, with the base left open. This symbol represents the surface of the inner side of the hand, and, as with all surface symbols, when it is followed by a direction symbol the surface faces in that direction.

The indication for palm facing is written next to the arm symbol, on the outer side. As this is a minor indication, it is customary to draw the direction symbols for palm facing narrower so that they do not distract the eye from the main symbol, the arm gesture.

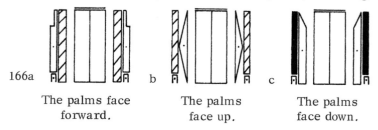

166a   b   c

The palms face   The palms   The palms
   forward.   face up.   face down.

To produce the stated facing direction for the palms in these examples, the lower arm must rotate. In the following examples palm facing is achieved through a flexion of the wrist. The exact performance may vary, for there is more than one possibility depending on whether or not there is a specific rotation in the lower arm. The resulting placement of the hand is usually described by stating the direction of the hand (see page 236).

166d   e   f

Cancellation of Palm Facing Indications

A palm-facing indication is considered in Labanotation to be valid only for as long as the arm gesture next to which it is written is valid.* With a new direction symbol the previous palm facing will be cancelled. To retain the effect of a previous palm facing (the rotated state in the lower arm and hand), the body hold sign is used.

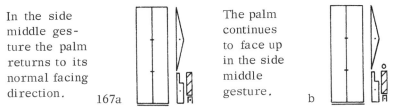

In the side middle gesture the palm returns to its normal facing direction.   167a

The palm continues to face up in the side middle gesture.   b

The hold sign for palm facing is in effect until specifically cancelled. Cancellation may be indicated by another direction symbol or by the "back to normal" sign ☉.** This sign is used to show the return of a part of the body to its normal carriage or state.

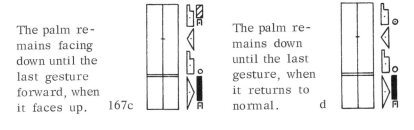

The palm remains facing down until the last gesture forward, when it faces up.   167c

The palm remains down until the last gesture, when it returns to normal.   d

UNWRITTEN ROTATIONS

In moving from one cardinal direction to another, the arms perform slight rotations of which the performer is often unaware even though they are observable to the viewer. These rotations are not written because they are considered to be the natural result caused by the structure of the limb in passing from one point to another. Specific rotations for the arms are given in Chapter 17.

* See Appendix A, note 4.   ** See Appendix A, note 5.

Raising and Lowering the Arms Laterally

Movements of the arms in the lateral (frontal) plane involves a continuous rotation, outward rotation as the arms are lifted and inward rotation as they are lowered. Note the unwritten rotations which occur in the following example.

Starting position: arms down, palms facing in.

1. As the arms lift to the side, there is a slight but constant outward rotation so that when the arms are horizontal the palms face forward.

2. This gradual rotation continues as the arms rise to place high. As a result, the palms end facing in toward each other.

3. The arms lower to side middle with a gradual inward rotation, which brings the palms to face forward again.

4. As the arms move to place low, the gradual inward rotation brings the palms to face in toward the body again.

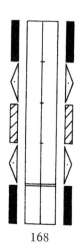

168

It is interesting to try to eliminate this natural rotation. The palms will face down when the arms are side middle, and out when the arms are straight up, producing a very twisted feeling. As soon as they are relaxed, the arms will return to their normal state, palms facing in.

Moving Horizontally from Forward to Backward

In carrying the arm from forward to backward via down, as in Fig. 169 (a), there is no change in the facing of the palm, and therefore no adjustment is necessary. But in carrying the arm backward via side a rotation occurs. In (b) no change is felt in the movement to the side, but from that point on the arm must gradually rotate inward in order to end with the palm facing to the right.

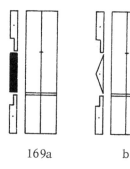

169a   b

If Fig. 169 (c) is performed without
any natural transitional rotation, the
arm will end in the forward direction
with the palm facing the left side. To
notate such an action an additional indication must be written - palm facing,
rotation or a back of the hand guidance.

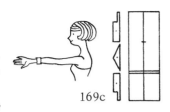

169c

Moving Vertically from Forward to Backward

When an arm passes from forward to backward
or the reverse via place high, a full rotation takes
place. In Fig. 170 (a) the arm experiences no rotation as it is raised and the palm is still facing
the right side. But as it passes into the backward
middle direction, the performer must rotate the
arm in the shoulder joint a full inward turn to assume the normal palm facing direction. In revers-
ing this movement, as in (b), the arm must first
make a full outward rotation on its way to place
high, after which there is no change.

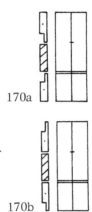

170a

170b

Full Arm Circles

In full arm circles a full rotation occurs, though the action of
rotating is not evenly spaced throughout the circular path.

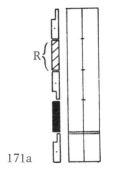

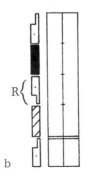

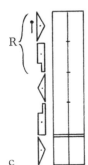

171a   b   c

In Figs. 171 (a) and (b) the letter "R" has been placed next to
the movement symbol during which the rotation takes place. In (c)
the rotation takes place over the last two symbols. It is, of course,
hard to perform a side middle arm gesture which crosses behind
the body, but when performed, the palm should end facing backward with the arm rotated inward.

UNWRITTEN FLEXIONS

The symbol in the arm column indicates a movement of the arm alone in its normally extended state. In gestures which cross the body, however, exact performance may vary according to individual flexibility of the shoulder joint, length of arm, and width of body. The arm may bend, but though there should be no marked effort to keep it straight, its bending is of little importance. Any specific bending or extension of the arm will be stated with the appropriate symbols (see Chapter 11).

In Fig. 172 the right arm crosses in front of the body and the left arm behind. It is expected that the right arm will bend slightly and that the left arm will definitely be bent, as this is a difficult position for most people to assume. Arm contractions need not be specifically written in such cases.

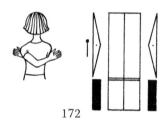

172

UNWRITTEN INCLUSIONS

To perform arm circles smoothly, in certain directions the performer must often include the shoulder area. This is true of a crossing circular gesture such as in Fig. 173 (a), and also for circular gestures which make use of the backward direction. Such inclusions can be kept to a minimum or even dispensed with by a loose-jointed individual; they should not be stressed and should disappear as soon as possible.

173a

To facilitate moving the arm in the backward direction, a slight inclusion of the shoulder area, called "opening the shoulder," is expected. Many people cannot achieve a true backward direction without it. Such an inclusion should disappear as soon as possible; it is not written unless the inclusion is to be given special emphasis.

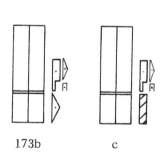

173b   c

READING STUDY IN PALM FACING

Measures 5 and 6 and 13 and 14 are repeated to the other side.
See Chapter 21 page 350 for repeat signs.

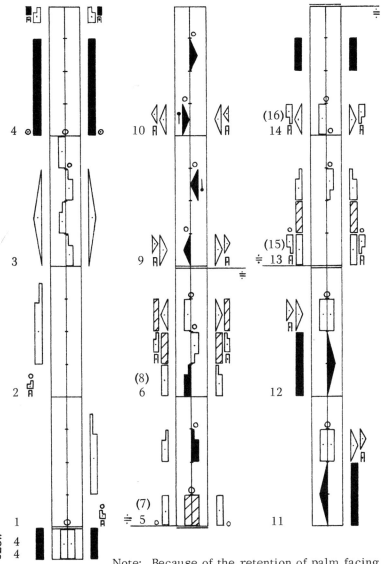

Note: Because of the retention of palm facing,
the palms will face up in measure 3.

174

THE EFFECT OF TURNING ON ARM MOVEMENTS

CARRIED ARM GESTURES

When there is no indication in Labanotation of movement for the arms, they are carried along with movements of the body as a whole. A position for the arms or for the free leg is retained during turns. During a turn the relationship which the arms have established to the body is retained; the arms are not held immobile, however, but may react slightly to the momentum of the turn. To indicate a rigidly held limb the body hold sign o is used.

During the turn the arms remain in front of the chest, but no effort is made to hold them completely still.

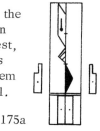

175a

The arms are shown by the hold sign o to be immobile during the turn.

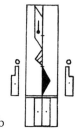

b

It is important to note the difference between physical change (movement within the body), e.g. movement of the arm which entails a change in the shoulder joint, and spatial change (movement in space), e.g. the arm passing through space as it is carried along with movements of the body. The rush of air against the limb imparts a sensation of movement even though the limb is inactive.

HORIZONTAL CURVES

Turns affect arm gestures in the horizontal plane. The path of an ordinary horizontal gesture is augmented or diminished in its passage through space according to whether the direction of the gesture and the direction of the turn are the same or opposite.

Simple Horizontal Curve

Fig. 176 (a) shows a simple horizontal curve performed without any accompanying turn. Such an ordinary curve is termed an "adequate curve." In this case the arm describes a half-circular path moving clockwise.

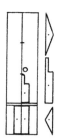

176a

Augmented Horizontal Curve

If the performer turns in the same direction as the path of his arm gesture, as in Fig. 176 (b), the gesture will be augmented. Its change of direction in relation to the body is the same, but its spatial path is extended. The performer has the feeling that, in relation to his body a much larger gesture has been performed.

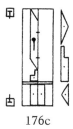

176b

Diminished Horizontal Curve

By turning into the direction opposite to the path of his arm gesture, the performer diminishes the gesture, as in Fig. 176 (c). He feels as though he has not gestured at all. The arm has changed its relationship to the body, but it has not moved in space. Such an action could be described as a turn in which the arm keeps its relation to a previously established room di-

176c

rection. In this example, the arm gesture started toward the left side of the room and remained in that direction. Thus it retained its relation to the Constant Directions in the Room while changing in relation to the Standard (Gravity Constant) Cross of Directions.

RETENTION IN SPACE - SPACE HOLD

The relation of a gesture to a room direction may be important enough to be described in those terms. Such description is needed when a limb is to retain a previously established direction in the room even though the rest of the body turns away from it. This retention in space, or "space hold," usually is needed in connection with turning. The sign for a space hold is a diamond, ◊.

In Fig. 177 (a) the performer starts facing the right side of the room. The right arm gesture remains forward from the body during the following turn. In (b) the space hold causes the right arm to retain its room direction during the turn. At the completion of the turn, the arm will end as a gesture backward from the body.

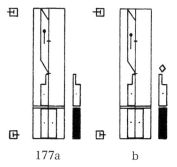

177a   b

Duration of a Space Hold *

A space hold lasts for the duration of a turn sign or other special indication in conjunction with which it is required. For each new movement requiring a space hold, the sign must be repeated.**

VERTICAL CURVES

Turns may affect arm gestures which describe vertical curves.

Simple Vertical Curve

Fig. 178 (a) shows a simple arm gesture which rises in the sagittal plane to forward middle. This is a two-dimensional gesture when it is not accompanied by a turn.

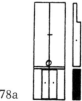

Deviating or Skew Curve   178a

When the same arm gesture is accompanied by a turn, as in (b), it takes the same path in relation to the body (the Standard Cross of Axes) but spatially it describes a three-dimensional path instead of a two-dimensional. This change is the normal result of combining these two actions so no additional indication is needed in the notation.   178b

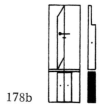

Undeviating Vertical Plane Curve

Where a two-dimensional curve is desired in spite of the accompanying turn, the indication must be given in terms of the relation of the gesture to the unchanging room directions. To write such an undeviating curve, the direction and level for the gesture are given as if no turn occurred, that is, into the direction established just before the turn began. Then, to counteract the normal effect of the turn, the space hold sign is placed within the arm gesture symbol. Thus during the whole movement, the limb must retain its relation to that direction in the room toward which the movement started. In (c) the performer starts by moving his right arm toward the right side of the room (a backward gesture from the body) and then keeps moving it toward that room direction during the turn. At the end of the turn his arm will be in front of his body. This final relationship of arm to body is not stated in the notation; it is the result of the combined action of the turn and the space hold.

* See Appendix B, note 4.   ** See page 306.

178c   d

In (c) the arm is being raised while the space hold is in effect. Compare this with (d), in which the raising of the arm is completed before the turn starts. During the turn no gesture occurs, so only the space hold is needed.

As an aid to the reader, the physical destination of a limb can be given as in (e), though this is not normally necessary. Figs. (f) and (g) show how the space hold sign is drawn within low and high symbols.   178e   f   g

CONTINUATION BOW

When a symbol must be carried over from the end of one staff to the beginning of another, a small angular vertical bow, the caret,* is used to indicate the continuity of the movement.

CONTINUATION OF A DIRECTION SYMBOL

When a movement starts at the top of one staff and continues over to the next staff, a full direction symbol is written at the top of the first staff and repeated again at the beginning of the next staff. To show that these two symbols are in fact one, the caret is placed both at the top of the previous staff and at the bottom of the new staff as shown in Fig. 179. Here the lowering of the arms starts at the

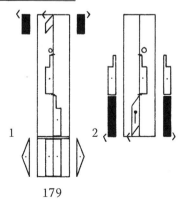

179

end of measure 1 and continues into measure 2. The turn which starts at the end of measure 1 also continues into measure 2.

* See Appendix B, note 5.

CHAPTER 10

Leg Gestures

The focus of a movement may be on a gesturing leg. This may be a functional action such as kicking a ball, or an expressive one. Leg gestures embellish steps, jumps, and turns, thereby changing their character and style. A leg gesture may touch or slide on the floor without taking weight. For purposes of notation, movements of the whole leg can be compared with movements of the whole arm, though the range of movement for the leg is more limited. Direction and level for leg gestures are determined by the line between the extremity of the limb, the foot, and the base, the hip.

CARRIAGE OF THE GESTURING LEG

In Labanotation the normal carriage of a gesturing leg is considered to be straight with a relaxed knee and foot. This natural carriage of the leg occurs in many folk dances. In several styled forms of dance, such as classical ballet, the leg is extended with the knee taut and the foot pointed (stretched). When any consistent use of the leg is basic to the style of movement it is indicated by a key at the start of the score (see page 484).

Rotated State of the Legs

Natural variations among individuals preclude consideration of any one particular form of rotation (inward, outward, or parallel) as being considered "normal." Direction and degree of rotation are stated at the beginning of the score in a key which applies to both steps and gestures. In the context of the movement, a slight inward or outward rotation may occur naturally as a physical need resulting from the leg's spatial pattern. Such slight rotations are often not observed by the untrained eye and in any case disappear automatically once the action is completed. Special changes in rotation should be written at the moment they occur.

If no rotation is stated the reader is expected to perform the movements in a natural manner. (For leg rotations see Chapter 17.)

PATH IN SPACE

Description of Motion or Destination

In the standard movement description of Labanotation, direction symbols state the destination to be reached, not the relative path of the movement. Place for a step is next to the previous support (usually the other foot). Place low for a leg gesture is straight down below the hip, next to the other leg. Thus a movement to the center line of the body is a movement to place. A gesture past the center line or away from it must be written with some other direction symbol. The following examples illustrate these differences.

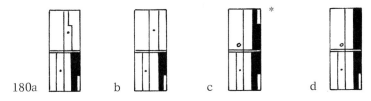

| 180a | b | c | d |

Step forward, past the left foot.   Step in place, next to the left foot.   Gesture forward, in front of the body.   Gesture in place, the leg ending next to the left leg.

Judged from the starting point, backward low, the movement in each of these examples is a forward directed one. But it is not written with a forward symbol unless the destination is forward of place, past the plumb line of the body.

Direct Path Leg Gestures

As with arm gestures, leg gestures move on a direct path from one point in space to the next. When these points lie close together, the leg will move in an arc. When the points are far apart, the leg will probably pass through another direction, often through place low. When moving between distant points, the leg will bend at the knee so that the extremity, the foot, can follow a direct path.**

* See Appendix B, note 6.   ** See pages 118-120.

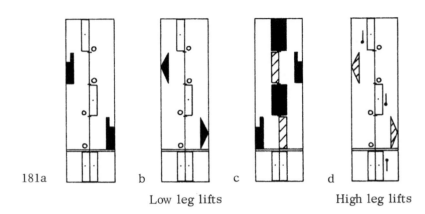

181a   b   c   d

Low leg lifts   High leg lifts

Straight Path Extensions of the Legs

The place middle direction can be used to show the foot passing as close to the hip as possible. When the foot has been drawn into place, it can then extend on a straight path into different directions.

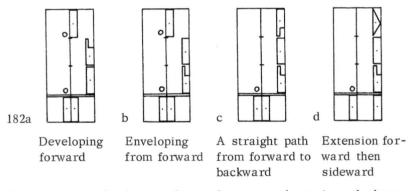

182a   b   c   d

| Developing forward | Enveloping from forward | A straight path from forward to backward | Extension for-ward then sideward |

Depending upon the degree of inward or outward rotation, the knee will be more to the front or more to the side in these patterns.

Circular Leg Gestures

A low outward leg circle   A low inward leg circle

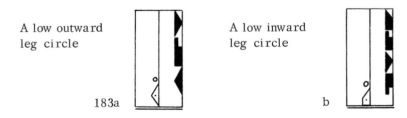

183a   b

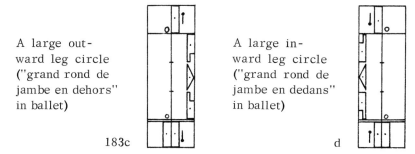

A large out-
ward leg circle
("grand rond de
jambe en dehors"
in ballet)

A large in-
ward leg circle
("grand rond de
jambe en dedans"
in ballet)

183c   d

Leg Swings

In a true swing the leg makes use of the force of gravity, so that
the downward motion is faster than the upward. Note how this is
indicated in the notation. A slight pause occurs before the leg
changes direction. The leg swings clear of the floor unless contact
with the floor is indicated (see Chapter 13 for touches and slides).

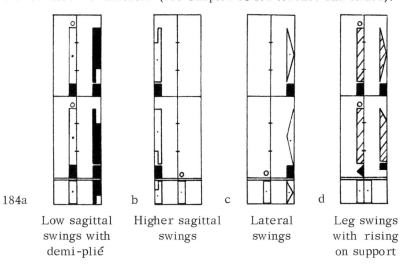

184a   b   c   d

Low sagittal   Higher sagittal   Lateral   Leg swings
swings with   swings   swings   with rising
demi-plié   on support

Carriage of Free Leg in Open Steps

In simple walking patterns carriage of the free leg is not emphasized; the transition between supports is accomplished in a natural,
appropriate manner. When walking forward, the free leg passes
close to the supporting leg on its way to begin the next step. When
there is a change of direction in open steps, this coming through
place is not considered necessary; if it is desired, it must be specifically written as illustrated in the following examples.

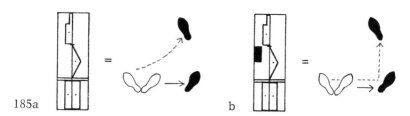

The dotted line represents the path of the free leg prior to the second step. Fig. 185 (a) illustrates the normal direct path. In (b) the use of place low is shown.

PLACE LOW LEG GESTURES

When the leg is brought to place low underneath the hip without actually touching the floor, the exact manner in which it is held will depend on the level of the accompanying support. If the support is high, the free leg can be straight with the foot almost as extended as the supporting foot. With a middle level support, the knee of the free leg is normally straight but relaxed, with the ankle flexed so that the foot is just off the floor. With a low level support the knee of the free leg must be bent. The degree of this bend will depend on the degree of bend in the supporting leg. When it is of importance, the exact degree of bending for the gesture can be shown (see Chapter 11).

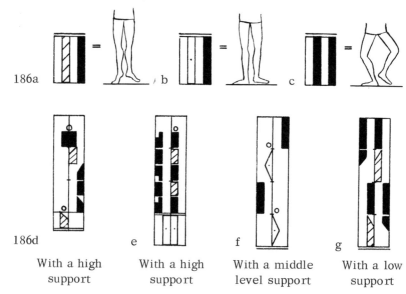

With a high support	With a high support	With a middle level support	With a low support

THE TIMING OF LEG GESTURES

LEGATO AND STACCATO

A break between the leg gesture symbols signifies a break
in the continuity of movement.
Legato movement results whenever one symbol follows another
without any break. In Fig. 187
(a) the left leg gesture is performed in a legato manner. In
(b) the same space pattern is
performed with staccato gestures.

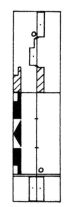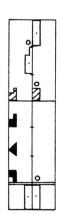

187a   b

STEPS WITH LEG GESTURES

A simple walking pattern can be embellished by use of accompanying leg gestures. Such gestures may serve as a preparation
for the step, or may follow it. When the gesture is slow and the
step itself quick, the gesture gains in importance and may become
the main feature of the movement. When the step is slow and the
gesture quick, it is usually the step which is featured.

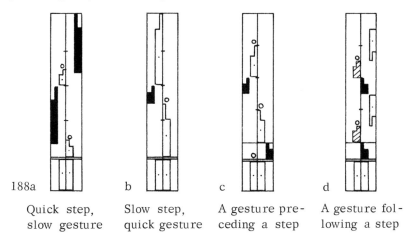

188a   b   c   d

| Quick step, | Slow step, | A gesture pre- | A gesture fol- |
| slow gesture | quick gesture | ceding a step | lowing a step |

Blending of Steps and Leg Gestures

The following examples range from complete separation of step
and leg gesture to the most fluent overlap of these two actions.

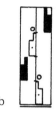

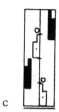

189a

b

c

A staccato perform-
ance; each action is
separated in time
from the next.

The weight comes to
rest before the leg
gesture starts. The
performance is not
staccato, however.

A slight overlap in-
dicates the start of
the gesture before
the center of weight
has come to rest.

In each of the above examples the action of
walking is interrupted, that is, the center
of weight comes to rest over the supporting
leg. It is possible to walk continuously with
the center of weight in constant motion and
at the same time to perform leg gestures.
This action is shown in Fig. 189 (d). The
leg gesture can overlap the last half of the
step symbol. More overlap than this is not
physically possible.

189d

THE STEP-GESTURE RULE

A leg gesture cannot occur at the same time as a transference
of weight, that is, a step. It may appear to the eye that a step
and a leg gesture are simultaneous, particularly if the action is
quick, but in fact the leg gesture starts a fraction of a beat later.
A truly simultaneous gesture and step can occur only when the
weight is lifted from the ground by means of a slight spring. Until the weight of the body is released from the foot, it cannot begin
to lift into the air and gesture. A simultaneous new support and
gesture occur in the darting movement called an "élancé."

Swift step and
gesture (call-
ed "piqué" in
ballet)

190a

Darting step-
gesture (call-
ed "élancé" in
ballet)

b

The same kind of action occurs in a cutting step (called a "coupé") in which one foot replaces the other as the support. In a coupé the weight usually stays in place; during the moment of lift off the ground one leg replaces the other. The degree of rise from the ground can vary from merely lifting the weight without lifting the feet from the floor to a full-fledged spring. When there is no lift from the ground, a stepping action must occur with the gesture following immediately.

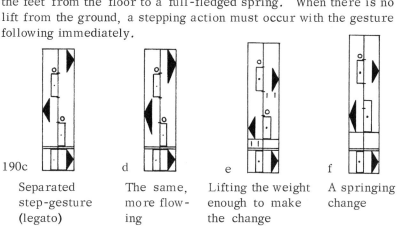

190c	d	e	f
Separated step-gesture (legato)	The same, more flow-ing	Lifting the weight enough to make the change	A springing change

Because of the difference in expression, it is important to be able to see clearly whether the movement is basically a stepping or a springing action, or only lifting the weight, as in (e).

Change of Level of the Support During a Gesture

Because a change of level in the supporting leg is not a step (a transference of weight), it is possible to change level while gesturing si-multaneously with the other leg.

191

AERIAL STEPS WITH LEG GESTURES

All simple forms of aerial steps, the five basic forms, can be em-bellished by leg gestures. These may include flexions and also beats, steps in which the legs contact each other while in the air. The simplest form of springs with leg gestures is that in which a specific direction for the free leg is stated at the time of landing.

SIMPLE SPRINGS WITH LEG GESTURES

A statement of the destination of the free leg at its moment of landing is sufficient for notating simple forms; movement of the leg in the air need not be written.

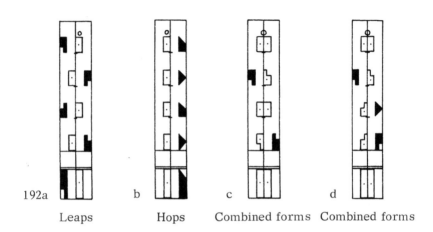

192a Leaps   b Hops   c Combined forms   d Combined forms

SPATIAL VARIATIONS IN THE USE OF LEG GESTURES

The character of the basic aerial forms changes according to the direction and timing of leg gestures. Variations in direction will be dealt with first.

Jumps with Leg Gestures

Because jumps take off from both feet and land on both feet, leg gestures can only occur while the body is in the air. As a rule these are simultaneous leg gestures. Note the difference in movement among the following:

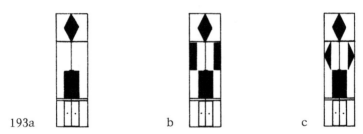

193a   b   c

No special gestures: the legs move out naturally to land in 2nd position.

The legs remain down, separating just in time to produce an open position.

The legs separate immediately in the air and so are ready for the open position.

In Fig. 193 (c) both legs gesture farther to the side than they normally would just to land in second position.

The following are variations in a jump from closed feet:

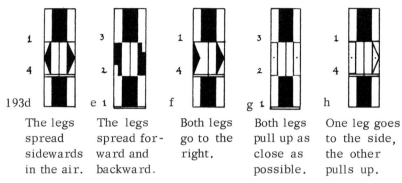

193d	e	f	g	h
The legs spread sidewards in the air.	The legs spread forward and backward.	Both legs go to the right.	Both legs pull up as close as possible.	One leg goes to the side, the other pulls up.

Step-Hop with Leg Gestures

Note the differences in the following sequences:

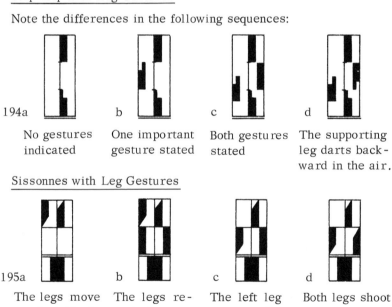

194a	b	c	d
No gestures indicated	One important gesture stated	Both gestures stated	The supporting leg darts backward in the air.

Sissonnes with Leg Gestures

195a	b	c	d
The legs move comfortably to produce the finishing position.	The legs remain down until the moment of landing.	The left leg gestures diagonally back at once.	Both legs shoot out at once.

In Fig. 195 (d) the right leg shoots farther forward than is required, landing diagonally forward. The extra energy needed to perform these gestures produces more brilliant jumps. Note that the direction of traveling is indicated by the landing support and not by the leg gesture.

Assemblés with Leg Gestures

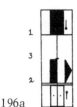 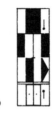  

196a   b   c   d

| A simple as-semblé start-ing with the leg out to the side | Bringing the legs immedi-ately together in the air | Lifting the right leg higher to the side in the air | Opening both legs while in the air |

Contact of the Legs During Jumps

In jumping the legs often touch while in the air. A horizontal bow ⌣ indicates this contact between the two legs.

197a   b   c   d

| The legs come in during the jump but do not touch. | The legs touch when they come in during the jump. | Example (b) written more simply | The legs remain together in the air and open on landing. |

In writing simple forms we need only show the contact bow as in Figs. 197 (c) and (d). It can be assumed that the legs will meet underneath the body and not in any other direction.

Beating the Legs During Jumps

In jumps the legs may beat, i.e. strike one an-other with sufficient energy to produce sound, the sound being affected by the kind of clothing worn. A strong accent sign ◄ or ➤ placed next to the ac-tive leg at the moment of contact signifies a beat. Position signs (pins) indicate the relationship of the legs when they touch. Fig. 198 (a) shows a jump in fourth position with the legs beating in the air.

198a

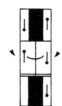

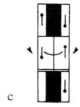

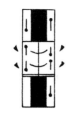

198b

c

d

| A beat while chang-ing 5th positions (an "entrechat royale" in ballet) | Changing the feet with a beat but returning to the same 5th ("entrechat quatre") | A double change with beats ("en-trechat six") |

In recording fully the correct technical performance of these balletic steps, a slight opening of the legs be-tween each beat ought also to be indicated. (For very small movements see Chapter 26.) In writing a brief version of the pattern as a memory aid for those who are already familiar with their correct performance we need only indicate an entrechat six, as in Fig.198(e).

198e

Cabrioles

The cabriole is basically a step-hop in which one leg beats against the other in the air. One leg rises into the air before the other and usually it is the second leg which does the beating.

A simple sideward cabriole form

199a

A forward cabriole, the left leg beat-ing the right

b

A double cabriole as done by a man

c

Note the pin ⧫ for "below" which indicates that the active leg con-tacts the other from below.

THE TIMING OF LEG GESTURES DURING AERIAL STEPS

The previous examples illustrating leg gestures during aerial steps have been simple in timing. In leaps, hops, and assemblés where one leg gesture starts after the other, the overlap in the timing of the gestures is important. How quickly one leg follows the other into the air can change the whole impetus and expression

of the action.   In addition to the interrelation of the actions of the
two legs, the relationship with the music or other accompaniment,
if any, must be stated.   The use of the time available is important.
Most jumps land on the beat.   Most preparations for jumps are
fast.   A slow preparation produces a heavy movement.   When a
step is used as the preparation for a take-off, it will be a fast, rebound step.   When the landing is also the preparation for the next
spring, it will be a fast rebound land-take-off.   When the landing
concludes the phrase, more time will be taken to allow for a controlled cushioning effect.   By performing the reverse of the above
statements a grotesque or comic effect may be achieved.   These
variations can easily be shown in Labanotation.

VARIATIONS IN PERFORMING A STEP-LEAP

In a step-leap pattern, there is usually an overlap in the action
of the leg gestures.   As the preparatory step is finishing, the free
leg begins to lift.   While it is still rising, the supporting leg lifts
and the body rises off the ground.   The beginning of the second
gesture indicates the moment the body is in the air.   If there is
no overlap at all in the performance of the leg gestures and a
step comes between as in Fig. 200 (d), an ordinary step-gesture
will result.

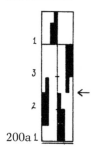 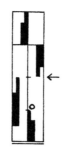 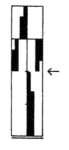 

| A step-leap with fluent overlap-ping gestures (the standard comfortable performance) | No overlap in the movement of the gestures (a less fluent leap) | A slow pre-paratory step and simultan-eous gestures producing a stilted leap | Step-gesture with no overlap of leg gestures (no rising into the air) |

In all the above examples, the arrow shows the moment that the
body rises into the air.   This is at the point when the support ends
or the second gesture starts.

Fig. 200 (e) shows a brilliant step-leap. The preparatory step is fast; there is an overlap of the first gesture with the step, and an overlap of the second gesture with the first. Though fast, these actions are fluent and harmonious. Both legs reach their destinations quickly, then hold still. This allows the body to shoot through the air unencumbered by movement, and produce the impression of suspension

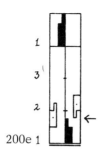

200e

VARIATIONS IN PERFORMING AN ASSEMBLE

Performances of an assemblé can range from stilted through comfortable to brilliant, as the following examples illustrate. In Fig. 201 (a) the left leg bends quickly on count 2 so that the body leaves the ground on the & of count 2, as indicated by the arrow. On count 3 the height of the jump is reached and by the following & the body is returning to the ground to land on count 1.

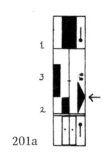

201a

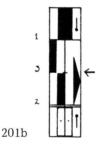

201b

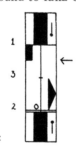

c

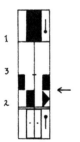

d

In Fig. 201 (b) the bending preparation on the left leg is slower and the rising into the air does not occur until count 3. This is a more earthbound performance. In (c) the left leg is already bent so that the preparation for the spring is static. The right gesture is faster but no rising occurs until the last moment when the left leg leaves the ground. The brevity of this moment in the air before landing produces a very stilted, earthbound assemblé. In contrast, (d) indicates a fast bending on the left leg and a fast right leg gesture for a quick take-off. The right leg then rapidly comes to place low to join the other leg and both legs remain motionless until the moment of landing. This lack of activity while in the air helps to produce a suspension in mid-air which results in an exciting and dynamic jump.

TURNS WITH LEG GESTURES

In pivot turns on one foot, the free leg can perform a variety of gestures during the turning action. The effect of the turn on these gestures is comparable to the effect of turning on arm gestures.

PIVOT TURNS WITH LEG GESTURES

Carried Leg Gesture

A previously established leg gesture is carried along during a turn, retaining its relation to the body. The body hold sign o may be used as a reminder that the leg must be kept particularly still.

In Fig. 202 (a) the step-turn is accompanied by a backward leg gesture (a "piqué arabesque" turn in ballet). The leg reaches its destination quickly so that it is not moving during most of the turn. Two full turns are performed. The preparation for (b) is from a second position (feet apart), from which a double turn ("pirouette") with the leg held to the side is performed. This ends by lowering the heel of the supporting leg; the gesturing leg remains out to the side.

202a   b

Simple and Augmented Horizontal Curves

Fig. 203 (a) shows a step followed by a half-circular leg gesture. In (b) this gesture is augmented by a pivot turn into the same direction. The impression of a larger gesture is given.

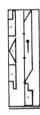

203a   b

Diminished Horizontal Curve

When the accompanying turn is in the opposite direction to a circular gesture, the effect is that of diminishing the gesture. Fig. 204 (a) shows the same gesture as in Fig. 203 (a) above performed with a quarter turn in the opposite direction. If a half turn occurs, as in (b), the result is the same as that of a space hold for the left leg.

204a   b

RETENTION IN SPACE - SPACE HOLD

When the leg is to retain its relation to a room direction, the space hold sign is used. Fig. 205 (a) shows a low step forward followed by a forward gesture toward the right side of the room. During the turn the right leg has a space hold; therefore it remains pointing toward that room direction. All during the pivot turn the leg changes its relation to the body, finishing backward. This rotation of the leg in the hip socket is known in ballet as "rotation," "dégagé," or "détourné." In (b) the right leg which starts as a backward gesture toward the left side of the room, ends as a forward gesture from the hip. No change of level in the supporting leg occurs in these two examples. Fig. (c) shows a swift rising turn in which the leg gesture produces a whiplike action. This movement is known as a "fouetté relevé" in ballet.

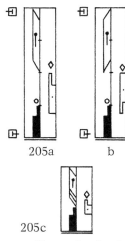

205a   b

205c

Fouetté relevé

Simple Vertical Curve

A simple vertical curve is shown in Fig. 206 (a). The limb rises in a two-dimensional curve, in this case in the sagittal plane. A simple lifting or lowering of the limb directly into any direction produces a vertical plane curve.

206a

Deviating or Skew Curve

When a simple rising or lowering leg gesture is accompanied by a turn, it produces a three-dimensional arc, that is, a deviating or skew curve, as illustrated in Fig. 206 (b).

206b

Undeviating Vertical Plane Curve

To indicate a two-dimensional curve while turning, we must state the relation of the gesture to the unchanging room directions. The gesture is written as though no turn occurs, and the direction stated is the one toward which the limb moves at the start of the action. The space hold sign within the leg gesture symbol states that the normal effect of the turn is counteracted.

Fig. 206 (c) shows a turn starting as the leg begins to move toward stage left. The space retention occurs all during the raising of the leg and ends only when the leg arrives at middle level. By then the action has become a backward gesture from the hip. The final result is the same as one in which the gesture is completed before the turn starts, and a space hold is in effect during the turn, as in (d). The important difference is that in (c) the leg rises gradually all during the turn, whereas in (d) it remains at the same level.

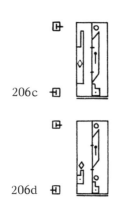

206c

206d

LEG GESTURES WITH AERIAL TURNS

Each form of aerial step can combine turning with leg gestures. The action strokes used for simple aerial turns are readily converted into specific leg gestures. Fig. 207 (a) shows a half-turn jump without any specific leg gestures;

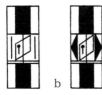

207a   b

in (b) the legs are shown to extend to the side. Steps which leave the ground from one support usually use a blended form of turn in which the turn starts on the support and then becomes aerial.

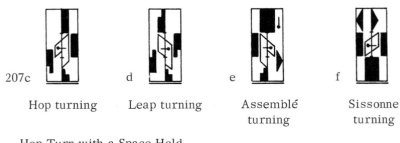

207c   d   e   f

Hop turning   Leap turning   Assemblé   Sissonne
                               turning   turning

Hop Turn with a Space Hold

The basic pattern of Fig. 206 (c) can also be performed as a hop turn in which the gesturing leg has a space hold, as in Fig. 208 (a). Because of the whiplike action of the leg, in ballet this step is called "grand fouetté sauté en tournant," or "fouetté sauté." Fig. 208 (b) shows a more brilliant execution of this step.

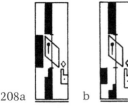

208a   b

Fouetté sauté

VARIATIONS ON A TURNING LEAP

The performance of a turning leap can be considerably varied according to the timing and the spatial pattern of the leg gestures.

Fig. 209 (a) shows the basic form: a leap turn. In (b) the left leg is shown to gesture forward and the right leg backward. The final position will be a support on the left leg with the right leg backward. As written here, this leap turn produces a fanlike effect, the legs performing arcs as they are lifted. When the legs pass

209a   b

each other closely, rising on undeviating curves, as though confined to a narrow space between two walls (a plane curve), (b) would be incorrect. Below are some variations on this basic form.

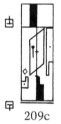    

209c   d   e   f   g

One variation of this leap uses a space hold, as in Fig. 209 (c). Here the quick preparatory step is followed at once by a fast gesture forward for the left leg. When the turn starts and the body leaves the ground, the left leg retains its direction in space, ending backward from the hip, while the right leg gestures backward. This backward gesture for the right leg is a fanning movement. When this is not wanted, it should be written as an undeviating curve as in (d). Fig. (e) shows the turn starting on the supporting foot while the left leg has an undeviating curve toward what started as a forward action. The turn continues in the air with the right leg down. When the turn is completed, the right leg whips backward while the left leg comes down; the legs change places in a scissorlike kick just before landing. The classical ballet version of this turning leap, called a "grand jeté en tournant en dehors," or "tour jeté" for short, is commonly written as (c), though (d) and (e) are more correct when performances of those specific forms are required. Fig. (f) shows the legs beating in the air; (g) is a more brilliant rendition, the turn occurring later.

CHAPTER 11

Distance – Space Measurement

An unqualified direction symbol indicates an ordinary-sized step or a normally extended gesture into the stated direction. The length of these symbols indicates the timing of the actions, a longer or shorter time spent in performing the given movement. The size of the movement in terms of the distance covered, that is, the space measurement, is stated with an additional indication. For supports, this greater or less use of space results in longer or shorter steps. For gestures, greater use of space results in the extension of the limbs and lesser use of space results in the contraction of the limbs, bending them to draw the extremity closer to the center. For both usages the concept of distance from center is the same.

THE SYMBOLS WHICH INDICATE DISTANCE

The principal signs used in space measurement are:

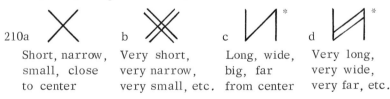

210a   Short, narrow, small, close to center

b   Very short, very narrow, very small, etc.

c   Long, wide, big, far from center

d   Very long, very wide, very far, etc.

The symbols are commonly called the "narrow" and "wide" signs, though in actual application, depending on the context, they may have any of the above meanings. Though different words are used, e.g. for ×: "a <u>short</u> step," "a <u>narrow</u> position of the feet," "a <u>small</u> distance from the center" (from place), "a <u>slight</u> bend" (contraction), the basic idea is the same.

* See Appendix B, note 7.

GENERAL INDICATIONS

Space measurement signs can be used by themselves, as in Motif Writing, to give a general statement of an action or to describe the idea of a movement.

211a	b	c
A starting position showing a general contraction of the whole body (very small, closed in)	General extension for the right side of the body (reach out, stretch)*	Traveling a long distance on a straight path

Such general statements allow for much freedom of interpretation; no exact degree of extension, contraction, or travel is given and no specific shape or spatial result is prescribed. All these may be notated in detail when required.

LENGTH OF STEPS

An ordinary step is the natural stride of the performer; therefore modifications of its length are based on the build of the performer rather than on any standard length in terms of inches or centimeters. Obviously four steps for a tall, long-legged person will cover more ground than will the same number for a short person. Exactness in measurement or in reaching a precise point on stage can be indicated but is seldom required for general purposes.

Natural Modifications in Length

Certain modifications in the length of steps occur naturally. High steps tend to be shorter than middle level steps, and in performing low steps there is a natural tendency to reach out and cover more ground. Forward steps are usually longer than sideward or backward steps and open steps are, of course, longer than crossing steps.

Indication of Length of Step

To modify the normal walking stride, the appropriate space measurement sign is placed before the direction symbol indicating a step. When used thus as a pre-sign, the space measurement sign and the direction symbol are considered a unit in indicating

* See Appendix A, note 6.

the timing of the action. Therefore the direction symbol is shortened by the length of the pre-sign (usually one square of graph paper) so that the over-all length indicating the timing is not changed. In the examples below each set of symbols indicates the same time value. Those in Fig. 212 (a) are half notes; in (b) quarter notes; in (c) eighth notes. The modified symbol occupies the same length of time as the plain symbol.

212
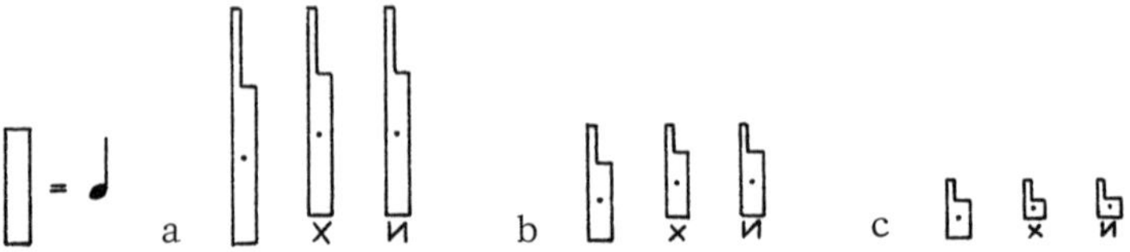
a
b
c

The two degrees of narrow (× and ⋇) and the two degrees of wide (И and ꟿ) which suffice for the general description of length of step are illustrated below.

213a
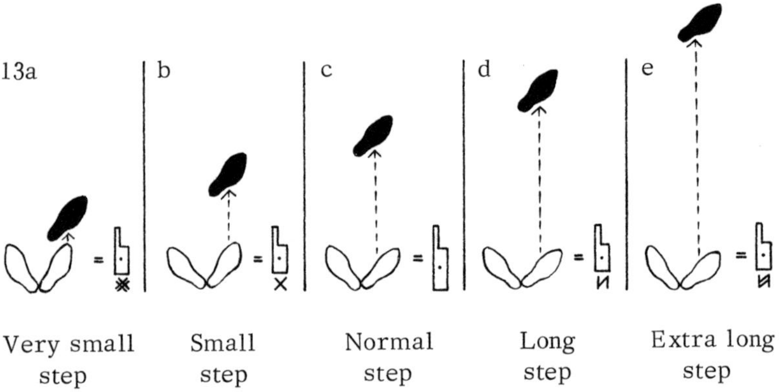
b
c
d
e
Very small step
Small step
Normal step
Long step
Extra long step

Finer degrees are shown by using the six degree scale given on page 162. Specific degrees for lengthening a step are on page 163.

Determining Length of Step

While great precision in notation is possible when it is needed, for general purposes the key to the size of steps should not lie in the distance between footprints, but rather in the movement used to take the step - the action of the legs and the traveling of the center of weight. One must observe

214
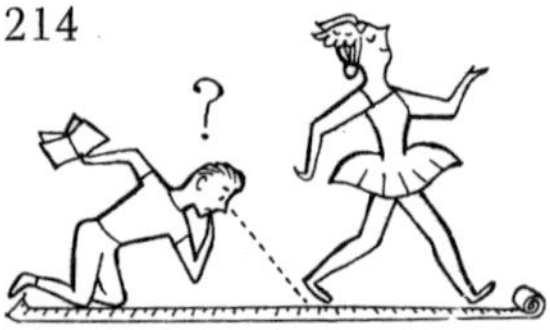
?

whether there is a drive to cover more ground than in a normal comfortable step, or whether the performer is holding back, thus producing smaller steps. Expending energy produces longer steps, and containing or lacking energy produces shorter steps.

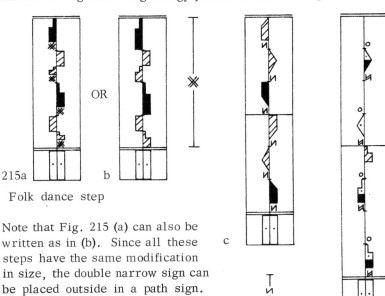

215a   b

Folk dance step

Note that Fig. 215 (a) can also be written as in (b). Since all these steps have the same modification in size, the double narrow sign can be placed outside in a path sign. Fig. (c) could be similarly handled by using ⊥.

c

d

NARROW AND WIDE POSITIONS OF THE FEET

The open positions of the feet may be narrow or wide in the same way that steps can be short or long. The appropriate pre-sign is placed under each direction symbol as in Fig. 216 (a) or centered under the two symbols as in (b). The width of a position of the feet is judged on the basis of the distance between the two feet, not on the distance of each foot from center (place).

216a   b

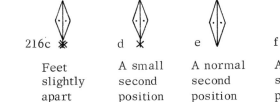

216c   d   e   f   g

| Feet slightly apart | A small second position | A normal second position | A wide second position | A very wide second position |

The distance of the separation of the feet is the same whether the position is reached through a jump, as in (h), or through stepping, as in (i). Because the pre-sign is considered part of the support indication, the moment of landing (the contact of the foot with the floor) is understood to occur at the start of the pre-sign. Below are examples

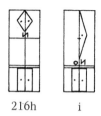

216h   i

of stepping or jumping into wider or narrower positions of the feet.

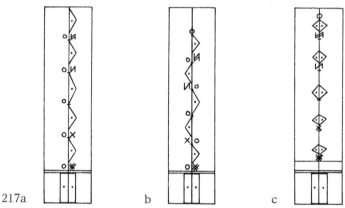

217a
Stepping out with the right foot

b
Stepping out alternately right and left

c
Jumping into increasingly wider positions

THE SIX-DEGREE SCALE OF NARROW AND WIDE

As a rule in Motif Writing only the two degrees of narrowing and widening are used. In the structural description of movement, finer degrees are needed for writing length of step and contraction of the limbs. These are provided by adding dots to the basic signs, thereby producing a scale of six degrees.

Degrees of Narrowing

The General Scale:

The Six Scale: 218

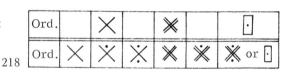

"Ord." represents the ordinary step length, or the normally extended limb. In stepping, the sixth degree is totally closed, i.e. it is equivalent to place.

Degrees of Widening

The minimum degree of width for a step is of course place, the maximum, "a split" or "stride" (the length of both legs). When the precise length of step must be observed, the distance of one step in the forward direction is stated as being two foot lengths from heel to heel when the whole foot is on the ground. The longest step is generally considered to be three and a half step lengths (seven times the foot length). More degrees exist for long steps than for short.

Scale for Long Steps. This scale for degrees of length applies only to steps. The limbs can only lengthen two degrees.

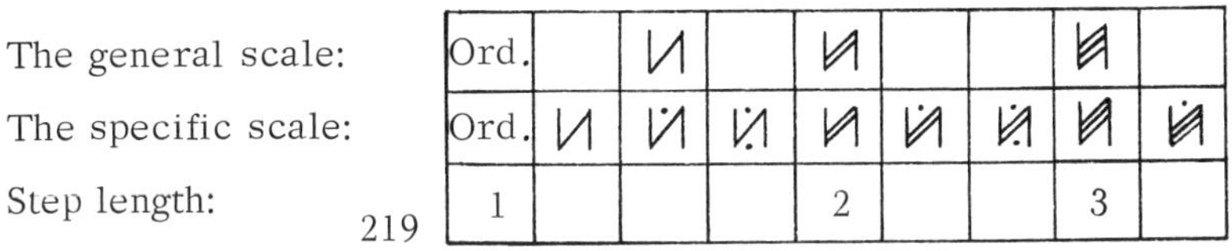

The general scale:	Ord.		И		�			�	
The specific scale:	Ord.	И	�	�	�	�	�	�	�
Step length: 219	1				2			3	

Fig. 220 illustrates the progression in degrees of widening an open position of the feet until a split is reached. The numbers given here refer to step lengths.

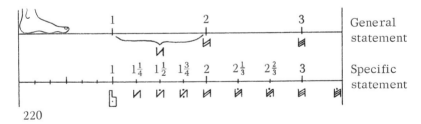

220

Observe that between place and a normal forward step there are six subdivisions; between one step length and two there are four; and between two step lengths and three there are only three. While this may not seem mathematically correct, it is physically practical, in that the dancer needs to make more distinctions between small steps than large.

Statement of Scale Used - General or Specific

Where no specific indication is given, the general usage is understood to apply. To indicate the specific scale for steps, the following statements should be made:

$$\times = \tfrac{1}{6} \qquad\qquad \text{И} = 1\tfrac{1}{4}$$

These indications are usually placed at the start of a score but
can appear outside the staff next to a statement which needs clarifying. In actual practice such indication of scale is only required
incidentally for the single symbols X and И, since any addition of
dots immediately denotes the use of the specific scale, and the
doubled signs ✳ and И are the same in both scales. Below are
examples in which the scale is stated. Fig. 221 (c) shows the statement of exact step length (see page 449 for the distance sign).

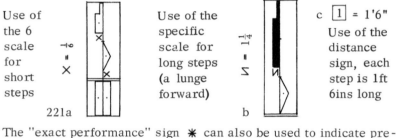

| Use of the 6 scale for short steps | Use of the specific scale for long steps (a lunge forward) | c ꠹1꠹ = 1'6" Use of the distance sign, each step is 1ft 6ins long |

221a   b

The "exact performance" sign ✳ can also be used to indicate precision in interpretation. (See page 356.)

NARROW AND WIDE GESTURES OF THE LIMBS

The narrow and wide signs are used to describe flexion (contraction) and extension of the limbs (arms, legs, hands) and to some
extent the whole torso (spine). In using less space, the limbs draw
in closer to the body, toward the point of attachment. In using
more space, the limbs extend away from the body.

EXTENSION

Analysis of Movement

Extension is the lengthening of a part of the body into the direction already established or into a stated new direction. The extremity of the limb, the free end, keeps its line of direction with
the base, the point of attachment.

Method of Writing

The space measurement signs И and И indicate extension.
Overextension (reaching out in space), which involves the part of
the body to which the limb is attached, is indicated by an extension
sign plus an inclusion sign (see Chapter 15). When used as a pre-
sign before a direction symbol, the space measurement sign modifies performance of a gesture in the given direction.

EXTENSION OF THE LEGS

In an ordinary leg gesture it is understood that the knee, ankle, and foot are relaxed. To indicate a straight leg, the symbol Ⱔ is placed in front of the direction symbol in the leg gesture column. Two degrees of extension are possible.

Knee, ankle and foot extended in one line.

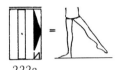

222a

Fully extended leg; lengthened to the utmost.

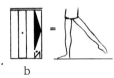

b

The difference between Ⱔ and Ⱔ in extending the leg is not easily seen in a drawing but the muscular effect is quite noticeable. The leg takes on a different appearance; there is a muscular lengthening in both directions, i.e. the muscles are "pulled up" and at the same time kinetic energy "projects" out through the foot. The limb is taut, but not tense: the energy is expended in the act of extension, causing neither stiffening nor cramp. Correct use of muscular relaxation will result in greater extension.

Only the two degrees of extension given above are possible within the limb itself. To extend further, to make greater use of space, the leg must pull out from the body so that the hip joint is involved.*

EXTENSION OF THE ARMS

The arm also has only two degrees of extension. It is normally held with a very slightly curved elbow and wrist. The hand is also curved, the degree of this curve being individual. In the first degree of extension, the elbow, wrist and hand straighten so that the whole arm becomes one straight line. In the second degree of extension, the limb lengthens further through the use of the muscles. This additional lengthening is only a small change spatially but it affects the expression of the movement considerably. The energy used for this extra extension causes neither stiffening nor cramp.

The arm is straight in one line.

223a

The arm is extended and taut.

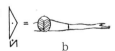

b

The difference between Figs. 223 (a) and (b) can be seen and felt muscularly but it is not easily drawn.

* See Appendix B, note 8.

FLEXION: CONTRACTION*

Contraction, also called "shortening" or "drawing in," is one form of flexion. The term "contraction" is used in its anatomical sense and not, as in certain contemporary dance techniques, specifically applied to a stylized movement of the torso.

Typical examples of contraction and extension which occur in everyday life are:

For the legs: pedaling a bicycle, braking a car, rowing a scull.
For the arms: boxing, archery, rowing, pushing furniture,
             opening an umbrella, planing wood.

In these actions we can see that the drawing in of the limb close to the center to make functional use of the force within the body is more important than any exact placement in space of the parts of the limbs. In dance, though such gestures as these are performed for expressive rather than functional reasons and an increase in energy may or may not be present, the basic actions of drawing in and of reaching out are physically the same.

Analysis of Movement

Contraction is the drawing in of the extremity of the limb (the free end) toward its base (the point of attachment or the fixed end). A contraction of the arm or leg involves a simultaneous flexion of two joints - the center joint of the limb and that at the point of attachment. For the arms these are the elbow and shoulder; for the leg, the knee and hip. In an extended limb, the extremity, the center joint, and the base are all in one line. In Fig. 224 (a) this line is represented by x-y, with z as the center joint. As the extremity y approaches the base x, the angle at z will decrease and the point z will be displaced in space. The greater the diminution of this angle, the greater the displacement. Thus in contracting the leg, the knee is displaced from its point on the line x-y while the foot and hip keep the original line of direction. It is important to note in (b) that neither section of the limb lies in the original line of direction, though the extremity and base do.

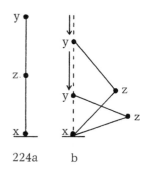

224a   b

* See page 319 for bending (folding), the other form of flexion.

Method of Writing

The symbol ╳ and its variants are used for gestures of the limbs to indicate contractions. The required pre-sign ╳, ╳ , etc., is placed in front of the direction symbol in the appropriate column for the arm, leg, or torso.

CONTRACTION OF THE LEG

In a contraction of the leg, flexion is understood to occur in the hip joint and in the knee, but not in the ankle joint. Any contraction in the ankle joint must be specifically stated.

Degrees of Contraction in the Place Low Direction

In these illustrations the leg is shown to be turned out and the foot to extend as is customary in ballet. The direction shown for the leg as a whole is place low, that is, straight down. Although the leg bends more and more, the foot retains the same relationship to the hip, remaining directly below it. As the bending increases the knee becomes more and more displaced to the side. It is important to recognize that the direction of the knee is not the direction of the leg as a whole.

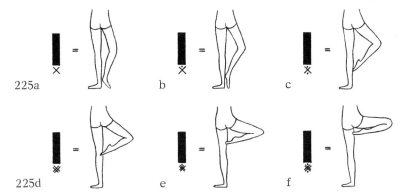

225a   b   c

225d   e   f

The direction of the knee's displacement will depend on the inward or outward rotation of the limb. Fig. 225 (c) above shows the effect of an outward rotation; (g) illustrates the same degree of contraction with the legs parallel. The notation here does not include the rotation (see Chapter 17).

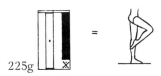

225g

A 90° contraction in the parallel state

Degrees of Contraction in the Side Low Direction

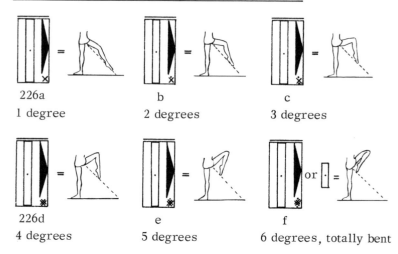

226a — 1 degree   b — 2 degrees   c — 3 degrees

226d — 4 degrees   e — 5 degrees   f — 6 degrees, totally bent

Note that the last degree of contraction for the leg cannot be performed by the limb alone; some outside assistance is required to pull the foot in that close to the hip.

Degrees of Contraction in the Forward Middle Direction

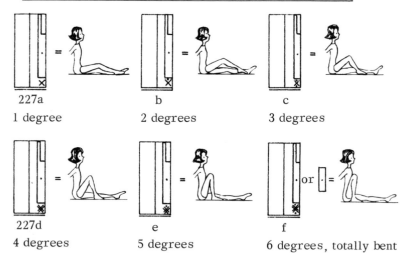

227a — 1 degree   b — 2 degrees   c — 3 degrees

227d — 4 degrees   e — 5 degrees   f — 6 degrees, totally bent

The above examples are illustrated with parallel legs in a sitting position on the floor where such positions commonly occur. The actions can also be performed with outward rotation.

CONTRACTION OF THE ARMS

The general direction for the whole arm, as stated by the direction symbol, is the line from the shoulder to the hand. In contractions of the whole arm, flexion occurs in the shoulder joint and in the elbow. Any flexion in the wrist or fingers must be written separately. A flexion of the elbow joint alone causes only the lower arm to change its direction in space and is therefore not an action of the whole limb.

When the arm contracts, neither its upper nor lower part remains in the originally stated direction. As the degree of bending increases, the elbow becomes progressively more displaced in space. Regardless of this displacement, the extremities of the limb, the hand and shoulder, retain the same spatial relationship. The exact direction of the elbow will depend on the degree of rotation, outward or inward, given for the limb as a whole.

Degrees of Contractions in the Forward Middle Direction

The following examples show the degrees of bending the arm in the forward middle direction. The illustrations are drawn as seen from above. Depending on the individual proportions of the parts of the limbs, it may be the center of the hand or the wrist which ends in front of the shoulder when total contraction occurs.

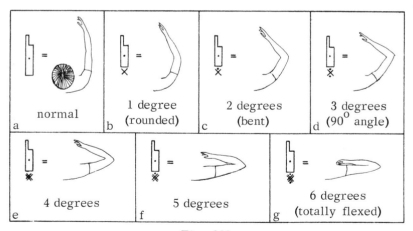

Fig. 228

As the arm contracts and the hand draws in to the shoulder, the elbow moves more and more to the side, ending side middle.

If this forward arm gesture is performed with the palm facing up (with outward rotation), the degree of bending will be the same, but the spatial result will be different because of the rotation. Instead of ending out to the side as in the previous examples, the elbow lowers gradually until it is straight down in a complete contraction, as shown below. The indication for the rotation of the arms is not given here (see Chapter 17).

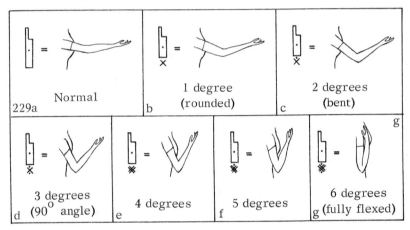

229a Normal	b 1 degree (rounded)	c 2 degrees (bent)
d 3 degrees (90° angle)	e 4 degrees	f 5 degrees	g 6 degrees (fully flexed)

An exact description of the final position reached can be given by stating the precise degree of rotation, the degree of contraction, and the direction of the limb as a whole. But if the final position to be reached, i.e. placement of the limb in space, is important it should be indicated by direction symbols for the parts of the limb. A description in terms of contraction using narrow signs should be employed whenever the action of drawing in the limb toward the center is of prime importance.

Contraction in the Place High Direction

The following example of a 90° contraction with the arm place high is illustrated with a normally held arm and with outward rotation of the limb.

Regardless of the rotation used the hand finishes above the shoulder.

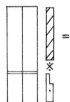

230

Arm with normal rotation

Arm with outward rotation

Contractions in the Place Low Direction

The following examples show the result of a 90° contraction of the arm in the place low direction using different states of rotation.

Regardless of
the rotation
used the hand
finishes below
the shoulder.
                    231

Palm facing in   Palm facing for-
toward the body   ward (outward
(normal rotation)   rotation)

DURATION OF NARROW AND WIDE SIGNS FOR GESTURES

Space measurement signs are not elongated to indicate an increase in the duration of the action.

Without Change of Direction - Sudden

Once the direction for the limb has been stated, we need only to write the isolated signs for sudden contractions or extensions which remain in the same basic direction.

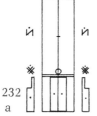

232
a

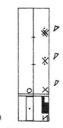

b

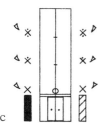

c

The arms contract   The contractions are not only quick but
quickly, then   are accented, i.e. sharp, staccato.
extend quickly.   (See page 478 for accent signs.)

Without Change of Direction - Sustained

When the limbs remain in the same spatial direction, the timing of sustained contractions and extensions can be shown by a duration line.* Repetition of the direction symbol is unnecessary. In Structural Description the action stroke means "perform this action in the simplest, most suitable way." Freedom in choice of action is shown by using the ad libitum sign $\{$. (See pages 354-5.)

* See Appendix A, note 6.

While contract-
ing and extend-
ing the arm and
leg remain in
the forward mid-
dle direction.

233a

The same leg ac-
tion but aware-
ness of the for-
ward direction is
emphasized; spe-
cific directions
given for the arm.

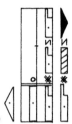

b

With Change of Direction

When a narrow or wide sign is placed before
a direction symbol it is considered as a unit with
that direction symbol with regard to timing. The
action of contracting or stretching is understood
to be spread over the amount of time indicated
by the direction symbol as well. Thus in Fig.
234 (a) the right leg takes two counts to contract
two degrees while it lifts into the forward middle
direction, and one count to extend while moving
to side middle. Though the symbol appears at
the beginning as a pre-sign, the action is spread
throughout the time available.

234a

When the same state of contraction or of extension is to be held,
the same pre-sign is stated for the new direction symbol. Without
this repeated pre-sign, the limb will return to its normal state.

Move the right leg
forward contract-
ing it two degrees,
then move it side
low, keeping the
same contraction.

234b

Move the right arm
to side right exten-
ding it two degrees,
then forward keep-
ing the same degree
of extension.

c

Motion or Destination

By themselves degrees of contraction state established destinations. In
going from a greater degree of contraction to a lesser, the action is one of extension. This may be written as in Fig.
235 (a) which states the motion of ex-

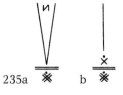

235a   b

tending, but in Structural Description usually destination is written
as in (b). (See pages 184 and 341 for $\vee$, $\wedge$ representing motion.)

TOTAL CONTRACTION VERSUS THE DIRECTION PLACE

Theoretically a fully contracted arm is at place (hand
close to shoulder); therefore
Figs. 236 (a) and (b) mean
generally the same thing. In
practice the choice of description depends on the expression
of the movement, for (a) emphasizes the spatial direction
(place) and (b) the action of
drawing in the limb. The a-
wareness of the action is different for the performer and
the resulting change of expression is observable to an onlooker.

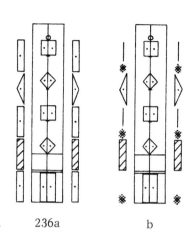

236a   b

READING MATERIAL: LEG AND ARM GESTURES

No statement of rotation is given for the following examples;
their performance is left open to interpretation. The effect of leg
rotation changes neither the basic direction nor degree of bending.

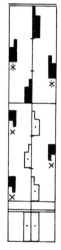 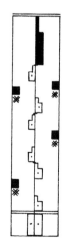 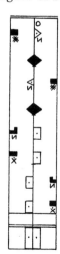

237a   b   c

Run with bent back-
ward gestures, then
a forward hitch kick
with bent legs.

Do two skips and
a gallop with the
legs pulled up
underneath.

Kick the leg out from
underneath on each hop.
Pull it in on sideward
springs.

READING MATERIAL

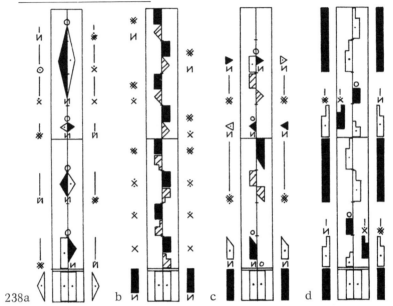

BENDING AND STRETCHING THE LEGS WHILE SUPPORTING

The signs X and И , when placed in the leg gesture column next to a support symbol, indicate the state of contraction or extension of the leg during that support.

Degrees of Knee Bends

The general indication of a low support, that is, of a support with a bent leg, shown by a shaded direction symbol, can be expressed more specifically by the use of the appropriate contraction symbol. The six degrees of contracting the legs can be shown solely through the use of the contraction signs; however, the convention of using middle level symbols when the leg is almost straight and low level symbols when the legs are definitely bent is applied, because these indications facilitate reading. The appropriate contraction sign is added to the appropriate level of support.

The following examples describing the six degrees of knee bends are illustrated with the legs both out-turned and parallel. The basic support and degree of leg contraction are the same regardless of leg rotations. The half knee bend (demi-plié) varies with different performers, generally falling between Figs. 239 (c) and (d); (f) is a full knee bend (grand plié) and (g) produces a squat.

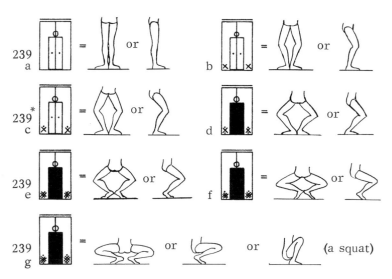

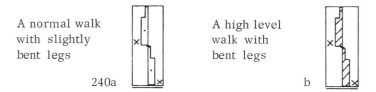

239 a   239 b   239 c*   239 d   239 e   239 f   239 g (a squat)

The exact degree of knee bend equivalent to an ordinary low level support is also left open. For some it is lower than for others. The commonly used degree probably lies between Fig. 239 (c) and (d). Once low level has been reached, from (d) on, the support is written as a low support with the additional information of the degree of knee bend. As the leg bending increases, it is common for the heels to leave the ground. The moment this must occur varies with the individual build of the performer. The exact use of the foot can be stated by adding the appropriate hooks to the support symbols (see Chapter 13).

Mod   Steps

The sign ✕ or И placed next to a step modifies the whole step. **

A normal walk
with slightly
bent legs

240a

A high level
walk with
bent legs

b

Note the difference between Figs. 240 (a) and (b) where the contraction sign modifies the step and (c) and (d) where it describes the free leg as it prepares to take the step which follows.

*See also page 401, Fig. 611. **See Appendix B, note 9.

Picking up the
free foot while
stepping in
place
240c

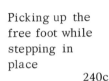

The same as
(c) but in low
level

d

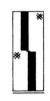

Length of Step with Contraction or Extension of Supporting Leg

Space measurement signs for length of step and degree of contracting or stretching the leg can be written side by side. Note the following combinations:

241

a

Short steps,
bent knees

b

Short steps,
stretched knees

c

Long steps,
stretched knees

d

Long steps,
bent knees

DURATION OF NARROW AND WIDE SIGNS FOR SUPPORTS

The sign x or и placed next to a support symbol modifies the whole symbol. In quick steps as in Fig. 242 (a), there is no time for differentiation in the moment when the contraction starts and when it is completed.

242a

In slow steps changes in leg contraction and extension can take place during the transference of weight. Bending can occur at the beginning, in the middle, or at the end of a step. Timing of the bending is shown by the addition of the action stroke (duration line).

242

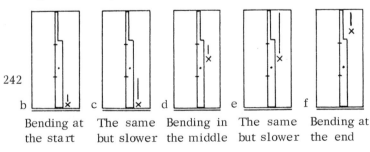

b — Bending at the start

c — The same but slower

d — Bending in the middle

e — The same but slower

f — Bending at the end

Note that in Figs. 242 (b), (c), and (d) the degree of contraction achieved is kept for the rest of the transference of weight. When the expanded staff is used, the x or ᴎ indication is placed in the space adjacent to the support column (the "a" column).

Change in Carriage of the Legs during Supports

When consecutive identical indications occur, the limb retains its state of contraction or extension. Only on the first indication will there be an actual change to that state of contraction or extension. Note the difference between Figs. 243 (a) and (b).

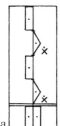

On the first step the right knee bends two degrees. This is cancelled when the left leg takes a normal middle level step. 243a

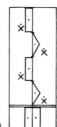

On the first two steps the degree of knee bend is achieved; on the next two steps it is maintained.   b

DISTANCE OF LEG GESTURE FROM SUPPORT

A low leg gesture should be at a 45° angle from the vertical line. Often the leg should be lower, nearer the other leg and hence also closer to the ground. Intermediate directions can indicate the precise directional point to which the leg moves, but a practical method of showing nearness to the support is to place the appropriate narrow sign in the support column of the gesturing leg. This follows the logic of distance from center applied to length of step.

Distance of Leg Gestures While Standing

The angle of a low leg gesture is modified the moment contact with the floor is indicated by the addition of hooks to the direction symbol (see Chapter 13). Before the leg actually touches the floor, it may be lowered two degrees from the normal 45° angle.

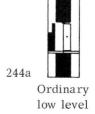
244a

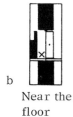
b

Ordinary
low level

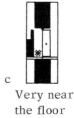
c

Near the
floor

Very near
the floor

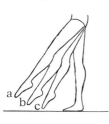

Distance of Leg Gestures during Jumps

The following examples illustrate variations in the distance of low leg gestures from the ground.

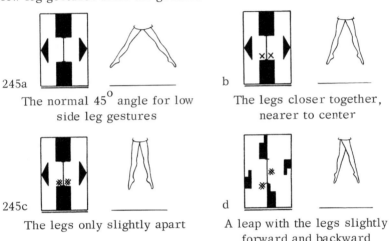

245a
The normal 45° angle for low side leg gestures

b
The legs closer together, nearer to center

245c
The legs only slightly apart

d
A leap with the legs slightly forward and backward

CANCELLATIONS

The rules for canceling space measurement signs which are used for length of step and for canceling contractions and extensions will be considered separately.

LENGTH OF STEP

A space measurement sign placed before a direction symbol lasts as long as that symbol is in effect. The particular pre-sign must be repeated if it is to apply to subsequent direction symbols.

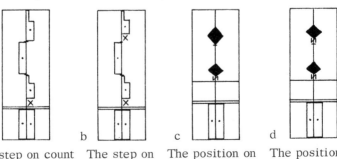

246a
The step on count 3 is a normal-sized step.

b
The step on count 3 is a small step.

c
The position on count 2 is of normal size.

d
The position on count 2 is a wide position.

When the size of step is shown by
placing the space measurement sign in a
path sign outside the staff on the right,
the size of all directional steps that occur during the length of the path sign is
affected. At the conclusion of the path
sign this modification ends. Therefore
in Fig. 247 the last step is of normal size. 247

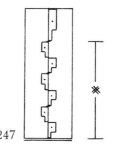

STATE OF LEG DURING STEP

The indication for the state of
the leg during a step, bent or extended, lasts only for the step
next to which it is placed; therefore in Fig. 248 (a) the right leg
steps in the normal manner on the
third beat. In (b) it is again bent. 248a

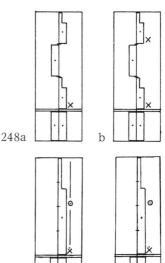

b

In a slow step, a particular state
of contraction or extension can be
shown to return to normal during
the course of the transference of
weight. In (c) the slight bending of
the leg during the first half of the
step disappears during the second
half. This return to normal is indicated by the back to normal sign ⊙. 248c
In (d) both these actions are sudden.

d

Retention of Bent or Stretched State for Steps

To show a series of steps to be performed
with bent or stretched knees, a retention sign
is placed over the space measurement sign.
This indication is cancelled by a return to
normal sign ⊙,* as in Fig. 249.

249

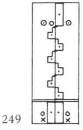

GESTURES OF THE LIMBS

The space measurement pre-sign is valid only as long as the
symbol before which it is placed is valid. To retain the same
state of contraction or extension, the pre-sign must be repeated.

* See Appendix A, note 5.

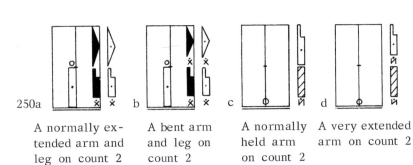

| A normally ex-
tended arm and
leg on count 2 | A bent arm
and leg on
count 2 | A normally
held arm
on count 2 | A very extended
arm on count 2 |

When the limb retains the same spatial direction but returns to the normal state after a contraction or extension, we can use the unqualified direction symbol or the back-to-normal indication. The first, Fig. 250 (e), emphasizes an awareness of the direction; the latter, (f), the normal state.

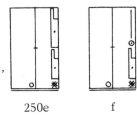

250e   f

Retention of Bent or Stretched State for Gestures

To keep a state of contraction or extension during a series of gestures without having to repeat the pre-sign for each direction symbol, a retention sign can be used when the pre-sign first appears, or the indication may be placed within an addition bracket.

In Fig. 251 (a) the two-degree contraction for the arm is cancelled on count 4. The back-to-normal sign ⊙ is used here as a pre-sign to indicate the normal carriage of the arm. In (b) the narrow sign is written in the adjacent column and tied to the arm column by a small horizontal bow ◡. The cancellation on count 4 also appears in this column. Note that because the starting position has no timing the indication can be written as in either (a) or (b).

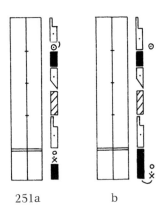

251a   b

For use of the addition bracket to eliminate repetition of the same pre-sign, see page 483.

CHAPTER 12

Floor Pattern, Paths

FLOOR PATTERN

A floor pattern is the design made by a dancer or several dancers performing steps which travel across and around the stage area. In a dance score indication of the path, direction, distance, degree of circling, etc. is part of the movement instruction. At the same time floor plans illustrating starting and finishing positions as well as paths are usually given alongside the movement staff to provide a visual aid. (For details of floor plans see Chapter 22.)

THE STAGE AREA*

The room or stage in which the per- former moves is represented by an open rectangle, the open side being the front of the room, the audience. Rooms and stages vary considerably in size and shape. Fig. 252 represents one of gen- eral proportions, greater in width than in depth. For individual needs the area can be scaled to an appropriate, relative size and shape.

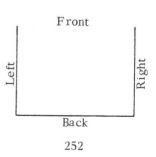

252

INDICATION OF THE PERFORMER

In the following floor plans which illustrate the performer's change of situation a white pin ♀ , which indicates a girl, is used to show the starting position, and a wedge △ to indicate her finish- ing position. The point of the pin or wedge indicates the direction in which she faces. (See page 365.)

* See Appendix B, note 10.

INDICATION OF PATH

A path across the floor is indicated on the floor plan by the use of an arrow which shows the progression from the starting point.

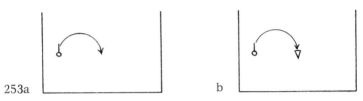

253a

b

The performer makes a half circle path to the right, ending center stage.

The same path with the finishing position shown: the performer ends facing the back of the room.

THE SPECIFIC AREAS IN THE ROOM

The specific parts of the room or stage are identified by representative signs.

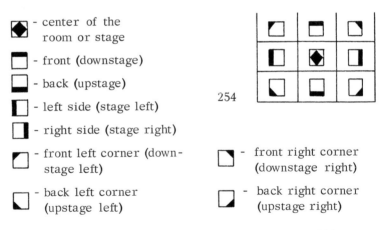

◆ - center of the room or stage

□ - front (downstage)

□ - back (upstage)

▌ - left side (stage left)

▐ - right side (stage right)

◤ - front left corner (downstage left)

◣ - back left corner (upstage left)

◥ - front right corner (downstage right)

◢ - back right corner (upstage right)

254

Additional area signs are given in the glossary, page 505.

GENERAL INDICATION OF PATHS

Notation of a specific choreographic work involves precise recording of paths; in many folk dances, for example, the paths are detailed and exact. But a general statement only is sufficient for many notation purposes; details may be added as desired.

BASIC SIGNS FOR PATH

Straight Path

The straight path sign, Fig. 255 (a), is the general indication for traveling on a straight line.
When placed next to a description of specific steps
it provides additional information regarding the
performance of those steps. (See page 84.)

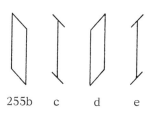

255a

Circular Path

The signs for circular path are
derived from the signs for turning.
The slanting parallel lines are connected by a central vertical line to
denote a path sign.   Fig. 255 (b) is
the parallelogram indicating a turn
to the left; (c) is the sign for a circular path to the left (counterclockwise); (e) is the turn sign for a circular path to the right (clockwise).
The length of the path sign indicates its duration. By following the
top slanted line, one can see clearly
the indication for circling left or
right as illustrated by the dotted
lines in (f) and (g).

255b   c   d   e

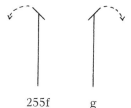

255f   g

GENERAL DESCRIPTION OF PATH

When freedom of interpretation is allowed, the following indications suggest the path desired, providing a progression from the
greatest possible freedom to more and more specific instructions.
In Motif Writing, where details are not stated, interpretation is
open to the performer.

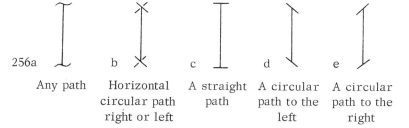

256a	b	c	d	e
Any path	Horizontal circular path right or left	A straight path	A circular path to the left	A circular path to the right

Size of path, direction of step, and amount of change of front during circular paths are left open to the performer. The sign for "any path" is derived from the ad libitum sign ⟩ or ∼ .

PATH APPROACHING

The aim of a path may be for the performer to move toward a person, object, or part of the room. This aim is stated as a focal point which may later be identified (see page 111). The action of approaching, of motion toward a focal point or state of being, is indicated by an elongated V sign. This sign was formerly called the increase sign and in some contexts is still used in that sense. The length of the sign indicates timing.

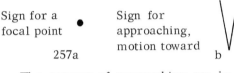

Sign for a focal point 257a

Sign for approaching, motion toward b

Approaching the focal point c

The concept of approaching can be combined with various indications for paths. Fig. 257 (d) shows a straight path approaching the focal point. In (e) approaching on a circular path produces an inward spiral path (see page 203).* 257d   e

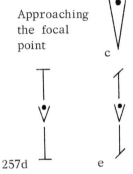

PATH WITHDRAWING

Motion away from a focal point or state of being is represented by an elongated inverted V , as in Fig. 258 (a). Fig. (b) shows withdrawing from a focal point. This indication combined with a path sign may show withdrawing on any path, as in (c), or withdrawing on a circular path (spiraling out) as in (d).* 258a b 258c d

A part of the room can be designated instead of a focal point. Fig. (e) shows any path moving away from the back of the room, while (f) shows a straight path approaching the front of the room. 258e f

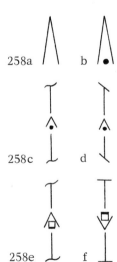

* See Appendix B, note 11.

STARTING POINT AND DESTINATION OF PATH

The appropriate stage area sign is placed to the left of the starting position to indicate where the performer is situated when he begins to move. This placement is used for Motif Writing as well as for structured scores.

Start in the center of the room in a low position, then perform a clockwise circular path.

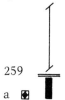

259

a

Start in the left upstage corner area facing the downstage right direction.

b

When a path arrives at the focal point, or reaches a person, object, or part of the room, the indication for this aim is placed at the end of the path sign and is tied to it with a small vertical bow. Fig. 259 (c) shows a straight path arriving at the focal point; (d) shows reaching the focal point on a circular path, and (e) arriving at the center area on any path.

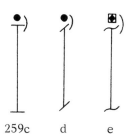

259c   d   e

GENERAL STATEMENT OF SIZE

Space measurement signs are used to indicate the general size of a path, the distance covered. Fig. 260 (a) shows any short path; (b) shows a very small clockwise circle, and (c) a very large counterclockwise circle.

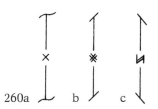

260a   b   c

SPECIFIC INDICATIONS OF CIRCULAR PATHS

A circular floor pattern can be achieved by a constant change in directional steps without any change of front, or by steps with a slight pivot between each step.

CIRCULAR FLOOR PATTERN

A circular floor pattern without a change of front can be described by a constant sequential change in the direction of each step. The circular floor pattern thus produced, however, is not true circling (a circular path), which must include a change of front as well.

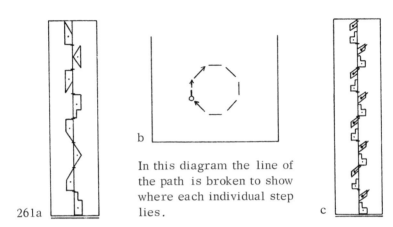

b

In this diagram the line of
the path is broken to show
where each individual step
lies.

261a

c

The step sequence shown in Fig. 261 (a) produces a circular
pattern as illustrated in (b). There is no change of front. In (c)
the step sequence produces the same pattern by an $\frac{1}{8}$ pivot turn
after each forward step. Though in both (a) and (b) a circular
shape results, the feeling is not the same as walking on a circular
path. The placement of the feet required in walking in a circle
and the gradual change of front are described on page 193.

AMOUNT OF CIRCLING

To show how much of a circle is to be performed, the vertical
line of the path sign is broken and the appropriate black pin is
placed inside to show the degree of turn, of change of front. This
usage of black pins follows that for turn signs (see Chapter 8).

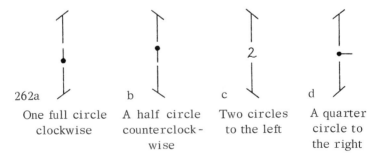

262a

b

c

d

One full circle   A half circle   Two circles   A quarter
clockwise   counterclock-   to the left   circle to
wise   the right

Interrelation of Segment of Circle and Degree of Turning

The segment of the circle, a quarter, a half, three quarters,
etc., and the degree of turning, the change of front, must agree.
In a whole circle the performer will end facing the direction in

which he started, in a half circle he will face the opposite direction, and so on. The following examples include front signs (stage
directions) to show this interrelationship. Note the placement of
the path signs on the right of the staff.*

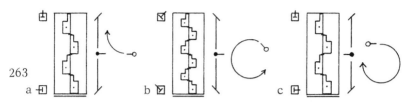

263

a

Start facing left.	Start facing left front,	Start facing right,
walk $\frac{1}{4}$ circle	walk $\frac{3}{4}$ circle counter-	walk $\frac{3}{4}$ circle
clockwise, end	clockwise, end facing	clockwise, end
facing front.	right front.	facing front.

Determining Segments of Circling

Many curved paths can be divided
into segments of a circle. Fig. 264 (a)
illustrates a path walked with forward
steps which can be broken into por-
tions of circling: $\frac{1}{4}$ circle clockwise,
$\frac{1}{2}$ circle counterclockwise, straight
for a few steps, $\frac{1}{4}$ circle counterclockwise and finally $\frac{3}{4}$ circle clockwise.

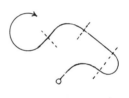

264a

This path is notated below.

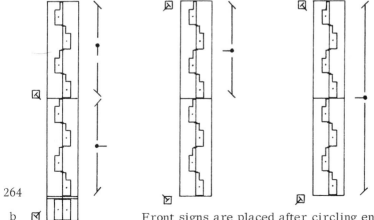

264

b

Front signs are placed after circling ends
when space allows.

* See Appendix A, note 7.

SIZE OF CIRCULAR PATH

The actual size of a circle is determined by:

1. The number of steps taken, and

2. The length of the steps.

The fewer the steps, the smaller the circle performed. The smaller the steps, the smaller the circle performed. Conversely, more steps or larger steps will increase the size of the circle. The indications for size of steps, short or long, are given in Chapter 11. If all steps are in place, the circling will occur around oneself.

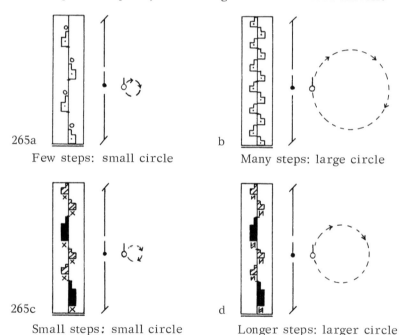

265a   Few steps: small circle

b   Many steps: large circle

265c   Small steps: small circle

d   Longer steps: larger circle

SITUATION OF THE CIRCLE

From any given point it is possible to walk eight different circles by using the eight main step directions: forward, backward, right left, and the four diagonal directions that lie between. Where the circle will lie in relation to the starting point will depend on the direction of the steps and whether circling is clockwise or counterclockwise. In every case the performer is situated at the circumference of the circle and travels around the circumference.

The performer does not start at the center of the circle. The center of the circle lies at a certain distance from the performer and is the point around which the performer moves. This point lies at right angles to the direction of the steps. The relation of the center of the circle to the performer remains constant throughout the path traveled.

In Fig. 266 (a) the white pin represents the performer. From this starting position he can describe any of the eight circles.

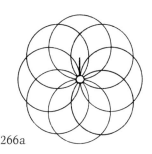

266a

Eight possible circles that can be performed from a given point

Fig. 266 (b) illustrates the following combinations of direction of steps with direction of circling:

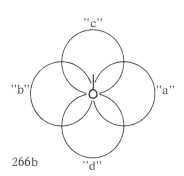

Circle "a" = ⌐ or ⌐

Circle "b" = ⌐ or ⌐

Circle "c" = ⟩ or ⟨

Circle "d" = ⟩ or ⟨

266b

Fig. 266 (c) illustrates the following combinations of diagonal steps and the direction of circling:

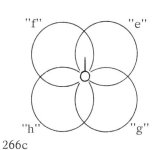

Circle "e" = ⟩ or ⟨

Circle "f" = ⟨ or ⟩

Circle "g" = ⟨ or ⟩

Circle "h" = ⟩ or ⟨

266c

Forward Steps

When we take forward steps, the center of the circle lies to our right when traveling clockwise and to our left when traveling counterclockwise. Note the dot marking the center of the circle.

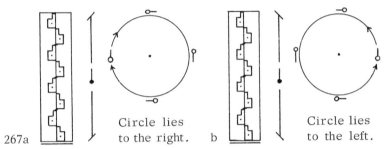

267a   Circle lies to the right.   b   Circle lies to the left.

Backward Steps

With backward steps, the center of the circle lies to our left when traveling clockwise, to our right when traveling counterclockwise.

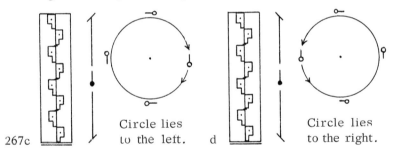

267c   Circle lies to the left.   d   Circle lies to the right.

Sideward Steps

When we take sideward steps to the right, the center of the circle lies behind us when we travel clockwise and in front of us when we travel counterclockwise.

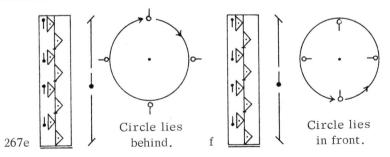

267e   Circle lies behind.   f   Circle lies in front.

If steps are taken to the left, the center of the circle will lie in front of us when we travel clockwise and behind us when we travel counterclockwise. In (g) and (h), though the choice of crossing in front or behind is left free, the line of the circular path must be kept.

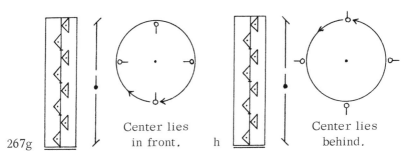

267g   Center lies   h   Center lies
                 in front.   behind.

Diagonal Steps

There are eight possible ways of walking circles using diagonal steps, of which four are illustrated here. In Fig. 268 (a) diagonally right forward steps moving clockwise produce a circle whose center lies diagonally backward right of the performer. In (b) the same steps moving counterclockwise produce a circle which lies diagonally forward left of the performer.

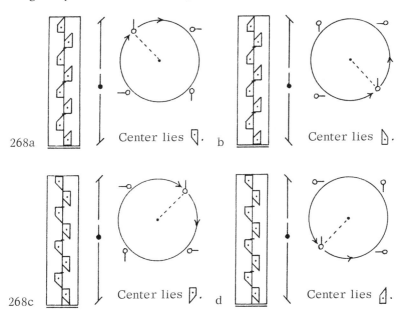

268a   Center lies ◁.   b   Center lies ▷.

268c   Center lies ▽.   d   Center lies △.

PERFORMANCE OF DEGREE OF CIRCULAR PATH

A circular path should be as true a full circle or portion thereof as possible. In walking a whole circle the performer should return to his starting point. If the number and direction of steps and
the degree of arc are given, there is a definite point in relation to
the starting point at which the performer should finish. We shall
explore quarter, half, and three-quarter circles here. In large
circles or portions thereof, the performer is at a greater distance
from the center than he is in small ones. Spirals, diminishing,
and augmenting shapes are discussed on pages 202-204.

A Quarter Circle

Whatever its size, the actual
shape of a quarter circle should remain a true arc. Fig. 269 (a) illustrates quarter circles of different
sizes. The extent of the path will
depend on the number and size of
steps taken. In each case the performer experiences a change of
front which is the same as that for
a quarter pivot turn to the right ⌐ .

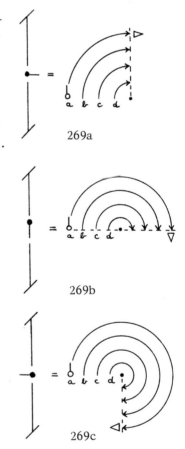

269a

A Half Circle

The performer describing a
half circle will end exactly opposite where he started and will
be facing the opposite direction.
In terms of change of front, the
result of (b) will be the equivalent of a half pivot turn ⦰ ,
regardless of the size of the
half circle.

269b

A Three-Quarter Circle

The change of front in walking a three-quarter circle as
in (c) is the same as that of a
three-quarter pivot turn ⦰ .

269c

Freedom in Interpreting Shape of Circular Path

The ad libitum sign ≀ placed next to the degree of circling, as in Fig. 270 (a), allows leeway in the amount of change of front and the circling in general. When the

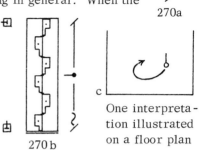

270a

change of front is specific but the shape of the curved path is not a true segment of a circle, the ad lib. sign is placed at the start of the turn sign, as in (b). Instead of calculating the exact degree of spiraling we draw the desired path in an ac- companying floor plan as in (c).

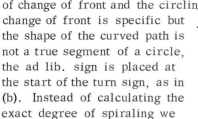

270 b

c

One interpreta- tion illustrated on a floor plan

PERFORMANCE OF STEPS ON A CIRCULAR PATH

The continuous action of turning while circling should be spread evenly over all directional steps. The starting step in walking on a circular path should be into the stated direction (forward in the examples below), but modified by the degree of curve which is to follow. In a large circle the first step hardly curves; in a very small circle the first step must curve sharply. When stepping and turning overlap completely, the turning action occurs in the body from the ankle up. Part of the turning occurs in the standing leg while the free leg prepares for the next step. Circling involves the automatic use of non-swivel turns; for this reason the steps

are taken with the feet placed on the curved line of the path. Note the difference in the placement of the feet between two steps with a ⅛ pivot turn, as in Fig. 271 (a), and two steps on a circular path as in (b) and (c). A parallel stance is used for the foot diagrams which illustrate the placement of the feet.

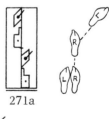

271a

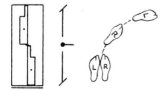

271b

c

The rotation of the legs to the right necessary for placing the feet on a circular path to the right is not usually written.

Simultaneous Step and Turn

A single step can be taken as though walking on a circular path. Fig. 271 (d) shows a
forward step occurring on a one quarter clockwise circle. This should be performed as
though it were the start of a whole circle of
four steps. In this way the step will be given
correct placement, degree of curvature, and
leg rotation. Note that the foot will be placed
on a diagonal line from the starting front,
part of the turning process being assumed by
the left leg as the right prepares to step.

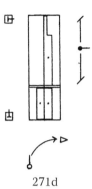

271d

Directional Steps and Steps in Place

When a sequence consists of directional steps and steps in place,
it is only the former that produce the actual path and therefore any
modification of the path refers only to these. In Fig. 272 (a) only
the forward steps will be long; the steps in place remain on the
spot. When steps are modified by a circular path sign, only those
steps which progress contribute to the curve and involve a change
of front. There is no change of front on the steps in place.

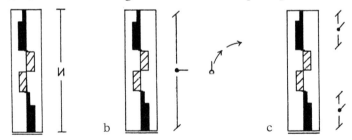

272a   b   c

In Fig. 272 (b) there will be no turning during the high steps in
place; the circular path action could have been written as in (c).
This separation is, however, unnecessary because of the above
rule regarding progression on a path.

Circling in Place

A special case occurs when all steps are
in place: the smallest possible circle is performed. Non-swivel turning occurs on each
step, and the turning action is spread evenly
over the stated number of steps.

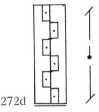

272d

Circling during Slow and Quick Steps

A slow step does not include more turning (change of front) than a quick step.
Thus in Fig. 272 (e) the degree of circling
is spread evenly over the five steps, though
the first alone is as long in duration as the
following four.   The path traveled will be
the same as that produced by five steps all
of equal time value.

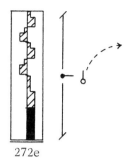

272e

REVOLVING ON A STRAIGHT PATH

Folk, ballroom, and other more complex forms of dance involve
the action of turning around one's own axis while stepping along a
straight path. In some cases this action can be analyzed so that
the direction and degree of turning for each step can be stated; in
other instances the number of steps or the total degree of revolving make an exact breakdown impossible. The following indications
illustrate how this form of movement is analyzed and written.

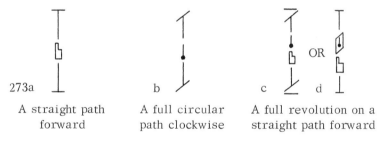

273a   b   c   d

A straight path   A full circular   A full revolution on a
forward   path clockwise   straight path forward

By combining Figs. 273 (a) and (b), the circular path of (b) is
straightened and made to fall on the path of (a). The straight path
encloses the circular path, and is dominant. When the revolving
is a pivoting action, it can be simplified to the version shown in (d).

The notation of Fig. 273 (c) does not provide information with respect to the number,
level, and timing of the steps taken. These
details can be shown as in (e). Five forward
steps travel toward the back of the room.
The direction of the steps is described according to the path to be followed as it appears at
the moment of starting. In relation to the performer, the direction of the step constantly

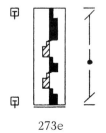

273e

changes as the body revolves. Because the direction of the path is given in the support column, it need not be indicated in the path sign. To perform a pattern such as Fig. 273 (e), the reader should first walk the straight path without any turning and then practice the given degree of turning spread evenly over the stated number of steps. These two actions can then be combined. To make this space pattern quite clear, three similar examples will be compared.

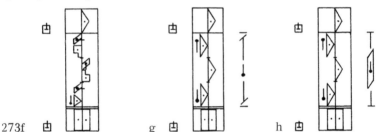

273f   g   h

Fig. 273 (f) shows three steps combined with pivot turns. The directions of the steps and the degrees of turning are such that a straight path toward the right side of the room results. There is swiveling on each step; the rate of turning is not constant. In (g) a full revolution is spread evenly over three steps which travel toward the right side of the room. There is no swiveling, each step is placed as though it were on a circular path. Fig. (h) is similar to (g) in all respects except that the turn sign within the straight path sign states that swiveling may be expected on each step.

Where there is no need to analyze the exact degree of turn for each step or where a large number or an unknown number of steps occurs, the indication for revolving on a straight path is suitable.

Jumps Revolving on a Straight Path

Traveling jumps, which must be written with a path sign, may travel on a circular path and may also combine revolving on a straight path.

Fig. 274 (a) shows four jumps with the feet apart circling a half to the right; there is no traveling. The dancer starts facing the front of the room and ends facing the back. Fig. (b) shows the same jumps traveling forward, producing a path. (See page 85.)

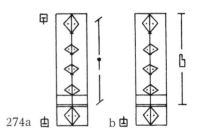

274a   b

Fig. (c) combines these two actions to produce the same path as if forward steps had occurred. In (d) the jumps travel toward the front of the room and the dancer turns constantly to end facing upstage.

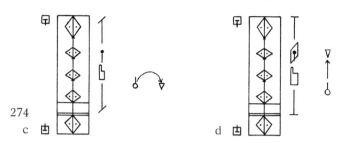

274

c	d
Traveling forward on a half circle clockwise	Revolving a half circle clockwise on a straight path forward

PIVOT TURNS ON A CIRCULAR PATH

Both pivot turns and jump turns can occur on a circular path. The usual progression on a straight path resulting from the step pattern and degree of turning is modified by the circular path. To determine the final facing direction, we add the amount of turning and circling when these are both in the same direction (e.g. turning right and circling clockwise), and subtract them when they are in opposition directions (e.g. turning left and circling clockwise).

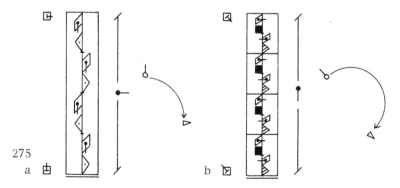

275

a   b

In Fig. 275 (a) the side steps followed by half turns to the right produce a straight path toward the right side of the room. This path is curved to become a quarter circle; thus the performer ends facing the right side of the room. In (b) the step turns also travel to the side. Here the performer starts facing left front and travels a half circle to the right to end facing back right.

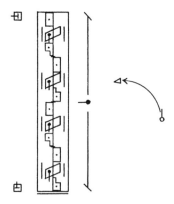

Fig. 275 (c) shows hops turning to the right on a circular path to the left (counterclockwise). The performer will end facing the left side of the room, as though he had walked an ordinary quarter circle to the left.

275c

REVOLVING ON A CIRCULAR PATH

The action of turning around one's own axis while traveling on a straight path can occur on a circular path. The revolving sign (turning) is placed within the circular path sign. To determine the final facing direction when both actions are turning in the same direction, we combine the degree of turning. When the turning directions are opposite, we subtract the degrees.

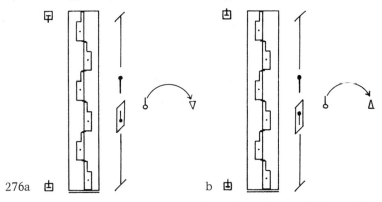

276a   b

Fig. 276 (a) shows a half circle to the right with forward steps during which there is one full turn around the dancer's own axis. The resulting total of one and a half turns causes the performer to end facing upstage. In (b) there is also a half circle to the right, but the performer revolves only a half turn around his axis. The sum of the two half turns is one full turn, which results in the performer ending as he started facing the audience.

Fig. 276 (c) shows a full revolution to the right on a half
circular path to the left. Because the turning directions
are in opposition, the amounts
will be subtracted so that in
this case the performer will
only achieve a half turn around
his own axis while walking on
a half circular path.

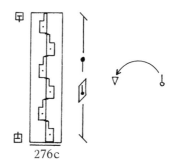

276c

Circular Path without Change of Front

If revolving on a circular path involves a certain degree of turning in one direction and an equal degree of circling in the other,
we can see that these degrees cancel each other so that a circular
path results with no change of front.

In Fig. 277 (a) the half revolution
right will cancel the half circling left;
the six steps are walked without any
change of front. (Fig. 261 (a) on page
186 showed a circular pattern produced by a change of directional steps.
Such a description of a circular pattern without change of front has obvious limitations, the most immediate
being that the idea of a circular path
is not directly stated.)

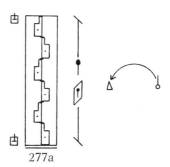

277a

Abbreviated Form for Circular Path without Change of Front

To simplify writing and reading a circular path without change of front, the convention is used of placing a space hold sign
within the circular path sign to indicate that
the front of the performer retains the same
space direction as at the start. The shape
of the circle, a whole, half, quarter, etc.
is indicated with a numeral or fraction, $\frac{1}{1}$,
$\frac{1}{2}$, $\frac{1}{4}$, etc. instead of by a black pin, as there
is no change of front to be shown which a
black pin would indicate. Fig. 277 (b) shows
(a) written in this abbreviated form.

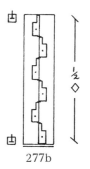

277b

FOCAL POINT FOR CIRCLE DANCES

In circle dances, the focal point for the group is automatically understood to be the center of the circle. The dancer relates to this center and is aware of facing it (facing in), having his back to it (facing out), having his right or left side to it, or having a diagonal relationship to it. In such dances the degrees of turning, an eighth, a quarter, etc. are usually replaced by the description of the new relationship of the performer to the focal point.

Indication of Front in Relation to the Circle

The front signs based on the directions in the room are not applicable to circle dances. The focal point ● (see pages 111, 112) is placed within the composite turn sign to describe the facing direction at the start of the score.

278

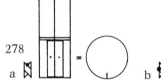

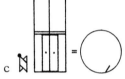

a   Focal point is in front (face the center of the circle). Side steps are required to keep on the line of the circle.

b   Focal point is to the left (left side is in to the center). Forward or backward steps are required to keep on the line of the circle.

c   Focal point is to the left front diagonal. Diagonal steps ⟋ or ⟍ are required to keep on the line of the circle.

When pivoting takes place on a circular path, the degree of turn is stated in terms of the projected new relationship to the focal point. In Fig. 278 (d) the performer starts with his left side in toward the center of the circle. After two steps forward, he pivots left until his right side is in toward the center of the circle. After two more steps he pivots right to face the center of the circle, and then after two more steps pivots right till his left side is again in toward the center of the circle. All these steps are on a counterclockwise path.

278d

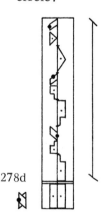

CIRCLING RIGHT OR LEFT

When used in Motif Writing, the composite circling sign, Fig. 279 (a), means that the choice of a clock-wise or counterclockwise path is left open. When used in the context of a full score, it means that steps should be taken in a clockwise or counterclockwise direction on the established circular path. Circular paths are understood to lie around a focal point; if this point is not obvious, it must be stated.

279a

In (b) the group in the circle facing counterclockwise will circle counterclockwise with the forward steps and clockwise with the back-ward steps. The situation of the focal point has been stated. Use of the composite circling sign, as in (c) eliminates the need to break down the indication for circling. It is understood that the path re-lates to the previously established focal point situated to the left of the dancers. (See page 371 for group indications.)

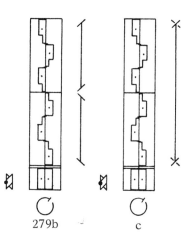

279b   c

Maintaining Circular Path with Mixed Direction Steps

In dance patterns using mixed directional steps, curving and change of front may take place on only some, not all of the steps. A good example is a pas de basque step in which the forward steps fol-low a circular path (or two parallel circular paths, to be exact), and the sideward steps are radial steps moving toward the focal point of the circle or away from it. To show that only forward or backward steps circle, the appropriate focal point indication is placed next to the start of the circular path sign, as in (d).

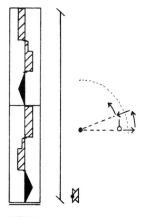

279d

In Fig. 279 (e) the focal point
is indicated at the start of the
composite circling sign to indicate which steps are to follow
the circular path. Here the
sideward steps will circle while
the forward and backward steps
will be radial, moving toward or
away from the focal point.   279e

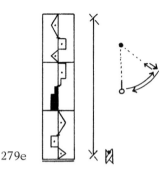

PRE-SCORE INDICATION FOR BALLROOM DANCES

In ballroom dancing, the line of direction into which the couple
progress is counterclockwise around the edges of the room. The
steps and turning patterns are adjusted to follow this line of progression. Where need be, the exact performance of the required
adjustments can be described, but a general statement for following this line of direction is enough for most purposes. The statement for the line of direction, shown
in Fig. 280, is placed at the start of
a score. The center of the room ▣
is shown to be on the left of the performer (see page 381 for the meeting
line) and the edges of the room, the
walls ◻ on the right, with the circular path going counterclockwise.
(See also page 431.)   280

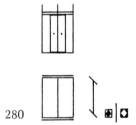

SPIRAL PATHS

The shape of a circular path diminishes as the focal point is ap-
proached, and conversely becomes larger as the distance from the
focal point increases. Such shapes become spirals when several
circles are performed. Spiral paths are often used in dances
where a certain location is to be reached on a circular path and a
certain direction is to be faced at the conclusion.

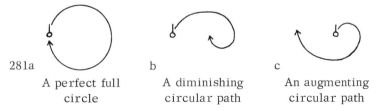

281a	b	c
A perfect full circle	A diminishing circular path	An augmenting circular path

General Indication of Spiraling

Spiral paths can be precisely measured and recorded with accuracy. For movement it is seldom necessary to go into such detail; a general indication is sufficient. Spiraling in is expressed as
approaching the focal point (center of the circle) on a circular path
and spiraling out as withdrawing from the focal point on a circular
path (see page 184). Degree of circling showing change of front is
shown as usual. For repeat signs used below see pages 350, 351.

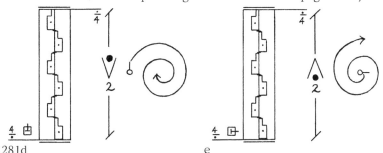

281d   e
Start facing front; with 24 steps   Start facing stage right; with 24
walk two inward spirals.   steps walk two outward spirals.

Equidistant (Constant) Spirals

Two distinguishable forms of spirals exist: those in which
there is an even rate of diminishing or augmenting the circular
shape and those in which the process increases.

Spirals in which the rate of increase or decrease is constant
are called equidistant or Archimedean spirals. These are shown
with a plain increase sign, and the degree of reduction or augmentation is shown by narrow and wide signs.

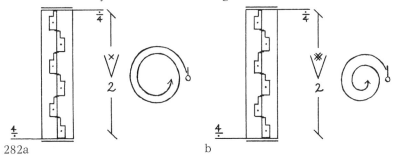

282a   b
Two equidistant inward spirals   Two equidistant inward spirals
to the left with a slight reduction   to the left with a great reduction

Increasing Spirals

When the rate of approaching or moving away from the focal point increases this fact is shown by doubling the increase sign. The resulting pattern can be compared to the shell of a snail, which, starting from a center, becomes increasingly bigger as it grows.

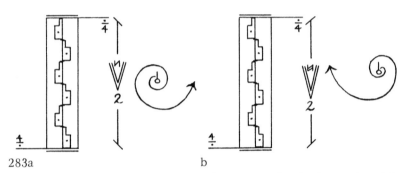

283a   b

Two outward spirals to the left   Two outward spirals to the right
becoming increasingly large   becoming increasingly very large

In dance scores it is seldom necessary to analyze exactly the spiral path covered. The shape of the path written on the floor plan sufficiently amplifies the movement description and gives the reader an immediate impression of the path to follow. The whole range of precise descriptions for spiral paths will be given in Book II.

Continuation of Path Signs

When a straight or circular path sign must be broken and continued on the following staff, a caret is used both at the top of the first and at the bottom of the next staff to indicate this continuation. In Fig. 284 (a) the half circular path continues from measure 34 to 35. If a path sign must be extended over three staves, it is best handled as in (b). Indication of the direction traveled or the amount of circling should be stated on the first staff so the reader has this information at the start.

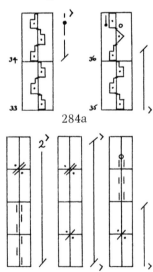

284a

284b

CHAPTER 13

Touch and Slide for the Legs

RELATIONSHIP BETWEEN TWO PARTS

A movement may be designed specifically to relate the performer, in some way, to another person or to an object. Its specific purpose (i.e., the projected relationship) is more important than the movement itself, and hence it is the aim rather than the action which is recorded. Such relationships may encompass degrees of contact ranging from glancing at, addressing, or gesturing toward the person or object from a distance to touching, grasping, and finally supporting the weight, either partially or fully. These possibilities are discussed in detail in Chapter 20. We shall first consider the common contact of the legs.

TOUCH

Touch, or contact between parts of the body or objects, is indicated by the use of a horizontal connecting bow.

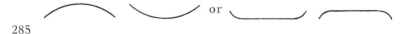

285

The connecting bow can be swung upward or downward, whichever the notator finds is more suitable in each context. The ends of the bow show the moment when a touch occurs.

Contact of the Legs

During jumps the legs may contact each other, beat together in the air, or be held together. The contact bow connects the two leg gesture symbols or is swung between the leg gesture columns when direction symbols for the leg gestures are not written.

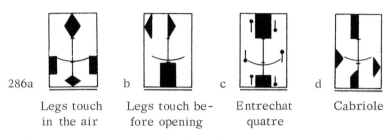

286a	b	c	d
Legs touch in the air	Legs touch before opening	Entrechat quatre	Cabriole

Contact of the Foot on the Ground

Small upward or downward hooks $\curlyvee$ $\curlywedge$, derived from the extremities of these bows, are used specifically to indicate the parts of the foot contacting the floor.

SPECIFIC PARTS OF THE FOOT

The following diagram illustrates the specific parts of the foot that contact the ground when gesturing or supporting the body. Terminology for these different parts varies considerably. Labanotation usage is given first, with familiar variations in parenthesis.

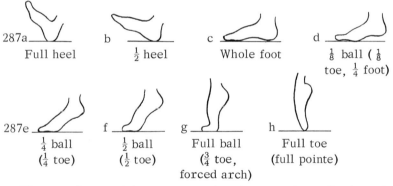

287a	b	c	d
Full heel	$\frac{1}{2}$ heel	Whole foot	$\frac{1}{8}$ ball ($\frac{1}{8}$ toe, $\frac{1}{4}$ foot)

287e	f	g	h
$\frac{1}{4}$ ball ($\frac{1}{4}$ toe)	$\frac{1}{2}$ ball ($\frac{1}{2}$ toe)	Full ball ($\frac{3}{4}$ toe, forced arch)	Full toe (full pointe)

The actual part of the toe contacting the ground usually depends on the direction of the limb.

Toe touch for a forward gesture   287i   Toe touch for a backward gesture   j

Key to Parts of the Foot

Different types of hooks show the different parts of the foot which contact the floor. These are combinations or modifications of the two basic hooks: the forward swinging hook $\llcorner$ or $\lrcorner$, which represents the front part of the foot, the toe, and the backward swinging hook ⌐ or ⌐, which represents the back part of the foot, the heel.

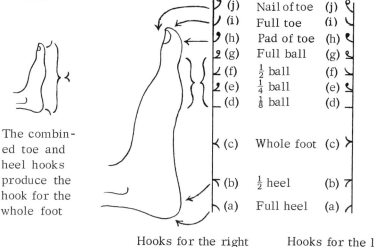

(j)	Nail of toe	(j)	
(i)	Full toe	(i)	
(h)	Pad of toe	(h)	
(g)	Full ball	(g)	
(f)	$\frac{1}{2}$ ball	(f)	
(e)	$\frac{1}{4}$ ball	(e)	
(d)	$\frac{1}{8}$ ball	(d)	
(c)	Whole foot	(c)	
(b)	$\frac{1}{2}$ heel	(b)	
(a)	Full heel	(a)	

The combined toe and heel hooks produce the hook for the whole foot

288

Hooks for the right support, left leg gesture symbols

Hooks for the left support, right leg gesture symbols

The two basic hooks, toe and heel, are modified by the addition of a straight line which represents the ball of the foot. Contact on the ball of the foot has four variations (four distinct angles of the foot in relation to the floor) occasioned by the raising of the heels (Figs. 287 and 288, d-g). These differences are the result of continuous extension in the ankle joint and the consequent bending of the metatarsophalangeal joints. The straight line also modifies the heel sign. The basic hooks are varied to provide a practical abbreviation for each position; they are attached to the direction symbol and modify the fundamental action being described. The whole range of hooks is used for both gestures and supports.

Placement of Hook

For Leg Gestures. The hook connects the leg gesture symbol with the support column representing the floor; therefore for leg gestures the hook is placed on the inside toward the center line.

289a   b

The hook modifies a low gesture, making it lower so that contact with the ground can result.

A low leg
gesture to
the side   289c

A side gesture
touching the
floor   d

For Supports. The hook is attached on the outer side of the support symbol, extending into the leg gesture column to indicate the manner of supporting on the ground. (See page 215.)

                                                        289e   f

Absence of Weight on a Touching Gesture

A clear distinction must be made between a true gesture, which carries no weight of the body and yet touches the ground, and a support, which is weight bearing. As long as a limb can be lifted without any shift of weight, its action is written as a gesture. Partial supports are given on page 448.

290a 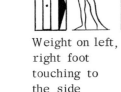   b   c   d

Weight on left, right foot touching to the side

Weight placed equally on both feet

Weight on left, right foot touching to the side

Weight on both feet, but more on the left

TIMING OF TOUCHING LEG GESTURES*

The length of the symbol for a free leg gesture indicates the length of time taken to reach the stated direction. By placing a hook on the leg gesture symbol we show contact with the ground taking place during this gesture. This may occur at the start of the gesture, at the end, or at any point in-between. Thus placement of a hook on the direction symbol has time significance. Care should be taken in the placement of hooks when an exact description is required. Whereas it is the end of the connecting bow ⌣ or ⌒ that indicates the moment of contact (limb with limb, etc.), it is the hook as a whole (regarded as a unit) that indicates the moment of contact of foot with floor. For starting positions such as those in Figs. 289 (a), (b), and (d) placement of the hook does not matter, since starting positions are not movement and have no time significance. Standard usage is to place the hook at the end.

* See Appendix B, note 12.

Terminating (Concluding) Touch

For an active touch, that is, a gesture which concludes as a touch, the hook is placed at the end of the direction symbol.

A slow legato movement con- cluding with a touch on count 3   291a

A fast staccato touch on the toe on count 1   b

Transient Touch

A touch can occur while the leg is en route from one direction to another.

On count 1 the foot low- ers to touch the floor at the start of the gesture, then progresses on its way as in a normal free gesture.   292a

Halfway to for- ward low, on count 2, the foot lowers to touch the floor, then lifts, ending free. b

Consecutive Touches

Where touching gestures appear one after the other, it is under- stood that the foot releases in order to touch again. Timing is not emphasized, since the release serves merely as a preparation for the next touch. For repeated touches in the same direction it is not necessary to restate the direction symbol; only the hooks need be drawn. If the rhythm should pose any problem, however, direc- tion symbols can be used for clarification.

293a

b

OR

c

In different directions   In the same direction

When the hooks are not attached to a direction symbol they are moved closer to the outer staff line for easier reading. They should not actually touch the staff line.

Timing for Terminating Touches

The hook as a unit states the moment of contact. Thus the action of extending the leg to reach its destination must oc- cur before the moment of touch. For the touch to occur exactly on the musi- cal beat the symbols should be written as in Fig. 294 (a). For a general des- cription of quick actions the convention is to write (b) which is clear and satis- factory for most cases. (See page 491.)

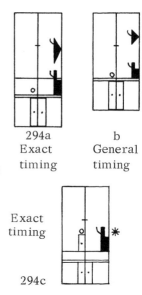

294a
Exact
timing

b
General
timing

If a literal performance of (b) is desired, the exact performance sign ✻ should be added.* In (c) the left foot lands on count 1 and the right foot touches on the follow "&" count. (See also page 356, Fig. 533.)

Exact
timing

294c

Retained Contact

A retained contact is a touch that has resulted from the move- ment of another part. A typical example may occur at the end of a simple step. Normally the free leg is raised clear of the floor after a step, but in a retained touch contact with the floor is kept. As the weight is transferred completely to one foot, the other is left touching the floor. Such touches are considered passive in that they happen as a result of an action elsewhere.

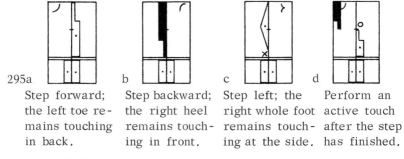

295a
Step forward; the left toe re- mains touching in back.

b
Step backward; the right heel remains touch- ing in front.

c
Step left; the right whole foot remains touch- ing at the side.

d
Perform an active touch after the step has finished.

In Figs. 295 (a-c) no direction symbol is needed in the leg gesture column, since no independent movement occurs. Fig. (d), being an action, requires a movement symbol.

* See Appendix B, note 13.

Bent or Stretched Retained Contact

When it is important to indicate the state of the leg in a retained touch, the appropriate notation ✗ or И is placed in the leg gesture column. If the action is slow, the duration line* can be used. Fig. 296 (a) shows a quick step ending with the left leg bent and touching on the ball of the foot; (b) shows a slower step forward at the end of which the right leg is stretched with the toe touching the ground.

296a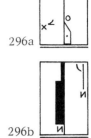

296b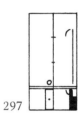

Fluent Transition between Parts of the Foot

When one touch has occurred and a fluent change to another part of the foot is to take place, the timing of this change is shown by a duration line.* In Fig. 297 the forward toe touch changes fluently to a heel touch, passing through the different parts of the foot on the way. The action is concluded on count 3.

297

CANCELLATION OF A TOUCH

A gesture which terminates in a touch remains touching until it is cancelled by another gesture, a step, or a release sign. The sign for a release is a broken hold sign ∽ or ⌇ . The action of releasing, letting go, is a small one; the foot should lift about an inch off the ground, not as high as in a normal low gesture. Note the differences in the movements described below.

The leg touches, then gestures side low at a 45° angle.

298a

The leg touches and releases on count 2, barely lifting from the ground.   b

The leg touches and releases immediately.

298c

A step cancels a previous touch (the foot is automatically released before stepping).   d

* See Appendix A, note 8.

SLIDING

SLIDING LEG GESTURES

A sliding gesture involves continued contact with the floor. To indicate sliding two hooks are used, showing a progression either on the same part of the foot or from one part to another.

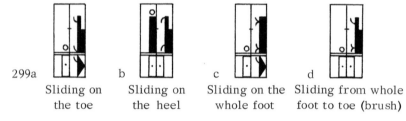

299a   Sliding on the toe   b   Sliding on the heel   c   Sliding on the whole foot   d   Sliding from whole foot to toe (brush)

Duration of Sliding Action

The contact can be sustained only momentarily or retained for a longer period. Placement of the hooks on a leg gesture symbol indicates the beginning and end of a sliding movement.*

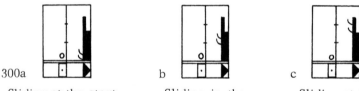

300a   Sliding at the start of the movement; the leg lifts to a normal forward low gesture.   b   Sliding in the middle; the gesture starts and ends free.   c   Sliding at the conclusion of the gesture; end touching.

The interval between two different hooks indicates the timing of the transition from one part of the foot to the other.

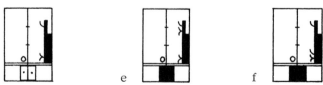

300d   Sliding with a continuous transition from whole foot to toe   e   Sliding on the whole foot until near the end; then transfer to toe   f   Immediate transition to sliding on the toe

* See Appendix B, note 12 (ii), (iii), and (iv).

Detailed Description of Sliding

A complete breakdown showing the use of each part of the foot can be made for detailed study of technique or research into different styles. Fig. 301 (a) illustrates in detail the transition from a toe touch to sliding on each part of the foot in turn until the action terminates in sliding on the whole foot (in the last third of the movement). In (b) sliding is on the ball of the foot until the very end of the movement when contact on the whole foot occurs. For general purposes such detail is not necessary, and description is best kept simple. In the careful analysis of fast footwork a longer basic unit for each beat should be used.

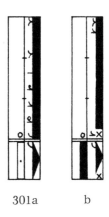

301a   b

Note that the signs ✗ or И, which appear before a direction symbol, are counted in the timing of the gesture; hence when sliding occurs at the start of the movement, as in Fig. 301 (b), the hook must appear alongside the ✗ or И sign.

Consecutive Transient Touches

Repeated touches which occur while the leg is moving must be written with release signs between each hook to distinguish them from continuous contact with the ground (sliding).

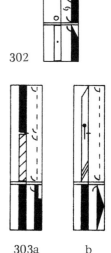

302

Resultant (Passive) Slide

Sliding may occur as a passive result of another action. No direction symbol is written, but instead a dotted line is used to indicate a passive reaction (see page 482). This line is comparable to an action stroke, but it shows passivity rather than activity. Without this line, the two hooks would appear to indicate two touching actions. In Fig. 303 (a) the right leg slides in and out as a result of a change in level on the left support. In (b) a resultant slide is produced by a turn.

303a   b

214 Touch and Slide for the Legs

READING MATERIAL: EXAMPLES FROM BALLET TECHNIQUE

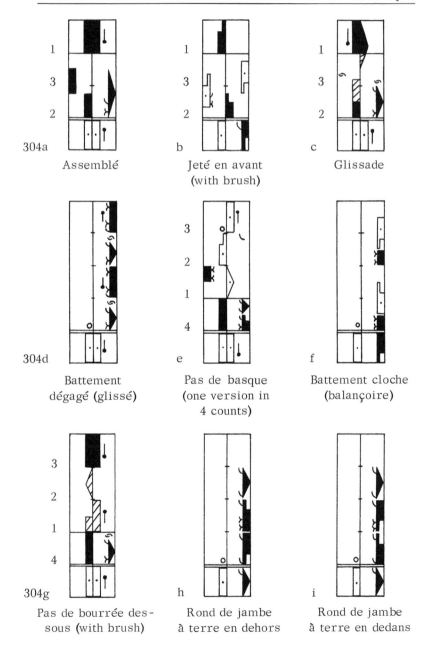

304a Assemblé

b Jeté en avant (with brush)

c Glissade

304d Battement dégagé (glissé)

e Pas de basque (one version in 4 counts)

f Battement cloche (balançoire)

304g Pas de bourrée dessous (with brush)

h Rond de jambe à terre en dehors

i Rond de jambe à terre en dedans

SUPPORTS QUALIFIED BY HOOKS

STEPS

The hooks that indicate parts of the foot touching are also used to qualify manner of a support. The hook extends from the support symbol into the gesture column on its own side of the staff. A single hook on the symbol for a step (a complete transference of weight, not a change of level) modifies the whole symbol. The hook is usually placed at the beginning of the symbol where the contact with the floor occurs. Note the following styles in walking:

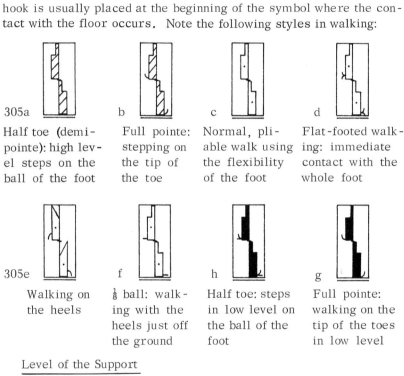

305a Half toe (demi-pointe): high level steps on the ball of the foot

b Full pointe: stepping on the tip of the toe

c Normal, pliable walk using the flexibility of the foot

d Flat-footed walking: immediate contact with the whole foot

305e Walking on the heels

f $\frac{1}{8}$ ball: walking with the heels just off the ground

h Half toe: steps in low level on the ball of the foot

g Full pointe: walking on the tip of the toes in low level

Level of the Support

To describe a qualified support, we must determine the basic level to which it belongs - high, middle or low - and then add the necessary modifications. Results are often rather similar in appearance. The feeling of a step should determine whether it is written as high level with flexed knees for example, or as low level with raised heels. A deep knee bend is a low support even though the heels are raised. The full range of use of parts of the foot may be combined with the degrees of bending and stretching the legs. Not all combinations are physically possible in all directions.

Transition in the Use of Parts of the Foot

If a change in the use of the foot is to be shown in one support symbol and two hooks are to be used, the placement of these hooks has time significance.

A continuous tran-
sition which rolls
from heel to whole
foot during a trans-
ference of weight   306a The rolling action
ends sooner,
transference of
weight continues
with no change.   b

The interval between hooks indicates the duration of a transition from one part of the foot to the other. If this is not a continuous change, a hold sign shows retention of the first indication, as in (c).

Keep the support
on the ball of the
foot until the last
moment.   306c An accent indicates
a more sudden
change; transition
is not fluent.   d

If weight is already on a foot, the manner of support is under-stood from the support sign; thus any subsequent change from that support will also have time significance.

In the forward step in (e) a whole foot
contact is understood; hence transition
to the ball of the foot as the knee bends
has time significance. The whole foot
hook could be stated as a reminder,   306e
as in (f) but this is not necessary.   f

Note that for contact of the whole foot with the floor it is the fi-nal result which is written, and not a heel sign to show lowering of the heel. Use of the heel sign means that weight is on the heel only with the rest of the foot off the ground. Compare Figs. 307 (a) and (c). To provide a direct description of a heel or toe drop, the ap-propriate hook for the active part is attached to a hold sign which indicates retention of the part already on the floor, making the com-bined sign ↗ or ↖ for a heel drop and ↘ or ↙ for a toe drop. Fig. 307 (b) illustrates a heel drop. (See also Spanish steps, page 222.)

Step on the
ball, then
lower heel.
         307a OR   b Start on the
ball, end with
weight only
on the heel.   c

SLIDING STEPS

A sliding transference of weight is indicated by two of the same hooks attached to a step symbol. During such a step, the sliding action is part gesture and part support. Contact with the ground should start as soon as possible without being given undue emphasis.

A Sliding Step from Place

When a sliding step starts from a closed position, the foot contacts the floor at once and the sliding transference begins.

A sliding step forward on the whole foot: the whole foot never leaves the ground. 308a

A sliding step to the side on the heel: the heel contacts the floor at once and continues to slide out. b

A familiar form of sliding step is the "chassé," frequently used in combination with a "coupé" (cut) step. Usually the knees bend before or during the sliding transference of weight.

309a

b

c

Chassé step rising

Chassé step lowering, ending on one foot

Chassé step lowering, ending in 2nd position

In Figs. 309 (b) and (c) the left leg bends with the weight still on it as the right foot slides out. In (b) all the weight is transferred to the right leg; in (c) the weight ends on both feet (a second position).

Fig. 309 (d) shows a combined chassé-coupé-chassé step in which the left foot cuts behind the right. The first chassé in (e) is preceded by a hop. This pattern, a temps levé chassé, is a skip in which the low sliding step is emphasized.

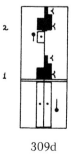 309d

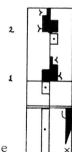 e

A Sliding Step from an Open Position

If the free leg starts from an open position, preparation for a sliding step will be partly free gesture and partly sliding step.

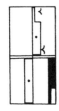

310a

b

The right foot contacts the floor as soon as possible on its way to place. Actual sliding on the whole foot does not start until place has been reached.	The leg will make a curve to reach the forward direction. Some free gesture will precede the sliding gesture and sliding support.

In the illustration for Fig. 310 (b), the dotted line shows the probable path of the free gesture. The leg will not move to place unless it is specifically instructed to do so, as in (c). Here the sliding step to the side will start next to the right foot (see page 144, Fig. 185).

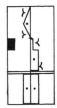

310c

Sliding into Place

In an ordinary step into place following an open leg gesture, as in Fig. 311 (a), the free foot moves at once to place and the weight is transferred throughout the time indicated. A sliding support into place is actually a sliding gesture terminating in a support. The sliding starts at once, but weight is not transferred until the end of the symbol.

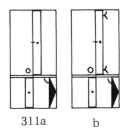

311a   b

SLIDING SUPPORTS

Sliding, such as happens in skidding or skating on a slippery surface, is one of the basic modes of progression. The term "sliding support" refers to a sliding action which occurs when the weight is already placed on the foot. There is no transference of weight and no transition from gesture to support as occurs in a sliding step.

Sliding into Open or Closed Positions of the Feet

In the échappé (escaping) action, page 82, Fig. 91, positions of the feet are changed through a slight spring which may include more or less actual sliding. In sliding supports there is no lifting of the weight; it rests fully on the floor, which must be sufficiently slippery for the performance to be possible.

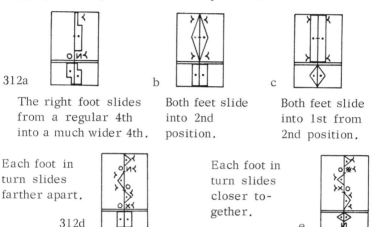

312a

b

c

The right foot slides from a regular 4th into a much wider 4th.

Both feet slide into 2nd position.

Both feet slide into 1st from 2nd position.

Each foot in turn slides farther apart.

312d

Each foot in turn slides closer to-gether.

e

Sliding on One Foot

In sliding on one foot, as in skating, the weight is placed on the new support before it starts to slide. The impetus for the move-ment is derived from the back foot which pushes away. Full details of recording skating will be given in Book II. For first notes, skating can be shown as in Fig. 313. The duration and direction of the sliding can be shown by a path sign outside the staff.*

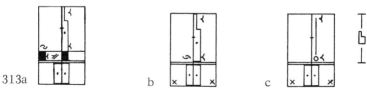

313a

b

c

The weight is shown to be entirely on the right foot before the sliding action starts.

The left foot re-leases from the floor as the slid-ing action starts.

During the path forward sliding on the whole foot occurs; weight is only on the right foot.

* See Appendix A, note 9.

READING MATERIAL: TAP DANCING

Time Steps and Breaks

Contributed by Billie Mahoney

Note: Specific details of style not given.

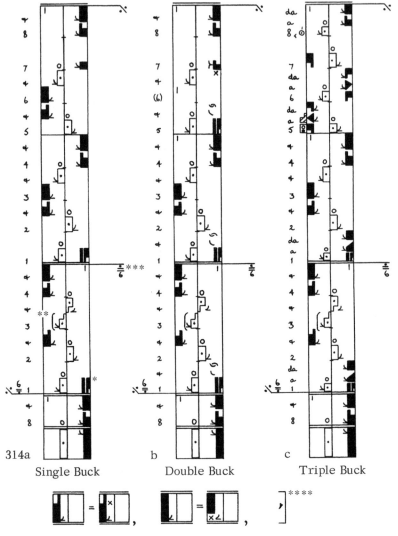

314a — Single Buck

b — Double Buck

c — Triple Buck

*See page 242. **See page 448. ***See page 350. ****See page 479.

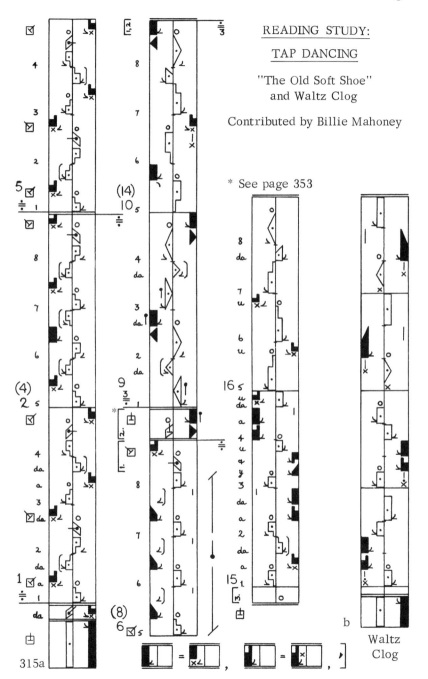

READING STUDY:

TAP DANCING

"The Old Soft Shoe"
and Waltz Clog

Contributed by Billie Mahoney

* See page 353

Waltz
Clog

READING EXAMPLES: SPANISH DANCE

Regional Steps and "Zapateado" (footwork)

Contributed by Felisa Victoria

Note: Specific details of style not given.

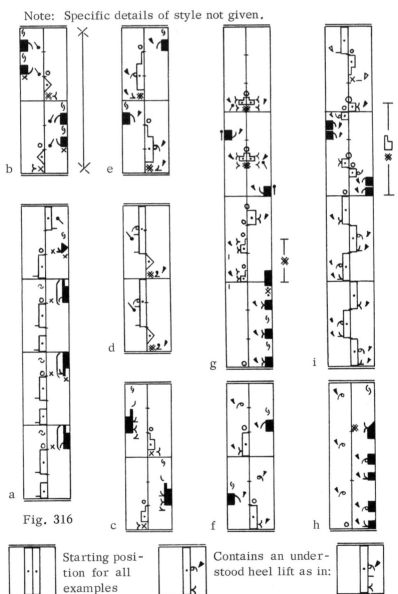

Fig. 316

b

e

a

d

c

g

f

i

h

Starting posi-
tion for all
examples

Contains an under-
stood heel lift as in:

CHAPTER 14

Parts of the Limbs

In Chapters 9 and 10 movements of the whole arm and whole leg were explored. When we deal with the parts of the arms and legs, individual joints as well as segments must be considered.

SPECIFIC PARTS OF THE LIMBS

Fig. 317 shows the signs for specific parts of the limbs. Used as pre-signs, they are placed before direction symbols to show movement of specific parts. With the exception of shoulder and hip signs, each symbol represents a segment of the limb for directional movement and the distal joint of that segment for touching, contraction, and extension.

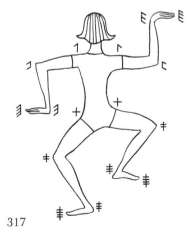

+   single hip

‡   knee (thigh)

‡   ankle (lower leg)

‡   foot

↑ ↾   shoulder

⊐ ⊏   elbow (upper arm)*

⋺ ⋲   wrist (lower arm)*

⋺ ⋲   hand*   317

* See Appendix B, note 14.

The parts of the arm have different symbols for right and left sides. Only one set of signs is generally used for the parts of the leg; right and left are indicated by placing the symbol on the right or left side of the center line of the staff. Where need be, right or left is indicated by drawing the signs thus:

318

Left hip	Right hip	Left knee	Right knee	Left ankle	Right ankle	Left foot	Right foot

Signs for the Whole Arm and Whole Leg

In a full movement description, the three line staff provides columns for movements of the whole arm and whole leg; therefore no pre-sign is needed for these limbs. But out of context and in Motif Writing a pre-sign is needed. The arm is represented as the limb below the shoulder, and the leg as the limb below the hip.

319

Sign for a limb	Left arm	Right arm	Both arms	Left leg	Right leg	Both legs

GENERAL STATEMENT OF ACTION FOR PARTS OF THE LIMBS

In Motif Writing a sign for a part of a limb followed by an action stroke indicates freedom in choice of an action for that part. This need not be an isolated action, but may be the main feature of a movement to which other parts of the body may contribute.

320a

An action of the right shoulder

b   An action of the left hand

c   An action of both shoulders

d   Simultaneous actions of the right knee and right elbow

Replacing the action stroke with a direction symbol makes the statement more specific. For Motif Writing the following mean:

320e   The main action is a forward movement of the left arm.

f   The main action is a backward movement of both elbows.

g   The main action is an upward movement of both hands.

CONTACT BETWEEN PARTS OF THE LIMBS

When parts of the limbs are brought into contact with each other, it is enough in many instances to write this result, the contact, without stating how it was achieved, that is, the action which produced it.

The horizontal connecting bow is used to indicate this contact between various joints. Note that the hand is included here, though it is not a "joint" in the sense that the shoulder, elbow, and wrist are.

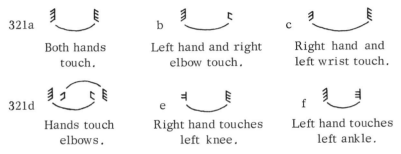

321a   b   c
Both hands   Left hand and right   Right hand and
  touch.   elbow touch.   left wrist touch.

321d   e   f
Hands touch   Right hand touches   Left hand touches
  elbows.   left knee.   left ankle.

The contact bow can be swung upwards or downwards. Below are two versions of the hands touching the shoulder.

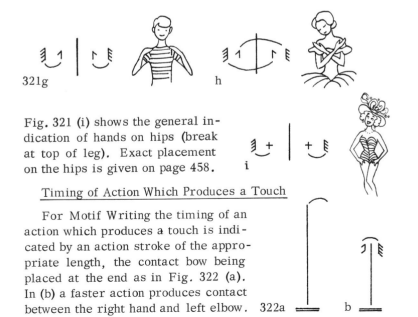

321g   h

Fig. 321 (i) shows the general indication of hands on hips (break at top of leg). Exact placement on the hips is given on page 458.

i

Timing of Action Which Produces a Touch

For Motif Writing the timing of an action which produces a touch is indicated by an action stroke of the appropriate length, the contact bow being placed at the end as in Fig. 322 (a). In (b) a faster action produces contact between the right hand and left elbow.   322a   b

INTERRELATION BETWEEN PARTS OF LIMBS

The following chart shows: (I) signs for the parts of the limbs; (II) their significance when combined with a contact bow; (III) their significance when combined with direction symbols; (IV) the minor segment which is excluded in the directional movement of its neighboring major part, being "left behind" or passively "carried along"; and (V) the minor segment which takes the same direction as, and acts as an extension of, the major segment.

I Sign	II Part Touched	III Part Moved into a Direction	IV Part Displaced but not Included in the Direction	V Part Included in Direction
⌐⌐	Outer edge of shoulder	Shoulder	Whole arm	--
⌐⌐	Elbow	Upper arm	Lower arm and hand	--
⌐⌐	Wrist	Lower arm (forearm)	--	Hand
⌐⌐	Hand in general	Metacarpus (base of hand)	--	Fingers
⌐⌐	Fingers in general	Fingers	--	--
+	Break at top of thigh	One side of pelvic girdle	Whole leg	--
‡	Knee	Thigh	Lower leg and foot	--
‡	Ankle	Lower leg	--	Foot (more or less)
‡	Foot in general	Metatarsus (base of foot)	--	Toes
‡	Toes in general	Toes	--	--

MOVEMENTS OF THE PARTS OF THE LIMBS

When we write movements of the parts of the limbs, two things must be considered - the segment that takes a new direction in space and the joint in which the action (flexion or extension) occurs. The same action could be described in two different ways: (1) spatial change, that is, movement of the part of the limb in a new direction; (2) anatomical change, the degree of flexion or extension of a joint. This latter description is given in Chapter 19.

Isolated movements of the parts of the limb follow the same principle established for the whole limb. Direction and level for the whole arm are determined by the relation of the extremity (hand) to the base or point of attachment (shoulder). The point of attachment (the base) is the joint in which articulation occurs.

Segment	Point of Attachment (Base)	Free End
Upper arm	Shoulder	Elbow
Lower arm	Elbow	Wrist and hand
Hand	Wrist	Fingertips
Upper leg	Hip	Knee
Lower leg	Knee	Ankle and foot
Foot	Ankle	Tips of the toes

To take a common example such as waving to say good-by, it can be seen that, once the arm is raised, it is the hand as a whole which moves in space, lowering and lifting. The action is made possible through flexibility in the wrist joint, but it is described as a hand movement in terms of direction and not as a movement of the wrist.

The best image to bear in mind in experiencing movement of isolated parts of the limbs is that of a puppet with strings attached to each joint and limb extremity. Puppets follow instructions (the strings that are pulled) since they are relaxed and allow for the natural pull of gravity. Although human beings do not move limply as puppets, but introduce dynamics and flow of movement, their use of direction and level is identical.

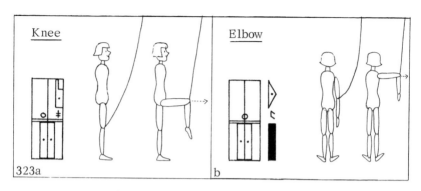

Knee (thigh) is
lifted forward.

Elbow (upper arm)
is lifted to the side.

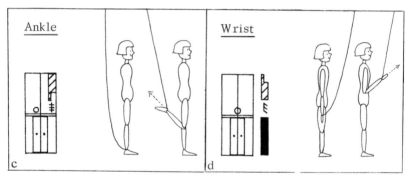

Ankle (lower leg) is
lifted backward high.

Wrist (lower arm) is
raised forward high.

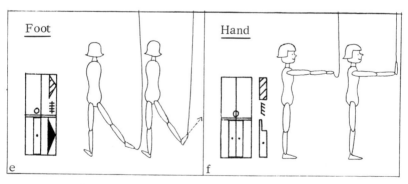

Foot is lifted
side high.

Hand is raised
place high.

LOCAL SYSTEMS OF REFERENCE

In writing a movement such as hand waving, the hand sign is followed by the sign for the direction in which the hand moves. To describe direction we must know to what the symbols "forward," "up,"
etc. refer, that is, the system of reference being used. Of the
three directional systems of reference presented briefly in the Introduction (see page 17), the system commonly used and hence automatically understood to be in effect is that in which the vertical line
of the cross of directions centered in the body is identical with the
constant line of gravity and the direction forward is that direction
in the room in which the performer is facing. This system of reference is called the Standard Cross of Axes. (See Chapter 25.)

Fig. 324 (a) shows the main cross
of directions centered in the body.
In an upright situation the vertical line in the body coincides with
the line of gravity. The lateral
(side to side) and sagittal (forward
and backward) directions are at
right angles to the vertical line.

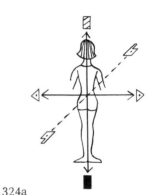

The main cross of directions is
duplicated exactly in the many
local crosses of direction situated one at each joint. All local   324a
directions are parallel to the
main directions of the Standard
Cross of Axes. Fig. (b) shows
the cross of directions situated
at the shoulder which is used
for the whole arm and also for
movements of the upper arm.
The center point, place, is at
the shoulder joint and all direc-   324b
tions are determined from there.

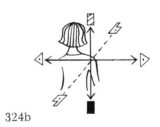

Parallel crosses exist also at the
elbow for movements of the lower
arm, and at the wrist for movements of the hand, Fig. (c). The
same principle holds true for local
systems at the hip, knee, and ankle. 324c

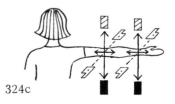

PARTS OF THE LEG

HIP

In analyzing movements of the hips it must be clear whether (1) one hip is the initiator or being emphasized; (2) both hips are involved; or (3) the whole area, the pelvic girdle, is acting as a unit. The body is so structured that one hip of necessity affects the other. The inactive hip may move in the opposite direction to the active or emphasized hip, except in the lateral direction, where it must move in the same direction. Or the inactive hip may serve as a pivot for actions of the other. The normal position for the hip is place middle, since it can be vertically raised or lowered.

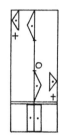
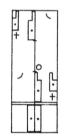
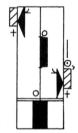

325a

Sway from side to side with parallel hip action.

b

Move the hip forward with each step.

c

Jazz step: lift the hip on the side of the free leg.

UPPER LEG (THIGH)

Movements of the thigh are guided by the knee. A familiar action is lifting the knee while marching or skipping. Direction and level for the knee, as for the whole leg, are taken from the hip. When the knee is raised the lower leg hangs down.

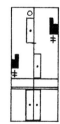

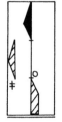

326a

Prances

b

Skips

c

A high knee lift

LOWER LEG

The ankle guides movements
of the lower leg. An isolated
use of the lower leg appears in
the can-can. In this step, the
upper leg is held out while the
lower leg beats rapidly in and
out or describes circles. Physio-
logically the lower leg is limited
in its range, but its directional

movements are varied by the placement of the upper leg and by allowing the thigh to rotate in the hip joint. The lower leg moves
from the knee joint; therefore direction and level in space are determined by the relation of ankle to knee.

In movements of the lower leg, the foot is understood to be carried along as an extension of the lower leg. If the foot moves into
another direction, it must be written separately.

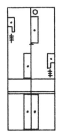  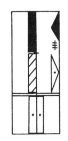 

327a
b

The lower leg is raised straight
back on each change.

The thigh remains out to the
side; only the lower leg moves.

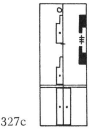  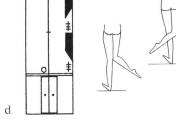

327c
d

The thigh remains for-
ward low; only the lower
leg moves back.

Here the lower leg movements
cause rotations of the thigh: first
it is in-turned, then out-turned.

FOOT

The foot symbol is used to describe directional movements of the foot in space. To establish the right idea one must think of the tip of the foot guiding the action. As with the lower leg, the foot is limited in its range of movement, direction and level being determined by placement or movement of the rest of the leg. The foot moves from the ankle joint and so takes its direction and level from there.

As with the lower leg, spatial indications for the foot can cause a passive rotation of the leg in the hip joint. The leg and foot are normally kept in line; that is, there is a straight line from the center of the knee through the center of the foot. Twisting or curling movements of the foot, such as are used in therapeutic exercises, involve rotations and flexions of the foot and ankle. These are discussed in Chapter 17, page 285.

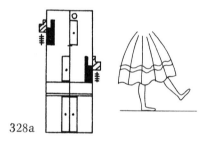 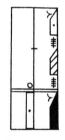 

328a

b

A peasant dance, with the foot turned up on each gesture

Impatience: lifting and tapping the foot

Note that the foot can be written in the third column out from the center when that column is not otherwise being used.

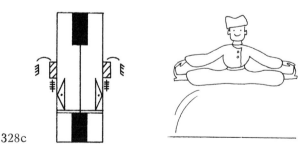

328c

Cossack jump: the feet point upward during the jump. Note the indication of contact between foot and hand.

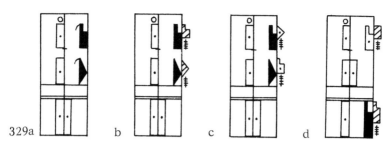

Fig. 329 (a) shows a gesture touching the floor on the heel; the ankle is flexed, the foot up. The instruction that only the tip of the heel is to contact the floor results automatically in ankle flexion. In (b) a similar movement occurs, but since the right foot is free of the floor its direction must be written. In (a) no leg rotation is indicated, the performer being left to do what feels comfortable or suitable. Fig. (c) shows the same general pattern but with parallel rotation on the first gesture and a turnout on the second, dictated by the position stated for the foot. In (d) the relation of the foot to the lower leg is the same on the second count as in the starting position, but as the leg is higher at the end, the foot direction must be shown to be place high instead of forward high. Note that the foot positions in Figs. (b), (c), and (d) would be written as ankle folding if the action of bending were more important than the direction in which the foot should point. (See pages 323, 327.)

USE OF COLUMNS FOR PARTS OF THE LEGS

Standardization in placement of indications on the staff facilitates reading; therefore the following usages have been established. Hip indications are usually written in the leg gesture column or in the body column, wherever there is room. The knee is written in the leg gesture column. Lower leg and foot indications are written in the leg gesture column, in the expanded staff additional "a" column, or, if need be, in the body column. As long as a pre-sign is used the indication is quite clear. A pre-sign can only appear in the support column when that part is taking weight.

Fig. 330 illustrates this range of placement on the expanded staff. Leg indications should always be placed in or near the leg gesture column. (See chart on page 491.)

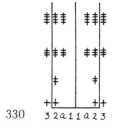

330

PARTS OF THE ARM

Movements of the parts of the arm are similar to those of the leg. The chief difference lies in the greater range resulting from the greater flexibility in the arm joints.

SHOULDER

The shoulder, though limited in range, has certain distinct movements. In this chapter simple movements of a single shoulder will be discussed; the shoulder area and shoulder section are given on page 250. The clavicle and shoulder blade form a girdle which in moving carries the top of the humerus with it. The normal position of the shoulder is place middle since the shoulder can be lowered as well as raised. Movements of the shoulders are those which can be performed without displacement in the rest of the chest. Common actions are lifting the shoulders in shrugging and pulling them back to achieve "good army posture."

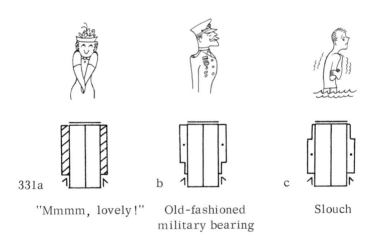

331a

"Mmmm, lovely!"   Old-fashioned   Slouch
                   military bearing

UPPER ARM

Upper arm movements are guided by the elbow. Direction and level are determined from the shoulder, as for movements of the whole arm. The lower arm is carried along. Note the everyday action depicted here, a nudging with the elbow.

When the upper arm moves in a definite direction, the lower arm may either take a specific direction or simply be carried along. The former case requires written instruction; the latter does not. When it is merely carried along, the lower arm may react slightly differently depending upon the starting point, the destination of the upper arm, and the speed with which the upper arm moves. Rule: when no instruction is written for the lower arm the simplest, least noticeable reaction should take place; anything specific must be stated. In the following illustrations the probable destination of the lower arm has been shown with dotted lines.

332a

Start with the arm up. Move the elbow to forward middle. The lower arm being carried along remains upward.

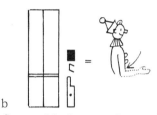

b

Start with the arm forward. Drop the elbow suddenly to place low. The lower arm remains forward.

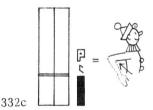

332c

Start with the arm down. Pull the elbow back quickly. The lower arm is illustrated as being not quite straight down, a result that can be expected from this sudden backward action.

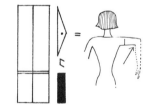

d

Start with the arm down. Raise the elbow to the side. The lower arm being carried along remains downward.

In (e) start with the arms up. Move the elbows to side middle. As in (a) the lower arms will follow maintaining the general upward direction.

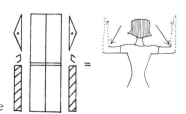

332e

LOWER ARM

The wrist guides movements of the lower arm. The hand does not follow limply, but is used as an extension of the lower arm. The structure of the elbow limits the range of action of the lower arm, but spatially this range is augmented by changes in placement of the upper arm and by allowing the upper arm to rotate. These rotations are unstressed and need not be written since they occur only to accommodate lower arm actions. Direction and level for the lower arm are determined by the relation of wrist to elbow; therefore upper arm placement needs to be known

An everyday example of a lower arm movement is this military salute. While the performer is aware of the hand approaching the forehead, the actual motion is one of the arm from the elbow down. 333a

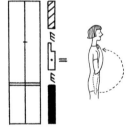

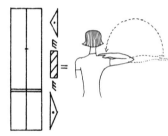

333b

c

Lift the lower arm until it is straight above the elbow from which it moves. It has performed a half circle.

Start with the whole arm to the side. Move the lower arm up and to the other side, ending with the hand near the shoulder.

HAND

The hand moves from the wrist, so its direction and level are determined by the relation of the extremity (fingertips) to the wrist. The range of spatial patterns which the hand can perform is augmented by the placement in space of the rest of the arm and by allowing rotation of the upper and lower arm to occur. Because exact direction and level for the hand will depend on the placement of the arm, the latter should be written first.

Simple directional movements of the hand follow the same general pattern as those of the foot but, with the greater flexibility of the arm, the hand can perform many more movements which require specific analysis. For many hand gestures it is important to state where the palm faces (see page 129). When the hand takes a new direction and nothing specific is stated, the palm faces the direction requiring the least arm rotation. In Fig. 334 (b) the palm faces down when the arm is down and up when the arm is up.

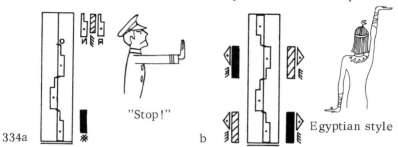

334a   "Stop!"   b   Egyptian style

Many hand movements are best described as flexions (bending) of the wrist. Details of such flexions are given in Chapter 19. Movements of the fingers are given in Chapter 27.

USE OF THE COLUMNS FOR PARTS OF THE ARMS

Fig. 335 illustrates the columns used for correct placement of notation for the parts of the arms.

Part of the Arm	Usual Placement of Notation	Acceptable Placement if Necessary
Shoulder	Body column	Arm column Subsidiary "b" column of expanded staff
Upper arm	Arm column	Outer adjacent, 5th column
Lower arm	Arm column	5th or 6th column
Hand	5th column, adjacent to arm column (when movement is simple)	6th or 7th column

Since pre-signs are used there is no problem of identification. The pre-sign for a part of the arm should appear in the support column only when that part is supporting, i.e. carrying weight.

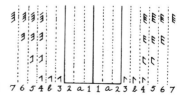

335 7 6 5 4 3 2 a 1 1 a 2 3 4 5 6 7

USE OF THE CARET

To avoid constant repetition of a pre-sign, an angular bow < or
> is used. This bow, called the caret, means "the same" and is
used to indicate movements of the same part of the body. The reader refers to the previously stated pre-sign. The caret must be
used in all cases where parts of the limb are written in the column
for the whole limb. Without a caret or repetition of the pre-sign, a
direction symbol in the leg gesture column refers to the whole limb.

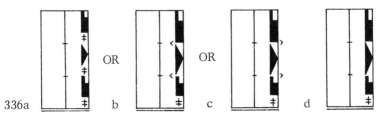

336a   OR   b   OR   c   d

In Figs. 336 (a), (b), and (c), each gesture is a knee gesture.
The caret can be placed on either side of a symbol, wherever there
is more room, as illustrated in (b) and (c). In (d) the absence of
the caret means that only the first movement is done by the knee;
the subsequent ones are gestures of the whole leg.

READING MATERIAL USE OF THE JOINT SIGNS

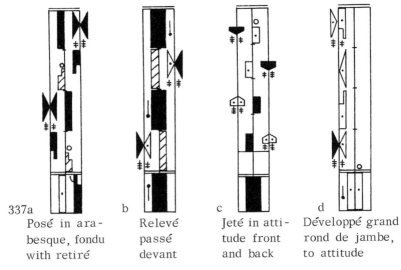

337a | b | c | d

Posé in ara-
besque, fondu
with retiré

Relevé
passé
devant

Jeté in atti-
tude front
and back

Développé grand
rond de jambe,
to attitude

To eliminate the need for pre-signs see page 242.

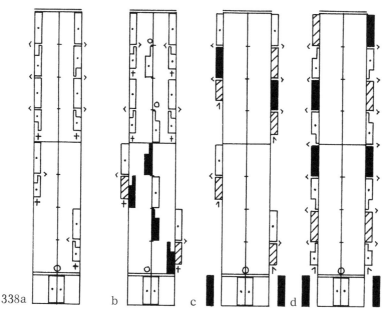

338a   b   c   d

Note that forward movement of a single hip causes a small rotation in the pelvic girdle. Both hips moving in opposite sagittal directions cause a distinct turn of the pelvis. When the emphasis is not on the initiation of the movement by a single hip, such actions are written as pelvic rotations (see page 301).

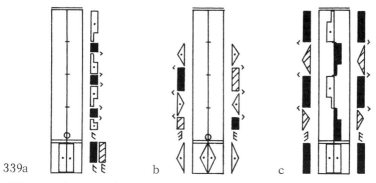

339a   b   c

Elbow swings, ending   Complete circles   Pendular movements
with the whole arm back   of the lower arm   of the lower arms

In Fig. 339 (a), after the starting position, nothing is stated for the lower arm; it is not important. In (b) and (c) rotations will oc- cur in the upper arm; these are understood and so are not written.

In the hand movements in Fig. 339 (d)
the simplest transition from one direction
to the next is understood to occur. Here
the hands will move to the opposite side
via down. A transition over forward or
backward would have to be written.   339d

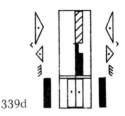

INDICATION OF TIMING

As with all pre-signs placed before direction symbols, indications
for the parts of the limbs are included in the timing of an action;
therefore motion starts at the beginning of the pre-sign.

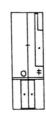

A thigh move-
ment starting
on count 1 and
taking two
full beats   340a

Hand move-
ments on counts
1 and 2, each
taking only half
a beat   b

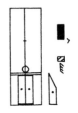

Note that in Fig. 340 (c) both the downward movement and the subsequent raising of the hand take
a whole beat, though the latter appears to be
slower because the direction symbol is longer.
Eliminating repetition of the hand sign through
the use of the caret allows more room for direction symbols.   340c

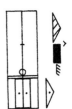

EXCLUSION OF THE PRE-SIGN IN TIMING

Where space is limited and it is desirable to omit the pre-sign
from timing indication, short double horizontal lines can be used
to signify the start of action. These are the same double lines
used at the start of a score to indicate where
movement begins. In Fig. 341 the pre-sign
for lower leg written before the double starting line is not counted in the timing of the
lower leg movement. For count 2 the small
double line shows that the lower arm pre-
sign is not included in the timing of the action.
Thus the lower leg moves backward sharply
on count 1, and the lower arm moves forward
sharply on count 2.   341

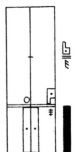

SIMULTANEOUS ACTIONS

When compound actions occur in which two or more parts of the limbs move simultaneously in different directions, the indications are placed side by side whenever possible.

Simultaneous Action Bow

When signs which are written one after the other should occur at the same time, they are tied with a curved vertical bow. This bow has time significance in that the start and finish of the bow indicate the start and finish of the overlap of the two actions.

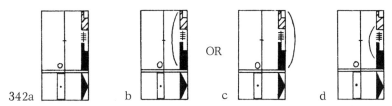

OR

342a   b   c   d

First move the   Perform both actions at once   The two ac-
leg forward,   as indicated by the bow, which tions partially
then lift the foot. can be written on either side. overlap.

Originally the simultaneous action bow had no time significance, and was always drawn small. Now the length of the bow shows the degree of overlap of two actions, i.e. the bow has time significance as in Fig. (b), (c), and (d) above. When, however, there is not

sufficient room for a large bow a very small bow is used to signify complete overlap. Thus, while in (e) the length of the bow indicates some overlap, in (f) the very small bow is understood to be an abbreviation of the largest bow possible and signifies complete overlap. Hence (f) has the same meaning as (b).

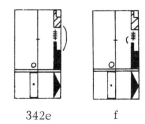

342e   f

DEVICES FOR ABBREVIATION

Most devices for abbreviation in writing belong to the shorthand version of the system used by notators, devices which are not given in this book. However, Division of the Column, and Attached Symbols have been so long in use that they have become part of the standard system and appear in finished scores and publications.

DIVISION OF THE COLUMN

Division of the column for the whole arm or whole leg makes it possible to write actions of the major parts (upper and lower limb) side by side without pre-signs. A direction symbol the full width of a column describes the whole limb; half width symbols indicate upper and lower segments.

For the Legs

We write the upper leg on the inner side, lower leg on the outer.

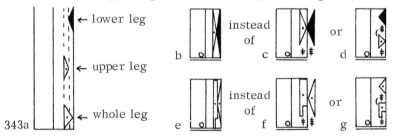

Figs. 343 (b), (c), and (d) show the passé (retiré), and (e), (f), and (g) the attitude positions for the right leg as used in classical ballet.

For the Arms

The upper arm is written on the inside (near the body column) and the lower arm on the outside.

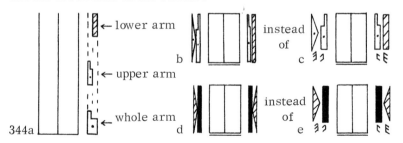

ATTACHED SYMBOLS

A small symbol attached to a normal width symbol is understood to mean the next segment of that limb, judged from the center of the body out. The smaller symbol is like a parasite in that it clings to the main symbol and takes the timing of the main symbol. For this usage, the expanded staff is preferred since it provides room for these additional indications.

For the Legs

The main symbol appears in the leg gesture column. The attached symbol representing the lower leg is placed beside the main symbol closer to the center line.

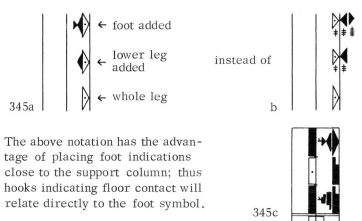

345a

b

The above notation has the advantage of placing foot indications close to the support column; thus hooks indicating floor contact will relate directly to the foot symbol.

345c

For the Arms

The main symbol appears in the arm column and the attached symbols are added on the outside.

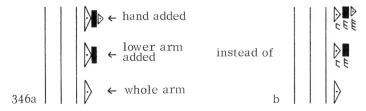

346a

b

CANCELLATIONS

A directional indication for the whole limb cancels any previous directional indication for its parts. Thus a whole arm indication will cancel an indication for the upper arm, lower arm, and hand, as these are part of the whole arm and hence instructions for them are contained within the instruction for the whole arm. The same is true of the whole leg and its parts. A movement of the whole arm does not cancel a previously established position for the shoulder, however, nor does a whole leg movement cancel a previously established position for the hip. In the examples below indications of the first count are cancelled on the third count.

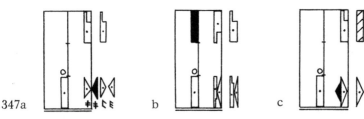

347a   b   c

A bent gesture of the whole limb will cancel a previous indication for a part of the limb. In Fig. 347 (d) the bent backward low gesture cancels the previous forward knee position. The bent sideward gestures of the arms cancel the previous forward lower arm positions.

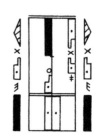

347d

BACK TO NORMAL

A return of a part of the body to its normal state or situation can be indicated either by an appropriate direction symbol or by a back to normal sign. The back to normal sign cancels a special state or situation such as twisting, flexing, or shifting. Under the Standard System of Reference it is common for arm and leg gestures returning to place low to be written with direction symbols. A back to normal sign used for an arm gesture means in the normal body alignment (an understood reference to the Cross of the Body axis).

Timing of a Return to Normal

The symbol ⊙ is followed by a duration line to show the timing used in returning to the normal state. As with other pre-signs, the symbol ⊙ itself is not elongated to show extension in time.

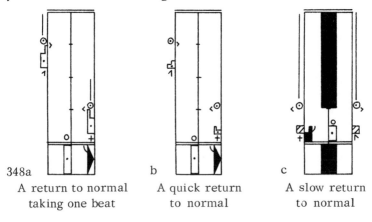

348a   b   c

A return to normal   A quick return   A slow return
taking one beat   to normal   to normal

RETENTION IN THE BODY (BODY HOLD)

The relation of a minor part of the body to a neighboring more major part may be retained while the limb as a whole is moved in space. For example, the hand may achieve a certain angle in rela- tion to the lower arm, and this angle may be retained (no move- ment occurring in the wrist) while the arm as a whole moves into another direction.

Fig. 349 shows a starting position with arm up and hand forward. The hand has a re- tention in the body (body hold) while the arm moves forward and down; flexion in the wrist is maintained. The hand is carried through space by the whole arm; as a result of the body hold its spatial direction changes until it ends back- ward middle.

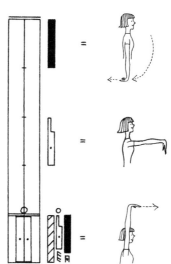

349

Cancellation of a Body Hold

To cancel the body hold sign either a new direction must be written for the hand or the back to normal sign ⊙ must be used.*

On count 4 the body hold is cancelled by the new di- rection indi- cated for the hand.

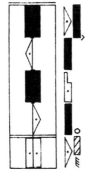

350a

On count 4 the body hold is cancelled by the return to normal sign.

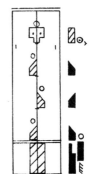

b

* See Appendix A, note 5.

RETENTION IN SPACE (SPACE HOLD)

The retention in space (space hold) was introduced in Chapter 8 in connection with turning. It can also be used to show that one part of a limb retains its relation to space, that is, its previously established direction in the Standard System of Reference, in spite of a change in direction of an adjacent major part. Since in retaining a spatial direction, the action in the joint is always the result of another movement, the rule is that the space hold symbol is vallid only for the same time as the movement which causes it. Thus the space hold sign must be repeated with each new movement indication unless a retention is indicated as in Fig. 354 (a).*

Compare Fig. 351 (a) with Fig. 349.

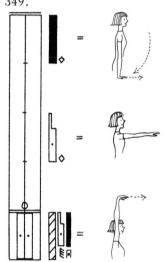

The arm starts straight up with the hand gesturing forward. While the arm is lowered through forward to place low, the hand maintains its space relation, i.e. its forward horizontal direction from the wrist. At the end of count 2 the arm and hand will both be forward middle, i.e. momentarily in line. At the end of count 4 when the arm is down, the hand will still be forward middle.   351a

Compare the next two examples, which start with the same position for the arm. Note the different result produced by the use of a body hold or a space hold for the lower arm.

In (b), as a result of the body hold, the lower arm will end exactly forward middle, the angle at the elbow remaining the same.

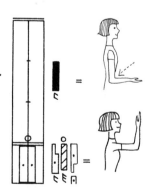

* See Appendix B, note 4.   351b

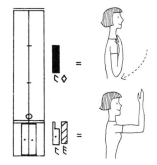

In (c) because the lower arm
has been given a space hold,
it remains in the vertical
direction. The elbow bend
necessary to achieve this is
understood and not written.

351c

Stated Destination Resulting from a Space Hold

For the reader's convenience a direction symbol may be used to show the final destination of a
limb as the result of a space hold. That such a
symbol signifies not a new action but the result
of the previous action is indicated by placement
of a small round bow by the base of the sign.

352

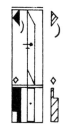

Modified Destination Resulting from a Space Hold

Where a change of level or slight directional adjustment occurs during the retention of a
spatial direction, the destination of the action
is written at the end, and the moment where
the change of level or other adjustment begins
to occur is indicated by an action stroke which
is tied to the indication of the destination. In
Fig. 353 the change of level starts halfway
through the movement; the right arm and left
leg end in middle level. Without the action
stroke and bow the adjustment would be sudden.

353

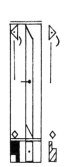

Cancellation of a Space Hold

As a rule the need for a space hold disappears once the
action which caused this need is over. Therefore a new
space hold sign is written for each new action. But where
space holds may occur continuously, the writer may wish
to warn his reader of this fact. In such cases the basic
retention sign o is used at the start, as in Fig. 354 (a),
remaining in effect until cancelled by the space release
sign, Fig. (b).

o
◇
354a

∿
354b

CHAPTER 15

Parts of the Torso, Inclusions

Movements of the torso and its parts can be described in a general way or in specific terms. The first general statement is the inclusion of the body in movements of the arms, legs, and head and in steps. The next general statement, developed from the basic idea of inclusions, is the special convention found suitable for their work by certain European colleagues; this convention in the use of direction symbols in the third columns for movements of the Upper Body (Upper Body Movements) is considered separately in Appendix D because of its special analysis of movement and use of direction and level. A further development in the progression toward being specific is the indication of the particular part of the body to be involved in an inclusion. Finally, actions of the torso and its parts can be described according to the specific part involved, and the kind of motion taking place. The specific parts of the body are presented first, and the specific actions are explored in detail in subsequent chapters.

SPECIFIC PARTS OF THE TORSO

The chief parts of the torso used in movement description are:

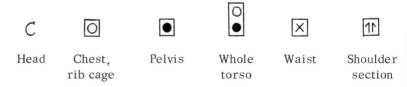

| Head | Chest, rib cage | Pelvis | Whole torso | Waist | Shoulder section |

Although the head is not technically a part of the whole torso, it is included here since its involvement in movements of the torso, chest, and shoulder section must be considered. Because of flex-

ibility in the neck the head can perform each of the basic types of
movement in a clearly defined way, and so provides a good example for investigating the various movement possibilities.

HEAD

The head, indicated by the letter C (caput - Latin for head)
moves through flexibility in the neck (cervical vertebrae). It is normally held straight up (place high) as an extension of the spine. It
is carried along in most actions of the shoulder section, the chest
and whole torso. The head, working through the neck, can perform the following actions: tilting, shifting, rotating on the longitudinal axis, and bending (curving). The head alone can rotate on a
lateral axis (comparable to a somersaulting action) and on a sagittal axis (comparable to a cartwheeling action). The neck alone can
contract and extend. Note that tilting, shifting and rotating which
are basically neck movements are not usually written as such.

CHEST

The chest (thorax, or rib cage) moves through flexibility in the
waist area (upper lumbar vertebrae). It is normally held in an upright position (place high). Movements written with the chest symbol are those in which this area of the body, which includes the dorsal vertebrae, moves as much as possible as a unit. The chest can
perform the following actions: tilting, shifting, contracting, extending, bending (curving), rotating and twisting on the longitudinal
axis and also a rotary movement on both sagittal and lateral axes.

PELVIS

The pelvic girdle, situated between hip joints and waist and
moving through the flexibility of these joints, is somewhat restricted in movement but is capable of: tilting, shifting, curving (limited
chiefly to a tilt with muscular differences), and rotating on its longitudinal, lateral and sagittal axes. Its normal position is place high.

WHOLE TORSO

The whole torso (rib cage and pelvic girdle moving as a unit) is
normally held vertically (place high) over the hip joints, the base
(point of attachment) from which direction is judged. The whole
torso is capable of the following actions: tilting, shifting, contracting, extending, bending (curving), rotating, and twisting.

WAIST

The waist area, comprising the lumbar vertebrae, is situated between the chest and pelvic girdle and acts principally as a "joint" for these parts. It is very limited in actual movement, being capable only of shifting, contracting and extending the vertebrae in its area. The waist sign is more often used in connection with touching or grasping than for movement indication.

SHOULDER SECTION (Upper Chest)

The shoulder section is that part of the spine from the bottom rim of the scapula up, the area of the upper chest which carries the shoulder girdle. In movement it is similar to the chest in that it performs limited versions of all the actions of which the chest is capable: tilting, shifting, twisting, contracting, extending and bending (curving). Many people lack sufficient flexibility in the upper spine to perform these actions clearly; nevertheless such movements of the shoulder section are possible.

SHOULDER GIRDLE

Isolated movements of the shoulder are discussed on page 234. The signs ⌐ and ⌐ , representing the left and right shoulder respectively, specify the outer edge of the shoulder (the acromion process) for touching, but the shoulder girdle (clavicle and scapula) for movement. The use of both signs together ⥣ indicates that both shoulders simultaneously perform the movement instruction.

Extended Shoulder Girdle Movements

The range of movement for a shoulder girdle working in isolation is limited. To increase this range the performer must involve part of the rib cage. Thus the addition of degrees of ⋈ to a shoulder movement means involvement of part of the rib cage on that side of the body. Similarly an inclusion of the body in a shoulder movement will affect the upper ribs on that side.

SHOULDER AREA

The area of the rib cage around a shoulder is indicated by the signs ⊓ and ⊓ . This area rarely initiates actions. It may be included in actions of the arm or of the shoulder on that side of the body; therefore the symbol is used mainly within an inclusion bow to specify the exact part to be included in a main action.

Note the distinction between the following:

355a   Shoulder girdle   b   Shoulder area   c   Shoulder section

Γ = Shoulder girdle, which can move without affecting the spine or rib cage.

[Γ] = Shoulder area, which includes upper ribs on that side of the torso; the spine will be affected and a lopsided displaced state of the rib cage is expected.

[ΛΓ] = Shoulder section of upper torso (spine included): in movement this section moves as a unit.

Only general movements of these parts are dealt with in this book; specific details and combined forms will be given in Book II.

AUGMENTED TORSO SECTIONS

The main subdivisions of the whole torso - chest and pelvis - can be augmented by including the waist area, thus enlarging the movement performed.

Augmented chest area: [O/X]   Augmented pelvic area: [X/●]

Augmented Chest Area

Rib cage and waist area moving as much as possible as a unit comprise the augmented chest area, also called "chest-plus-waist" as the symbol indicates. Inclusion of more of the spine results in an enlarged thoracic movement, but no noticeable action occurs in the hip joints.

Augmented Pelvic Area

Pelvic girdle and waist area moving as much as possible as a unit comprise the augmented pelvic area, also called "pelvis-plus-waist" as the symbol indicates. Such pelvic movement includes the spine in the waist area, below the rib cage, but no noticeable action occurs in the upper spine.

Each of the aforementioned parts of the torso performing each of the listed actions will be discussed.

These are the main activities; finer subtleties such as tensions in body areas, movement description in terms of paths of the parts of the body will be given in Book II.

AUGMENTED BODY SECTIONS

Tilts of the torso may include more than just the torso itself; an adjacent part may move with the torso as a unit. A familiar example is the backward tilt which hinges at the knees, torso and thighs moving as a unit. Other examples can include the arms or a gesturing leg. To indicate this unit in movement, the extremities of the unit are written within a box.

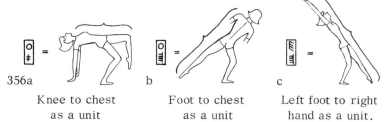

356a

    Knee to chest
       as a unit

b   Foot to chest
        as a unit

c   Left foot to right
        hand as a unit.

USE OF THE COLUMNS FOR THE SPECIFIC PARTS

To facilitate reading, there is a preferred use of the right and left third columns for parts of the torso. As illustrated here chest and shoulder girdle are placed on the right, whole torso and pelvis on the left. As long as the pre-sign is used, however, the indications could be placed on the other side or in 357 other gesture columns. The support column can only be used when weight is placed on that part of the body.

SPECIFIC ACTIONS FOR THE PARTS OF THE TORSO

The general description of body actions, those which result from inclusions in arm and leg gestures and steps, will be discussed first. For a specific description the three main actions which can be performed by the parts of the torso are:

      TILTING,   ROTATING (twisting),   SHIFTING

A fourth, Facing, is the result of the three basic actions.

These actions will be explored in this and subsequent chapters.

INCLUSIONS, RESULTANT MOVEMENT

In movement involving two related parts, such as the arm and the upper body, one part may initiate the movement while the other follows, or both may act simultaneously. The movement of one part may therefore be described as leading, accompanying, or following the other.

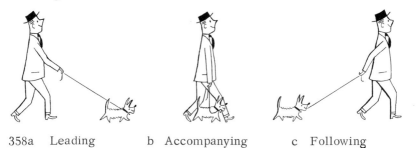

358a   Leading   b Accompanying   c Following

Now let us consider the analogous case of a limb. The hand may lead the arm, Fig. 359 (a), may travel in unison with the arm, (b), or may be led by it, (c).

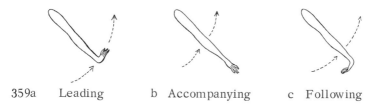

359a   Leading   b Accompanying   c Following

The notation for part leading is given on page 463. Accompanying takes place when similarly directed movements occur for both body and limb simultaneously. The most familiar form of following, resultant movement, is inclusion of the body in an arm gesture. Other passive and resultant movements will be fully discussed in Book II.

INCLUSION OF THE BODY IN ARM GESTURES

A direction symbol in the arm column indicates a gesture of the arm alone. The body should not participate in such movements except for the few instances where some flexibility in the shoulder area may be needed to facilitate performance, as in a backward arm gesture. The inclusion of the body in an arm movement means that the upper section of the torso participates in the direction of the arm movement. All resulting inclinations and twists of the upper body should be performed in such a way that they are the natural accompaniment to and augmentation of a similarly directed arm movement. In certain directions the range of arm gesture and swing is increased when the body is included in the action. Below are some simple everyday examples of arm gestures in which the upper body is included.

In reaching for an object that is close at hand, the arm need only extend to pick it up. But if the object is further away the body will have to be included to reach the object comfortably.

360a

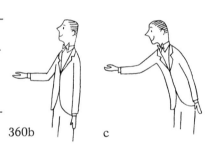

If no body movement is included in a handshake, the person seems cold, standoffish. Warmheartedness is shown by inclining toward the person being greeted, that is by including the upper body in the arm gesture as in (c).

360b

c

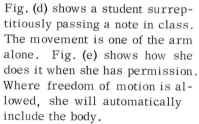

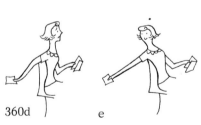

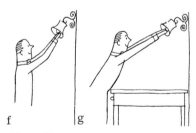

360d   e   f   g

Fig. (d) shows a student surreptitiously passing a note in class. The movement is one of the arm alone. Fig. (e) shows how she does it when she has permission. Where freedom of motion is allowed, she will automatically include the body.

Fig. (f) is a person using both hands to fix a light bulb which is forward high but within easy reach. In (g) he is unable to get near the light, and so must include his body in the action.

In dance such inclusions of the upper body in arm movements occur for expressive and choreographic reasons. While in functional movements the arms are used as much as possible in front of the body, in dance all directions are used. The description of body movement in terms of an inclusion purposely allows a certain leeway in performance. Where precision is necessary, the resultant body movement can be analyzed and recorded in detail.

THE INCLUSION BOW

To show that a part of the body is included in another movement, a vertical bow is used. This bow is curved at the ends and straight in the middle so that it can be drawn in the column of the part of the body to be included. This bow differs from the simultaneous action bow already discussed in that the latter is curved throughout its length.

361a

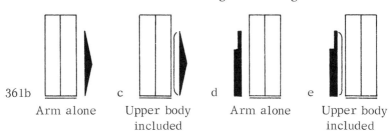

361b   c   d   e

Arm alone   Upper body   Arm alone   Upper body
             included   included

Note that the inclusion bow connects the arm gesture symbol to the body column, being drawn from the arm gesture symbol into the third column. The following examples show generally the effect of a body inclusion in an arm gesture. These illustrations provide the idea; the interpretation need not be precise.

Inclusions in a Lateral Direction

The upper body inclines into the direction of the arm gesture. The lower the arm gesture, the lower the inclination.

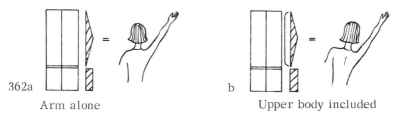

362a   b

Arm alone   Upper body included

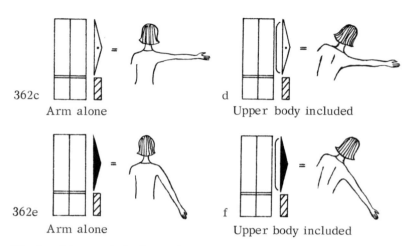

362c Arm alone   d Upper body included

362e Arm alone   f Upper body included

The head is carried along when the upper body tilts. Degrees of tilt are approximate; it is expected that there will be variation according to movement context. These examples can be taken as a general guide. The arm need not be extended, since inclusions can occur with a bent arm.

Inclusions in a Sagittal Direction

When both arms move in the same sagittal direction, as in Fig. 360 (g), an inclusion of the upper body produces a tilt in that direction. Fig. 363 (a) illustrates such a forward inclusion in low level.

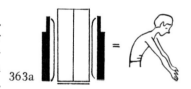

363a

When only one arm moves in a sagittal direction, an inclusion of the upper body produces a twist as well as a tilt. The one arm causes that side of the body to be brought forward (or backward in a backward gesture), producing a rotation in the upper body as well as an inclination.

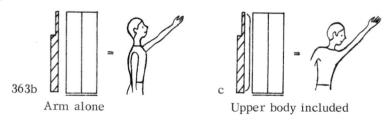

363b Arm alone   c Upper body included

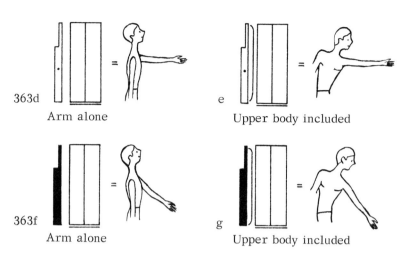

363d Arm alone

e Upper body included

363f Arm alone

g Upper body included

It is important to note that the twist in the upper body does not affect the head. The head inclines with a tilt, being carried along as an extension of the upper spine, but does not turn as a result of body inclusion in an arm gesture. The pelvis should not be affected at all in any upper body inclusions.

Arm gestures in diagonal directions also produce a twist as well as an inclination, but this twist is less than in a forward or backward direction.

In balanced inclusions in the sagittal direction (that is, when one arm is forward to the equal degree that the other is backward) the tilt will be negated but the twist will remain.

363h

i

The degree of twist is less for (i) than for (h). In both (h) and (i) no tilt occurs and the head is not affected, but remains facing the original direction.

Inclusions in Gestures Crossing the Body

When the right arm gestures to the left side of the body, or vice versa, the resultant upper body movement may vary according to the path of the arm gesture.

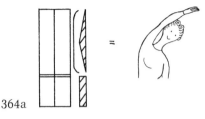

An inclusion in the crossed side high direction results in an inclination in that direction. Without the inclusion the arm would be across the face.

364a

In Fig. 364 (b) the forward low arm gesture produces a tilted and twisted accompaniment in the body. Therefore, in reaching the crossed side low direction, a tilt to the right could result. In (c) the arm moves via side high which produces no twist, so an inclination of the body to the left will result. It will be found that in certain patterns inclusions may be open to interpretation. How the body should react can be stated by writing an indication for the Upper Body (see Appendix D) or by specific means given in Chapters 16, 18 and 19.

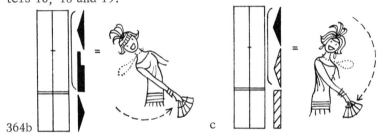

364b   c

TIMING OF INCLUSIONS

The inclusion bow has time significance: inclusion of an indicated part of the body begins where the bow begins, and ends where the bow ends. If the bow lasts the length of a direction symbol it is valid for as long as that symbol is valid. No specific cancellation is necessary.

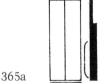

365a

Inclusion starts with the arm gesture but finishes halfway through.

b

Inclusion occurs all during the arm gesture

c

Inclusion starts only halfway through the gesture.

SPECIFYING PART TO BE INCLUDED

The specific part of the body to be included may be stated within the inclusion bow. While this allows for a more specific statement, there will still be some leeway in interpretation. In sagittal, diagonal and crossed side directions a one sided inclusion produces a twist. In Figs. 366 (a-d) a twist occurs. Inclusion of one
side of the torso in a sagittal direction as in (d) produces a twist.

366a   b   c   d

The shoulder only is in- cluded in the arm gesture.   The hip is in- cluded in the leg gesture, (pelvis turns)   Specific hip inclusion in crossing step   Hip and shoul- der inclusion in the forward step

In the case of upper body inclusions in movements of the head,
the bow is not drawn into the body column, but is drawn on the left
side of the head indication toward the staff.

The upper body is included in the head tilt.
366e

Head twists be-
yond the normal
range, involving
the upper spine. f

Inclusion of a body area produces a tilt but no twist. This is because the whole area is involved, not just one side as in (d) above.

Whole torso in-
clusion in the arm
gesture, produces
a slight forward
tilt.   366g

Whole torso in-
clusion in the for-
ward leg gesture
produces a slight
backward tilt
(counterbalance). h

DEGREE OF INCLUSION*

By using the signs И and X a greater or
lesser degree of inclusion can be shown.
The amount of upper body involved and the
spatial range of the gesture will be increased for Fig. 367 (a) and decreased for (b). 367a

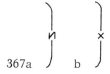

* See Appendix B, note 15.

CHAPTER 16

Tilting (Inclining)

ANALYSIS OF TILTING

Tilting, also called inclining or "taking a direction," means movement of a part of the body away from its normal position into another direction in space. The free end describes a portion of an
arc, but in the standard description this curved path in space is
not recorded. Instead direction symbols are used to state a new
destination for the free end of the part of the body concerned.
This part moves as a unit from its base, or point of attachment,
the point of reference from which directions and levels are judged.

To understand tilting the parts
of the torso, imagine a chair being tilted. In Fig. 368 (a) a chair
is in its normal upright position.
In (b) the chair has been tilted to
the right and is now at an angle,
the free end slanting in its right
side high direction. The point of
attachment (joint) from which it
moves is the base of its right leg.
When the chair slants upward it is

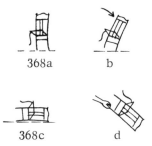

368a   b

368c   d

in high level. In (c) it is side middle, level with the point from
which it is moving. Fig. (d) shows it slanting downward, side low,
below the point of reference which is the base of the leg where it
is being held. Although the term tilting is not used for arms, gestures of the whole arm in one piece which take a new direction
could be called tilts in that they employ the same basic kind of action. To clarify analysis of level for the head and torso, we will
make a comparison with arm gestures in the high area.

Because the head, chest, and whole torso have place high as their normal situation, tilting these parts is comparable to tilting the whole arm when it starts place high. Fig. (e) illustrates the head and right arm starting place high. In (f) they have tilted right side high, and in (g) forward high. The arm does not reach middle level until it is horizontal, parallel with the floor. This is true also of head, chest, and whole torso tilts; they do not reach middle level until the longitudinal axis of that part of the body is horizontal.

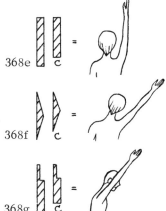

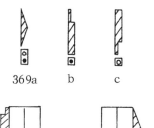

METHOD OF WRITING TILTS

Tilting is written with a direction symbol following the pre-sign for that particular part of the body. Fig. 369 (a) shows a sideward high tilt of the whole torso. Fig. (b) shows a forward high tilt of the pelvis; and (c) a backward tilt of the chest.*

369a   b   c

When consecutive tilts occur a caret is used to avoid repetition of the pre-sign. Careful use of the caret is particularly important for indications placed in the third column, as a direction symbol without a pre-sign in the third column* means an Upper Body movement. (See Appendix D.)

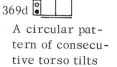

369d

A circular pattern of consecutive torso tilts

An Upper Body movement after a chest tilt

TIMING OF TILTS

The pre-sign is included in the timing of an action; therefore the direction symbol which follows is shortened accordingly. In Fig. 370 the forward tilt of the whole torso takes the same amount of time - one beat - as the return to place high.

370

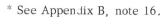
* See Appendix B, note 16.

DEGREE OF TILTING

The stated direction and level indicate how far the part of the body tilts. For general purposes the cardinal directions are used; when necessary intermediate directions can be given. The latter, as well as very slight tilts, are explained in Chapter 26.

CANCELLATION OF SIMPLE TILTS

A tilt is cancelled by a subsequent tilt into another direction or by a return to the normal situation. This normal situation can be indicated by the direction place high for the upright standing position, or by the return to normal sign ⊙ followed by a duration line to show timing.* Because the return to normal sign will also cancel any accompanying twist, it may not always be suitable. If a place high symbol is written, the emphasis is on a return to that direction; if a back to normal sign is written, the emphasis is on a resumption of the normal position within the body. The former description stresses direction, the latter body alignment.

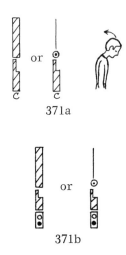

371a

371b

TILTING SPECIFIC PARTS OF THE TORSO

In discussions of tilting it is understood that the starting position is with the whole body in the normal upright position.

Tilting the Head

The free end of the head is the crown, its point of attachment is the base of the neck. In tilts of the head it is understood that head and neck incline as a unit. From the normal upright position as an extension of the spine the head can tilt in various directions in high level. A middle level head tilt occurs when the crown is on a horizontal line with the base of the neck. For most people this requires a slight giving way in the thoracic spine, that is, an inclusion of the upper spine. To tilt the head into low level while in an upright standing position, we must either include more of the spine or tilt the chest or torso in the same direction.

* See Appendix A, note 5.

Movements of the head are written on the right side of the staff outside any indications for arm and hand. The pre-sign C is used for actions of tilting and rotating; facing and shifting require special pre-signs. Once the head pre-sign has been stated, it is understood that all subsequent direction symbols in the column refer to that pre-sign. If there is a considerable gap, the head pre-sign can be repeated to reassure the reader. Because the head is written apart from other indications, carets are only used where clarification is needed, as when changing from the actions of tilting or twisting to those of facing or shifting.

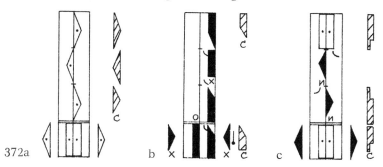

372a   b   c

In Fig. 372 (a) it is understood that all tilts are of the head. Where a gap occurs as in (b) the pre-sign can be repeated. Only a small gap is illustrated here. In (c) the head tilts forward on the first side step, then resumes the backward tilt when the feet close.

A circular pattern can be made by tilting consecutively in the directions forward, right, backward, and left as in (d). This "circling" of the head is not a rotation, for no rotary action or twisting occurs. Such patterns are frequently performed with the addition of rotations to augment and facilitate the circular action.

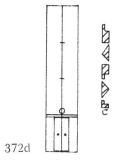

372d

Tilting the Whole Torso

The whole torso moves as a unit in one piece from the hips. The hip joints are considered the point of attachment (point of reference), and the base of the neck the "free end." Though the head is not included in the analysis of direction and level, it is carried along and follows the line of the spine established by a whole torso tilt. The normal position for the whole torso is straight up above the hips, i.e. place high. When the torso tilts, there may be a slight natural curvature in the direction of the tilt; the pre-sign И must be added in order to specify a completely straight torso. If, however, a slight curvature is specifically desired, the pre-sign Х must be added.

Movements of the whole torso are generally written with the whole torso pre-sign in the left third column, but since the identifying pre-sign is always used, they may be written in the right third column or in any free column. The whole torso indication should be placed in the support column only when the weight of the body rests on that part, i.e. when the body is lying down.

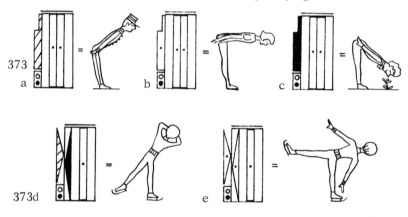

Tilting forward can occur with the weight on both feet or on one foot. If the performer tilts to the side while supported by both feet, he may find it impossible to get a true whole torso tilt, that is, to move his chest and pelvis as a unit; one leg must be free. He can strive to tilt from the hip joint, but as there is little play in the hip joint, usually the action is better described as a chest-plus-waist tilt. (See page 267.)

Natural Pelvic Shift During Whole Torso Tilts. When the whole torso tilts forward, it is natural for the pelvis to shift slightly backward in order to maintain the line of balance, i.e. so that the center of gravity can remain vertically over the center of the support. This adjustment is not written. If, however, the weight is to be kept forward or specifically shifted backward, special instruction must be written. Similar adjustments to maintain balance occur in torso tilts in other directions. Shifting the center of weight is given in Chapter 24.

Tilting the Chest

The chest (rib cage) uses the vertebrae at the waist as its axis of movement. Thus the waist is its point of reference and the shoulders its "free end." The head is carried along and follows the line of the spine established by a chest tilt.

Normal position for the chest is place high, straight up above the waist. A performer in an upright standing position cannot tilt his chest to horizontal level (waist level) without involving his lower spine. When the lower spine is involved the action is des- cribed as an augmented chest tilt. If the action involves the hip joint it becomes a tilt of the whole torso. In true chest tilts, the pelvic girdle should not be displaced at all.

Tilts of the chest are written with the chest pre-sign in the right third column.* Because the pre-sign is always used, however, the indications may be written on the left side if need be or in any free column. The chest sign must not be placed in the support col- umn unless the body rests on that part, as in lying down.

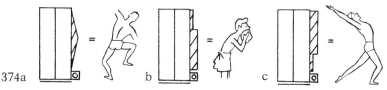

374a   b   c

When the chest is tilted the area is displaced as a unit. There may be a slight rounding in the spine, but any narrowing or collaps- ing in the direction of the tilt must be written with contraction or bending (curving) signs.

Tilting the Pelvis

The pelvic girdle, situated between the hip joints and waist, tilts through flexion in the hip joint or joints and the lumbar verte- brae. Normally the pelvis is held directly above the hips, i.e. place high. As with the whole torso, the "point of attachment" is the hip joint, while the upper rim of the pelvis is considered the "free end" though its freedom is limited by the upper spine. Be- cause the chest is displaced (carried along) in pelvic tilts, how- ever, the effect of a free end can reasonably be achieved. Tilts of the pelvis are, in fact, tilts of the whole torso in which the chest does not join. Whereas in a whole torso tilt the line of the whole

* See Appendix B, note 16.

spine is in the stated direction, in pelvic tilts only the lower spine takes this direction, the upper spine remaining upright. It is as though the chest has an unwritten space hold.

Tilts of the pelvis are written with the pelvis pre-sign in the left third column. Because the pre-sign is always used, however, the indications may be written on the right side or elsewhere. The pelvis sign appears in the support column only when the weight of the body is on that part, as in lying down.

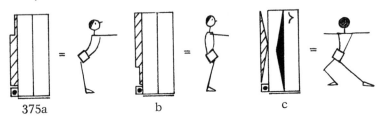

375a   b   c

In pelvic tilts the upper rim is displaced, moving in the stated direction so that the line from the base of the spine to the waist slants in that direction. The chest remains vertical but is carried along, i.e. displaced in space, by the tilting pelvis.

From the forward middle position of the whole torso, the chest lifts to place high. The pelvis remains horizontal.   375d

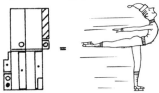

Automatic Pelvic Tilts. When a backward middle leg gesture is written it is understood that, because of the structure of the hip joint, in order for the leg to reach this level the pelvis must tilt forward. Only a small degree of backward leg gesture can be performed without affecting the pelvis. This understood adjustment in the pelvis need not be written; it is not a pelvic movement to be described as such. The degree of pelvic tilt will depend on the build of the individual performer. The same is true of a place high leg gesture, some pelvic inclusion must occur.

Fig. 376 (a) shows a backward middle leg gesture as in an arabesque; (b) shows a high kick via side.   376a

b

Tilting the Shoulder Section

The shoulder section (upper chest, upper spine) can tilt in the same way as the chest, but its movement is smaller and more limited in range. There is no definite point providing an axis for such tilts, as the waist does for the chest; therefore it is usual for movements forward and backward to be flexions, i.e. that section of the spine arches or curves over rather than tilts as a unit. If the movement is a true tilt, however, it should be written as such.

Tilts of the shoulder section are generally written with the pre-sign 🄼 in the right third column. The indication may also be written in the left third column or where space permits. The shoulder section sign will appear in the support column only when the weight of the body is on that part.

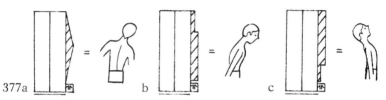

377a   b   c

Tilts of the shoulder section are usually rather slight; for the notation to be quite accurate, use should be made of intermediate directions given in Chapter 26.

Tilts of Augmented Torso Sections

Augmented Chest: 🄾 In tilts of the augmented chest (chest-plus-waist) the movement is based lower in the spine than in tilts of the chest alone; the hip joints are not affected, however, as they are in whole torso tilts. Much of the difference between chest and chest-plus-waist tilts may be observed and felt as muscular rather than as significantly spatial. Compare the following examples.

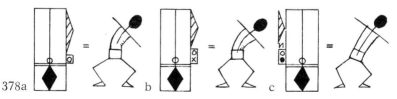

378a

| A chest tilt: the rib cage moves from the waist. | An augmented chest tilt: the waist is involved. | A stretched whole torso tilt: the hip joints are affected. |

The position in Fig. 378 (c) - feet
apart and knees bent - allows some
action in the hip joints, but the line
of the spine is not as straight as in
(d), where the weight on one foot
allows for a true straight torso tilt. 378d

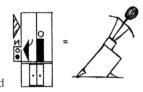

Tilts of the Augmented Pelvis 🔲. A pelvic tilt can include the
spine higher up into the waist area. The rib cage should not be affected. Some people may be able to keep only the shoulder section
and head unaffected; this depends on the individual build. Usually
the break comes in the mid-dorsal vertebrae.

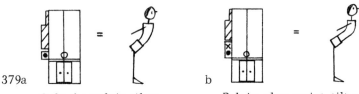

379a

Only the pelvis tilts;
the chest remains
upright.

b

Pelvis plus waist tilts;
only the shoulder section
remains upright.

Augmented Whole Torso . The whole torso can be augmented by
including the head in its actions so that the spine from pelvis to
head moves as a unit. In movements of the ordinary whole torso
(the more commonly used description) the head accompanies the action, but there is no special feeling of keeping in one piece and
some play may be expected. When the sign 🔲 is used there will
be no such play.

Pelvis to head moving as a
unit: the line of the spine
must be quite straight from
base of pelvis to top of head.   380

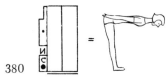

Progression in Tilting the Segments of the Spine from the Top

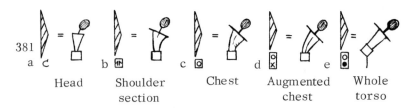

381
a c   b   c   d   e

Head   Shoulder   Chest   Augmented   Whole
        section   chest   torso

Progression in Tilting the Segments of the Spine from the Bottom

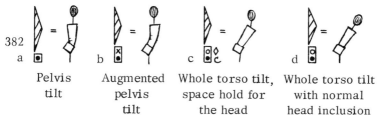

382

a Pelvis
tilt

b Augmented
pelvis
tilt

c Whole torso tilt,
space hold for
the head

d Whole torso tilt
with normal
head inclusion

Tilts of Augmented Body Sections

When a limb or part of a limb moves as a unit with the whole torso or part of the torso, the signs for the extremities of this unit are placed within one area sign. (See page 252.)

Direction and level of the tilt are judged from the indication at the bottom of the augmented body sec- tion sign. In Fig. 383 (a) the girl tilts sideward from the whole foot (tip of toes) to her head.

In (b) the line of inclin- ation to the right is from the left foot to the left hand. Details on the inverting of these body sections are given on page 273.

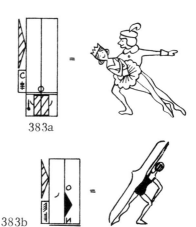

383a

383b

LIMBS CARRIED DURING TORSO TILTS

Rule: a major part of the body carries along a minor or de- pendent part. This rule is applicable to the action of turning the whole body, to tilting, * and to rotating (twisting).

When no directional change is written for the limbs (arms, leg, or head) and a torso tilt occurs, the torso carries the limbs with it. A body hold sign is not needed theoretically, but is added as a reminder. If a limb is to remain in the previously established dir- ection, a space hold (retention in space) must be written.

* See Appendix A, note 10.

Retention in the Body. The arms are carried along.

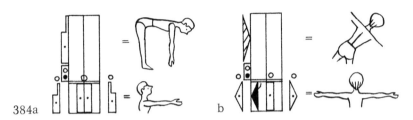

384a   b

Retention in Space. The arms retain the spatial direction.

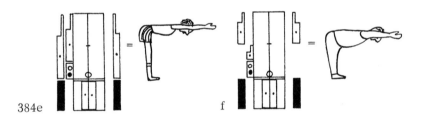

384c   d

Note the results when gestures of the limbs occur at the same time as or follow a torso tilt.

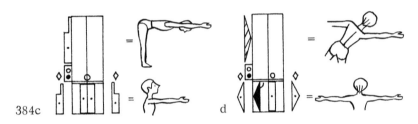

384e   f

In Fig. 384 (g) a body hold and in (h) a space hold follow naturally from the physical need or from physical habit.

The arms cannot easily perform a space hold here; a body hold is logical and expected.   384g

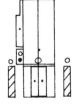

The arms tend to return to the side of the body, so a space hold results.

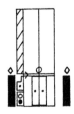

h

CANCELLATION OF INTERRELATED TILTS

Rule: a movement of a major part of the torso cancels the result of a previous movement of a minor part.

Cancellation of Head Tilts

It is understood that the head normally follows the line of the
spine in tilts of the shoulder section, chest and whole torso; therefore since the head is carried along, a tilt of one of these parts
cancels the result of a previous head tilt.

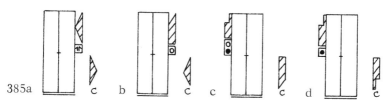

385a

In Figs. 385 (a), (b), and (c) the head tilt on count 1 is cancelled
on count 2. In (d) the head tilt is not cancelled by the pelvic tilt.

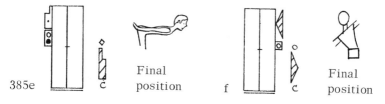

385e   Final   f   Final
              position   position

If the direction of a previous head tilt is to be retained when a
whole torso, chest, or shoulder section tilt occurs, a retention in
space must be shown, as in Fig. 385 (e). If the angle of the head
in relation to the shoulders is to be kept, a retention in the body
must be used, as in (f).

Cancellation of Shoulder Section and Chest Tilts

A chest or whole torso tilt
will cancel a previous shoulder section tilt, as in Figs.
386 (a) and (b). A whole torso
tilt cancels a previous chest
tilt since the whole torso indication includes the chest: (c).

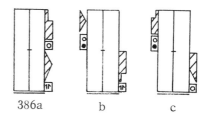

386a   b   c

To maintain the result of a previous chest tilt, a retention either in space or in the body must be used; the latter is more likely to occur. Figs. (a), (b), and (c) below illustrate such a body hold and its subsequent cancellation.

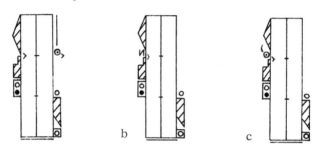

387a   b   c

In Fig. 387 (a) the chest tilt is shown to return to normal on count 3 while the torso is tilting to the left. In (b) the stretch sign for the whole torso on count 3 signifies alignment of the chest into a straight line with the pelvis; thus the previous bend in the spine must be cancelled. In (c) the back to normal sign is used as a pre-sign to describe a normal whole torso tilt to the left. Regaining the normal alignment will cancel the previous chest tilt.

Cancellation of Pelvic Tilts

A whole torso tilt cancels a previous pelvic tilt since the whole torso indication includes the pelvis. In Fig. 388 the sideward pelvic tilt is cancelled by the forward whole torso tilt.

388

Cancellation of Augmented Chest Tilts

Augmented chest tilts are cancelled in the same way as are tilts for the chest. Thus an ordinary chest tilt will cancel a previous augmented chest tilt. Involvement of the spine in the waist area is treated as an inclusion; thus if it does not appear in the following indication, it is understood to have returned to normal.

An augmented chest tilt is cancelled by a tilt of the whole torso.

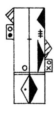

389a

An augmented chest tilt is cancelled by a plain chest tilt.

b

Cancellation of Augmented Pelvic Tilts

An augmented pelvic tilt is cancelled in the same way as are plain pelvic tilts, by a tilt either of the whole torso or of the pelvis. Involvement of the spine in the waist area is treated as an inclusion; thus if it does not appear in the following indication it is understood to have returned to normal.

An augmented pelvic tilt is cancelled by a tilt of the whole torso.

390a

An augmented pelvic tilt is cancelled by a plain pelvic tilt.

b

INVERTED BODY SECTIONS

For each of the symbols 🔲 , 🔲 , and ◉ it is the base of that part of the body which provides the point of reference from which direction and level are judged. It is possible to describe direction and level from the reverse point of view, e.g. shoulder to hips for the whole torso, when this best suits the expression or idea of the movement. For such description the symbol is inverted. The whole torso becomes 🔲 . The waist indication is added to 🔲 and ◉ to show what part is considered the base. 🔲 describes the line from waist to hips; 🔲 describes the line from shoulders to waist.

391a

b

The feeling is of the lower part moving away, backward, not of the upper part moving forward.

From chest to knee the whole torso slants forward low, the downward slant being stressed.

CHAPTER 17

Rotation of the Limbs

GENERAL INDICATION OF ROTATION

The basic meaning of the signs Ʋ and Ø is rotation of an entity, i.e. a turn of the whole unit. In Motif Writing where freedom of interpretation is desired, the signs Ʋ and Ø mean turns of the body as a whole. To indicate rotation within the body, such as a rotation of an area or a twist of a limb, the hold sign o is placed within the turn symbol. Such use of a hold sign signifies a retention within the body (usually at the point of attachment), as a result of which the specific part indicated cannot rotate freely as a unit.

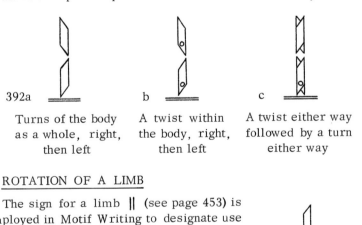

392a	b	c
Turns of the body as a whole, right, then left	A twist within the body, right, then left	A twist either way followed by a turn either way

ROTATION OF A LIMB

The sign for a limb ‖ (see page 453) is employed in Motif Writing to designate use of an individual limb rather than of the body (torso and limbs) in general. Fig. 393 (a) shows a twist to the right for a limb. Signs for the specific limbs (see page 224) are used for rotations or twists of those parts.

393a

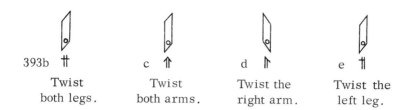

393b ╫	c ⇑	d ↾	e ⇃
Twist both legs.	Twist both arms.	Twist the right arm.	Twist the left leg.

SPECIFIC INDICATION OF ROTATION, TWIST

In Structured Description the three-line staff is used, and rotations of torso and limbs are shown by turn signs in the appropriate columns. For arms and legs pre-signs are not needed; for other specific parts of the body they are. Once the turn sign is placed in the column or is preceded by a specific pre-sign, the physical limitation of the turning action is automatically understood; it is not generally necessary (as it is in Motif Writing) to add the hold sign within the turn sign.

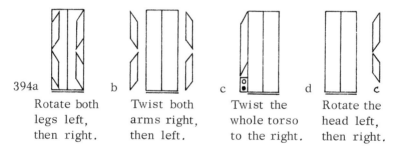

394a	b	c	d
Rotate both legs left, then right.	Twist both arms right, then left.	Twist the whole torso to the right.	Rotate the head left, then right.

ANALYSIS OF ROTATION, TWIST

A rotation or twist of a part of the body is understood to be around the longitudinal axis of that part. In the normal standing position this is the vertical axis.

Distinction between "Rotation" and "Twist"

A part of the body, such as the head, rotates in one piece. There is no twist in the part itself, the twist occuring in the joint or segment at the point of attachment. For this action the specific term "rotation" has been chosen. Where the free end is able to rotate farther than the base, a twist within the limb itself is bound to occur. For this the specific term "twist" is used. A few parts of the body are capable of both actions. For example there may be a twist in the torso or a rotation of the whole torso.

Analysis of Rotating. Fig. 395 (a) illustrates an object which can move as a
unit through a flexible joint or segment
at its base. The free end is marked x-y
and the base z. In (b) the object has rotated $\frac{1}{2}$ to the right producing a twist in
the base. This action could be described 395a
as a twist in the base which carried the
attached object along with it. The choice
of description will depend on whether
emphasis should be on the displacement
of the object or on the action in the base.
In the case of the head, the description is
usually of the head rotating rather than of
the neck twisting, though head rotation 395c
can only be achieved through flexibility in
the neck vertebrae.

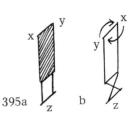

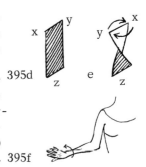

Analysis of Twisting. Fig. 395 (d) illustrates an object with a free end at the
top, x-y, and a point of attachment at the
base, z. In (e) the free end has been
twisted to the right. Only the extremity 395d
reaches the degree of half a twist. The
resulting twist within the object can clearly be seen. Such an action happens frequently within the arm and spine. Fig. (f)
illustrates such a twist in the lower arm. 395f

Method of Writing Rotation or Twist

In Structural Description the unqualified turn signs 〖 and 〗
represent for each part of the body the form which is suited to it or
commonly used by that part. These are:

Rotation as a Unit	Twist within the Limb
Head, hand, pelvis, whole leg, foot	Whole torso, whole arm, low-er arm, whole leg, lower leg

The chest and shoulder section can rotate as a unit only when
slight degrees are used but with the greater degrees the action becomes a twist; therefore twisting is taken as the basic action for
this part. Interpretation of turning for the whole leg varies considerably, therefore neither form is taken for granted as the ex-

pected action. When desired, rotation as a unit (each part turning equally) is indicated by placing the sign for equal = either in the turn sign, or within a vertical bow adjacent to the turn sign.

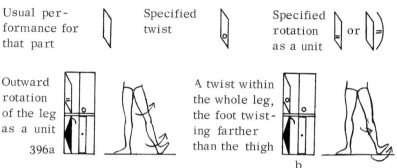

Usual per-
formance for
that part

Specified
twist

Specified
rotation   or
as a unit

Outward
rotation
of the leg
as a unit

396a

A twist within
the whole leg,
the foot twist-
ing farther
than the thigh

b

Unwritten Rotations

Some rotation usually occurs when the limbs are moved in dif-ferent directions. Minor changes as a rule are not recorded, be-ing the natural result of anatomical structure and not themselves intentional. If, as in the medical field, a record should be re-quired of such minor changes, subtle details must be indicated. See also page 231.

Meaning of the Composite Turn Sign

When placed in a support column the composite turn sign signi-fies a choice of either a right or left turn. In a gesture column it signifies neither right nor left, but the untwisted state.

Turn either way,
right or left. 397a

Arms and legs
are in the un-
twisted state. b

DEGREE OF ROTATION

There are four possible ways to describe the amount of rotation or twist of a part of the body. Two are based on two of the three systems of reference (the Constant and Body Crosses of Axes). Not all of these four methods are suitable for all parts of the body, the first and third being more suitable to describe rotations of the limbs. All are given here for future reference.

1. The qualitative (sensed or felt) description in terms of little or much twist away from the normal state.
2. The amount of rotation judged from the previous front.

3. The specific (quantative) degree of twist from the normal untwisted state.

4. The destination of the front of that part of the body in relation to the room (stage) directions.

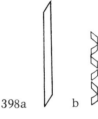

An empty turn sign indicates freedom of choice, the amount of turn being left open to the interpreter. When very quick turns occur one after the other as in (b) the signs are often left empty, as at this speed only a small amount of rotation is usually accomplished.   398a   b

1. Qualitative Description of Degree

When the amount of rotation or twist away from normal is to be described more by feeling than by actual measurement, narrow and wide signs are used. Fig. 398 (c) states a very small amount of twist to the left followed by an equally small amount past normal to the right and finally, a good deal of twist to the left.

398c

2. Amount of Rotation

The black pin placed within a turn sign states the amount of rotation judged from the previous front. This description was applied to pivot and jump turns of the whole body (see Chapter 8). Fig. (d) states $\frac{1}{8}$ rotation to the right from the previously established position, followed by $\frac{1}{4}$ to the left. Black pins describe motion; white pins and straight pins describe destination.   398d

3. Degree of Twist or Rotation from Normal

A white pin placed in a turn sign states the degree of twist away from the normal untwisted state for that part of the body. In Fig. (e) there is a twist to the right $\frac{1}{8}$ away from normal, followed by a twist to the left $\frac{1}{8}$ away from normal. If the starting position is the untwisted state, (f) shows the amount of rotation needed to achieve the actions in (e). The white pin is derived from the sign for the Cross of Axes   398e   f
in the Body ⭧ (see pages 417, 425).

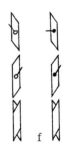

4. Destination of the Front

Indication of the room or stage direction in which a part faces at the end of a turn can be applied to parts of the body in the same way as it can to the whole body (see page 109). This method of description applies mainly to the head. The straight pin (tack) indicating stage direction is taken from the Constant Cross of Directions in the Room. Thus ⊥ = ⯐ , ✓ = ☑ etc. Fig. 398 (g) describes first a rotation to the right which ends facing downstage right, followed by a rotation to the left which ends facing stage left. The degree of rotation the first action will cause depends on where in the room the performer is facing at the start of the action.

398g

ROTATION OF THE LEGS

Leg rotation may happen as an isolated movement, or it may occur in conjunction with other basic actions, thereby giving these actions a particular style or expression. Leg rotation is in effect only an addition to the basic movement pattern, and hence does not change any of the rules regarding supports, leg gestures, jumps, touches, slides, etc.

The whole leg rotates in the hip socket, the point of attachment to the torso. In general the leg rotates as a unit when only slight degrees of rotation occur; in exaggerated degrees the foot (extremity) will twist further than the thigh. A general interpretation is expected unless either a twist or rotation as a unit is specified.

INWARD AND OUTWARD ROTATION

Direction for rotations of the legs is usually described verbally as inward or outward. For the right leg an inward rotation is a turn to the left, an outward rotation a turn to the right; the reverse is true for the left leg. No one state of rotation is called "normal" in Labanotation, but the common situation in which the feet are parallel is indicated by the composite turn sign.

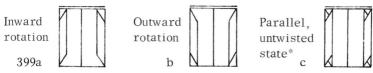

Inward
rotation

399a

Outward
rotation

b

Parallel,
untwisted
state*

c

* See Appendix B, note 17.

The not quite parallel position with the heels together and toes slightly apart is shown by placing the sign for "freely" (ad lib.) inside the composite turn sign.   399d

Degree of Rotation

Description of degree of rotation for the legs is usually in terms of the amount of rotation away from the untwisted state. This may be qualitative (No. 1, page 278) or quantative (No. 3, page 278), the latter being more precise.

Starting parallel, rotate the right leg inward slightly, then outward a good deal.   400a

Similar to (a), but described by degree from the untwisted state: $\frac{1}{8}$ left, $\frac{1}{4}$ right.   b

SIMULTANEOUS GESTURE AND ROTATION

The turn sign is usually placed within the leg gesture column for rotations of the whole leg. When a change of direction occurs at the same time as a rotation, the turn sign is placed in an adjacent column (the expanded staff provides room for such adjacent placement), or may be written after the direction symbol with the two indications tied to show that they occur simultaneously. In general it is preferable to write simultaneous indications side by side.

      OR   OR

401a   b   c   d

Leg rotation following a gesture

Gesture and rotation occurring simultaneously

Alternate possibilities for writing simultaneous gesture and rotation

Fig. 401 (b) shows the preferred way of writing simultaneous gesture and rotation. Other possibilities for placement are illustrated in (c), where the rotation symbol, placed in the body column, is tied to the leg gesture by a small round horizontal bow, and (d), where rotation and leg gesture, both in the leg gesture column, are shown to occur simultaneously by a round vertical bow. (See page 96 for details on the use of the simultaneous action bow.)

With an augmented staff there is the further possibility of using an attached indication, as in (e). Here
rotation is indicated by a small turn sign attached to
a normal-sized leg gesture symbol, the former taking
the same timing as the latter.   401e

CANCELLATION OF ROTATIONS

A specifically stated rotation remains in effect until cancelled by
another rotation or by a back to normal sign ⊙ when the "normal"
state has been established at the outset of the score (see page 291).

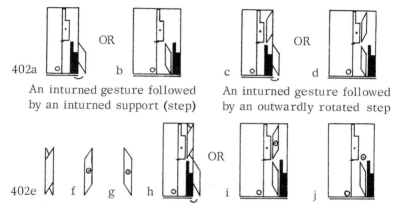

402a   OR   b   c   OR   d

An inturned gesture followed   An inturned gesture followed
by an inturned support (step)   by an outwardly rotated step

402e   f   g   h   i   OR   j

If "normal" is designated as the parallel state, then cancellation of a rotation can be indicated either by the composite turn sign
as in Fig. 402 (e), or by a back to normal sign within the appropriate turn sign, as in (f) and (g). In (h) and (i) the leg which was
turned inward on the gesture is untwisted on the following step.
Fig. (j) shows the use of the sign ⊙ above the rotation symbol when
the column is free and the meaning is clear.

Cancellation of Attached Rotation

The attached symbol by its very nature indicates dependence on the major symbol to which
it belongs; thus when this major indication is no
longer in effect, the rotation attached to it is also no longer in effect. Such automatic cancellation provides an advantage in the quick writing of
momentary rotations. Attached rotations also momentarily cancel

403

a previously stated rotation. In Fig. 403 the step following the inturned leg will be in the previously prevailing state of rotation.

Retention of a Rotation

Certain directional movements for parts of a limb cause rotations in that limb (see pages 231 and 236). Such resultant rotations do not cancel a previously stated rotation.

In Fig. 404 the previously stated outward rotation of the legs is not cancelled by the right lower leg gesture, which causes the thigh to turn in. On the following step the leg is again outwardly rotated.

404

Reminder of Retention of a Rotation

Although a rotation is held until cancelled, the context of the movement may induce the reader to forget the rule and to negate the rotation automatically. A hold sign may be used as a reminder to retain a rotation. In Fig. 405 an inward rotation for the right leg is held until measure 3; all steps and gestures of the right leg are turned in up to that point.

The state of rotation in effect can be indicated at the start of each new page or, if need be, on each staff as a reminder. The state of rotation for the legs in effect at the end of measure 3 is carried over to the next staff where it is written before a double bar line.

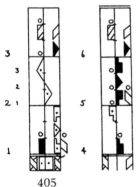

405

ROTATIONS OF LEG GESTURES

Rotations which occur during leg gestures may occur at the start of a gesture, suddenly during a gesture, or be spread over the whole gesture.

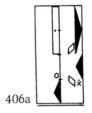  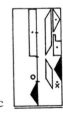 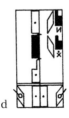

406a   b   c   d

Sudden rotations at start of gesture   Rotation finishing ahead of gesture   Continuous rotation, in then out   Rotation with contraction and extension

Rotations of Touching Leg Gestures

A rotation does not cause a release of a previous touch. When a hook is attached to a rotation sign, the leg remains in the same direction, but performs a fresh touch in addition to the rotation.

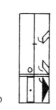

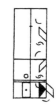

407a

b

c

| The toe remains touching the floor during rotations. | The toe repeats the touch, as the leg rotates. | Rotation occurs during the specific release between touches. |

A leg rotation has a greater visual effect when the leg is bent.

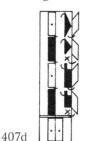

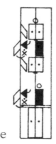

407d

e

f

g

Note that in (g) the leg bends and stretches in the forward direction as it rotates in and out, sliding on the toes.

Placement of X and И in Relation to Rotations

Note the difference in meaning between a space measurement sign written within a turn sign (where it describes the degree of rotation), and a space measurement sign in front of a turn sign in the gesture column (where it describes the state of the limb, bent or stretched). Fig. 408 (a) shows a small inward rotation, (b) a bending which occurs during the rotation. Fig. (c) states a good deal of outward rota- tion, (d) stretching which occurs during outward rotation. The X or И symbol is included in the timing of the action as when used with a direction symbol.

408a   b

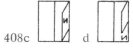

408c   d

LEG ROTATIONS DURING JUMPS

Many examples of leg rotation occur during leaps, hops, jumps, etc. Though the change of rotation usually occurs while in the air, for a simple statement the rotation sign is written next to the landing symbol. The following are some well known patterns.

In (e) and (f) the rotation distinctly occurs while in the air and must therefore be written as such.

Read the following examples at tempo.

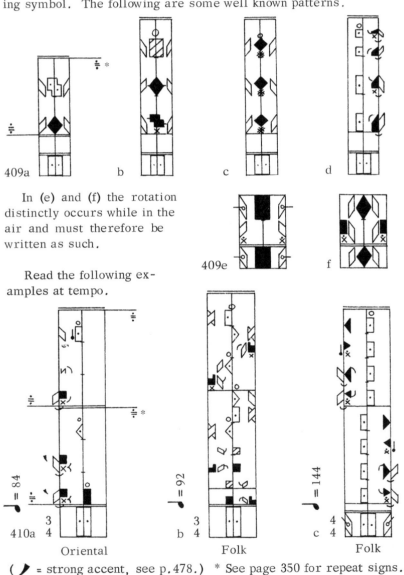

409a   b   c   d

409e   f

410a   Oriental   b   Folk   c   Folk

(♪ = strong accent, see p.478.) * See page 350 for repeat signs.

A familiar example
of rotated supports
is the Charleston.
Note the difference
in the description
of leg gestures in
these two examples.

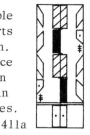 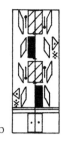

411a   b

"Charleston!"

ROTATION OF THE KNEE

Strictly speaking, the knee cannot rotate; it
can, however, activate a rotary movement in the
center of the leg. In a knee rotation the hip and
foot remain as immobile as possible, rotary action occurring through flexibility in hip and ankle joints. Outward knee rotations are often
used as an exercise to counteract knock-knees.

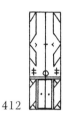

412

ROTATION OF THE LOWER LEG

A rotation of the lower leg is a twist of
the leg in one piece from the knee down.
Its range of movement is limited by the
flexibility in the knee joint. To understand the action, sit on a chair with the
heel of the foot resting on the floor. Rotate the lower leg in and out. There
should be no action in the thigh; movement
occurs only from the knee down. Rotation
of the lower leg will cause the foot to
move from side to side; such movement,
however, is not an action of the foot itself.

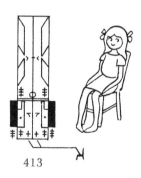

413

ROTATION OF THE FOOT

A foot can be rotated either while supporting or while gesturing.
A familiar form of supporting foot rotation is "rolling the ankle."
Because weight is on the foot rotation visibly affects the ankle,
which is slightly displaced in space. Ankle displacement, however,
is only the result of the rolling over (rotation) of the foot. When
such foot rotations are performed as gestures there is no displacement of the ankle, as the foot itself is free to move.

As an example, stand with feet parallel and slightly apart. On the first count
the feet rotate out (foot inversion), causing the weight to shift to the outside of
the feet, thus stretching the outside of
the ankles. On the second count reverse
the procedure. The feet rotate inward
(foot eversion), throwing the weight onto
the inside of the feet (as in flatfootedness),
thus stretching the inside of the ankles.

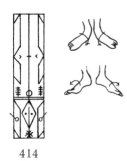

414

Do not confuse foot rotations with rotations of the whole leg
while supporting. The latter is discussed below.

ROTATED SUPPORTS

Rotations can occur both during transferences of weight (steps)
and also while the weight is fully supported on the foot or feet.

During Transference of Weight

In a quick step the actual
change in the state of rotation
occurs before the weight is
transferred, that is, while
the foot extends to start the
step. Because the action is
quick, it is sufficient to
write the rotation as occurring with the step. In Figs.
415 (a) and (b) there will be
no doubt as to how it should
be performed.

415a

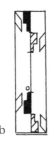
b

Quick steps alternating outward and inward rotation

In slow steps there is time
to rotate during the transference of weight. Thus, if the
state of rotation to be used is
established in the preparation,
the rotation sign is written at
the very start of the step and
does not continue during the
process of transferring the
weight, as in (c) and (d).

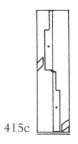
415c

d

Slower steps: the rotated state
is established at the start.

When a rotation occurs throughout the process of stepping, the
rotation symbol extends to cover the entire step symbol.

Starting paral-
lel, the legs ro-
tate outward all
during the trans-
ference of weight
to the right foot.
In the second
measure the
legs rotate in
slowly during
the step to
the left.

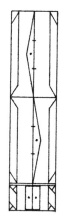

416a

The legs start
bent and paral-
lel, feet to-
gether. The
slow step for-
ward starts in-
turned on the
heel and gradu-
ally turns out
as weight is
taken over and
the toe lowered.

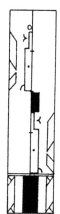

b

Weight Remaining on the Support

On Two Feet. When the weight is on both feet, the legs can rotate in or out, either one at a time or both together, the latter in a
parallel or a symmetrical manner.

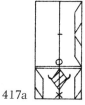

417a

Right leg rotating
in and out on
pointe

b

Parallel rotations
on the balls of
the feet

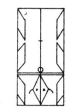

c

Symmetrical
rotations on
the heels

A leg rotation with the weight on the whole foot causes considerable friction; usually either the heels lift slightly so that the
swivel occurs on the ball of the foot, or the ball lifts slightly so
that the swivel is on the heel. Appropriate hooks are used to indicate placement of the weight on the ball or heel. When nothing
is stated interpretation is left open, but the common practice is
for weight to be on the ball of the foot. When weight must be kept
on the whole foot, whole foot hooks must be written.*

* See Appendix B, note 18.

In Figs. 418 (a) and (b) the swivel
is understood to be on the ball of
the foot, though it is not specifically stated.

 418a

 b

In (c) weight is on the whole foot during
the inward and outward rotations. The
center of the foot will remain where it
is, toes and heels will be displaced
equally during the rotation.

 418c

On One Foot: A rotation may coincide with a change in level on
the supporting leg.

The high forward
step is turned out.
An inward rotation
occurs during the
change of level in
place. The swivel
will be on the ball
of the foot while
the heel lowers. 419a

The low forward
step is inturned;
the leg turns out
as it straightens,
swiveling on the
ball of the foot,
the heel just off
the ground.

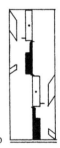 b

Adjustment of Position through Leg Rotations

If the foot is rotated on its heel, the ball will be displaced in
space, and vice versa; therefore rotations can change foot positions.
By rotating one or both legs and alternating use of ball and heel, we
can change from closed to open positions, and from open to closed.
The specific part of the foot to be used is indicated by adding the appropriate hook to the
support while rotation occurs.

Fig. 420 (a) shows opening both feet to
a wider second position, ending with the
weight on the whole foot. Hooks are attached to the support symbols, needed here because a change of level takes place.

 420a

When support symbols are absent, as in (b) and (c), hooks are written as though attached to supports but are placed closer to the center line without touching it.

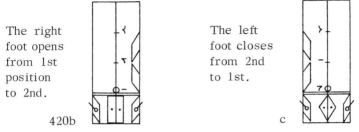

The right foot opens from 1st position to 2nd.

420b

The left foot closes from 2nd to 1st.

c

Traveling by Means of Leg Rotations

By using parallel or symmetrical rotations for both legs and alternating in the use of ball and heel, the performer can move to one side or the other. Such progressions are well known from Russian folk dances and also from Oriental and jazz dancing.

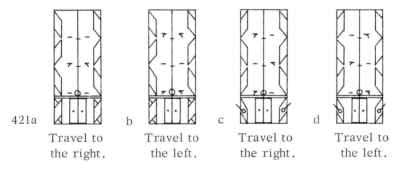

421a

Travel to the right.

b

Travel to the left.

c

Travel to the right.

d

Travel to the left.

When traveling is really the aim of such rotations, a path sign can be written outside to indicate at once to the reader the direction into which he is to travel. If the traveling direction is stated, it is not necessary to repeat hooks for the parts of the foot. The distance traveled can show the degree of rotation: the greater the rotation the more distance covered, the smaller the rotation the less distance covered. Such traveling can also occur on one foot, particularly if momentum is used. Fig. (e) is the same as (d) but with the path sign added to facilitate reading.

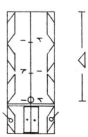

421e

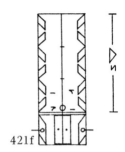

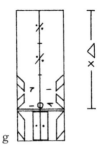

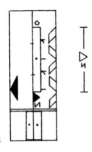

421f

g

h

Travel a long dis-
tance to the right.

Travel a short dis-
tance to the left.

Travel on one foot
to the right.

In Fig. (f) hooks have been given on the first two rotations as a
lead-in; since the path has been indicated it is assumed the reader
will understand the action is to continue. In (g) use has been made
of repeat signs (see page 347). In (h) the quick long step provides
momentum for traveling on one foot. Note in this example the gradual rising to middle level after the initial step.

Sliding of Part of the Foot

The free part of the sole of the foot can be shown to slide along
the floor. Note the difference between the following examples:

With the weight
on the heel, the
legs rotate in
and out. The
ball is just clear
of the floor. 422a

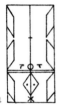

The same, but
the ball of the
foot slides a-
long the floor
during the
rotation

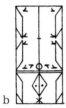

b

KEY SIGNATURES FOR LEG ROTATION

At the start of a dance score, whether it is an exercise or a
composition, a statement is usually made with respect to leg rotation, i.e. whether legs should be turned out, parallel, or (possibly)
turned in. In ballroom dancing as a rule legs are parallel; classical ballet demands extreme outward rotation; many folk dances call
for the legs to be almost parallel, toes slightly apart. The statement of leg rotation to be used throughout a piece is given as a key
signature, a separate pre-graph indication at the start of the score,
and is thereafter considered the standard state for that score.

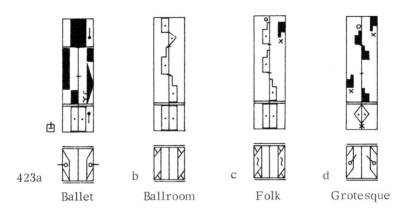

423a   Ballet   b   Ballroom   c   Folk   d   Grotesque

STATEMENT OF NORMAL

The symbol for normal ⊙ can be used in a score to indicate a return to the rotated state given in the key signature (which establishes the "normal" at the beginning of the score).

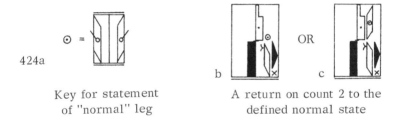

424a

Key for statement   A return on count 2 to the
of "normal" leg   defined normal state

Fig. 424 (a) is an example of a pre-graph statement appearing at the start of a score. Subsequently a change in rotation can be cancelled by writing the normal sign as in (b) where the cancellation of the rotation can be understood, or as in (c), where it is specifically stated that an outward rotation occurs until the defined normal state is reached.

ROTATION OF THE ARM

An arm rotation occurs around the longitudinal axis of the limb. Flexibility of the arm joint allows a range of possibilities for rotations and twists, but the movement is usually a twist in the arm rather than a rotation of the arm as a whole. In this respect arm rotations differ from leg rotations; in the latter it is common for the leg as a whole to rotate.

TWIST IN THE WHOLE ARM

An unqualified turn symbol indicates a twist in the arm. The hand (extremity) will rotate further than the upper arm (base). The degree of twist is judged according to the amount achieved by the extremity. Fig. 425 shows twists in the arms.

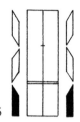

425

ROTATION OF THE WHOLE ARM IN ONE PIECE

An equal sign placed within a turn sign in the arm column signifies equal rotation of all parts, i.e. rotation of the limb as a unit. Such rotations (involving no twist within the arm itself) are rare and usually require action in the shoulder joint. (If the emphasis of the movement is in the shoulder, notation for a shoulder movement should be used.) Fig. 426 illustrates rotations of the whole arm as a unit.

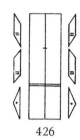

426

Direction of Twist

An outward twist is written with a turn to the right for the right arm and to the left for the left arm (away from the center line). An inward twist is written with a turn to the left for the right arm and to the right for the left arm (toward the center line).

Outward twists 427a   Inward twists b

When the arms are down or forward, it is easy to see and feel which is an outward twist and which an inward. When the arm is held high overhead, however, a seeming contradiction takes place. What was an outward twist now appears to be an inward twist, and vice versa. The arm must be lowered in order to determine the direction of the twist. A solution for the average right-handed person is to remember that, thanks to standardization, such activities as screwing on jar lids, light bulbs, radiator caps, and the like, are twists to the right (outward for the right arm, inward for the left) and those of unscrewing are twists to the left (inward for the right arm, outward for the left).

Degree of Twist

The methods of indicating degree of twist listed on page 277 are applicable to twists of the arm. Because of the nature of arm ges-tures and the fact that the normal, untwisted state is not always readily felt or observed, description is often either in terms of little or much (No. 1, page 278) or in terms of destination of the front of the extremity, that is, where the palm ends facing. The latter description refers to the Standard directions, as explained on page 130. Destination in terms of room directions (as in No. 4, page 279) is rarely used for the arms. If only palm facing is indi-cated, the action is usually one of a twist in the lower arm. For a twist of the whole arm, the palm facing indication is placed at the end of the turn sign to give the destination. Fig. 428 shows similar actions written in four different ways. Each version stresses a different aspect of the movement; therefore the choice of notation rests on what best describes the action.

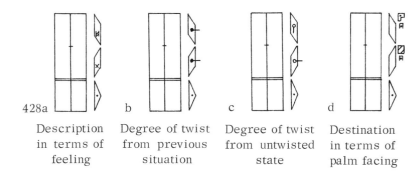

428a   b   c   d

| Description in terms of feeling | Degree of twist from previous situation | Degree of twist from untwisted state | Destination in terms of palm facing |

In Fig. 428 (a) the right arm starts out to the side in an untwist-ed state, palm facing forward. On count 1 a slight outward twist occurs; on count 2 a great deal of inward twist occurs. The des-criptions of (b), (c), and (d) are more precise. In (b) from the starting position the degree of twist is first outward $\frac{1}{4}$ right, then inward $\frac{3}{4}$ left, resulting in the palm ending facing backward. In (c) the outward twist is $\frac{1}{4}$ right from the untwisted state; on count 2 the inward twist is $\frac{1}{2}$ left from the untwisted state, resulting in the same final position as in (b). In (d) the degree of outward twist is described in terms of the final facing direction for the palm, straight up; the inward twist ends with the palm facing back. Be-cause of the clear destination for the palm this last description is often easiest to read.

PLACEMENT OF ROTATION SYMBOL

When there is no change in the previously established position for the arm, turn signs can be placed within the arm column as in the above examples. When the arm changes direction during a twist, the turn sign is placed beside the arm gesture.

Because the turn sign is placed adjacent to the arm direction symbol on the outer side it is understood to refer to the arm. If there should be any doubt, the turn sign can be tied to the arm gesture with a small curved horizontal bow as in Fig. 429 (b).

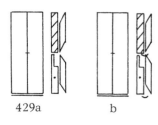

429a   b

The turn sign can also be attached to the direction symbol, in which case it is written considerably smaller. Fig. (c) is the same movement as (a) and (b). The attached symbol takes the timing of the main symbol.

429c

CANCELLATION OF ROTATIONS, TWISTS

The rules for cancellation are exactly the same as for the legs (see page 281). A rotation or twist remains until it is cancelled, unless it is written as an attached sign as in Fig. 429 (c), in which case automatic cancellation occurs as soon as the indication to which the turn sign is attached is no longer in effect.

ROTATION OF THE ELBOW

The elbow cannot truly rotate; it can, however, activate a rotary movement in the center of the arm. This limited rotation takes place through the upper and lower part of the arm while the extremities, shoulder and hand, remain quiet. This movement appears in Oriental dance and in a less exaggerated form in other styles. The "lifting" or "dropping" of the elbow is actually a slight rotation of this kind. The easiest way to perform the movement fully is to grasp a stationary object, such as a barre. Concentration can then be focused on the independent movement of the elbow. The effect of such elbow rotation is more readily seen when the arm is bent for then the action produces a marked spatial displacement.

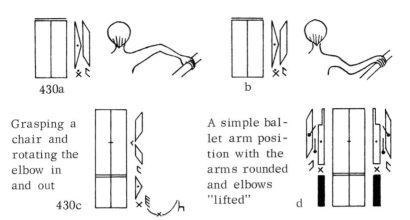

430a   b

Grasping a   A simple bal-
chair and   let arm posi-
rotating the   tion with the
elbow in   arms rounded
and out   and elbows
         430c   "lifted"   d

TWIST IN THE LOWER ARM

The lower arm can twist but it cannot rotate. In the untwisted state the inside of the elbow and wrist are in line. Twists of the forearm are written with the wrist symbol. The forearm twists in-

ward (pronation) and outward (supination) from the elbow down; no change need oc- cur above the elbow. The hand reacts as an extension of the lower arm, having no movement or importance of its own. If the hand is at an angle to the lower arm, lower arm twists will cause it to move in space as in Fig. 431 (d).

431a

Pronation of
lower arm

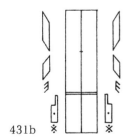

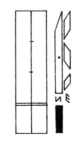

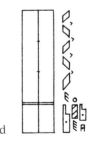

431b   c   d

ROTATION OF THE HAND

Rotations of the hand are comparable to those of the head: the hand is able to turn as a result of a twist in the lower arm, the head as a result of a twist in the neck. When emphasis is on the hand rather than lower arm action, a hand movement is written.

The plain rotation sign is used to signify a turn of the hand in one piece. A different expression will result if the movement is described in terms of the lower arm.

Quick rotations of the hand overhead: the amount of rotation is not important.

432a

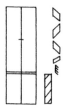

The degree of rotation can be indicated where need be.

b

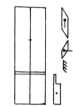

TWIST IN THE HAND

To some extent a twist can occur in the hand from wrist to fingertip. A slight twist can be observed in the metatarsus but it will be more pronounced in the line of the phalanges. Such twists (usually accompanied by spread fingers) can be seen in East Indian dancing. The hold sign placed within the turn sign indicates a twist within the hand, as shown in Fig. 433.

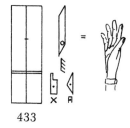

433

CIRCLES OF THE HAND

Circles of the hand are usually a combination of circular space pattern and rotation. The rotation permits a greater range of movement.

Limited circle, with no rotation (body hold given as a reminder)

434a

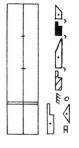

Circle augmented by rotations

b

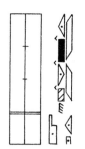

The choice of several methods of description in the analysis of complex hand movements allows for proper placing of the desired emphasis. Further details on hand movements appear in Chapter 27; still greater refinements will be given in Book II.

CHAPTER 18

Rotation of the Torso and Head

ROTATIONS OF SPECIFIC PARTS OF THE TORSO

Discussion of rotations of specific parts of the torso - head, shoulder section, chest, pelvis, and whole torso (see Chapter 15) - will be concerned first with the body in the normal vertical position and second during or after a tilt of the body.

A rotation of a part of the body as a unit and a twist occurring within a part of the body (both explored on pages 275 and 276) are applicable to the specific parts of the torso, as are the indications for degree of rotation given on page 278.

ROTATIONS OF THE HEAD

The head has a range of $\frac{1}{4}$ to $\frac{3}{8}$ from normal in rotating in either direction. Rotations of the head are written with the pre-sign C in the head column outside the staff on the right.

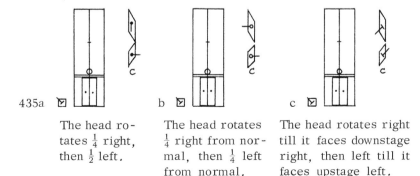

435a The head rotates $\frac{1}{4}$ right, then $\frac{1}{2}$ left.

b The head rotates $\frac{1}{4}$ right from normal, then $\frac{1}{4}$ left from normal.

c The head rotates right till it faces downstage right, then left till it faces upstage left.

The physical movement and final position for each of the preceding examples are the same. The intention (expression, emphasis) of the action dictates the choice of description.

Very slight
rotation from
right to left
saying "no"
gently.
436a

Large head
rotation from
left to right,
saying "no"
vehemently
b

TWISTS IN THE WHOLE TORSO

An unqualified turn sign represents a twist in the whole torso.* In such a twist the chest and shoulder section rotate farther than the pelvis. Thus from ankle to shoulder line there is a continuous spiral. Degree of twist is determined by the free end. The head and arms are carried along in a torso

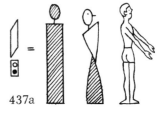

437a

twist. Such a twist produces a divided front. The original front for the body as a whole is maintained by the support, usually the feet. Direction for arm gestures and tilts of the head, chest, and whole torso are judged from the front of the shoulder section (line of shoulders). Direction for steps relate to the untwisted part, the previously established "Stance." Details on divided front, Stance, and use of other systems of reference are given on pages 307-310.

437

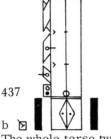

b

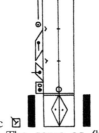

c

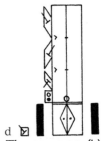

d

The whole torso twists left ¼ from normal, then right ¼ from normal, finally returning to the untwisted state.

The same as (b) but written as the amount of twist left and right from the previous front.

The same as (b), but written by stating the room direction to be faced at the end of each twist.

*See Appendix B, note 19.

A very slight whole torso twist
to the right, the same to the
left, then a great deal of twist
to the right

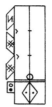

437e

ROTATIONS OF THE WHOLE TORSO AS A UNIT

In rotations of the whole torso (chest
and pelvis moving as a unit) there is no
twist in the spine; torsion is in the legs,
i.e. in the hip, knee and ankle joints.
To specify an equal rotation of all the
parts rather than a twist, the sign = is
written in or beside the turn sign. It is
easier to perform such rotations of the
whole torso as a unit when supporting on
only one foot. The figure here is shown
standing on two feet to illustrate that
there is no change in the situation of the
feet; rotation occurs from the ankle up.

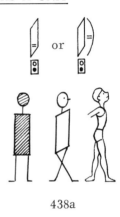

438a

When such whole-torso rotations are followed by a change of
front, the action is best described as a non-swivel turn (fixed-base
or "blind" turn - see page 113).

The body returns
to its original
front; there is
no intention of
change of front,
but just a rota-
tion of the whole
torso as a unit.

438
b

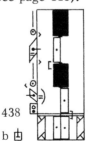

The performer
abandons the old
front; hence the
action is basi-
cally one of turn-
ing and thus is
written as a non-
swivel turn.   c

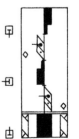

In the above examples the legs are indicated as starting in the
untwisted, parallel state. This given state of rotation should be
retained; if it is momentarily changed through rotation of the torso
or through a non-swivel turn, it must be regained. Use of inward
or outward rotation for the supporting leg augments or diminishes
torso rotations and non-swivel turns; therefore it is important to
know what leg rotation is in effect at the start.

TWISTS AND ROTATIONS OF THE CHEST

Twists of the chest are written with the chest pre-sign ◙ followed by ◖ or ◗ . When rotation as a unit is specifically to be produced, the sign = is placed within the turn symbol. The chest can rotate as a unit between $\frac{1}{8}$ and $\frac{1}{4}$ (depending upon the individual body structure) before a marked twist appears. The greater the degree of rotation, the more the shoulders will twist away from the front established by the base of the waist area. The head is carried along in a chest rotation or twist.

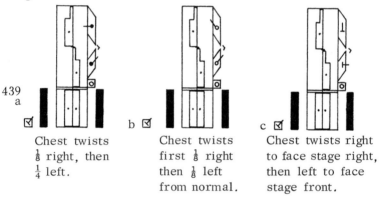

439
a

Chest twists
$\frac{1}{8}$ right, then
$\frac{1}{4}$ left.

b

Chest twists
first $\frac{1}{8}$ right
then $\frac{1}{8}$ left
from normal.

c

Chest twists right
to face stage right,
then left to face
stage front.

The physical movements in the above examples are the same, but each description provides a different intention, awareness, or expression, particularly (c). Note use of a caret to avoid repeating the chest pre-sign, necessary in this column since a direction or turn sign without any pre-sign placed in the third column refers to Upper Body Movements (see Appendix D). The caret may be written on either side of the symbols, wherever there is more room.

TWISTS OF THE SHOULDER SECTION

Twists of the shoulder section (upper chest), written with the pre-sign ▥ , are similar to twists of the chest, but more limited. In itself the upper chest cannot twist more than $\frac{1}{16}$ from normal; thus it is common for description to be in terms of little or very little twist. Fig. 440 shows a slight twist of the shoulder section to the left, then to the right. Such usage is called "épaulement" in classical ballet.

440

ROTATIONS OF THE PELVIS

The pelvic girdle by itself rotates in one piece through flexibility in the waist area and in the joints of the supporting leg or legs. The chest should not be visibly affected. Pelvic rotations are written with the pre-sign ◙ .

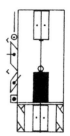

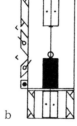

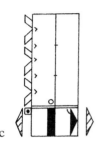

441a Pelvis rotating ⅛ right, ¼ left, then returning to normal.

b The same, written as the degree of twist from normal

c "Shaking" the hips, fast rotations from side to side

In (c) the pre-sign ◙ is placed before the double starting line and so is not included in the timing of the rotation. Thus the first rotation sign can be written the same length as the others. Compare this with (b).

A rotation of the pelvic girdle is caused by bringing one hip forward and the other backward at the same time. The action may be written with single hip signs, but the degree of rotation achieved will be more clearly indicated if it is described as a pelvic rotation. The former description emphasizes hip joints and direction, the latter the pelvic area and rotation.

Bringing the right hip diagonally forward and the left hip diagonally backward as in (d) produces approximately an eighth rotation of the pelvic girdle to the left as in (e). 441d

e

CANCELLATION OF SIMPLE ROTATIONS

A rotation or twist in one direction is valid until cancelled. A return to the normal untwisted state is shown by the composite sign 🛆 or by the back to normal sign ⊙ . Because the back to normal sign will also cancel any accompanying tilt or shift, when only the rotation is to be cancelled and the tilt or shift is to remain, the back to normal sign must be placed within a turn sign.

The four possible descriptions for degrees of rotations shown in Fig. 442 (a) are cancelled by any of the indications in (b). Those in Fig. (c) are cancelled by the indications in (d). In each case the normal untwisted state is produced.

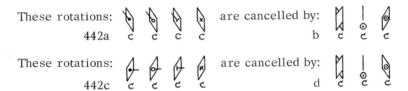

These rotations: 442a   are cancelled by: b

These rotations: 442c   are cancelled by: d

The examples above are for the head, but the same rules apply also to all parts of the torso.

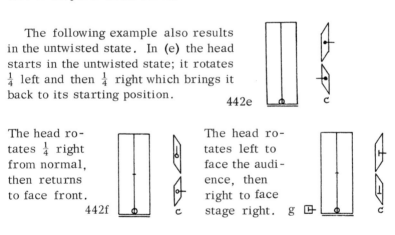

The following example also results in the untwisted state. In (e) the head starts in the untwisted state; it rotates $\frac{1}{4}$ left and then $\frac{1}{4}$ right which brings it back to its starting position. 442e

The head rotates $\frac{1}{4}$ right from normal, then returns to face front. 442f

The head rotates left to face the audience, then right to face stage right. g

Because the performer is facing stage right in (g), the turning of the head to face that direction produces the untwisted state.

INTERRELATION OF PARTS OF THE TORSO IN ROTATIONS

A rotation for one part of the body may affect a previous rotation of another part. Two parts of the torso may rotate at the same time in opposite directions or in the same direction but to different degrees.

Rule: when a major part rotates it carries with it the attached minor (dependent) part.

Spatially Augmented Rotations

A rotation of a major part augments spatially a rotation in the same direction of a minor part. For instance, a rotation of the head to the right appears to be augmented by a twist of the whole torso to the right. Within the body the head rotation has not increased, but when judged from the outside directions, its spatial result has been increased. The following examples illustrate accumulative rotations.

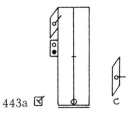 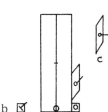 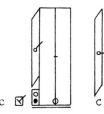

443a

The rotated head is carried around farther in space through the twist in the whole torso.

b

The chest twist (which automatically includes the head) is followed by an additional head rotation.

c

While the whole torso twists $\frac{1}{8}$ right, the head rotates an additional $\frac{1}{4}$ right.

In each of the above examples the head ends facing upstage. Note the following results of accumulative rotations:

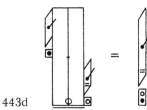 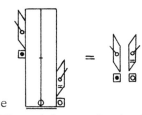

443d

$\frac{1}{8}$ rotation of the chest followed by an $\frac{1}{8}$ rotation of the pelvis in the same direction gives the same result as $\frac{1}{8}$ rotation of the whole torso moving in one piece.

e

The pelvic rotation in the opposite direction does not cancel the previous chest rotation; the result is as though both had rotated at the same time.

Spatially Diminished Rotations

Rotation or twist of a major part such as chest or torso spatially diminishes a rotation in the opposite direction of a minor part such as the head. Within the body one rotation does not cancel another, but the spatial effect may be cancelled. For example the effect of a head rotation in one direction is changed by a whole torso rotation in the opposite direction.

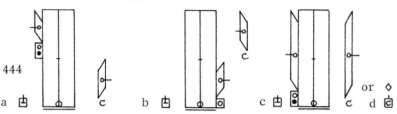

444

| The head is carried along in its rotated state with the whole torso rotation. | The head is carried along with the chest rotation, and then rotates on its own. | The head rotates to the right simultaneously with a whole torso twist to the left. |

In each of the above examples the head ends looking toward the starting front, in this case the front of the room. Fig. (c) could be described in terms of the face remaining toward the audience, i.e. having a space hold, as in (d). (See page 342 for Facing.)

CANCELLATION OF INTERRELATED ROTATIONS

As a rule the greater part cancels the lesser. A rotation or twist of the whole torso in one direction cancels any previous rotation of the pelvis, chest, or shoulder section in the other direction.

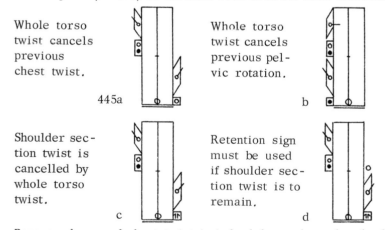

Whole torso twist cancels previous chest twist.

Whole torso twist cancels previous pelvic rotation.

445a

b

Shoulder section twist is cancelled by whole torso twist.

Retention sign must be used if shoulder section twist is to remain.

c

d

Because degree of chest twist is judged from where the shoulder line finishes, a shoulder section twist is understood to be cancelled by a chest twist in the opposite direction.

The shoulder
section twist
is cancelled
by the chest
twist.
        445e

The chest twist
is not totally
cancelled by
the shoulder
section twist.   f

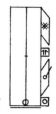

Unless a retention is specified, the tendency in movement is for one part that is closely connected to another to relinquish its previous state of rotation in order to take part in the following rotation of an immediately adjacent part. If, as in (f), it is hard to retain an uncancelled rotation the hold sign may be used as a reminder.

GESTURES COMBINED WITH TORSO ROTATION

When a gap in a gesture column indicates no movement for that limb, no change occurs, that is, no action by that part of the body.

CARRIED LIMBS AND DEPENDENT PARTS

Rule: when a major part of the body rotates or twists it carries with it the attached minor parts. The head and arms are carried during torso, chest, and shoulder section twists, as in Fig. 446 (a); the leg is carried during pelvic rotations, as in (b). Pelvic rotations do not affect the chest, arms, or head. In each case it is as though the limb had an understood body hold.* To retain spatial directions a space hold must be used.

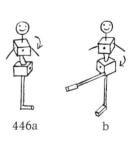

446a   b

Figs. 446 (c-f) illustrate the application of the above rule to arm and leg gestures.

The arms
are carried
along, re-
maining in
front of the
shoulders.
        446c

The arms
are carried
along, re-
maining to
the side of
the shoulders.
        d

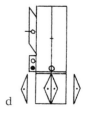

* See Appendix A, note 10.

The leg is carried along, remaining in front of the hip.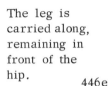

446e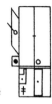

The leg is carried along, remaining be- hind the hip.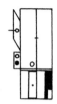

f

In each of the above examples the relationship of limbs to body is maintained as though the body hold o had been written.

Space Retention for Gestures During Twists

When a limb is not to be carried along in a twist of a major part, a space hold is written for it. (See usage of space hold with pivot turns, as explained on pages 136-139 and 154-157.)

447
a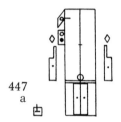

b

c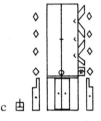

Arms remain to- ward audience while torso twists.

Arms remain to- ward audience while chest twists.

Arms retain their room direction dur- ing upper chest twists.

To eliminate the need for repetition of a space hold sign, the notator may use a duration line, as in Fig. 447 (d), the addition bracket (see page 483), as in (e), or the retention sign o as in (f) (see page 247, Fig. 354).

447d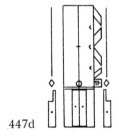

e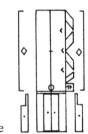

f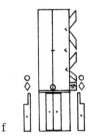

Note the following examples for the head illustrating the range from a specific body hold to a space hold. The same range can be applied to the whole torso, limbs and parts of the limbs.

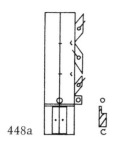 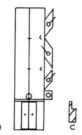 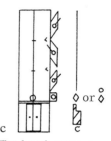

448a	b	c
The head is kept motionless as though it were a solid part of the shoulders.	The head is carried along with the chest but there is some flexibility; some "play" is expected.	The head retains its spatial direction while the chest rotates.

DIVIDED FRONT: DETERMINING DIRECTION

When the body as a whole is in the normal upright untwisted situation, front is taken to be that wall or corner of the room which the body is facing. This front establishes the direction forward and hence the whole cross of directions. Rotations of the torso or of its parts produce a divided front, that is, the coexistence of two or more "fronts." The physical front of a part of the torso may no longer coincide with the front established by the body as a whole. The question then arises as to how directional indications are to be interpreted. To what does a forward symbol refer - the main front or the physical front of the individual part which has twisted?

Meaning of the Term "Stance"

The main front established by the body as a whole is called "Stance." Stance is retained by that part of the body which does not twist away from the established front. When upper parts of the body twist, Stance is the base, the support. In cases where twists occur in the lower part of the body, an upper part such as the head, arms or shoulders may retain the established front and hence be termed the Stance. The following discussions will deal with twists of the upper parts of the body, the feet retaining Stance.

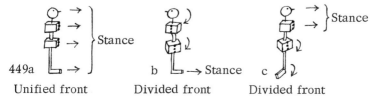

449a	b	c
Unified front	Divided front	Divided front

The Idea of "Base" and "Free End" for Parts of Body

Each part of the body which can twist has a "base" (point of attachment) and a "free end" (extremity), as discussed on page 32. The base is that part not included in the twist, beyond which the twist takes place. The free end of a twisting section is its own extremity, or upper "rim," the opposite end to the base.

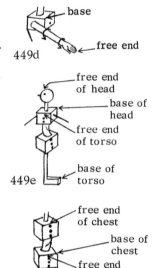

In an arm twist, as in Fig. 449 (d), the base is the shoulder section (line of the shoulder), the free end is the hand.

In a whole torso twist, Fig. (e), the base is the feet, the free end the line of the shoulders. For the head the base is the shoulders, the free end the crown.

For the chest, Fig. (f), the base is the pelvis, the free end the shoulders. For the pelvis the base is the feet, the free end the upper rim of the pelvis.

Choice of Description for Direction

When a divided front occurs there are two or three choices in describing direction:

1) Stance - directions related to the front established by Stance.
2) Part-Twisted - directions in relation to the front of the free end of the part twisting or twisted.
3) Base-of-Twisted-Part - directions in relation to the front of the base of the part twisting or twisted. This possibility is not required when the base of part twisting and Stance are the same.

Rule: when twists occur-

1) Gestures (tilts) of a twisted body section (torso, pelvis, chest, shoulder section or head) relate to the front of the free end of that section (a Part-Twisted description).
2) Gestures of a limb (arm or leg), whether twisted or not, always relate to the front of the base (shoulder or pelvis) of that limb. This Base-of-Twisted-Part description is the natural one and therefore was applied in Chapter 17 without explicit discussion.
3) Steps take direction from Stance regardless of other twists.

The arms take direction from the line of the shoulders.

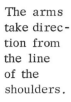
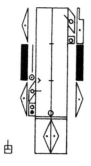

450a

The knee gestures forward from the hip; the step takes its direction from Stance, i.e. toward the audience.

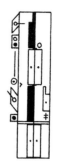

b

Use of Two Fronts

The steps travel toward stage left (the original front); arms move forward from the shoulders. Two different forward directions are being used at the same time.   450c

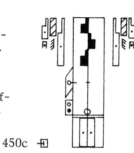

USE OF KEYS FOR DESCRIPTION OF DIRECTION

When it is more suitable to describe direction for tilts and gestures by a system of reference other than the established rule, the appropriate key is given.

Key of Stance*

The Standard System of Reference Key ✦ is combined with the space hold sign ◇ to make the Stance Key ✦ (key for the Standard Directions according to the Untwisted Part).

The Stance key, placed outside the staff on the left, is in effect until cancelled by another key. Fig. 451 shows the result of using this key. The direction forward is the same spatial direction for all parts of the body. Such unity in directional description is often desirable.   451

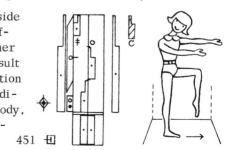

* See Appendix B, note 20 (ii).

Key for Twisted-Part[*]

The Standard Key ✛ is combined with the body hold sign O to produce the Twisted-Part Key ⬦ (Standard Directions according to the Front of the Free End of the Individual Twisted Part).[*] Because of the rule stated on page 308, this key is the understood reference for twists of the parts of the torso and the head and is therefore needed only to cancel other keys.

In Fig. 452 (a) the Stance key is used for the knee lift when the pelvis rotates and the chest, head and foot retain Stance. For the subsequent whole torso twist direction for the knee is more suitably judged from the pelvis, therefore the Standard key is used to cancel the Stance key. When the key is placed as a pre-sign before a direction symbol, as in (b), it refers only to that symbol and is therefore automatically cancelled.   452a

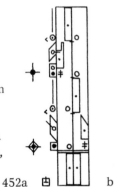
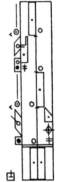

Key for Base-of-Twisted-Part

The key for Stance ⬦ is combined with a body hold sign O to produce the Base-of-Twisted-Part Key ⬙ (Standard Directions according to the Base of the Individual Twisted Part). The addition of the body hold sign expresses the idea of a Base (Stance) within the body. For orthographical purposes the sign is simplified by placing the body hold sign at the base of the cross ⬦.

In Fig. 453 torso and head start twisted; no degree of twist is stated. The chest automatically takes direction from its free end (the shoulders) tilting left, then right. The Base-of-Twisted-Part Key placed next to the head indication and tied to it with a small bow instructs the reader to interpret head directions according to the line of the shoulders. Thus the head tilts left and right in line with the chest tilts. The key is in effect until cancelled by either ⬦ or ⬦ .

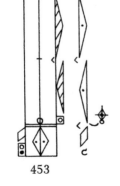

453

[*]See Appendix B, note 20 (iii).

PATHS OF GESTURES DURING A TWIST

Arm and leg gestures which occur during a torso twist normally produce skew curves (three dimensional curves). Undeviating
curves (two dimensional, plane curves) require use of a space hold
or of the Stance key. Note: these different curves were discussed
on pages 138 and 155 in connection with pivot turns.

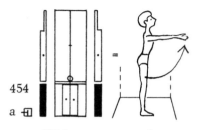   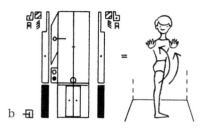

454

a

Without a turn a plane
curve results.

The arms make a skew curve as
they rise to forward middle.

To produce undeviating plane curves during rotations and twists,
a space hold sign must be placed within the gesture symbol, as in
(c), or direction must be described according to Stance, as in (d).

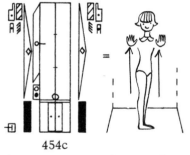   OR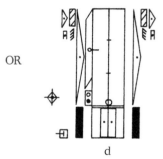

454c

The arms move undeviatingly
toward what was the side direction at the moment of starting the movement.

d

By using the Stance key the
arms will move on a direct
line toward the audience, producing the same result as (c).

COMBINED TWIST AND TILT

The following examples illustrate combinations of tilting and twisting for the whole torso and for the head. The chest is not illustrated separately as it follows the same rules and patterns as those
for the whole torso.

THE WHOLE TORSO

Although the whole torso as a unit tilts from the hip joints, the direction of such tilts is usually described in relation to the front of the shoulder section, the shoulder line.

Separate Twist and Tilt

When a tilt follows a twist an undeviating plane curve (a two dimensional curve) is produced. In Fig. 455 (a) the whole torso twists $\frac{1}{4}$ to the right and then tilts forward, toward stage right. In (b) this same action is described from Stance by adding the Stance key.

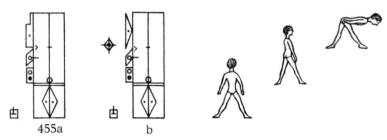

455a   b

Combined Twist and Tilt

When a twist and a tilt are combined for one part of the body, the resulting path in space is a skew curve (three dimensional curve).

In Fig. 455 (c) the $\frac{1}{4}$ twist to the right is combined with a forward tilt (judged from the free end of the torso) so that a skew curve results.

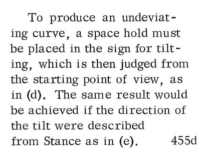

455c

To produce an undeviating curve, a space hold must be placed in the sign for tilting, which is then judged from the starting point of view, as in (d). The same result would be achieved if the direction of the tilt were described from Stance as in (e).

455d

or

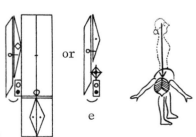

e

THE HEAD

Rotation (Twist) of Base of Head

When a torso, chest or shoulder section twist occurs the head is carried along. Unless the head has an additional rotation of its own or a space hold its front is the same as that of its base, the shoulder section.

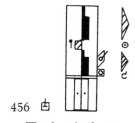

456

The head tilts over the right shoulder.

Separate Rotation and Tilt

Following a rotation, the head takes direction from its own front (the nose) unless a key is stated. The examples below illustrate a head tilt written from the understood key ⊕ and from Stance ◈ .

$\frac{1}{4}$ rotation to the right followed by a tilt to the left from ⊕, forward from ◈.

 457a   or   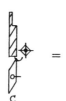 b   =

Combined Rotation and Tilt

Because the head takes its direction from its own front Fig. 457 (c) produces a skew curve. The head follows a three dimensional path as it rotates and tilts toward the nose, ending with the face over the right shoulder.

457c

 =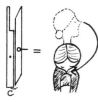

To produce a two dimensional plane curve, either a space hold must be placed within the direction symbol, as in (d), or direction must be described from Stance, as in (e). Here the head tilts in what is the forward direction at the start.

457d   e

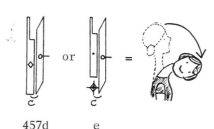

OFF-VERTICAL ROTATIONS: TWISTING, WHEELING

Two forms of rotation are possible when the torso is off the vertical line: (1) twisting around the longitudinal axis of that part of the body, (2) wheeling, a rotation around the unchanged vertical axis (the line of gravity of the Standard Cross of Axes) which passes through the point of attachment. In a wheeling movement of a part of the body the extremity describes a circular path.

x,y

Fig. 458 (a) illustrates the upright position of the body in which the vertical line of gravity is marked "x" and the longitudinal axis in the body is marked "y". In the upright standing position these two axes coincide.

458a

x,y

Twisting - Rotation around the Body Axis*

Rotation around the longitudinal axis of the part of the body is the understood and unwritten rule for the signs ◖ and ◗ . When the whole body is on the ground as in (b), the action produced is called Log Rolling. When it is the torso and not the whole body which is rotating, a twist similar to but more limited than log rolling occurs.

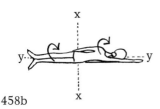

458b

In (c) the torso has tilted forward horizontal. The vertical line of gravity, x-x, remains unchanged, while the body axis, y-y, has moved with the torso as it tilted.

458c

In (d) the whole torso in the tilted situation twists ¼ to the right around its own longitudinal axis. The result is that the top of the head remains where it is, but the face and the shoulder section now face the side.

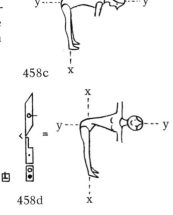

458d

* See Appendix B, note 21.

When this kind of rotation is
applied to the head, the following movement results: starting
from a tilted position forward
high, the head twists around its
own axis $\frac{1}{4}$ to the right, to end
facing the right; (f) shows the
final position.

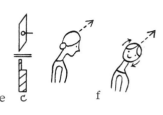

458e c   f

Wheeling - Rotation around the Constant Vertical Axis*

When a tilted part of the body rotates
around the constant vertical axis the extremity of the limb, the free end, describes a path in space. This action is
similar to that of a wheel, and is often
called wheeling to differentiate it from
the previously described twisting.

459a

Fig. 459 (a) shows a wheel, the front
of which is marked by a bow. Fig. (b)
shows a person tilted forward with a
corresponding bow on her head.

459b

As the wheel revolves around the vertical axis, the bow describes a circular path
to the right. In this illustration $\frac{1}{4}$ circle is
described.

459c

In a similar wheeling action of the whole
torso, the top of the head, like the bow,
makes a circular path in space, as illustrated in (d).

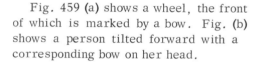

459d

In (e) the head is shown in a wheeling
action. Starting with the nose over the
left shoulder, it wheels to the right over
forward and ends up over the right shoulder. A total of a half circle is described
by the top of the head.

459e

* See Appendix B, note 21.

Such rotations are usually written as circular paths. The signs ʆ and ʅ have an understood vertical line axis. Degree of change from the previous situation is shown by a black pin, and degree of rotation from the untwisted state by a white pin.

Starting from the tilted position forward high, the head wheels around the vertical axis which passes through the base of the neck. The result of $\frac{1}{4}$ wheeling to the right is a position with the nose over the right shoulder. Fig. (g) shows this ending position.

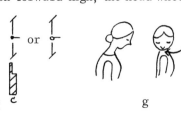

459f

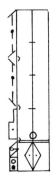

From a position twisted to the right, the whole torso tilts forward, wheels $\frac{1}{2}$ circle to the left, then $\frac{1}{2}$ circle to the right. A vertical axis is understood.

459h

The whole torso describes a circular path without change of front. Compare this with Fig. 277 (b) on page 199. This could be written as a series of tilts as in Fig. 369 (d), but the circular path best indicates the intention and over-all pattern.

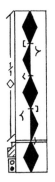

i

USE OF KEYS FOR ROTATIONS, TWISTS*

In any rotation the axis used can be specifically stated by placing the appropriate key within the turn sign.

460a

A turn, rotation around the longitudinal axis in the body

b

A turn, rotation around the vertical line of gravity (Standard Cross of Axes)

c

A turn, rotation around the vertical axis in the room (Constant Cross)

Figs. (b) and (c) are equivalent as long as the room does not tilt. For ordinary turns or rotations the key in (a) above is not needed, this being the understood axis. Wheeling may be writ-

* See Appendix B, note 21.

ten as in (b) instead of
with a circular path sign.

Fig. (e) describes the
same action as (d).

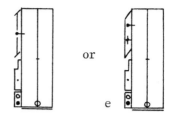

460d   e

Body Axis for Head Wheeling

When the torso is tilted it may not be possible to describe head wheeling around the constant vertical axis; a body reference is usually more suitable.

The action of head wheeling can be described as occurring around the longitudinal axis in the torso by placing the key for the Body Cross of Axes within the path sign.

In (f) the whole torso is tilted forward and the head is (hanging) down. The body axis is the extension of the spine as illustrated by the line y-y.

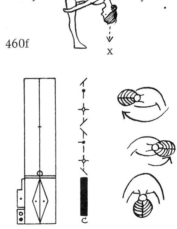

460f

Fig. (g) shows the notation of this starting position, and the subsequent head wheeling $\frac{1}{4}$ to the left followed by $\frac{1}{2}$ to the right.

460g

CANCELLATION OF KEYS

When placed outside the staff on the left a key is in effect until cancelled by the Standard Key or another key. When placed under a direction symbol or within an addition bracket the key is in effect only for the duration of that action or that addition bracket. If the need for a key results from a rotation or tilt in the body and such rotation or tilt is cancelled, the key is no longer needed and so is "cancelled" until a later rotation or tilt when it is again in effect.

CHAPTER 19

Specific Contraction and Extension; Bending; Gestures on a Straight Path, Shifting

ANALYSIS OF FORMS OF FLEXION IN THE BODY

Flexion in the body can occur in different ways, and movements which appear similar may in fact be based on different principles or concepts. "Flexion" is used here as a general term to cover the different possible forms. In everyday parlance the terms "flexing" and "bending" are often interchangeable, as are "flexing" and "contracting." In Labanotation, however, "contracting" and "bending" have specific meanings, substantiated by the dictionary definition of the words. (Note: only examples that are generally met will be presented here; greater detail will be given in Book II.)

ANALYSIS OF CONTRACTING

Contraction, according to the dictionary,* means: "to draw together or nearer, to shorten, narrow." The analysis on page 166 of contraction with reference to the arm and leg is applicable to other parts of the body. If a part has several joints rather than one central joint, a contraction results in the part becoming curved rather than angular.

ANALYSIS OF BENDING (FOLDING, CURVING)

Bending, according to the dictionary,* means: "to be moved out of a straight line or away from a given line, to crook, to be curved." When a limb is bent at a joint, its free end moves on a curved path away from the original line of direction and toward the base of the limb which retains its original direction. When there is one central joint, an angle is produced in the limb. For this form

* Webster's New International Dictionary, second edition, 1950.

of bending the term "folding" is used. When there are several joints, as in the spine, bending produces a curve in that part of the body. This action is termed "curving" or sometimes "curling".

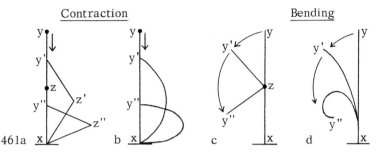

	Contraction		Bending	
461a	b	c	d	
One central joint	Multi-jointed	One central joint	Multi-jointed	

Contraction	Bending
Path: Straight. The extremity "y" draws in toward the base "x" on a straight path.	Path: Curved. The extremity "y" approaches the base "x" on a curved path.
Line of Direction: The extremity maintains the same directional relation with the base.	Line of Direction: The base which does not move maintains the original line of direction.
Displacement: The central joint "z" is displaced out of the original line of direction.	Displacement: The free end is displaced from the line of direction as it moves toward the base.
Involvement of Other Joints: The joint at "x" must also articulate.	Involvement of Other Joints: No other joint is involved.

SPECIFIC CONTRACTION AND EXTENSION

The symbols X and ✖ indicate contraction in general. The term "contraction" is given its anatomical meaning (see page 166). Specific statement may involve modification of the symbol to indicate three-dimensional rather than the usual two-dimensional contraction (see page 460), or modification to show the physical direction of the contraction (toward which surface of a limb contraction occurs, i.e. which surface becomes concave).

PHYSICAL DIRECTION OF CONTRACTION

When no directional change is indicated a contraction occurs toward the natural anatomical "inner" (or "front") surface of the part of the body concerned. For the legs the "inner" surface is the back. Interpretation of "front" surface is as follows:

hand	-	palm	foot -	sole
arm	-	inside of elbow & wrist	ankle -	instep (upper) side
neck	-	throat side	knee -	knee cap side

When combined with a tilt (directional change) a contraction normally occurs toward the same surface as the physical direction of the tilt. (Note that, depending on the situation of the body, this body direction may or may **not** coincide with a spatial directional description.) For exceptions to this rule and where specific contractions need to be stated, a meeting line representing the performer (—, |) is used in conjunction with the contraction sign to indicate toward which body surface the action occurs. Note the following:

462a X b X̄ c X| d |X e X̄|

Contract over the front.	Contract over the back.	Contract over the left side.	Contract over the right front diagonal.	Contract over the left back diagonal.

Note that the diagonal direction is indicated by a combination of forward and side, or backward and side meeting lines.

The degree of contraction is shown as usual (see page 167). Fig. (f) shows a 4-degree contraction over the left side, and (g) a 2-degree contraction over the right back diagonal side.

※| |x̄

462f   g

Specific Contraction of the Elbow

When a joint is contracted the parts of the limb on either side move toward one another. The greater the contraction of the joint the closer these parts become. A contraction of the elbow has the same effect as a contraction of the whole arm. In the final degree the lower arm and upper arm will meet.

The elbow contracts toward its front (inner) surface.

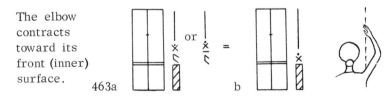

463a   b

Specific Contraction of the Wrist

In a contraction of the wrist the lower arm and hand move toward one another. This action can be seen clearly if the arm is placed palm down on a table. As the wrist contracts, it is displaced upward and the extremity of the hand approaches the elbow, the base of the "limb" of which the wrist is the central joint. Some flexion in the elbow joint must also occur.

A 3-degree contraction of the wrist toward the front surface.

464

Starting position

Specific Contraction of the Knee

A contraction of the knee produces the same result as a contraction of the whole leg while gesturing. The thigh and lower leg approach one another and the knee itself is displaced in space.

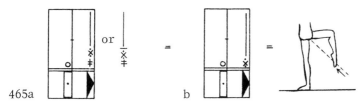

465a   b

Specific Contraction of the Ankle

A familiar example of ankle contraction occurs in kneeling when the lower leg rests on the floor with the foot extended. When the front of the ankle is contracted the ankle is displaced upward while the foot draws closer to the lower leg. Some bending of the knee joint will occur.

A 3-degree contraction of the ankle toward the front surface.

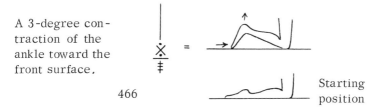

466

Starting position

General Contraction of the Whole Torso

When nothing specific is stated, the symbol X used for the whole torso means a contraction over the front surface. (Such a contraction could be written as concaving the front surface X ; the meaning is unchanged.) The torso is normally capable of three degrees of contraction, though some people can achieve more. Figs. 467 (a-d) illustrate contractions of the whole torso in the upright direction. As the contraction increases, the center part (waist) is displaced backward while the base of the neck (extremity of the whole torso retains its line of direction over the hips (the base). The pelvis gradually slants more and more backward. The head continues the curved line established by the spine.

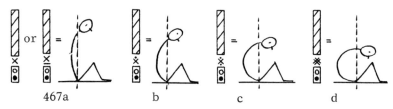

467a   b   c   d

Specific Contractions of the Whole Torso

For contractions toward other surfaces of the whole torso the specific contraction signs must be used. It is important to observe that in each case the free end, the base of the neck, remains over the pelvis regardless of the physical direction of the contraction.

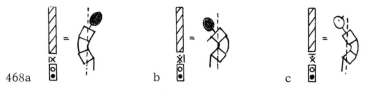

468a   b   c

Contraction toward   A 3-degree contrac-   A 2-degree contrac-
the right side   tion to the left   tion over the back

In all such contractions the result will include a tilting of the pelvis. If the contraction is over the left, as in Fig. 468 (b), the pelvis will tilt to the right; if over the back, as in (c), the pelvis will tilt forward. These actions contrast strongly with that of bending (folding) in which the base of the spine does not move. Specific contractions are applicable to the chest, and to some extent to the foot and hand (see Chapter 27). Full details will appear in Book II.

SPECIFIC EXTENSION

While extension of a part of the body produces a straight line, extension (stretching) of one side produces a convex surface on that side. The combination of the appropriate meeting line and the extension symbol indicates such extension of a particular surface. The curve produced is not to be confused with the form of hyperextension which is in fact an action either of folding or of contracting "backward" i.e. in the opposite physical direction to normal.

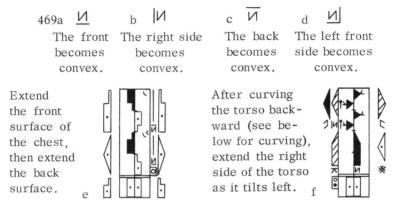

469a   b   c   d

The front becomes convex.	The right side becomes convex.	The back becomes convex.	The left front side becomes convex.

Extend the front surface of the chest, then extend the back surface.   e

After curving the torso backward (see below for curving), extend the right side of the torso as it tilts left.   f

BENDING (FOLDING, CURVING)

While "bending" is the general term for this action, the term "folding" is suitable for a single joint, the action being the same as in folding a piece of paper. A multi-jointed part of the body resembles the frond of a fern when performing this action and so the term "curving" or "curling" is usually more appropriate.

METHOD OF WRITING FOLDING

The basic sign for folding, ⩒ , is derived from a combination of the concepts of contracting and approaching (see Fig. 257 (b), page 184); the meeting line again represents the performer.

| Contraction sign: | ✕ | Approaching sign: | ∨ | Meeting Line: | ─ , ╱ , etc. |

Specific Folding

Since certain joints can fold in more than one direction (the spine, for example), it is important to indicate toward which surface the folding takes place; therefore the meeting line is used as the base of the folding symbol in a way comparable to its use for specific contractions and extensions.

470a $\underline{\vee}$ b $\overline{\wedge}$ c $\rangle\!\!\!\!\backslash$ d K

Folding over
the front

Folding over
the back

Folding over
the left

Folding over
the right

The diagonal directions can also be shown:

470e $\nearrow\!\!\!\!\downarrow$ f $\nwarrow\!\!\!\!\vee$ g $\nearrow\!\!\!\!\uparrow$ h $\nwarrow\!\!\!\!\wedge$

Over the left
front diagonal

Over the right
front diagonal

Over the left
back diagonal

Over the right
back diagonal

The above symbol group takes the name "K signs" from the shape of Fig. 470 (d).

Degree of Folding

The method of indicating the six degrees of folding is derived from that used for contraction signs. All six degrees exist though many parts of the body cannot achieve the extreme degrees.

471 $\underline{\vee}$ $\underline{\dot{\vee}}$ $\underline{\ddot{\vee}}$ $\underline{\vee\!\!\!/}$ $\underline{\dot{\vee\!\!\!/}}$ $\underline{\ddot{\vee\!\!\!/}}$

1st   2nd   3rd   4th   5th   6th

Regardless of how the sign is turned, the first dot appears within the V. Note that only the V, and not the base line, is doubled. A third degree always produces a right angle at the joint that bends.

472 K $\nwarrow\!\!\!\!\wedge\cdot$ $\overline{\wedge}\!\!\!\cdot$ $\rightarrow\!\!\!\uparrow$ $\rangle\!\!\!\uparrow$ $\Rightarrow\!\!\!\downarrow$

1st   2nd   3rd   4th   5th   6th

Comparison Between Folding a Single or Multi-jointed Part

The following illustrations, applicable to any direction, show the six degrees of folding a single joint and a multi-jointed part. Note that for the latter the extremity ends curved in snail fashion.

Folding (Single Joint):

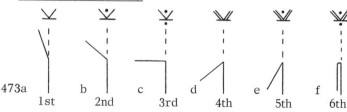

473a   b   c   d   e   f

1st   2nd   3rd   4th   5th   6th

Curving (Multi-jointed Part):

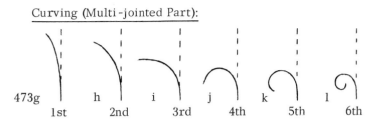

473g   h   i   j   k   l
1st   2nd   3rd   4th   5th   6th

The degrees illustrated above give the theoretically desired curvature. In practice each part of the body capable of this action varies
in the degree it can achieve, the hand coming closest to the ideal.
For movement one should consider the idea, a curving in slightly
or as much as possible, rather than measuring exact angles.

INDICATION OF TIMING

The indication of timing for the action of folding follows the
same usage established for narrow and wide signs when these are
applied to gestures.* (See pages 171, 172.)

Without Change of Direction

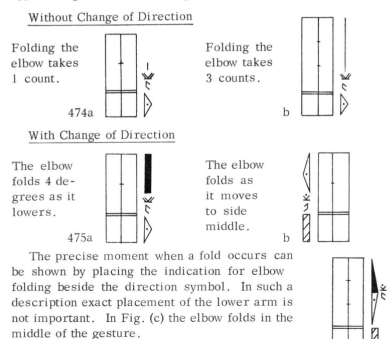

Folding the
elbow takes
1 count.

474a

Folding the
elbow takes
3 counts.

b

With Change of Direction

The elbow
folds 4 de-
grees as it
lowers.

475a

The elbow
folds as
it moves
to side
middle.

b

The precise moment when a fold occurs can
be shown by placing the indication for elbow
folding beside the direction symbol. In such a
description exact placement of the lower arm is
not important. In Fig. (c) the elbow folds in the
middle of the gesture.

475c

* See Appendix A, note 6.

FOLDING A JOINT

When a joint folds the distal limb (that farther from the center of the body) moves and approaches the proximal limb (that nearer the center). In folding the elbow the lower arm moves toward the upper arm; in folding the wrist the hand moves toward the lower arm, and so on.

Folding the Elbow

The elbow normally folds only toward the inner surface which is considered the front. Hyperextension is folding backward.

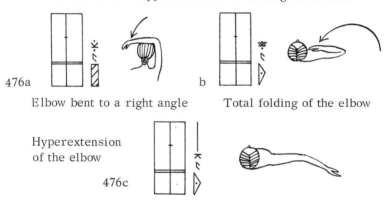

476a

Elbow bent to a right angle   b   Total folding of the elbow

Hyperextension
of the elbow

476c

In most instances the above results could have been described in terms of a spatial change for the free end, but emphasis would then have been on space pattern, rather than on what is happening in that particular joint. The action within the joint will be the same whether there is a slight rotation of the upper arm one way or the other, whereas the spatial result will be changed by any variation in rotation.

Specific Folding of the Wrist

The following examples illustrate use of the K signs in different degrees and directions for the wrist. The starting position with the wrist in its normal alignment is shown in Figs. 477 (a) and (d) so that subsequent changes are more clearly seen.

477a   b
    Starting position

Compare (b) with Fig. 464.

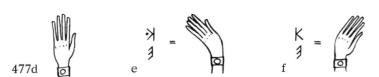

477d   e   f

The indication ⤢ always refers to the front surface of that part of the body (see list on page 320). When a general folding action is required, i.e. no particular surface is to be indicated, the sign for unspecified folding ⤡ is used. In this sign the ad lib. sign replaces the meeting line.

Specific Folding of the Hip

The hip joint can fold in all of the eight possible directions. A hip fold may produce a lifting of the leg or a tilt of the whole torso, depending on which part of the body takes the role of "base." When the weight is indicated as being on the legs, the torso will be considered the "free end" and therefore be the part to move in space toward the legs, the "base." The hip indication is placed in the appropriate column.

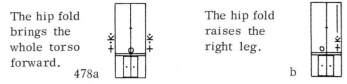

The hip fold brings the whole torso forward. 478a

The hip fold raises the right leg. b

Folding the Knee

Except in the case of hyperextension (folding into the opposite direction from normal), the knee can fold in only one direction, toward the back surface. This physical direction remains the same whether the leg is rotated in or out. Usually an isolated knee fold produces a gesture of the lower leg. Placement of the lower leg is not important and depends on the leg rotation used.

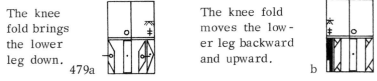

The knee fold brings the lower leg down. 479a

The knee fold moves the lower leg backward and upward. b

Specific Folding of the Ankle

When the ankle folds only the foot moves; there is no action or displacement in the lower leg.

Compare this example of
folding the ankle while
kneeling on a chair to the
contraction of the ankle
while kneeling on the
floor in Fig. 466.   480

A Demi-plié Described in Terms of Folding the Joints

To illustrate application of these signs Fig. 481 (a) shows a
demi-plié (lowering into a half knee bend) written in the standard
way and (b) shows the same action described in anatomical terms,
i.e. the specific folding and stretching of the appropriate joints.
Outward rotation is specified.

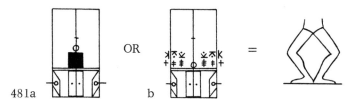

OR

481a   b

Note the sideward folding in the hip joint which results from the
turn-out. The advantage of the Labanotation convention used in
Fig. 481 (a) is obvious. The description in terms of folding is
needed for detailed study and research.

CURVING A MULTI-JOINTED SECTION

Curving (Folding) the Arm

Fig. 482 (a) illustrates the arm curving (folding) in from the
forward direction. Having too few joints, the arm cannot achieve
a true curve, but the idea of the movement is that of folding in like
the frond of a fern. Fig. (b) shows a contraction in the same direction to illustrate the difference between these two forms of flexion.

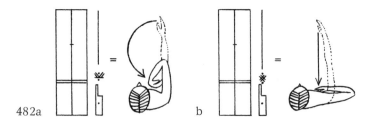

482a   b

Bending (Curving) the Whole Torso

The whole torso rarely can achieve more than four degrees of curving. The action of curving can be performed sequentially or can be led by the head, but these indications must be added (see Chapter 27). The torso can curve in any of the eight directions. The familiar instruction "bend backward" for the whole torso is usually a curving action. Curving is often combined with lengthening (⋀) to produce an arch (an extended curve) as in (c). Curving may be combined with a change of basic direction.

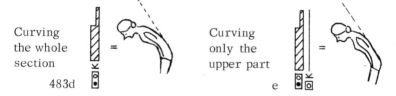

483a   b   c

It is important that, even for the first degree, curving be a movement of the whole spine which from the base up leaves the original line of direction and not a displacement of the upper spine.

Curving
the whole   =
section
483d

Curving
only the   =
upper part
                                   e

CANCELLATION (UNFOLDING)

Unbending or unfolding is the reverse of bending or folding. To produce the action of unfolding, a part of the body must already be bent or contracted. If the aim of unfolding is to return to the normal state, a back to normal indication is written. When motion is more important than destination (see page 172), the action of unfolding may need to be stated for its own sake.

Method of Writing Unfolding

The basic sign for unfolding A is derived from the signs for extension, withdrawing (see page 184), and the meeting line. A "forward" unfolding means unfolding from some degree of ⋁ or ⋉. A "right" unfolding occurs after some degree of K or |X, and so on.

The basic sign is turned as needed to show the eight directions.

484a A	b V	c ⋖	d X
From the front	From the back	From the left	From the left front diagonal

The above symbol group takes the name "A signs" from the shape of Fig. 484 (a).

Degrees of Unfolding

When a specific destination (state or situation) is required, it is usually written in terms of the desired degree of folding or curving. A description of unfolding is usually in terms of motion, rather than destination. For this reason the degrees A, A, A, etc. are not commonly used unless such destination is required. The completely unfolded state would be the last degree A. When the destination is the normal state, the symbol ⊙ may be added to the unfolding sign A .

CANCELLATION

The rules for cancelling indications for specific forms of extension, contraction, and bending follow those established for narrow and wide signs applied to gestures (see page 179). In some cases a specific contraction or bending may be cancelled by an unfolding.

Further details on use of X and K signs will appear in Book II.

GESTURES ON A STRAIGHT PATH, SHIFTING

Shifting is the term given to displacement of a part of the body on a straight line. Because of the structure of the body a perfectly straight path for each part may not be possible, but the aim of a shift is to move on a straight line.

GENERAL INDICATION OF STRAIGHT PATH GESTURES

In Motif Writing the basic action of the whole body moving on a straight path in the room is written with the straight path sign, Fig. 485 (a). This same sign is used in Structural Description to show any modification of the path produced by the indications in the support column. See page 85, Fig. 95 (b), illustrating traveling jumps.

485a

The straight path sign is modified as in (b)
to indicate either a gesture in which the extremity of a limb follows a straight path or a displacement of an area of the body on a straight
path. The addition of the body hold sign o in-
dicates restriction of the action within the body. 485b
Note the following differences:

A turn of the whole body followed by traveling on a straight path for the whole body 485c 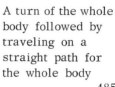	A twist within the body fol- lowed by a ges- ture on a straight path d	

General Statement for Limb or Area of Body

Indication for a straight path gesture may be made more specific by addition of the signs ‖ (limb) and ☐ (area). Because of the
structure of the limbs only an extremity can follow a straight path.

The extremity of
a limb describes
a straight path.
486a ‖

An area moves on
a straight path.
This action is
called "shifting."   b ☐

General Statement for Specific Part of the Body

A general indication of movement on a straight path can be
given for specific parts of the body. By stating the part of the
body, the physical limitation of the action is clear, therefore it is
not necessary to add the body hold sign within the path sign.

The hand (extremity
of the arm) describes
a straight path.
486c

The chest moves
on a straight
path (shifts).
d

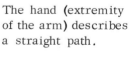
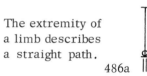

SPECIFIC INDICATION OF SHIFTING

As specific gestures of the arms and legs on a straight path are
usually described by other means (e.g. use of place for gestures
of the arms, page 120), the following discussions concentrate on
shifting body areas. In Structured Description the part of the body,
timing, direction, and degree of shift are shown.

ANALYSIS OF SHIFTING

Shifting, movement on a straight line, can be a major action, a movement as big as the physical limitations of that part of the body will allow, or it can be a minor action, a very slight displacement in space. Minor displacements are indicated through the use of pins, see Chapter 26. Shifting a body area is made possible through mobility in the neighboring part or parts of the body. Fig. 487 (a) illustrates a shifting action for a part of the body, such as the head, which is free at one end. The action in the neck makes it possible for the head to move on an approximately straight line.

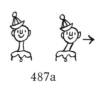

487a

Fig. 487 (b) illustrates a shifting action for a part which is confined between two other parts, such as the pelvis. The pelvis can shift because of mobility in hip and ankle joints and in the vertebrae in the waist area. The normal situation for a part which shifts is ⍰ , i.e. center.

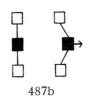

487b

METHOD OF WRITING SHIFTS*

A shift for a specific area of the body may be written with the sign for that area followed by the appropriate direction symbol placed in a straight path sign. Fig. 488 (a) shows a forward shift of the chest. The path sign may be shortened to become the pre-sign **I**, which can be placed directly after the indication for the part of the body, as in (b), which shows a left-right chest shift. The practical abbreviation commonly preferred is to combine the part of the body sign with the small path sign as in (c), which shows a left-right head shift with a pause in the normal position in between. Fig. (c) could also be written with an addition bracket (see page 483) as in (d). In (b), to be precise, double carets should be used to make clear that the next direction symbol refers to both pre-signs.

* See Appendix A, note 11.

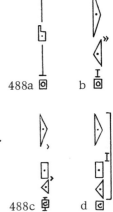

488a   b

488c   d

DEGREE OF SHIFTING

The degree or distance of a shift can be shown by placing the appropriate space measurement sign, narrow or wide, before the direction symbol. A normal-sized shift is that which is comfortable for the performer. Less than this distance would be a small or very small shift. In a large shift the part of the body moves as far as possible without involving other neighboring parts, while in a very wide shift the neighboring part or parts are involved to make this greater distance possible.

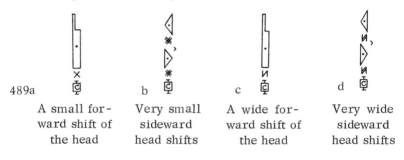

489a

A small for-	Very small	A wide for-	Very wide
ward shift of	sideward	ward shift of	sideward
the head	head shifts	the head	head shifts

b   c   d

SHIFTING SPECIFIC AREAS OF THE BODY

Shifting the Head

The head shifts through flexibility in the neck vertebrae, the chief axis of the head remaining vertical. The boxed pre-sign is customarily used to stress the idea of its being the movement of an area. The pre-sign ⚡ would not be wrong.

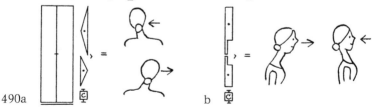

490a

Shifting the head right and left   Shifting the head forward
                                            and backward.

Shifting the Chest

The chest shifts through flexibility of the vertebrae in the waist area. The pelvis should not be affected in a small or normal-sized shift of the chest. The head is carried along in its normal placement on the shoulders.

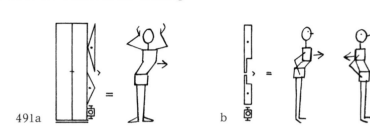

491a   b

Shifting the Pelvis

The pelvis shifts through flexibility in the waist vertebrae and the legs. The chest should be affected as little as possible. In a large shift some accompanying pelvic tilt will occur.

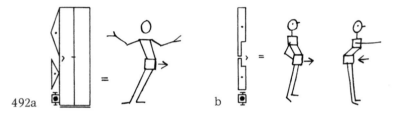

492a   b

A movement similar to a pelvic shift can be written with the single hip signs. When both hips move forward, the result is a bulge similar to a forward pelvic shift, but the motivation is an action of the hips rather than a displacement of the pelvic girdle as a whole. In the case of movement of the single hip there is more articulation in the groin, the hip joint.

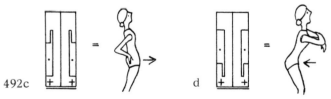

492c   d

Shifting the Whole Torso

The whole torso, moving in one piece, can shift slightly in the different directions. In a whole torso shift the head is carried along. With respect to displacement of weight a whole torso shift, when the feet are supporting, can be compared to a center of gravity shift (see pages 402, 403), but the emphasis of the movement is different. In a whole torso shift the emphasis is on displacement of the chest and pelvic areas moving as a unit. In a center of gravity shift awareness centers on placement of weight.

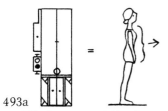
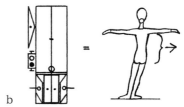

493a   Whole torso shifts forward.   b   Whole torso shifts to the right.

LEVELS OF SHIFT

When the body is in an upright standing position, its areas (head, chest, pelvis, and whole torso) usually shift on the horizontal plane. The chest and head, with some limitations, can also shift into high and low levels. Such actions usually include a slight tilt which is not emphasized and which disappears as soon as the action is over.

The chest shifts forward high then backward low.
494a

The head shifts right side high then left side low.
b

When the whole torso is tilted, direction and level of a shift of a body area adjust accordingly. Fig. 494 (c) shows the chest shifting toward the floor and then toward the ceiling while the whole torso is tilted forward horizontal.

494c

CANCELLATION OF SHIFTS

The result of a shift will be cancelled by a shift in another direction, by a return to place, or by the back to normal sign.

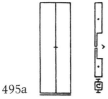

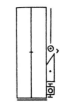

495a   A backward head shift cancels the previous forward shift.

b   After a shift to the left the pelvis returns to place.

c   After shifting diagonally, the chest returns to normal.

CHAPTER 20

Relationship

INDICATIONS OF RELATIONSHIP

The aim of certain basic movements may be to establish a parti-cular relationship or contact between two parts of the body, be-tween one part of the body and the floor, or between a part of the body and an object or another person. The range of such possible relationships is given in the order of increasing involvement. Such a relationship, or "contact," may be visual, as in looking at a person from a distance, or may be physical, as in touching.

ADDRESSING

The basic sign for establishing a relationship is the sign for addressing. This may be drawn ⎯⌣ or ⌣⎯ or inverted ⎯⌢ or ⌢⎯. The horizontal line of this sign extends from the staff or column of the active person, the one initiating the relationship. Within the cup is placed an indication of the person, object, or part of the room being addressed. Mutual addressing is written ⌣⎯⌣ or ⌢⎯⌢.

General Description

In Motif Writing when the purpose of an action is to address someone or something, the choice of action may be left to the per-former, or a specific form of movement may be indicated.

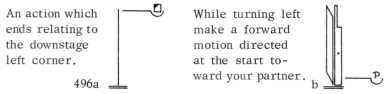

An action which ends relating to the downstage left corner.

496a

While turning left make a forward motion directed at the start to-ward your partner.

b

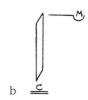

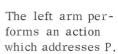

497a   b   c

The left arm per-	The head turns to	The right and left
forms an action	address a person	hands mutually ad-
which addresses P.	identified as M.	dress one another.

Specific Indication

In Structural Description an indication of addressing may modify the interpretation of the direction symbol depending on the location of the person, object, or part of the room being addressed.
The direction symbol given may therefore be an approximation of
the direction used. In the following examples the staff is written
for performer A who relates to performer B.

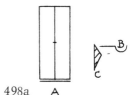 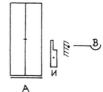

498a   A   b   A   c   A

A's head tilt speci-	A points at B	A turns and steps
fically relates to B.	(see page 455)	toward B.

NEARNESS, CLOSENESS

When a part of the body is near another part, an object, or another person, this closeness is indicated by the dotted horizontal
bow ⟍⟍___⟋ or ⟋‾‾⟍ .

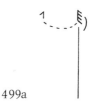 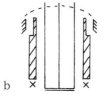 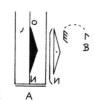

499a   b   x   x   c   A

An action which results	The hands finish	A reaches out until
in the right hand being	near each other.	his hand is near B's
near the left shoulder.		shoulder.

CONTACT, TOUCH

The horizontal bow indicating touch (contact bow) was presented on page 205.

500a

b

c

An action resulting in the right hand touching the left elbow

Right hand touching the waist, left hand touching the left shoulder

Hands touching opposite elbows

Indication of Active Side

In most contexts it is obvious which part is active in producing a touch (e.g. the hands in Fig. 500). When the active side must be specified the horizontal bow is thickened on the appropriate side.

Right side is active.

501a

Left side is active.

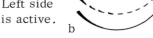

b

Right hand moves to be near the left.

501c

The left elbow moves to touch the right knee.

d

SUPPORT, CARRY

When one part of the body takes weight, or supports an object or another person, the relationship bow becomes angular. The sign for supporting is ╰───╯ or ╭───╮ . It is usually drawn ╰───╮ or ╭───╯ to indicate which part is supported and which is supporting. At the lower end is placed the object, person, or part which is supporting (when nothing is stated the floor is understood) and at the upper end the person or part being supported.

502a

b

c

In Motif Writing: an action resulting in a support on the floor

In Motif Writing: an action resulting in sitting on a chair

Supporting on the right knee on a bench

ENCLOSING, SURROUNDING

An enclosing relationship can be shown by adding the contraction sign ×. When contact occurs such enclosing produces grasping. The × within the bow is placed nearer the active part. The
active part enfolds the passive part; degree of contraction is influenced by the shape of the passive part. The thumb is generally
used in opposition to the fingers in a grasp. Grasping the hands
with penetration, shown by ⋇, means the fingers intertwine.

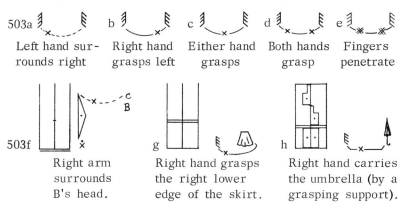

503a	b	c	d	e
Left hand sur- rounds right	Right hand grasps left	Either hand grasps	Both hands grasp	Fingers penetrate

503f   g   h

Right arm   Right hand grasps   Right hand carries
surrounds   the right lower   the umbrella (by a
B's head.   edge of the skirt.   grasping support).

PASSING, TRANSIENT RELATIONSHIP

Each of the relationships, addressing, nearness, touching, etc.,
may occur in passing, that is, the relationship may be established,
momentarily sustained, and then relinquished. This momentary
sustainment is indicated by doubling the relationship indication.

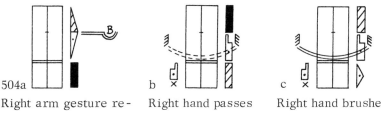

504a   b   c

Right arm gesture re-   Right hand passes   Right hand brushes
lates in passing to B. near the left hand.   the left.

RETENTION OF A RELATIONSHIP

A single contact bow (relationship indication) shows a momentary relationship. Whether this is retained for more than the moment usually depends on what comes next. When no obvious can-

cellation occurs in Structural Description the contact is expected to remain. For retention to be specifically stated despite other activities, the sign o is placed after the relationship indication.

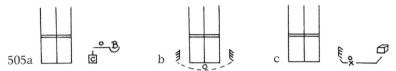

505a
                b   c

Keep looking at B,   Keep the hands   The box is to be kept
gaze follows if B moves. near each other.   in the right hand.

Continuous sliding for arm gestures is expressed as the retention, i.e. continuation, of the sliding relationship; hence the use of the hold sign to produce this result.

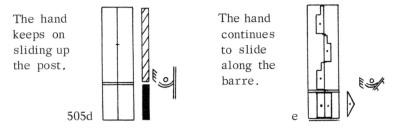

The hand
keeps on
sliding up
the post.

505d

The hand
continues
to slide
along the
barre.

e

CANCELLATION OF A RELATIONSHIP

A relationship may be cancelled by another action which obviously invalidates the previous relationship, or it may be specifically cancelled by the release sign. When a retention sign has been used, and a release must be given, it is placed over the part of the body actively releasing.

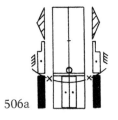

506a
                b 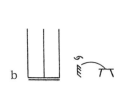   c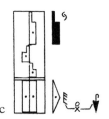

The clasped hands   The hand immedi-   The umbrella is
release automati-   ately releases   released (dropped)
cally when the arms from the table.   on the third step.
open to the side.

TOWARD AND AWAY

A performer may gesture toward or away from a part of his body, another person, an object, or a part of the room.

General Description

To show a movement toward a direction, person, object, or part of the room, the appropriate sign for that direction, person, etc. is placed within the approaching sign (see page 184).

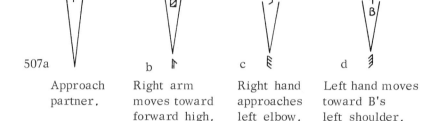

507a	b	c	d
Approach partner.	Right arm moves toward forward high.	Right hand approaches left elbow.	Left hand moves toward B's left shoulder.

The appropriate symbol is placed within the sign for retreating to indicate movement away from a person, object, etc.

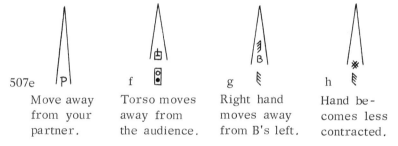

507e	f	g	h
Move away from your partner.	Torso moves away from the audience.	Right hand moves away from B's left.	Hand becomes less contracted.

Structural Description

Indications for motions toward or away can be placed within the columns on the staff.

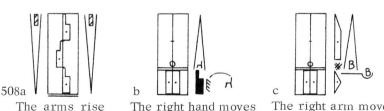

508a	b	c
The arms rise during the steps.	The right hand moves away from the chair.	The right arm moves away from B.

CANCELLATION OF TOWARD AND AWAY

Because the actions of approaching or withdrawing are motions rather than destinations, their results do not need to be specifically cancelled. Any subsequent action will cancel the resulting state or position which has been achieved.

FACING

The action of facing is that of directing any surface of the body, such as the palm, toward a direction, object, or person. The question "Where are you facing?" or "Where is your front?" refers to the body as a whole and is answered by a direction in the room indicated by the front signs 凸, ☑, etc. (See pages 104-107). The questions "Where do you look?" "Where is your head facing?" "Where is your chest facing?" "Where are your palms facing?" refer to the performer's directions, his Standard Cross of Axes, and are written with direction symbols following the appropriate pre-sign for that surface.

Analysis of Facing

Facing is the result of other basic actions such as tilting, rotating, singly or combined. The importance of this result requires that facing be given a specific description.

In facing, the surface in question is aimed in a stated direction much as one would focus a camera, turning and tilting it as required. The physical movement which produces facing includes an outwardly directed focus or projection which the actions of turning and tilting do not contain.

General Indication of Facing

The sign for "a surface" in connection with the addressing sign is used to state the basic fact of facing.

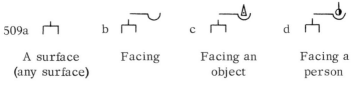

509a	b	c	d
A surface (any surface)	Facing	Facing an object	Facing a person

For indications in (c) and (d) see page 365.

Specific Indication of Facing

The sign for a surface of a part of the body must be used to write facing for that part.* A surface is described as one or other of the outer sides of an area.

An area ☐   Front ☐ surface   Back ☐ surface   Right front ☐ surface

A pin placed on an area sign indicates which surface is being de-signated. Within the box is placed the part of the body in question. The chest, pelvis, and whole torso are already box signs.

Front surface of the head, the face 〔c〕   Back sur-face of the chest 〔O〕   Front sur-face of the whole torso 〔O•〕

The appropriate direction symbol is placed after the indication of a particular surface to state facing that direction. The length of the direction symbol gives the timing of the action. The address-ing sign used for a general statement of facing is no longer needed.

FACING FOR SPECIFIC PARTS OF THE BODY

Head Facing

The symbol for face 〔c〕 is followed by the appropriate direc-tion symbol.* The head normally faces forward middle; to face in different directions it will tilt, turn, or tilt and turn at the same time. In the following illustrations each example of head facing is accompanied by a description of the same action in terms of tilting and rotating. These are only approxi-mate, as the head does not make quite the same use of the neck in the action of facing as in tilting. The sign for similar 〈 (see page 354) placed next to the tilting in-dications denotes this inexactness.

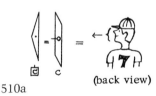

510a

(back view)

Head facing left

Facing forward high   510b 〔c〕   =   =

Facing forward low   c 〔c〕   =   =

* See Appendix B, note 22.

These are the most common directions in which the face looks. If a performer faces a direction which requires both tilting and turning, he can best determine the destination to be reached by first looking in the direction stated and then adjusting to the level. The action is then performed as one movement with the same end result.

When timing need not be indicated, note the following abbreviations giving the destination of the movement.

510d

Chest Facing

The chest does not have as wide a range of movement as the head and so is more limited in its ability to face different directions. There are times, however, when such a description is desirable. The chest normally faces forward middle.

511

a   b

The chest faces diagonally;   The chest faces diagonally low;
a rotation must occur.   a rotation plus the tilt occurs.

Shoulder Section (Upper Chest) Facing

A facing movement of the chest in forward or diagonal high directions is often actually a facing of the front of the shoulder section (upper chest). For the whole chest to face in these directions a greater adjustment in the spine is required.

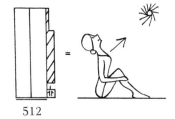

512

Facing for Other Parts of the Body

If need be, any part of the body can be shown to face a direction by combining a pin with the boxed indication for that part of the body. Fig. 513 shows the front of the knee facing left forward diagonal.   513

CANCELLATION OF FACING

Examples of cancellations for facing given here for the head
are applicable to other parts. A previous facing indication for the
head will be cancelled by another facing indication, or by the return to normal sign. A facing indication will usually be affected
and hence cancelled by a rotation of the head, and in certain instances by a tilt of the head. In certain contexts a tilt will not
cancel a facing direction.

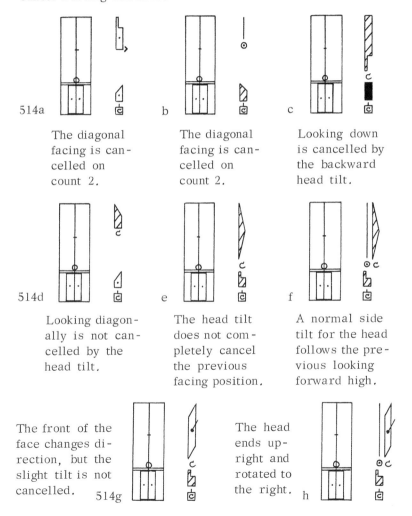

514a   The diagonal   b   The diagonal   c   Looking down
        facing is can-   facing is can-   is cancelled by
        celled on   celled on   the backward
        count 2.   count 2.   head tilt.

514d   Looking diagon-   e   The head tilt   f   A normal side
        ally is not can-   does not com-   tilt for the head
        celled by the   pletely cancel   follows the pre-
        head tilt.   the previous   vious looking
                                facing position.   forward high.

The front of the
face changes di-
rection, but the
slight tilt is not
cancelled.   514g

The head
ends up-
right and
rotated to
the right.   h

CHAPTER 21

Repeat and Analogy Signs

REPEAT SIGNS

A variety of repeat signs facilitates writing, particularly for the notator working at speed. Repeated material should be written out fully in the final draft of a score as a rule; however, repeat signs which refer directly to material on the same page are acceptable.

REPEAT SIGNS PLACED WITHIN THE STAFF

The sign for a simple identical repeat is taken from music notation* ⁄ . The slanting line is doubled to show a repeat "to the other side," i.e. alternating sides, a laterally symmetrical repeat.

Repeat the same (an identical repeat).   Repeat to the other side (lateral symmetry).

Lateral symmetry means the exchange of right and left in the use of the body and in direction:

 means:

Such an exchange is illustrated in Fig. 515 below, (b) being laterally symmetrical to the pattern in (a).

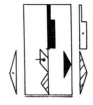

515a   b

* See Appendix A, note 12.

Repeat signs always refer to the last notated measure unless another measure is indicated. The repeat sign is centered in the space on the staff to which it refers.

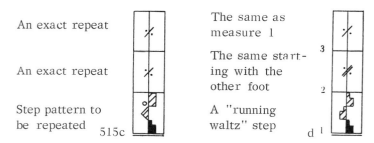

An exact repeat

An exact repeat

Step pattern to
be repeated   515c

The same as
measure 1

The same start-
ing with the
other foot

A "running
waltz" step

Size of the Repeat Sign

As a visual aid the size of a repeat sign
reflects the length of the section (area) on
paper in which the sign is centered. Repeat
of a count is written quite small, repeat of
a whole measure larger, and repeat of
several measures larger still. In these examples a small unit has been taken to con-
serve space. Fig.
516 shows repeats
for: (a) one count;
(b) one measure;
(c) two measures;
(d) four measures. 516a

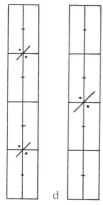

b   c   d

Repeats Bridging Two Staves

When a repeat sign falls in an area
of two staves, the repeat sign is placed
at the top of the first and again at the
bottom of the following staff. A caret
is added to each repeat sign to signify
that the second is simply the conclusion of the first. In Fig. 517 measures
1 and 2 are repeated on alternate sides
three times (a total of four performances of the material) before a two-
measure conclusion.   517

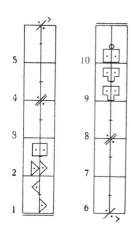

Defining the Area to be Repeated

If an area to be repeated does not coincide with established bar lines, dotted horizontal lines are used as a visual aid to indicate the repeated area. In Fig. 518 (a) a movement which takes three counts is repeated within four count measures. Even if this were written out fully, as in (b), the dotted lines would still be used to assist in reading and understanding the phrasing.

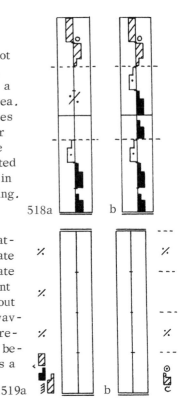

518a   b

Repeat Signs Within a Column

When a small movement is repeated several times, it is easier to state the movement once and then to indicate with tiny repeat signs its subsequent repetition, rather than to write it out fully. Fig. 519 (a) shows the hand waving repeatedly, while (b) shows a repeated nod of the head, with a pause between. Dotted lines can be used as a visual aid.

519a

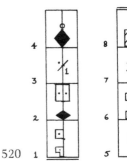

b

Specific Measure to be Repeated

To refer to a particular measure in describing a repeat, the notator replaces the dot at the bottom of the repeat sign with the number of the measure in question.

An identical repeat   A laterally symmetrical
of measure 1   repeat of measure 4

The simple sequence in Fig. 520 includes as many repeats as possible for the purpose of illustration only. Fully written out notation would obviously be easier to read. Measure 3 shows an identical repeat of measure 1; measure 5 is measure 1 done with the other foot; measure 7 shows a repeat of measure 2.

520

Modification of Repeated Material

When repeated material includes slight variations which are easy to read, the repeat signs can be used with the changes indicated. If such changes are complex it is better to write out the whole sequence. In Fig. 521 the first two measures are repeated to the other side, but at the very end of the fourth measure a quarter turn occurs as a preparation for the next pattern. Measures 7 and 8 are an exact repeat of 5 and 6 but arm gestures have been added.

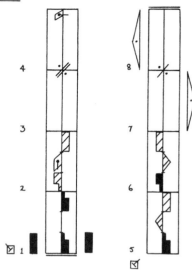

521

Reminder of Repeated Material

When a complex movement phrase which has already been described in detail appears again, it is permissible to give an outline of the movement and to indicate outside the staff on the left in parentheses the measure numbers where it is written fully. Fig. 522 states that measures 65 and 66 are the same as measures 15 and 16. Even if the material is completely written out, such an indication will help the reader who would otherwise have to study the symbols with care to see if the movement is actually the same in every detail.

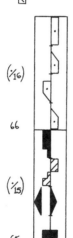

522   65

REPEAT SIGNS OUTSIDE THE STAFF

For exercises or short studies designed to be repeated several times, there is no need to draft out each repeat as in a regular dance score. The exercise is written once and the repeats are indicated outside the staff. The slanting signs ⁄ and ⁄⁄ are modified to ÷ and ≑ and are placed at the beginning on the left and at the end on the right of the section to be repeated. Extended horizontal lines enclose the section. If a sequence is to be performed more than twice, the number of times is written in place of the inner dot of the repeat sign. Thus the number four states the sequence is to be performed once and then repeated three times (a total of four times). The repeat in Fig. 523d starts on the upbeat.

Short Sectional Repeats*

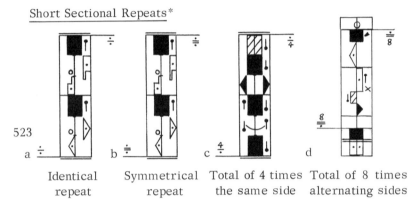

523

a

| Identical repeat | Symmetrical repeat | Total of 4 times the same side | Total of 8 times alternating sides |

Longer Sectional Repeats

For longer sections containing shorter repeats, the extended lines are bent to enclose the whole section, and the repeat sign is incorporated in this slanting extension. Fig. 524 (a) shows two measures which are repeated twice (a total of three performances of this material) followed by two unrepeated measures, making a total of eight measures. These eight measures are then performed again. In (b) the eight measures are repeated to the other side. Note the indication of measure numbers. Fig. (c)

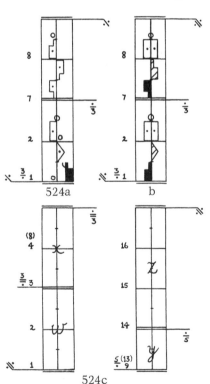

524a   b

524c

* See Appendix B, note 23.

shows such longer sectional repeats used for a sequence which involves more than one staff. The device of enclosing the repeated
section helps the eye to see the beginning and end of what is to be
repeated. In this example theme "w" is performed, then theme
"x" is performed three times, alternating sides; theme "y" is performed a total of five times followed by "z." All sixteen measures
are then repeated to the other side.

Repeats Used with Path Signs

In sectional repeats in which a circular path occurs, care must
be taken to indicate clearly whether the circling is included in the
repeat, or whether the step pattern is repeated during one circular
path. Note placement of the repeat signs in the examples below.

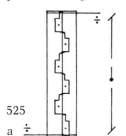
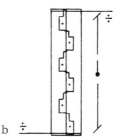
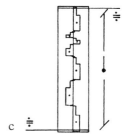

525

a

Take 12 steps to walk   Take 6 steps to walk   Walk a circle to the
a complete circle.   a circle; 2 circles   right in 7 steps; re-
                  are walked in all.   peat to the left.

En Croix Repeats

A pattern derived from exercises at the barre is that in which a
theme is performed to the front, to the open side, and to the back.
The side direction may be employed again in returning. Ballet terminology calls this pattern "en croix," from the French for cross.
The repeat sign ÷ has been modified to show en croix repetition.

A return to the side direction is shown by doubling the side line.

En croix signs are placed outside the staff, in the same manner as
sectional repeat signs.

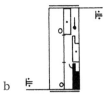

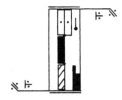

526a 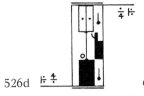 b c

| Perform this to the front, side, and back. | Perform this to the front, side, back, and side. | Perform this front, side, back, then all to the other side. |

Note the addition of a number to indicate the total number of times an exercise is to be performed:

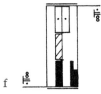

526d e f

| Perform 4 times forward, 4 times side, 4 times backward. | Perform this exercise en croix twice. | Perform this exercise en croix a total of 8 times. |

Labeling a Section - Reprise Signs

A reprise is the repetition of a phrase of movement which appeared earlier in a dance, other material having appeared in between. The section so to be repeated is identified by being enclosed between extended horizontal repeat lines, one at the beginning, one at the end, to each of which is attached a box in which is placed an identifying mark, usually a letter. Fig. 527 (a) shows a phrase labelled as a reprise with the letter A. Later on, when this material is to be repeated, the reprise sign (identifying box) is used with the extended repeat lines enclosing a short section of staff, as in Fig. (b). The nature of the repeat, identical or symmetrical, is indicated by the use of the appropriate repeat sign placed within the staff.

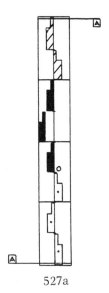

527a

Figs. (c) and (e) illustrate alternate ways of writing (b) and (d) respectively; the boxed letter identifying the reprise replaces the lower dot of the repeat sign.

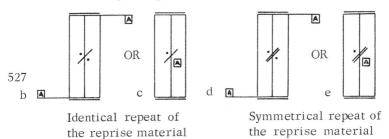

527
b

| Identical repeat of | Symmetrical repeat of |
| the reprise material | the reprise material |

<u>First and Second Ending</u>

It is common in sectional repeats for a modification to occur on the last repeat, as a bridge into the next sequence. The device to differentiate a second from a first ending is borrowed from music notation. An angular vertical bracket is placed alongside each of the two endings on the left of the staff. Inside each bracket is the number of the ending. The first ending may be placed within thickened lines to draw attention to the material to be omitted on the last reading. In Fig. 528 a movement sequence of four measures is performed three times. For the first two times the phrase ending on measure 20 (measure 24 on the repeat) contains circling in place. On the last repeat (third ending, measure 28) the circling is omitted and instead the legs merely straighten.

Note that numbers of repeated measures are written in parentheses. Where measures repeat several times usually only the last set of numbers is given.

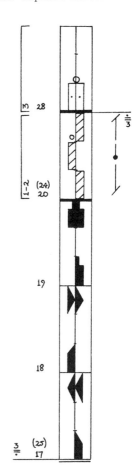

528

First and Second Beginning

The same device can be used to indicate that the beginning of a sequence is to be altered on the repeat. In Fig. 529 the turn required at the start to face the corner of the room becomes $\frac{1}{4}$ turn on the subsequent repeats so that each corner is faced in turn. Note the numbering of the measures and use of parentheses to help the reader follow the sequence.

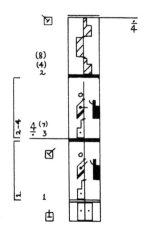

529

ANALOGY SIGNS

Analogy signs are used to abbreviate the score. Their greatest value is as an aid to quick writing, though they may appear in the finished score. The analogy signs are:*

Similar: ⌣ or ⟩

Exact: ✳

Equal: ══

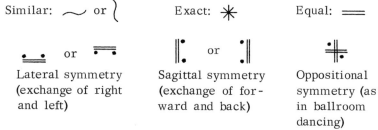

Lateral symmetry (exchange of right and left)

Sagittal symmetry (exchange of forward and back)

Oppositional symmetry (as in ballroom dancing)

SIMILAR

The similar sign is also known as the ad libitum sign since it appears where freedom in performance is allowed. The sign may be used for the whole staff generally, or in specific columns.

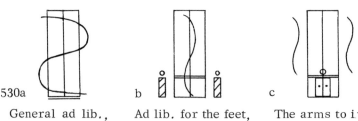

530a General ad lib., free improvisation

b Ad lib. for the feet, with arms held

c The arms to improvise freely

* See Appendix A, note 12, and Appendix B, note 24.

In Structural Description an ad lib. sign
is added to a duration line to indicate timing
of actions such as flexing and extending,
thereby allowing freedom in choice of spatial
pattern and manner of performance. Compare (d) with Fig. 233 (a) on page 172.

530d

When placed next to movement indications, the similar sign
means "on the order of," "similar to," "along the lines of."
Freedom is allowed in performance of the written material.

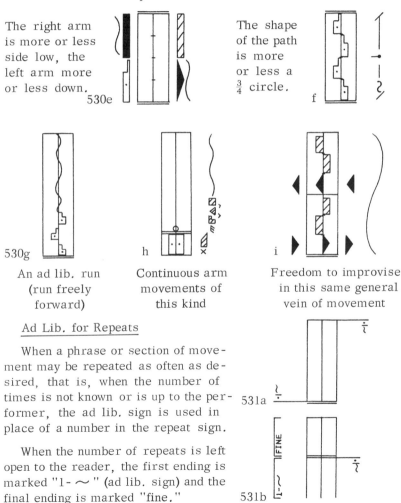

The right arm
is more or less
side low, the
left arm more
or less down.
530e

The shape
of the path
is more
or less a
$\frac{3}{4}$ circle.
f

530g

An ad lib. run
(run freely
forward)

h

Continuous arm
movements of
this kind

i

Freedom to improvise
in this same general
vein of movement

Ad Lib. for Repeats

When a phrase or section of movement may be repeated as often as desired, that is, when the number of
times is not known or is up to the per-   531a
former, the ad lib. sign is used in
place of a number in the repeat sign.

When the number of repeats is left
open to the reader, the first ending is
marked "1- $\sim$ " (ad lib. sign) and the
final ending is marked "fine."   531b

EXACT PERFORMANCE

When a detailed description is written the reader is aware that exactness in performance is needed. But exactness in interpretation may also be required for movement recorded in what appears to be simple, general terms. The use of the asterisk ✻ * placed next to particular symbols alerts the reader that these are to be given their precise, literal meaning, being performed without any leeway at all.

The exact performance sign may be written as a key at the start of a score as in Fig. 532, or it may be placed next to a particular symbol, as in Fig. 533 (c), or placed within a vertical bow or bracket to modify several symbols as in Fig. 534 (c).

532

Exact Timing

The convention established to indicate timing for steps and gestures** suffices for general purposes; only in particular cases does a simple indication require precise interpretation. At such times the exact sign is placed next to the indication in question.

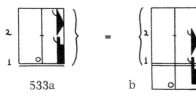

533a	b	c
Toe touches occur on counts 1 and 2 (general timing).	The notation specifies that the touches occur precisely at the start of counts 1 and 2.	Precise performance of the touches a fraction before counts 2 and 3 (on the "u" subdivision).

Exception to Stated Key

Particular details of style which are to be used throughout are stated as a key signature at the start of a dance score. When such a key signature must be cancelled at some point in the score, the notator may use either the back to normal sign (signifying the normal state for that part of the body) or the exact sign (signifying that the symbols are to be read with their exact meaning).

*See Appendix B, note 13. ** See Appendix C, note 4.

In Fig. 534 (a) the key states
that middle level supports
mean steps with slightly bent
legs. On counts 3 and 4 of
(b) the normal middle level
support is to be used, as
shown by the use of the back
to normal signs; (c) is the
equivalent of (b) but with the
exact sign placed within a
vertical bow.

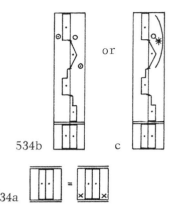

534b   c

534a

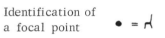

EQUAL

The equal sign = has certain obvious uses:

Indication of
an object   ⚔ = sword

Identification of
a focal point   ● = ⊀

When used below or at the
side of the staff, the equal
sign shows that one person performs the same movement as
another. Fig. 535 (a) shows
at the start of a score that A
and B are to be alike. Fig. (b)
shows B joining A on the third
measure, and states that B is
now to do the same as A. This
statement facilitates reading.

A = B

535a   b

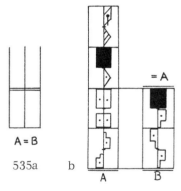

= A

A   B

SYMMETRICAL

There are two possibilities in the use of symmetry: lateral
symmetry and sagittal symmetry.

Lateral Symmetry

In lateral symmetry right becomes left in the use of the sides
of the body, in direction, and also in turning.

⋮ OR ⋮   means   ◁=▷ ▷=◁ ◁=▷ ◁=▷

A sign for lateral symmetry is used under the staff to show one person constantly moving symmetrically to another. In Fig. 536 B is to produce movement laterally symmetrical to A's; (i.e. "the same to the other side"). The sign can be drawn with the dots above or below; in this context above is preferable.** Note the use here of a comma.

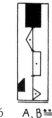

536   A, B≌

Sagittal Symmetry

In sagittal symmetry the pattern balances in respect of the forward and backward directions. The same side of the body is used, and the sideward directions remain the same, but the direction of turning is reversed.

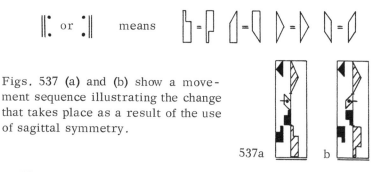

Figs. 537 (a) and (b) show a movement sequence illustrating the change that takes place as a result of the use of sagittal symmetry.

537a   b

The sign for sagittal symmetry can be used below the staff to indicate that one person constantly moves in this form of symmetry to another. In (c) B performs steps that are sagittally symmetrical to A's, that is, he moves backward where A moves forward and vice versa. The sign is drawn with the dots facing the indication of the person.

537c   A, B:‖

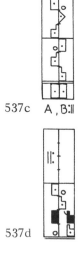

Fig. 537 (d) shows the sign used within the staff as a repeat sign to mean that the preceding measure should be reversed in respect to sagittal symmetry. Such usage is practical in writing exercises.

537d

* See Appendix B, note 25.   ** See Appendix A, note 13.

In (e) the sign is used outside the
staff attached to the extended horizontal
line. Note that the dots face in, toward
one another. Here the movement pattern
is repeated four times alternating forward and backward.

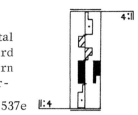

537e

OPPOSITION*

The combination of lateral and sagittal symmetry, called "opposition," is most commonly met in ballroom dancing. In this
form right and left are exchanged, as are forward and backward.
The opposite side of the body is used, but the turning direction remains the same, as the result of a double change in turning direction - once for lateral and once for sagittal symmetry. The sign
for opposition is a combination of the other two signs.

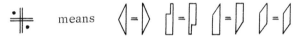

The opposition sign can be placed below the
staff to show that one person constantly moves
in opposition to another. Here the woman (W)
performs "the ballroom of" the man (M).

538a

The use of opposition as a
repeat sign should only be for
rough notes, as this form is
not easily interpreted. The
sign is used in the same way
as the symmetry signs, both
within or outside the staff.

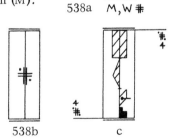

538b   c

---

* See Appendix B, note 24.

CHAPTER 22

Scoring

DRAFTING THE DANCE SCORE

A sequence of written movement is referred to as a dance score when it is a dance composition, that is, a piece of choreography, comparable to the score of a musical composition. The term "kinetogram" is used for any written sequence. This may be an isolated movement pattern, an exercise, or a complete movement sequence. In a full dance score the action and the musical accompaniment, if any, must be related.

COORDINATION WITH THE MUSIC SCORE

As a rule it has been found more practical to have in one book the dance score which is to be used in rehearsal by the ballet master and dancers, while the accompanying music is in a separate book for the pianist. Because in Labanotation timing of each step and its composite parts is indicated by the relative lengths of the movement symbols, music notation is not needed to indicate the timing or rhythm of individual actions. Thus a dance score can exist independently from a music score. In special cases it is desirable to place an outline of the accompanying music alongside the dance score, but as a rule the existing music score is used for rehearsals, coordination between dance and music being achieved through numbered measures.

By numbering the measures of the music score so that they tally with the dance score, dancers and musicians can readily coordinate at any given moment. The number of a desired measure need only be called out to locate at once the place in the score.

Music measures are numbered above the treble stave, under it, or below the bass stave, according to where there is most room. Once placement has been established, it should be followed consistently. Fig. 539 (a) shows placement below the treble stave.

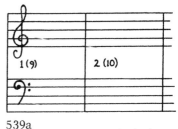

When sections in the music are repeated, a second set of numbers written in parentheses appears after the first. In the illustration here measure 1 becomes measure 9 on the repeat; measure 2 becomes measure 10 and so on.

539a

Measure numbers for a dance score are written on the left of the staff outside any stage direction signs, as in Fig. 539 (b). Any section numbers or letters in the musical score which may be referred to by the musicians should also appear on the dance score. These indications are usually boxed or encircled letters or numbers. This example shows a number 1.

Each new section or complete dance begins with new numbering, starting again from 1. An upbeat measure is numbered 0 (zero).

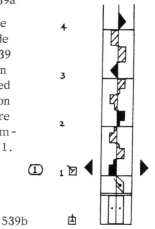

539b

Indication of Musical Cuts in the Dance Score

Not all the music in a printed score may be used for a dance; to facilitate coordination between dance and music scores it is important that note be made of which edition of the music is being used and of the measures which have been cut. It has been found practical to number the music measures throughout disregarding cuts; the numbers are there for future reference should the cuts be restored. Note of a cut must be made in the dance score, as in Fig. 540, either (a) or (b).

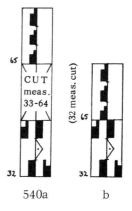

540a   b

SCORING FOR SEVERAL PERFORMERS

A dance score is comparable to a music score in that all parts are joined together by a line at the start of each page. A separate staff is needed for each individual dancer; only one staff is needed for a group moving in unison. In the illustrations below holes for a ring binder are shown on the inside margin of each page.

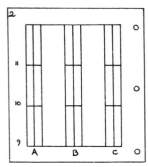

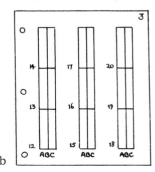

541a

Each dancer is given
a separate staff.

b

Unison movement allows
condensation of the score.

SCORING OF ENTRANCES AND EXITS

An entrance is usually shown on the score by attaching the appropriate stage area sign to a horizontal line extended to the left of the staff. This is understood to be the moment when the performer enters. The horizontal line extends to the right to show an exit and has attached to it the appropriate stage area sign. In Fig. 542 A is shown to enter from the downstage left wing, while B shortly after exits into the upstage right wing.

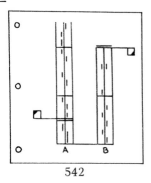

542

Complete information on scoring, layout of staves, handling of musical introduction, etc. will be given in Book II.

FLOOR PLANS

In recording dances for a group it is important to be able to see at a glance the dancers' positions on stage and how one formation changes into another. These floor plans or stage plans are also useful for a solo figure. Examples of the use of floor plans were

given in Chapter 12, pages 181 and 182. In the dance score the
floor plans are written from the dancer's point of view. (Director's plans are given on pages 378 and 379.)

PLACEMENT OF THE FLOOR PLANS

In the movement score floor plans should be placed as close as
possible to the notation to which they refer. Practical use should
be made of available space.

Under the Score Line

When all the staves on a page
are in use floor plans are placed
at the bottom, side by side if
there is more than one, in two
rows if there are many.

543a

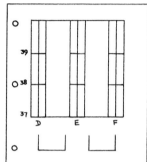

At the Side of the Score Line

When an empty staff leaves
space at the side of a page floor
plans are placed there, thus allowing room for an extra measure of dance. Such placement
makes it possible to relate a
plan directly to the movement
it describes. When a plan shows
the floor pattern for several
measures, the appropriate measure numbers are placed adja-   543b
cent to it.

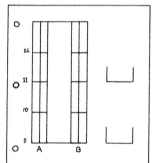

Within the Score Line

In general interruption of the score
line is avoided, but at the end of a section of the dance it may be broken to
leave room for a floor plan. This has
the advantage of focusing attention on
the arrangement of the dancers on
stage at an exact point in the score.

543c

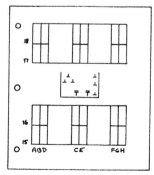

FLOOR PLANS FOR FOLK DANCES

In many folk or country dances the action is set in relation to the "top" of the room, where the musicians are seated. As there is no proscenium and no sense of having an audience it is customary in drawing floor plans of such dances for the notator to use a square or rectangle in which the top of the room is placed toward the top of the page.

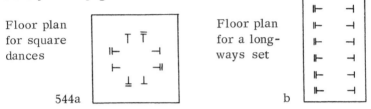

Floor plan for square dances

Floor plan for a long-ways set

544a   b

COORDINATION OF FLOOR PLANS WITH MUSIC SCORE

To coordinate floor plans with the music score, the notator places the appropriate music measure number at the left of or below the floor plan. Fig. 545 (a) shows measure 6 to 8.

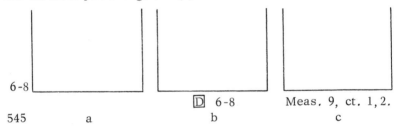

6-8

$\boxed{D}$ 6-8   Meas. 9, ct. 1, 2.

545   a   b   c

Fig. 545 (b) shows Section D, measures 6-8; (c) states the counts as well, using the abbreviations "ct." for count and "meas." for measure. ("Bar" may also be used.) Counts may also be indicated by enlarging the measure number and making the count number small, e.g. 9 1,2 or $9^{1,2}$.

Indication of Sequence of Action

Several paths can be written on one floor plan even though they are not performed simultaneously. The sequence of action is indicated by labeling the paths 1st, 2nd, 3rd. The exact spacing musically between the actions will be given in the movement score.   546

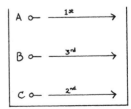

INDICATION OF THE PERFORMER

Pins or wedges are used to indicate individual performers on a stage plan.

Starting Position Pins

Two standard sets of pins indicate starting positions: straight pins (tacks) and round pins.

| Girl | Boy | Person | Girl | Boy | Person |

The sign for a "person" may be used to indicate either male or female, when differentiation is not important.

The point of a pin or tack indicates the direction faced. The dancer is understood to be standing on the head of the pin or at the point of the tack where the two lines meet ⌐. Placement of the pin on a stage plan indicates where on stage the performer is located.

Finishing Position Wedges

In special cases when both starting and finishing positions must be shown on the same plan, a wedge is used to indicate the latter. The point of the wedge indicates where the performer is facing.

Girl △   Boy ▲   Person ◭

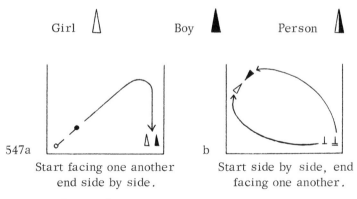

547a   Start facing one another   b   Start side by side, end
        end side by side.   facing one another.

Various Shaped Pins

Other kinds of pins may be used, such as ⅄ , ⅁ , to identify people or objects. These should be identified in a glossary given at the start of the score. A chosen set of pins must be used consistently throughout the score.

RELATIONSHIP OF THE PERFORMERS

Juxtaposition of pins representing the performers illustrates the latter's relationship. A few possibilities are given here.

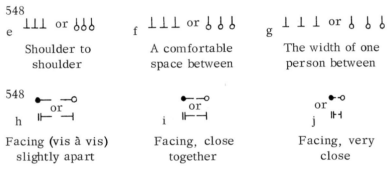

548

a ⊥⊥ or ⌡⌡   Side by side facing the same way

b ≒ or ⌽   Back to back (dos à dos)

c ⊥⊤ or ⌽⌿   Side by side facing opposite directions

d ⊥⊥ or ⌽   One in front of the other

Distance between Performers

The space between pins can give some indication of the proximity of the performers.

548

e ⊥⊥⊥ or ⌿⌿⌿   Shoulder to shoulder

f ⊥⊥⊥ or ⌿ ⌿ ⌿   A comfortable space between

g ⊥ ⊥ ⊥ or ⌿ ⌿ ⌿   The width of one person between

548

h ●— —○ or ⊩— ⊣   Facing (vis à vis) slightly apart

i ●—○ or ⊩—⊣   Facing, close together

j or ●-○ or ⊩⊣   Facing, very close

Size of Pins in Relation to Size of Floor Plan

Pins used on floor plans can give an indication of the size of the stage area used in relation to the performer. Although stages vary considerably in size, the impression can easily be given of a dancer on a very large or a very small stage. Care should be taken to indicate the right general relationship. Performance in a small area calls for a smaller plan or a larger pin in relation to the size of the stage area drawn.

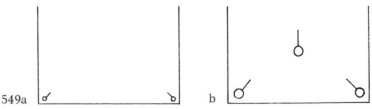

549a   Two dancers on a large stage   b   Three dancers on a small stage

Pins should illustrate as correctly as possible the relationship of the dancers to one another as well as to the stage area. Of the two floor plans given below, the first is correctly drawn, the second a poor copy which suggests a different arrangement

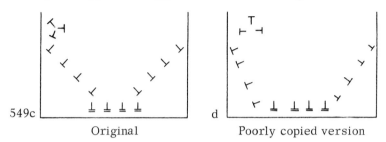

549c   Original   d   Poorly copied version

Comparing (c) and (d) above note the difference between: (1) the slanting lines of four girls each, (2) the relationship of trio members to one another, (3) the relationship of trios to stage left line, and (4) the relationship of the line of boys at the back to the two lines of girls. Choreography must be represented as faithfully as possible; therefore care should be taken in copying scores.

USE OF ARROWS

Arrows are used on floor plans in an obvious way to indicate movement. The arrow head should indicate the point on stage at which the path finishes. Note that pin and movement arrow are separated by a small space.

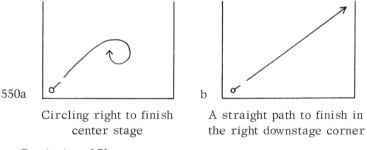

550a   Circling right to finish   b   A straight path to finish in
                  center stage   the right downstage corner

Continuity of Plans

For continuity it is important that one floor plan pick up spatially where the previous one left off. A change in facing direction may have occurred, but the position on stage should tally. Note the following examples:

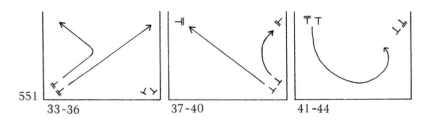

551 33-36   37-40   41-44

Choice of Starting or Finishing Description

In standard usage pins on a floor plan show where the dancers start and arrows the path which is followed, as in Fig. 552 (a). When occasionally statement of an ending position is more practical, the arrow begins where the dancer starts and ends at a pin showing the destination of the path, as in (b).

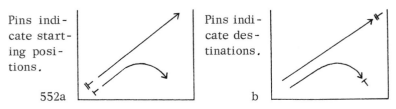

Pins indi-
cate start-
ing posi-
tions.

552a

Pins indi-
cate des-
tinations.

b

Suggestion of Step Direction

The direction of steps producing a path on stage may in most instances be indicated by the relationship between the pin and the point at which the arrow starts. Note the following.

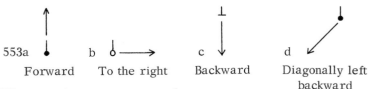

553a   b   c   d

Forward   To the right   Backward   Diagonally left
                                      backward

When turning occurs on a path these indications no longer hold true, but they can give a good first impression of the movement they illustrate. In Fig. 553 (e) the finishing position is shown on the stage plan. A turn must occur, but how, when, and to which side can only be known from the movement description.

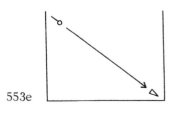

553e

A girl ends upstage right
facing that corner.

Entrance and Exit

To indicate an entrance a pin is placed offstage (outside the stage area) in the appropriate wing, its facing direction signifying that direction faced by the dancer when actually entering. To indicate an exit the arrow must extend beyond the stage area outline through the appropriate wing.

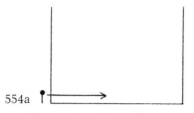

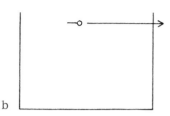

554a   b

A boy enters from the upstage   A girl exits into the first
left corner, facing upstage.   downstage right wing.

Crossing Paths

When the paths of two dancers or of two groups cross, a solid line is drawn for the person passing in front (i.e. who has the "right of way") and a broken line for the person passing behind. In Fig. 555 the boy passes behind the girl.

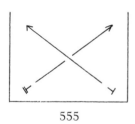

555

Retracing Paths

When a performer retraces his steps on a path, the arrow showing this returning path is drawn slightly shorter and starts within the head of the first arrow. In some cases a double-headed arrow is suitable. When many such paths occur one after the other, it is unnecessary to draw each one, but it is a help to show where the last one finishes.

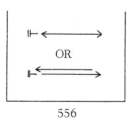

556

Single or Multiple Paths

When possible a single arrow is used to signify progression of a couple or a group. Arrows representing more than one person are either double or wedge-shaped with a number inside the wedge ⑥. Fig. 557 (d) below could be written with the sign ③ instead of ↑.

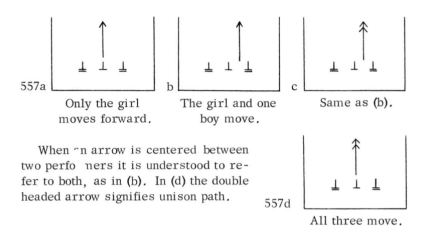

557a   Only the girl   b   The girl and one   c   Same as (b).
moves forward.   boy move.

When an arrow is centered between two performers it is understood to refer to both, as in (b). In (d) the double headed arrow signifies unison path.   557d

All three move.

<u>Unison Movement for Ranks and Files</u>

A number of individual pins representing dancers may be either joined by a line or included in a bracket to indicate that a rank or file moves as a unit.

Four girls in a straight line move forward as a unit.   558a

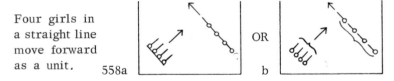

OR   b

GENERAL GROUP INDICATIONS

Two special cases require a method of indicating group shapes or arrangements in a general way (without a pin for each performer): (1) when a group has been established and remains static for some time, and (2) when a detailed composition of a group may not at first be known (as when the notator is making his first quick notes). In both cases the following abbreviations may be used:

<u>General Indication of Formation</u>

Showing the general shape of the group   559a   b   c

A solid group is shaded, a linear formation left empty. Figs. 559 (a) and (b) are solid shapes; (c) is a linear triangular formation. The following are abbreviations of common formations:

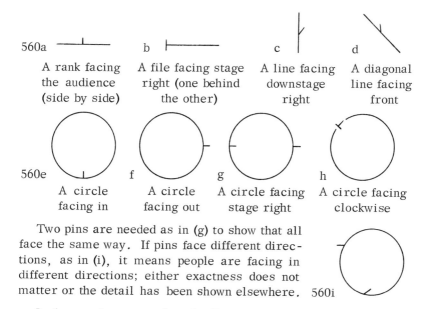

560a
A rank facing
the audience
(side by side)

b
A file facing stage
right (one behind
the other)

c
A line facing
downstage
right

d
A diagonal
line facing
front

560e
A circle
facing in

f
A circle
facing out

g
A circle facing
stage right

h
A circle facing
clockwise

Two pins are needed as in (g) to show that all
face the same way. If pins face different directions, as in (i), it means people are facing in
different directions; either exactness does not
matter or the detail has been shown elsewhere. 560i

In the previous examples the linear indication does not specify
whether the performers are men or women. This is indicated by
use of a white or black pin.

560j
A circle of girls
facing in

k
A circle of boys
facing counter-
clockwise

l
People in an "open
circle" facing
clockwise

Indication of Number of Performers

A number placed in a circle indicates the number of performers.
A single person not facing in any particular direction can be shown
on a stage plan by o , ● , or ◖ .

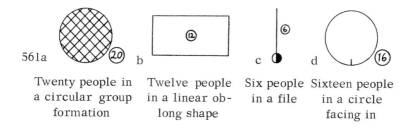

561a
Twenty people in
a circular group
formation

b
Twelve people
in a linear ob-
long shape

c
Six people
in a file

d
Sixteen people
in a circle
facing in

General Indication of Group Action

The overall pattern of group shape and group movement on stage can be shown.

The general stage action indicated in Fig. 562 shows a group of ten people who enter upstage left and move across to the upstage right corner, and a line of three people who enter downstage left and face the group in the corner.

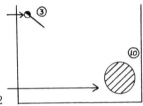

562

Indication of Couples in Group Formations

A formation can be shown by the use of black and white pins to consist of couples arranged with the boy on one side of the girl.

A file of 6 people arranged in couples, each boy behind a girl   563a

A rank of 8 people arranged in couples, each girl on the boy's left

b

Sixteen people, in a square, arranged in couples, each boy on the left of his girl   563c

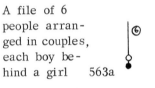

Twelve people in a circle, facing in, each girl on the boy's right

d

ENLARGEMENT OF FLOOR PLAN

A particular change in formation on stage may need to be shown in detail. It is not necessary to enlarge the entire stage area, but just to show the performers in question. The enlargement is usually a square, "lifted," so to speak, from the stage plan.

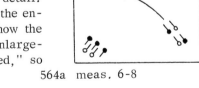

564a meas. 6-8

The action which should occur in the upstage left corner in Fig. 564 (a) is enlarged for clarity in (b) and (c).

564b meas. 6

c meas. 7-8

QUANTITY OF FLOOR PLANS

The number of floor plans needed depends on the frequency and complexity of paths and changes in formations. When a dancer or group stays virtually on the spot, or travels only slightly away and returns, it is not necessary to draw new floor plans. When complex interweavings occur it may be necessary to give a separate plan for each performer, showing the path and the people between whom he passes at each point. Although in group dances there may be no change of formation for some time, it is helpful to have the positions on stage reiterated frequently. There may be a need in rehearsal to start reading in the middle of a score, and so all devices which help the reader pick up the thread of the action quickly are desirable. The reader must always be borne in mind in the writing of any score.

IDENTIFICATION OF THE PERFORMER: PRE-STAFF SIGNS

Performers require identification, both for the score and for floor plans. Letters of the alphabet are usually selected, and the following usages have been found practical - though no hard and fast rules are established, since each piece provides its own particular needs. The identification chosen must be kept throughout the score.

Solos

In most cases a solo requires no special identification. The title of the piece usually establishes whether it is a solo for a man or a girl. If need be, the appropriate pin can be placed under the movement staff at the start as a pre-staff sign, enclosed in a circle to distinguish it from a movement indication pin. This encircling is not needed in the floor plans.

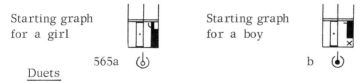

Starting graph
for a girl

Starting graph
for a boy

565a

b

Duets

For a simple duet, it is often enough to use the appropriate pin as in Fig. 566 (a). One can also state B, G (boy, girl), as in (b), or M, W (man, woman), or M, F (male, female). The lettering may be in capitals or in lower case (m,w; m,f). The appropriate letter is placed beneath each staff. On floor plans, when there is only one couple, the pins suffice to identify the dancers.

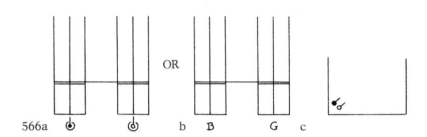

566a   b   B   G   c

Partners, Couple Dances

Many group dances involve couples which need not be specifically identified. It is enough to indicate the relation of the two dancers and the number of couples involved. A circle surrounding two pins signifies "a couple," and a stated number refers to the number of couples, not to individuals.

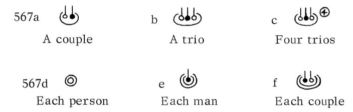

567a   b   c

A couple   A trio   Four trios

567d   e   f

Each person   Each man   Each couple

A double circle means "each;" thus each man, each woman, each couple, etc. may be shown.

Established partners, that is, couples whose members are identified with each other throughout a dance, may be represented by particular choice of letters or numbers. In folk dances it is common for couples to be given numbers: first couple, second couple, and so on. Thus identification can be: M1, W1, M2, W2, M3, W3, etc. On floor plans only the number need be added to the pin.

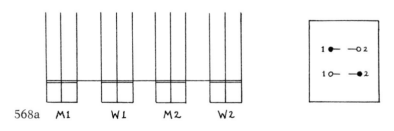

568a   M1   W1   M2   W2

When couples have a distinct identity, that is, play a particular character in a ballet, such individuality may be shown in the choice of letters. Each girl is given an identifying letter to which M is added for her partner. On the stage plan only the letter need be used; pins distinguish boy from girl as in Fig. 568 (b)

A - girl in red   MA - her partner
B - girl in blue   MB - her partner
C - girl in pink   MC - her partner

568b

Large Group or Crowd

When a group consists of members without specific individuality, it may suffice to name the group and to indicate the number of people involved. It is not expected that at any point one particular performer will be singled out. Statement can be made as to the number of men and women in the group.

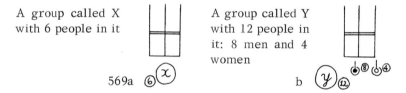

A group called X with 6 people in it   569a

A group called Y with 12 people in it: 8 men and 4 women   b

Smaller Groups and Corps de Ballet

In some group situations the dancers work as a unit and have no individual significance, but at certain points one may need to keep track of each individual in the group. For such situations it is practical to give a letter to the group and to number the dancers in it. Generally the group letter need be stated only once on each floor plan, but if the group breaks up the individual members may be identified by letter and number.

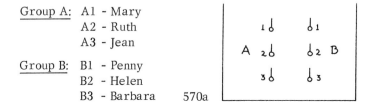

Group A: A1 - Mary
           A2 - Ruth
           A3 - Jean

Group B: B1 - Penny
           B2 - Helen
           B3 - Barbara   570a

When the dancers are in their own group, identification can be kept simple, as in Fig. 570 (a) or (b). Should the dancers mix, each individual will require full identification as in (c).

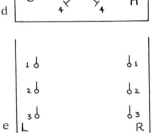

570b

In certain ballets the corps keeps its position on stage for the greater part of the time. The stage left group usually balances the stage right group and those dancers who are in the front remain in front or return to the front after an all-over change of formation. Groups on stage left may be given lower letters, while those on stage right are given higher letters. In (d) each dancer in group G has a counterpart in Group H.

c

d

When groups stay for the greater part of a dance on one side of the stage or the other, the lettering can reflect this by being L for stage left and R for stage right. Members of such groups would then be L1, L2, L3, etc. and R1, R2, R3, etc. as in (e).

e

Large Corps de Ballet and Ensembles

Use of odd and even numbers is helpful to identify individuals in large groups which move in an orderly and symmetrical way. Some large ballets and ensembles, such as the Rockettes at Radio City Music Hall, use formations which require this means of identification. Stage left dancers are given odd numbers and their counterparts on stage right even numbers. Dancers in front are given low numbers and those in the back higher numbers. When groups mix together and later separate, it is then easy to see where individuals belong. In this type of ballet the actual steps are usually simple, the dancer's problem being to find where she belongs and where she must go at each change in formation. Such a system of numbering helps her keep track of her place.

```
  1 ⊥      ⊥ 2                        3⊬     1⊬
  3 ⊥      ⊥ 4                         4⊬    2⊬
  5 ⊥      ⊥ 6               ⊥  ⊥              12  11
  7 ⊥      ⊥ 8               5  6             ↑  ↑
  9 ⊥      ⊥ 10
571a  11 ⊥   ⊥ 12          b        ⊬8    ⊬10
                                   ⊬7     ⊬9
```

A two-line formation   Couples form a circle,
                                  facing clockwise

Dance Dramas

Individual letters should be given in a dramatic dance work in which each dancer has an individual character to portray. These letters may be based on the characters, e.g. H - hermit, Y - youth, M - mother, but as this is not always satisfactory, it may be found better to start at the beginning of the alphabet. The device of giving lower letters to girls and higher letters to boys aids quick identification.

A - the young girl   If there are more than 26 characters
B - her mother   in the dance, single letters may be
J - her father   used for girls and double letters for
K - her suitor   (etc.)   boys.

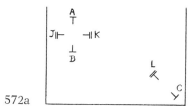

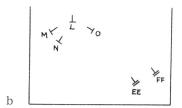

572a   b

PLACEMENT OF IDENTIFICATION BY THE STAGE PINS

In an identification of performers on a stage plan, it is important that letters be easy to read and also that their presence on the plan does not destroy the visual impact of group formations. Letters should be placed upright and near the base of the pin.

Letters are   Letters are too
well propor-   B   ⊣ K   large and should   ꟸ   ⊣ ⋊
tioned and   ⊤   not be placed   ⊤
correctly   ⊣ J   sideways or   ⊣ ⌐
placed.   573a   upside down.   b

Dramatis Personae

At the start of a dance score the list of characters (dramatis personae) should be given. This list provides the identifying letter used for each character portrayed. For library purposes the list can state who performed the roles in the original production or at the time the work was notated.

> A - young girl (Margot Fonteyn)
> B - her lover (Rudolf Nureyev)

Current Cast List

At the time a score is being used for a particular group or company, the list of those dancers presently performing the roles can be inserted. A practical method of doing so is to attach the list to the back cover so that it can be folded inside the score when not in use, and folded out to be in sight no matter which page is being turned. The list may be updated if changes occur.

574

STAGE DIRECTOR'S PLANS

Heretofore we have discussed and illustrated stage plans, written from the performer's point of view, which appear throughout a score next to the movement notation they illustrate. A complete set of plans drawn from the point of view of the audience, however, is most valuable to a director, who must visualize the staging of an entire work. In the director's plans the rectangle representing the stage is drawn upside down.

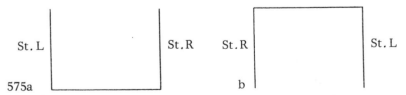

In the performer's score	In the director's score

Group arrangements on a director's plans are the same as in the full score, but upside down, as illustrated below.

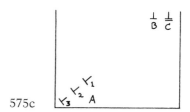

575c

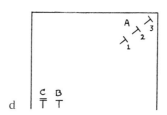

d

Floor plan as it appears in   Floor plan as drawn in the
the dance score   director's set of plans

The director's plans are usually
placed in the back of a dance score,
attached so that they can be removed
and used separately when needed.
The standard sequence in which
these plans are arranged is the ordinary reading direction, starting at the
top and reading from left to right.

575e

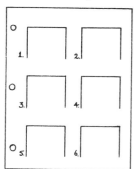

REPEAT SIGNS FOR SCORING

The repeat signs given on pages 346-349 can be freely used in the
process of notating a work, but in a finished manuscript care
should be taken to use only indications which can be followed easily. As a rule reference should be made only to material on the
same page as the repeat signs.

REFERENCE TO ANOTHER PERFORMER

In the repeat signs ╱ and ╱╱ the upper dot can be replaced by
a letter to refer to a specific person.

Perform the same   Perform the opposite side
as A is doing now: of what A is doing now:

In the following examples B performs the same as A, while C
performs the "other side" (the laterally symmetrical version) of
what A is doing. It is presumed that B is only temporarily the
same as A; therefore the two staves are not combined for such a
short time. Repeats can be centered in each measure, as in Fig.
576 (a), or one large sign can be centered on the staff to cover a
whole page, as in (b).

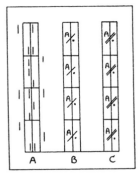
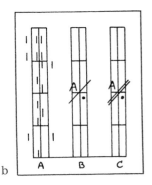

576a

b

Fig. (b) is preferable to (a).

For shorthand notes reference can be made to another performer and to another measure; in the final score such indications
usually should be written out for the reader's benefit.

Do the same as $A\!\!\!/_4$ Do the "other side" $B\!\!\!/_9$
A did in meas. 4   of B in meas. 9

REPEAT SIGNS WITHIN FLOOR PLANS

For simplicity both in reading and
in writing, repeat signs may be used
within the floor plan, particularly
where identical actions occur. There
may be four groups on the stage, as
illustrated in Fig. 577, each of which
performs the same change in formation. Pins and arrows are shown for
one group; repeat signs indicate that
all groups are to do the same. It is
presumed that the other groups have
been described in recent plans so that
no doubt exists as to their identity.

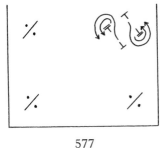

577

All four groups
are alike

RELATIONSHIP INDICATIONS IN THE SCORE

While floor plans indicate relationships of the dancers and are cor-
related to the movement score, it is advantageous to pinpoint within
the movement score the exact moment at which a relationship occurs or changes. For such indications either a meeting line is
used or stage plan pins are inserted within the movement score.

THE MEETING LINE

The meeting line is a stroke placed on the right side of the staff to indicate that a specific performer meets or passes another person at that moment. The angle of the meeting line and placement of an indication for the other person is read from the point of view of the performer beside whose staff the symbol is placed. Identification of the other person may range from a general statement signifying "someone" to indication of a specific individual.

578a ◎   b ◎   c ◉   d ◉

Each has a person   A person is   A girl is in   A man is
in front, i.e. face   behind you   front of you   behind you
   each other.

578e A╱   f ╲J   g y   h Z

A is diagon-   J is diagon-   Y is above   Z is below
ally left in   ally right in   you.   and behind
front of you.   front of you   you.

The addition of a pin to the most suitable meeting line is needed to show a vertical relationship or any three-dimensional situation.

The meeting line may signify either the moment of passing (to show the relation of two dancers at that point) or the aim of a path (establishment of a certain position in relation to another performer at the destination).

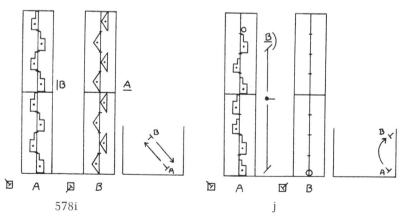

        578i   j

B passes on the right side   The aim of A's path is to
of A; A passes in front of B.   end with B in front of her.

FLOOR PLAN PINS WRITTEN IN THE SCORE

Straight back pins (tacks) used for stage plans can also be placed alongside the movement score to facilitate reading sequences in which there is partnering.

In Fig. 579 (a) A and B start back to back. B turns toward A who walks around and takes an arabesque placing her left hand on his right shoulder and her right hand on his right wrist. A and B then face each other and B lifts A (carries with grasping, hands on waist). Placement of stage pins within the score makes it easier to relate movement instructions directly to stage placement. These pins, extracted from the floor plan, are easy to read when performers face any forward or sideward direction, but become more difficult to read when they face backward on stage. In such cases the meeting line may prove more practical. In the following examples first the relationship of the dancers one to another

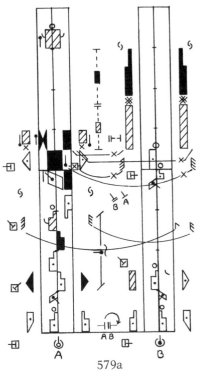

579a

is shown, then two possible placements of this relationship on stage.

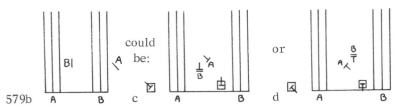

579b

The diagonal relationship of A and B is the same whether they are facing downstage or upstage. Fig. (b) is the same regardless of how this relationship is placed on stage; (c) is easy to read, whereas (d) may not be so easy.

CHAPTER 23

Supporting on Various Parts of the Body

KNEELING, SITTING, LYING

In lowering the body to the ground, the performer usually follows the sequence of passing through kneeling, sitting, and lying in the forward or side direction. In the backward or diagonally backward direction, the progression may omit kneeling. In rising the reverse process usually takes place. Many variations exist in transitions from standing on the feet to supporting on the floor on other parts of the body. Changes of support can occur while the body is on the floor. Only the simplest and most commonly used will be dealt with in this book; complex floor work and acrobatics will be presented in Book II.

GENERAL STATEMENT

In Motif Writing the broad statement of an action which results in a support is made more specific by indicating which part of the body takes the weight. (See page 338 for the support sign ⌐.)

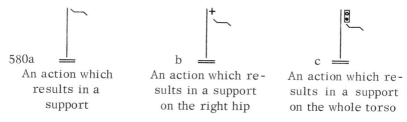

580a	b	c
An action which results in a support	An action which results in a support on the right hip	An action which results in a support on the whole torso

SPECIFIC STATEMENT, ABBREVIATED DESCRIPTION

When the full staff is used a description of supporting on different parts of the body can still be kept simple, in a way comparable to Motif Writing. Placement of signs for specific parts of the body in the support columns indicates that those parts are carrying the body's weight. Direction symbols placed in the support columns normally signify standing on the feet. Signs for the feet are used to write a broad statement of weight on the feet without specifying direction. A head sign in either right or left support column indicates supporting on the head.

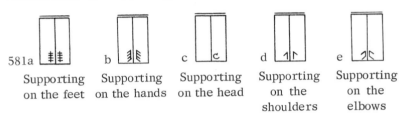

581a
Supporting on the feet   b Supporting on the hands   c Supporting on the head   d Supporting on the shoulders   e Supporting on the elbows

KNEELING

For the weight to be placed on the knee the body must be lowered until the knee touches the floor. Such lowering is understood in brief statements and need not be written, but when timing or other detail must be shown, lowering should be specifically indicated.

Weight is placed on the right knee (bending the left leg is understood).   582a

The left leg bends and weight is then also placed on the right knee.   b

SPECIFIC DESCRIPTION OF KNEELING

Kneeling is comparable to standing in the use of direction and levels, and in shifting the weight. The use of the lower leg to help keep balance is comparable to use of the foot in standing.

Levels of Kneeling

A convention is used to indicate the three main levels of kneeling comparable to the three main levels established for standing on the feet.

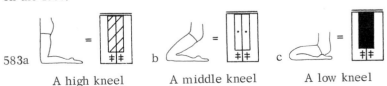

583a   A high kneel   b   A middle kneel   c   A low kneel

In a high kneel the body is as high as possible on that support, the hips being directly over the knees. The thigh is vertical and the weight is on the knee itself with the lower leg resting on the floor. In a low kneel the body is as low as it can be on the knees, which are totally bent; weight is centered over the ankles, hips resting on heels. In a progression from a high to a low kneel the weight is first centered over the knees, then over the lower leg, and finally over the ankles. Middle level is the point between a high and a low kneel. Although the weight is no longer on the knee itself in a low or middle level kneel, because of common usage the position is written as a kneel and not as a support on the lower leg.

Direction of Kneeling

Direction of kneeling and walking on the knees is comparable to that for stepping. Place is beneath the center of weight and directions are judged from center or from the previous knee support. The foot of the kneeling leg usually contacts the ground in the process of kneeling as a help in lowering the weight, but as a rule this contact is not written. The direction of the kneel is judged by where the knee and not the rest of the leg is placed.

584a

b

The right knee supports in place next to the left foot.

The right knee "steps" backward from the previous support.

A low forward step often leads into a kneel. In an ordinary sized step the knee will support approximately next to the other foot. A long step must be taken to produce an open forward-backward (fourth position) kneel.

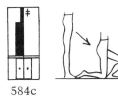   or

584c

d   e

Kneeling after an ordinary step

Kneeling at the end of a long step (fourth position kneel)

Fig. (e) states the motion (direction and level) of lowering into a kneel. From the starting position the left foot takes a long step forward (three degrees) while at the same time the body lowers to a forward support on the right knee. Each support is judged from the starting point where the feet were together.

When all the weight is on the knee in a starting position, the notation may be as in Fig. 584 (f) or as in (g), which uses the attached symbol. Partial weight is discussed on page 448.

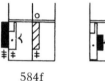

584f   g

In performing the position of (f) people often have the impression that foot and knee share the weight equally. Fig. (h) shows the weight equally divided.

584h

Placement of the Lower Leg

The lower leg rests on the ground to help maintain balance in kneeling. Any definite placement of the lower leg must be written. This may be a lift off the ground as in Fig. 585 (b) below, or a placement on the floor resulting from thigh rotation, as in (c).

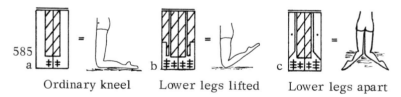

585 a   Ordinary kneel   b   Lower legs lifted   c   Lower legs apart

The standing position prior to a kneel may dictate placement of the lower legs. The following examples show movement into a kneeling position, and the destination stated as a position.

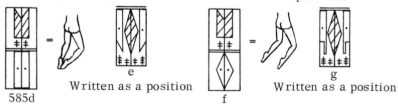

585d   Written as a position   e   f   Written as a position   g

For Fig. 585 (d) start with the feet together, kneel forward into a second position kneel (direction is judged from place). Fig. (e) shows the result of this action written as a starting position.

Use of the Ball of the Foot

When the lower leg rests on the ground, the question arises as to whether the ankle and foot are extended with the instep touching the ground, or whether the ball of the foot is on the ground with the ankle flexed. When nothing is stated, the choice is left open to the performer. The movement context may suggest one or the other usage. If this detail is important it must be written. For an extended foot the ankle may be shown to be stretched, or the top of the foot to contact the ground. The sign ⟨o⟩ placed in a leg column refers to the foot. The white circle in the sign indicates the top of the foot, the upper side. Contact with the floor is indicated by using the neutral contact hook ∪ .*

The toes are
tucked under in
preparation for
taking weight

586a

Instep touching the
floor. This could
be written as ankle
extended:

b

WALKING ON THE KNEES

Walking on the knees is comparable to walking on the feet with respect to direction of steps, shift of weight, etc. The knee pre-sign must be used to show that each direction symbol in the support column refers to the knees. Once the pre-sign has been stated, however, a caret < or > may be employed to indicate reference to the part of the body previously stated.

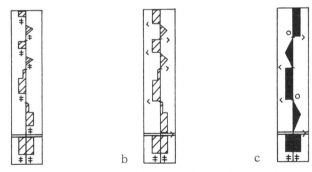

587a   b   c

Fig. 587 (b) is the same as (a) but written with carets instead of repeated knee pre-signs. Fig. (c) shows low steps on the knees.

* See Appendix B, note 26.

Size of Steps on the Knees

An ordinary step on the knee is the size that is naturally comfortable for the performer. This size is automatically reduced as
the kneeling level is lowered; only relatively small steps can be
taken in low level. Reduction in size is understood and generally
need not be indicated. With effort
larger knee steps can be taken.
Pre-signs for length are used as
with ordinary steps. When distance covered is important the
number of ordinary walking step
lengths traveled can be indicated
in a path sign placed alongside
the notation. (See page 449.)

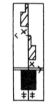 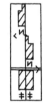

588a   b

Short steps   Long steps

Change of Level on the Knees

Change of level on the knees can occur in place or during transference of weight. Observe that though there is a backward displacement of the center of gravity in sinking to a low from a high
kneel, the description is still one of lowering in place.

From standing,
lower to the
knees. Follow
this by sinking
and rising on
the knees.

589a

Step into a high
4th position on
the knees, then
sink, closing the
knees together.
(Note use of a
staple for pos-
ition writing.)

b

Combination of Support on Knee and Foot

A direction symbol in the support
column without any pre-sign or caret
always means supporting on the foot.
The transition from supporting on
the foot to supporting on the knee
may alternate sides, as in Fig. 590
(a), or the weight may be taken onto
the knee of the same leg, as in (b)
which shows a knee crawl.

590a   b

When weight is placed at the same time on one knee and the other foot, the level of the kneel automatically modifies the level of the foot support. Therefore the exact level of the foot support need not be stated.

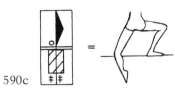

590c

A high support on the knee automatically dictates the level of the right support.

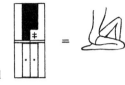

d

A low kneel dictates that the low support on the left leg will be extremely bent.

The sideward step on the left foot automatically adjusts the level of the right leg to ordinary low level.

590e

Transition from Kneeling to Standing

Because a direction symbol in the support column without any pre-sign means supporting on the foot at the stated ordinary step level, Fig. 591 (a) shows an ordinary forward low step and (b) an ordinary forward middle level step following a high kneel. Fig. (c) shows the transition from low to middle level which will occur in (b) but which generally need not be written. Fig. (d) shows standing up in place after kneeling. In (e) a high step follows a low kneel. The unstated but understood transition is: rising to a high kneel, place the right foot forward to take the weight, and rise while the weight is being transferred. In such a simple description no part of this transition is important or in any way to be stressed. In this example it happens too quickly for the performer to be concerned with details.

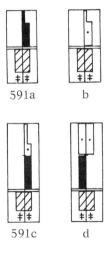

591a   b

591c   d

591e

SITTING

Sitting, i.e. supporting on the hip bones (the tuberosities of the ischia), is written by placing the hip sign in the support column. When the weight is on one hip, the other is slightly off the floor.

Sitting on both hips
592a

Sitting on right hip
b

Sitting on left hip
c

The general sign for hip + has two interpretations: (1) for touching - the break at the top of the leg, and (2) for supporting - that part of the lower pelvis which normally takes the weight in a sitting position, either on both hips or on one hip. Specific signs for parts of the single hip area are seldom needed; they will be presented in Book II.

SPECIFIC DESCRIPTION OF SITTING

Levels of Sitting

The level of sitting is determined by the previous point of support. If the performer starts standing on the floor, a middle level sit will be on the floor; a high level sit will be on an object above floor level. Sitting on the floor in low level can occur only when the floor slants downward.

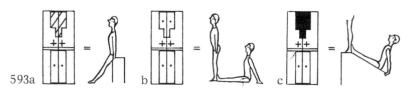

593a

A high level sit: above the previous point of support

A middle level sit: horizontal with the previous point of support

A low level sit: below the previous point of support

Legs Resting on the Floor

When sitting on the floor, though the hips are supporting, it is understood that the legs will normally be resting on the floor. All such leg gestures are in middle level. It is not possible to perform low gestures unless one is sitting above floor level, as on a table, etc.

594

Legs just off the Floor

The legs may be lifted slightly from the floor, either in a starting position, or as a release from touching.

Starting position with the legs just above the floor 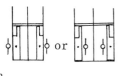 595a

Releasing the legs from the floor after an understood contact b

In Fig. 595 (a) the pin for above ◊ modifies the main direction symbol. (See Chapter 26 for the use of pins and deviations.)

Specific Contact of the Legs with the Floor

A definite sliding action may occur in changing positions of the legs resting on the floor. Where they are applicable hooks for the various parts of the foot are used to indicate touching or sliding on the floor. When contact is of the whole leg or of an unspecified part, the neutral contact indication ⌣ is used.*

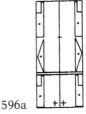
596a

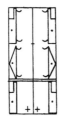
b

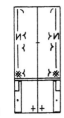
c

No specific performance is stated; sliding may occur.

Sliding the legs is indicated.

As the legs bend, slide the whole foot on the floor; when they stretch, slide whole foot to heel.

Distance of Sitting**

A support on the hips may be either close to or far away from a previous support on the feet. For practical purposes the length of the leg has been taken as the measurement of distance, providing a six-degree scale identical with that for contraction of the legs. When no distance is indicated the hips support at the full length of the legs. The shorter the distance, the more the legs will be bent. The following examples show no details of transition from standing to sitting, but only a broad statement of the result to be achieved.

* See Appendix B, note 26.   ** See Appendix B, note 27.

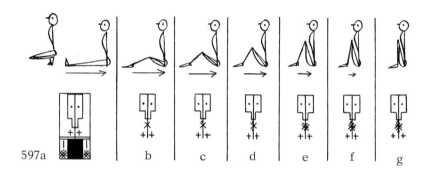

597a | b | c | d | e | f | g

Description of Starting Position

The starting position for sitting may be described in two ways. Fig. 598 (a) shows weight on the hip with direction and degree of contraction for the legs; (b) shows direction and distance of sitting from an unwritten but understood standing position. The latter method will produce the desired direction and degree of contraction for the legs. If leg rotation is important it should be added.

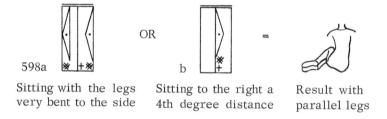

598a   OR   b   =

| Sitting with the legs very bent to the side | Sitting to the right a 4th degree distance | Result with parallel legs |

WAYS OF SITTING DOWN ON THE FLOOR

The following examples show some typical transitions from standing to sitting. Specific details are not given. When sitting follows a support on the knee the distance of the support on the hips will automatically be the length of the thigh; no space measurement need be added.

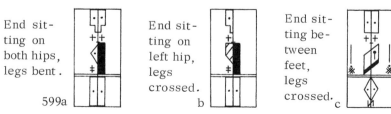

End sitting on both hips, legs bent.

599a

End sitting on left hip, legs crossed.

b

End sitting between feet, legs crossed.

c

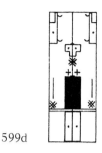 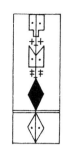 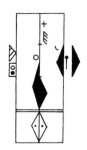

599d   e   f

End sitting with   End sitting between   End on right hip and
both legs forward.   legs, knees on floor. hand, leaning to right.

LYING, SUPPORTING ON THE WHOLE TORSO

For starting positions the most direct description of lying is to
write the whole torso sign indicating with a pin which side is taking
the weight. The signs for the main whole torso surfaces are:

Front [symbol]   Back [symbol]   Right   [symbol]   Left   [symbol]
                                   side   side

Symbols for lying prone or supine may be placed in either the
right or left support column; to indicate lying on the side, however,
the symbol should be placed in the appropriate column so that the
center line will not obstruct the pin.

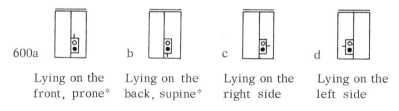

600a   b   c   d

Lying on the   Lying on the   Lying on the   Lying on the
front, prone*   back, supine*   right side   left side

SPECIFIC DESCRIPTION OF LYING

Placement of the Limbs

When no indication is given for placement of arms and legs, a
simple or comfortable position may be assumed.

All gestures of the arms and legs can only be in middle or high
level while lying on the floor. The examples below show possible
placement of the limbs for the main starting positions.

* See Appendix B, note 28.

601a   b   c   d

In Figs. 601 (a) and (b) arms and legs are in their normal anatomical position with the legs extended and the arms by the side of the body. In (c) the right arm is out to the side, resting on the floor, the left arm is along the body. In (d) the limbs are drawn in. For analysis of direction and level for the limbs while lying on the floor see pages 418 to 420.

Level of Lying

When the performer is lying on the floor the level of support is middle. High level lying occurs if the floor slopes upward, i.e. if the new point is higher than the previous support, low level if downward, i.e. lower than the previous support.

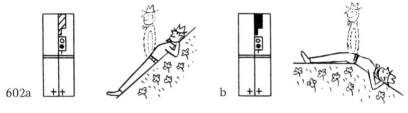

602a   b

Lying back on an up-   Lying backward on a
hill slope (higher   downhill slope (lower
than level of hips)   than level of hips)

WAYS OF LYING DOWN

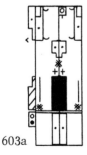   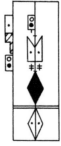   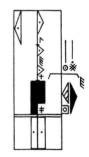

603a   b   c

Lying supine   Lying supine be-   Lying on right side
after sitting   tween the legs   after dropping on to
backward   after kneeling   right knee and hip

CANCELLATIONS

SPECIFIC RULES FOR SITTING AND LYING

As soon as supports occur on parts of the body other than feet and knees, the following departures from the previously establish-ed rules take effect:

1. A space in the support column no longer means absence of sup-port. Springing into the air, jumping up from sitting or lying is a specialized action which must be specifically written.

2. Limbs at floor level are understood to rest on the floor unless written as being above floor level.

3. The addition of a new support such as a hand does not automati-cally mean that all the weight is taken on that part of the body; it will be an addition to the existing supports.

4. From the context of the movement or from release signs it can be seen when certain supports are released. For example, when a dancer is sitting and supporting on one hand a subsequent upward gesture for the appropriate arm will automatically re-lease weight from that hand. Details on mixed supports, walk-ing on all fours, acrobatics, etc. will be given in Book II.

UNDERSTOOD CHANGE FOR CENTER OF GRAVITY

In changes of level while supporting on the feet or on the knees there is in fact a change in the situation of the center of gravity. This change is understood even though it is not specifically stated with a center of gravity indication. Similarly, when a dancer lowers through kneeling or sitting to lying or rises through sitting or kneeling to standing, there is an unwritten but understood change in the center of gravity (see Chapter 24).

Note the following rule:

Changes in level of the center of gravity which are indicated by change of supports can be cancelled by a subsequent change of sup-port. An unqualified direction symbol in the support column is un-derstood to mean an ordinary support on the foot in the stated level.

The following examples give only an outline of the action. The process of shifting the weight to one knee and other necessary ad-justments are not stated.

604a

b

c

| Rising from the knees by stepping forward | Rising from sitting by stepping onto the right foot | Rising from lying by stepping forward on the left foot |

CANCELLATION OF LYING

Raising any part of the torso from a lying position will release weight from that part. Note the following examples:

605a

b

c

By being moved back-ward high, the chest no longer is weight-bearing.

The whole torso lifts backward high, leaving the weight on the hips.

Shifting the pelvis upward places the weight on the shoulders and feet.

CANCELLATION FOR MIXED SUPPORTS

Specific gestures for a limb which is supporting, for instance, when on all fours, will automatically release weight from that limb. When no specific direction is stated the release sign is used.

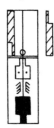

606a

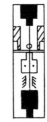

b

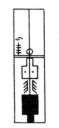

c

Gestures for left leg and right arm release weight from left foot and right hand.

Because both legs gesture the weight is momentarily placed on both hands.

As (a), but only a slight lifting of hand and foot shown by release signs.

READING MATERIAL: KNEEL, SIT, LIE

Three Delsarte Falls from "Fundamental Training Exercises"
ⓒ 1970 by Ted Shawn

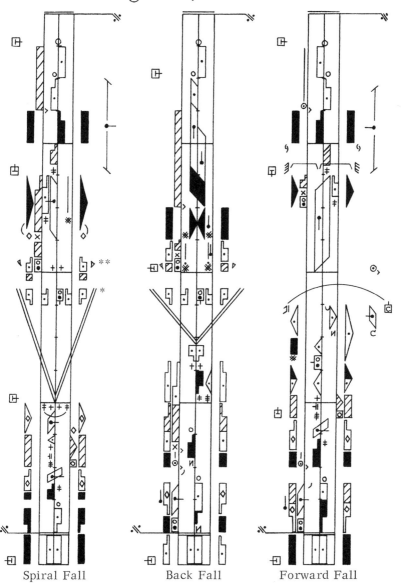

Spiral Fall   Back Fall   Forward Fall

Fig. 607   * See page 468   ** See page 478

CHAPTER 24

Equilibrium, Loss of Balance

THE CENTER OF GRAVITY

The center of gravity, or center of weight, is that point in the body from which or on which the body can be suspended or poised in equilibrium. For the purposes at hand the terms "center of gravity" and "center of weight" are interchangeable. The center of gravity has no fixed location in the body, its exact position depending on the build of the individual and on the position taken. When the arms are raised the center of gravity rises; when the trunk bends it lowers. At certain moments it can even lie outside the body itself, as will be explained in Book II. For general purposes, however, in a normal erect standing position the center of gravity is understood to be located in the upper sacral region, or, in broader terms, in the upper area of the pelvic girdle.

THE LINE OF GRAVITY

The line of gravity is an imaginary vertical line passing through the center of gravity. No matter what the position or angle of the body, the line of gravity remains vertical. The center of gravity is directly above the feet in a normal standing position. As seen in profile, the line of gravity passes through the ear and hip and just in front of the ankle bone.  608

UNSPECIFIED CHANGES FOR THE CENTER OF GRAVITY

The following actions include a major change for the center of gravity without such a statement being made:

1. Progressions of the body as a whole through transference of

weight, e.g. walking, as in Fig. 609 (a).

2. Progressions across the floor through springing, traveling leaps or jumps, etc. as in (b).

3. Changes in level of supports; rising and sinking as in (c).

4. Vertical rising into the air as in (d), where an extra high spring is indicated by the path sign outside.

5. Supporting on different parts of the body, changes from standing to kneeling, sitting, etc. as in (e).

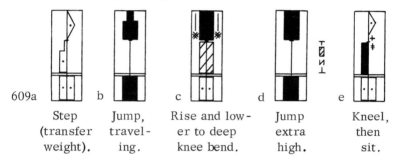

609a	b	c	d	e
Step (transfer weight).	Jump, traveling.	Rise and lower to deep knee bend.	Jump extra high.	Kneel, then sit.

SPECIFIED CHANGES FOR THE CENTER OF GRAVITY

Action of the center of gravity is specifically described for:

a) Shift in balance, variation in placement of weight over the supporting surface

b) Loss of balance, falling

c) Special situations of the center of gravity in relation to the point of support as are needed in acrobatics, gymnastics, etc.

METHOD OF WRITING CENTER OF GRAVITY

The symbol for the center of gravity is ● *. (Note that this sign is also used for a focal point when placed outside the staff or when placed on the edge or corner of a turn sign to indicate turning to a focal point; see page 111.) Defined changes in the situation of the center of gravity are indicated by the center of gravity sign with a direction symbol or a position sign (pin). Indications for center of gravity movements are usually placed in the left third column. The right third column or either of the leg gesture col-

___
* See Appendix B, note 29.

umns may be used when these are free. The indications may be placed outside the staff when the usual columns are full.

GENERAL SITUATION OF THE CENTER OF GRAVITY

Direction and level for movements of the center of gravity are judged from the point of support. This point of support may be a chair, table, another person, etc., but is usually the floor. In the normal upright position, the point of support (the feet on the floor) is place middle: ⊡ , and the situation of the center of gravity is place high: ⬚ , being directly above the point of support.

The Main Levels for the Center of Gravity

When the body is in balance the center of gravity is in place, that is, on the line of gravity. The three main levels on this line of gravity are:

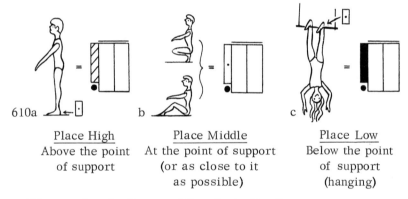

Place High	Place Middle	Place Low
Above the point of support	At the point of support (or as close to it as possible)	Below the point of support (hanging)

610a   b   c

Distance for the Center of Gravity in Standing

To provide a scale of measurement for general purposes of movement notation (where scientific exactness is not necessary), we adopt a convention of measuring distances in terms of body lengths, these being easily observed.

The distance of the center of gravity in a normal standing position is considered to be the length of the legs from the point of support. The center of gravity is lowered toward the point of support by bending the legs. A scale of six degrees of lowering coincides with the six degrees of contracting when the legs are in place. Both scales indicate destination: the exact degree of contraction to be reached or the degree of distance from the point of support.

The Six-Degree Scale on the Vertical Line*

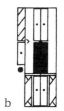

611

Deep Knee Bends

The emphasis of a movement in which the knees bend and thereby lower the body to the floor may be on either the leg contraction or the descent of the center of gravity. This difference in emphasis may be shown by the choice of description. Even a slight lowering may be described as an action of the center of gravity. The following examples illustrate use of the center of gravity description. See page 175 for knee bends written in terms of leg contractions.

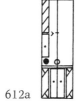

612a   b

Deep knee bend with feet parallel (squat)

The same, showing the low support as well

In Fig. 612 (a) no change of level has been written in the support column; it is understood that the usual way to lower the center of gravity while supporting on the feet is to bend the legs. The low

* See Appendix B, note 30.

support need not be indicated, but common practice includes it as a reading aid, as illustrated in (b), (c), and (d).

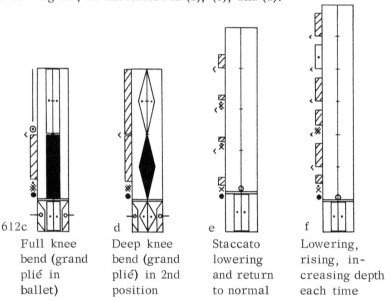

612c	d	e	f
Full knee bend (grand plié in ballet)	Deep knee bend (grand plié) in 2nd position	Staccato lowering and return to normal	Lowering, rising, increasing depth each time

A return to normal for the center of gravity may be written with the back to normal sign as in Fig. 612 (c), or, when the rising is to be stressed, with the place high symbol as illustrated in (d), (e), and (f). Fig. (d) illustrates correct level for the knee bend in second position in classical ballet.

STABILITY, BALANCE, EQUILIBRIUM

As long as the line of gravity falls within the area of the base of the support, the body does not fall. The line of gravity in supporting on the feet must fall within the area of the foot or, when the weight is on both, the area bounded by the two feet. In general the larger the area, the greater the stability. Thus it can be seen that standing with the feet apart is a more stable position than standing on one foot on half toe.

Shift of Weight

When nothing specific is written it is assumed that the body is in balance. The precise centering of any shift of the line of gravity over the area of the supporting base is indicated by middle level pins (tacks). The whole range of these pins is applicable to

shifting the center of gravity. Center (in
balance) is shown by the center pin which
may be drawn ⧾ or ⧿. A center of gravity shift is not to be confused with a pelvic shift in which the pelvis is displaced
from its normal position in the body.

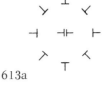

613a

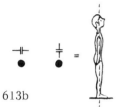 = 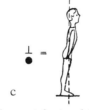 = 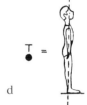 =

613b

The weight is centered.	The weight is shift-ed forward over the metatarsal joint.	The weight is shifted backward over the heels.

c   d

Certain actions require an automatic adjustment of weight in
order to maintain balance. Such adjustments need not be written;
only exceptions are indicated. A typical example is the tilting forward of the whole torso. For the performer to maintain centered
balance the pelvis must travel slightly backward. It is possible to
keep the weight forward by muscular control. It is also possible
to shift the weight much farther back than is necessary, as illustrated in (g).

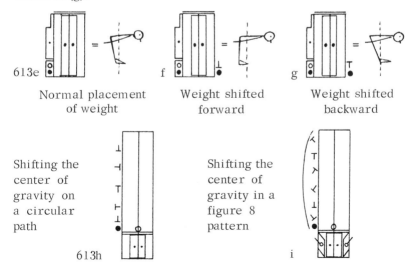

613e

Normal placement of weight	Weight shifted forward	Weight shifted backward

f   g

Shifting the
center of
gravity on
a circular
path

613h

Shifting the
center of
gravity in a
figure 8
pattern

i

For consecutive shifting movements as in Fig. (i) the vertical bow helps to show phrasing (continuity of action). A passing state is expressed by placing the pins within a similar round vertical bow, as in Fig. 614 (c); at the end of this bow an automatic return to normal is understood. (See deviations, page 443.)

Timing of Center of Gravity Shifts

Duration of a shift for the center of gravity may be shown by a duration line following the pin (destination) or the pin within an increase sign (motion). If the result of a shift is not to be kept, the shift may be indicated within a vertical "passing state" bow.

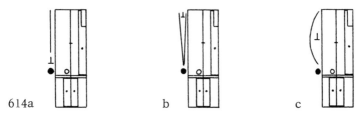

614a   b   c

In each of the above the weight is taken forward while the leg is raised. The forward shift of the center of gravity takes two counts. In Fig. 614 (a) the center of gravity ends forward; in (b) it ends forward of its previous situation and in (c) it has returned to normal at the conclusion of the passing state bow.

Retention of Center of Gravity Shift

The weight can be kept shifted in a specific direction during subsequent steps, etc. This placement of weight may be important for technical or expressive reasons. The hold sign o used as a reminder to retain placement of weight must later be cancelled by a return to normal indication.

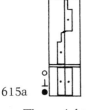 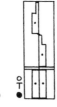 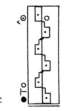

615a   b   c

The weight is kept shifted forward.	The weight is kept shifted backward.	The weight is kept shifted to the right until the feet close.

Elimination of Natural Resilience

In a normal walk a natural resilience results in a slight up and down movement of the center of gravity. This resilience is greater in running, and occurs during slight springs in middle level. Such natural pliancy of the legs is not specifically written. When it should not occur and the center of gravity should be kept at a precise level, the hold sign o is used after the center of gravity sign. The following examples indicate a walk and a run without any rise and fall and a jump in which the legs leave the ground but the body does not rise, as occurs in terre à terre steps in ballet. Fig. 616 (d) states that the level established when kneeling is to be retained in the steps which follow; there will be no raising of the center of gravity and no pliancy. If pliancy is to be permitted the ad lib. sign) is placed next to the retention sign, as in (e).

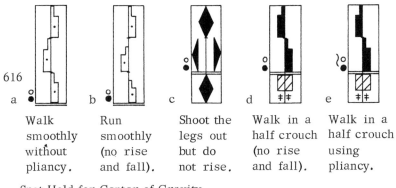

616

a Walk
smoothly
without
pliancy.

b Run
smoothly
(no rise
and fall).

c Shoot the
legs out
but do
not rise.

d Walk in a
half crouch
(no rise
and fall).

e Walk in a
half crouch
using
pliancy.

Spot Hold for Center of Gravity

When the center of gravity holds its situation during a directional step, the sign for a retention on the spot ◈ (spot hold) is used to counteract the normal displacement in the direction of the step.

During fast side to side steps, the center of gravity remains on the same spot (no right and left shift). 617a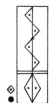

Center of gravity does not move with the step, it remains where it was. b

In Fig. 617 (b) the center of gravity does not move to the side on the step producing a momentary off-balance situation. The above actions can only happen at a reasonably quick tempo.

The center of gravity can remain centered, traveling on an undeviating path,
even though the steps zig-zag. Fig. (c)
illustrates a typical example. Normally
diagonal steps take the center of gravity
from side to side, but as the steps are
at a reasonable speed the center of gravity can be held centered, at the same
time traveling on a straight line forward.
The path sign outside shows the undeviating aim to be straight forward (see page
451 for undeviating aim).

617c

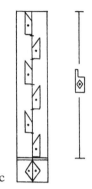

MOBILITY, CENTER OF GRAVITY LEADING

In an ordinary walk the center of gravity is understood to be set
in motion at the start of each step. Normally the center of gravity
moves forward as the free leg extends and contacts the floor in preparation for taking over the weight of the body. In both Figs. 618
(a) and (b) the center of gravity starts
to move in anticipation of the new step
approximately at the moment indicated
by the arrow. Until that point the
weight is understood to be centered.
Whether the leg gestures forward prior
to the step as in (b) or not, the center
of gravity will start moving forward at
this point.

618a

b

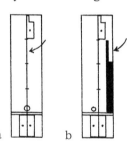

To indicate that the center of gravity
is set in motion sooner and to show the
timing of the motion, the symbol for the
center of gravity displacement is placed
within a vertical bow which slightly over-
laps the following step. Fig. (c) shows
this occurring without any preliminary
gesture and (d) with a preceding forward
leg gesture.

618c

d

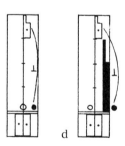

In continuous steps in one direction, the center of gravity keeps
moving in that direction. When a step in place occurs the center
of gravity may or may not come to rest, depending on what follows
and on the speed of progression. Note the following examples:

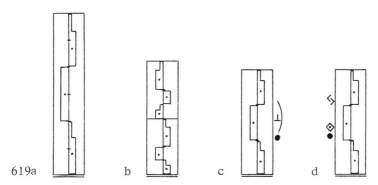

In slow steps, as in Fig. 619 (a), it is natural for the center of weight to come to rest on the step in place and difficult to keep it moving at a slow speed. Conversely, it is difficult to keep the center of gravity from continuing to move forward when such a pattern is performed quickly, as in (b). When continuation of movement of the center of gravity is important, it is indicated as in (c); when the center of gravity must remain centered for the step in place, a spot hold is written as in (d) and cancelled on the following step.

Momentary Loss of Balance

A slight falling movement (a tombé in ballet) results when the center of gravity passes beyond the base support and hence is momentarily unsupported before weight is taken over by a new support. This is expressed as center of gravity "leading," and written with the center of gravity sign by itself within a vertical bow. (See part leading, page 463.) Fig. 620 shows a typical example in which a tombé occurs before a long step. By the end of the bow the falling action has ceased.

620

FALLING, PRECIPITATION, LOSS OF BALANCE

When the center of gravity moves away from the base of the support, loss of balance occurs and the body is falling. Once balance is lost the body will continue to fall until a new point of support is provided.

Note that in a jump there is no point of support. The center of gravity is carried along in the body and hence there is no balance or imbalance. Loss of balance could occur on landing, i.e. on the establishment of a new point of support.

Direction of Center of Gravity Movement

Falling is written with the center of gravity sign followed by the appropriate direction symbol. Direction and level for center of gravity movements are judged in relation to the point of support.

Backward middle is backward of and on the same level as the point of support. Backward high is backward of and higher than the point of support. Forward high is forward of and higher than the point of support. Forward middle is forward of and on the same level as the point of support. The six degrees of distance used on the vertical line (see page 401) are also applicable to distances on the horizontal and slanting lines. Full details of these will be given in Book II.

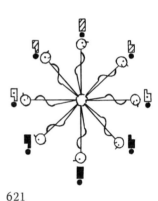

621

Incomplete Fall

In an incomplete fall the weight is usually caught while the center of gravity is still in the high area, before the body reaches the ground. Loss of balance can be sudden or can occur gradually. Regaining balance may be gradual, though most often it is rapid.

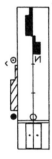

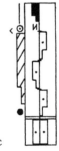

622a

Balance is lost over counts 1 and 2, and regained on count 3.

b

Balance is lost on count 1, and not regained until count 4.

c

Balance is gradually lost during the first 3 steps and is regained on the 4th.

A state of imbalance cannot physically be held. Fig. (b) is possible because the body is in motion. The physical sensation on counts 2 and 3 is that of running down hill.

Falling to the Floor

When the body falls to the floor, the level of the center of gravity changes to middle, horizontal. Below are two common falls written without any specific performance details.

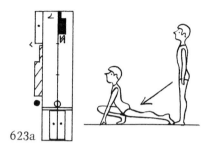

623a

b

The fall is caught by a lunge on the right foot. The center of gravity is then centered above the new support.

A backward falling, known as a "prat fall."

When the new support after a fall is on a part of the torso such as the hips, as in Fig. 623 (b), the fall is concluded. The center of gravity has reached floor level and is supported on a part which has no "limb" to provide distance from the point of support, so no cancellation of the center of gravity in motion is needed.

Falls Written without Specifying Center of Gravity Motion

By using the signs for body sections (see page 252) the notator can show movements which include the action of falling. When emphasis is on the center of gravity motion, it should be included in the description.

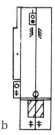

624a

b

Falling backward: the chest to ankles moving backward middle in one piece.

Falling forward: the chest to knees moving forward middle in one piece.

CANCELLATIONS

Changes of Level

1. A change of level written with a contraction sign is automatically cancelled by the next indication unless a hold sign is used.

625a An ordinary low level step forward follows the deep knee bend.

b Degree of bend remains.

c The degree of knee bend is held until cancelled when the feet close.

2. A change stated in terms of the center of gravity must be cancelled by: (a) another center of gravity indication,
(b) a return to normal for the center of gravity, or
(c) a support on a part of the body other than the feet.

  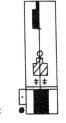

626a The center of gravity remains down until the step forward when it comes part way up.

b The center of gravity returns to normal, i.e. normal level for a low step.

c Kneeling cancels the previous center of gravity level. The final step is a normal level support.

Miscellaneous Cancellation Rules

Cancellation of center of gravity displacement (shifting) is shown as in Fig. 615 (c) or by using the sign ⊣⊢ . Center of gravity leading has automatic cancellation as with all passing state indications (see Fig. 620). Elimination of natural resilience is cancelled by ⊙ . Falling is cancelled as indicated in Figs. 622 (a-c) and Figs. 623 (a) and (b).

SPECIFIC SITUATION OF THE CENTER OF GRAVITY

Distance for the center of gravity when supporting on the feet was given on pages 400 and 401. The distance may be greater or less if the support is on other parts of the body. Description of such distances, sufficient for the recording of all movement other than the most scientifically detailed, is based on the convention of using body lengths to determine distance for the center of gravity from the point of support.

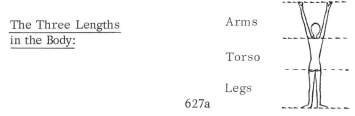

The Three Lengths
in the Body: Arms

                                Torso

                                Legs
                    627a

Indication for more than one length:

$\bigvee$ = $1\frac{1}{2}$ body lengths $\bigvee\hspace{-6pt}\bigvee$ = 2 body lengths

In an upright position the center of gravity is one body length - the length of the legs from the point of support. In a hand stand there is a greater distance - the distance of the arms plus the torso - two body lengths. When the center of gravity is above the point of support, the distance is always described in terms of degrees of place high; when it is below the point of support the distance is in terms of degrees of place low; when it is at the point of support, or as close as is physically possible to the point of support, it is at place middle.

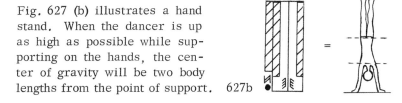

Fig. 627 (b) illustrates a hand stand. When the dancer is up as high as possible while supporting on the hands, the center of gravity will be two body lengths from the point of support.   627b

The following tables illustrate a progression from the greatest distance above the point of support to examples at the point of support, and also a progression from the greatest distance below the point of support up to the point of support. Use of these possibilities in acrobatics, gymnastics, etc. will be given in Book II.

Levels of Center of Gravity Supporting on Various Parts of the Body

Above Point of Support   (Levels on feet given on pages 400 and 401.)

Scale: × = 1/3 (general statement)

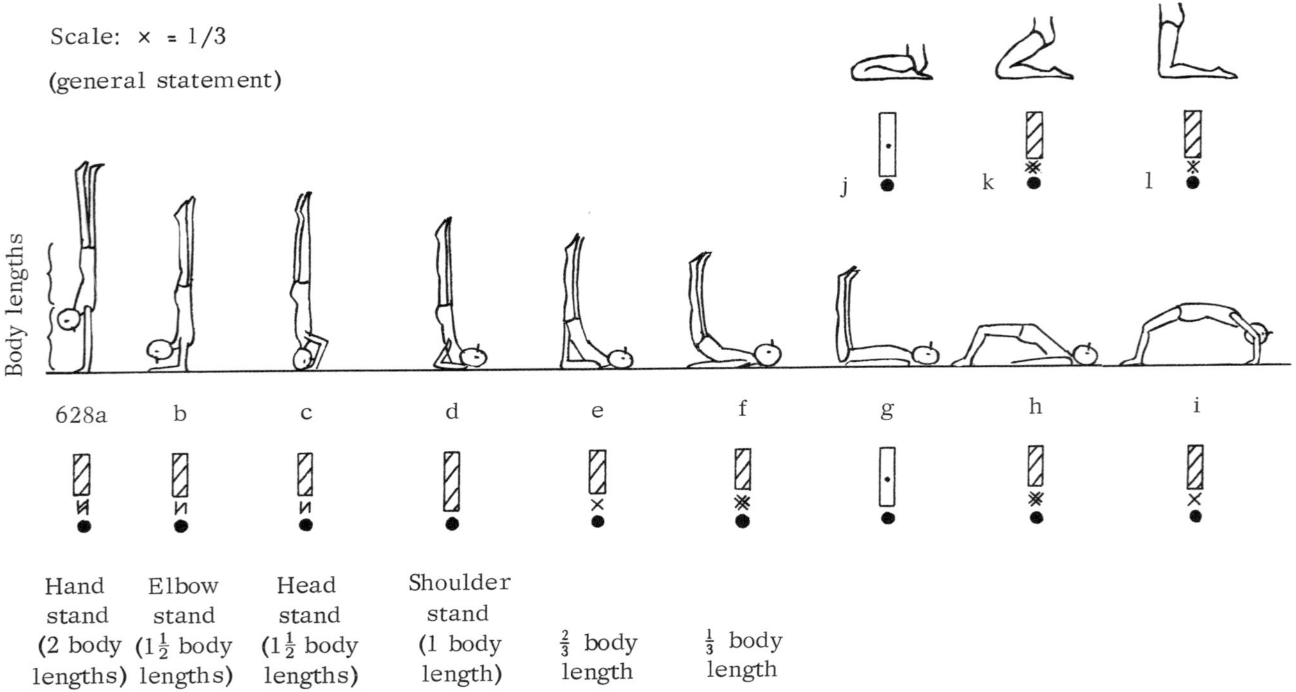

Body lengths

628a   b   c   d   e   f   g   h   i

j   k   l

Hand stand (2 body lengths)   Elbow stand ($1\frac{1}{2}$ body lengths)   Head stand ($1\frac{1}{2}$ body lengths)   Shoulder stand (1 body length) $\frac{2}{3}$ body length $\frac{1}{3}$ body length

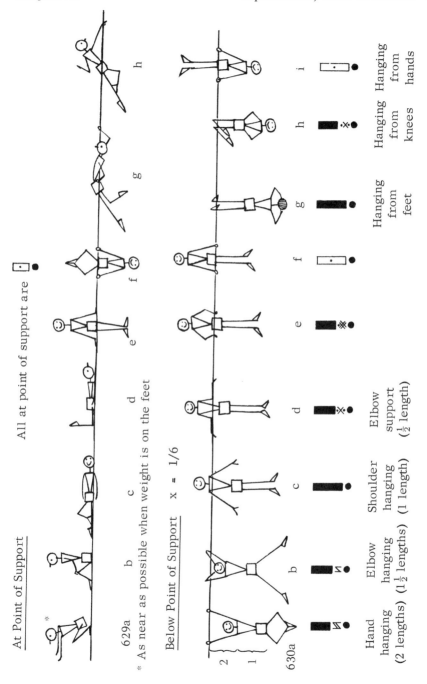

At Point of Support

All at point of support are

629a

b   c   d   e   f

* As near as possible when weight is on the feet

Below Point of Support   x = 1/6

630a   1   2

b   c   d   e   f   g   h   i

Hand
hanging
(2 lengths)

Elbow
hanging
(1½ lengths)

Shoulder
hanging
(1 length)

Elbow
support
(½ length)

Hanging
from
feet

Hanging
from
knees

Hanging
from
hands

CHAPTER 25

Systems of Reference

ANALYSIS OF DIRECTION

When actions are described in terms of direction, be it spatial destination or motion toward a direction, the reader must know what system of reference is in effect. How will a command such as "Hands up!" be interpreted?

"HANDS UP!"

Here are two distinctly different reactions to the command "Hands up!" The two barbers who are standing automatically raise their arms overhead toward the ceiling. There is no question as to where "up" is for them. But the two clients lying down have chosen different "up" directions. One has taken his arms "over his head," while the other is reaching for the ceiling. This difference lies in the system of reference each has used. The client with his arms raised toward the ceiling has in mind the constant line of gravity in which up is always toward the ceiling and down toward the floor. The client with his arms over his head is thinking of his own physical directions, in which up is headward and down is footward.

How should the instruction "point forward" be interpreted? Is the direction forward to be toward the front of the room, toward the direction in which the body as a whole is facing, or the direction in which the front of the chest is facing? When one is standing upright facing the front of the room these three possible interpretations are all the same, but in other situations they may differ.

In this cartoon A is pointing to the audience, the front of the room; B is pointing to where his whole body is facing; C is pointing to the direction forward from his chest, while D, who is standing upright and facing the audience, is doing all three of these things.   626

Each of these three possibilities is based on a directional system of reference, a cross of axes. Of these three, one is considered the standard and is automatically understood to be in effect; the other two require keys.

Reference has already been made in preceding chapters to one or other of these crosses of axes. In this chapter we bring together for comparison information on all three.

THE THREE CROSSES OF AXES

A cross of axes is comprised of three lines intersecting at right angles. From the point of intersection each line goes out in two opposite directions into infinity. It is from this central point, called "place," that all directions are judged. (See page 24, Fig. 7.)   627

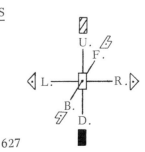

The three crosses of axes used in describing direction are:*

1. ⟟ The Standard Cross of Axes: The direction forward is determined by where the performer is facing (his personal front): up and down remain constant.

2. ⟟ The Cross of the Body Axes: Direction is established by the build of the body, up being "headward," down being "footward," forward being "chestward," etc.

3. ⟟ The Constant Cross of Axes: The established directions in the room.

Note: all three crosses of axes are centered in the performer and all three coincide when the body is in the upright position and facing the front of the room.

THE STANDARD CROSS OF AXES

The name Standard has been given to the system of reference most commonly in use. In the Standard Cross of Axes, the vertical line (line of gravity) remains constant. When the performer tilts away from a normal vertical standing situation, the Standard Cross of Axes does not tilt. The performer relates his movements to this "vertical constant" frame of reference. Therefore up is always toward the ceiling or sky and down toward the floor or ground. The other dimensional directions, forward, backward, right and left, lie at right angles to the vertical line of gravity. (See page 24, Fig. 7, and page 229, Fig. 324.) The direction forward, established by the personal front of the performer, is that wall or corner of the room which he is facing when in the normal upright, untwisted position. Once this direction is known the sideward and diagonal directions fall into place. After each turn a new front is established and this becomes the new forward direction.

The symbol for the Standard Cross ✛ (a cross superimposed on the center of gravity sign ●) represents a cross of axes based on the line of gravity. (For this reason the system is sometimes called the Line of Gravity Cross of Axes.) Reference to directions based on the Standard Cross of Axes may be abbreviated to "Standard directions," "Standard side middle," etc. Specific examples of its use will be presented on a chart for comparison with the Cross of Axes in the Body, following an investigation of the latter.

* See Appendix B, note 20.

THE CROSS OF THE BODY AXES

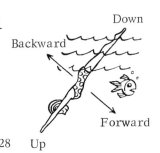

The cross of directions based on the build of the body has its "up-down" dimension in the body's longitudinal axis (line of the spine). "Chestward" and "backward" represent forward and backward body directions, while the right and left sides of the body provide right and left directions. Fig. 628 shows the directions when diving. When the performer turns and changes front this cross of directions turns with him; when he tilts away from the line of gravity it tilts with him. It is the system of reference most applicable when either the force of gravity does not exist as in the weightless state or when there is no defined area, no floor or ground to which the performer can relate.

The key for the Cross of Body Axes ⊕ is a cross centered on a circle. (Throughout the Laban system indications which are based on or appear in a circle refer to physical aspects.) The Cross of the Body Axes may be called the Body Cross, and directions referred to as "Body-forward," "Body-side middle," etc.

A floor must of course exist for steps (transference of weight). This at once establishes a "down," a gravitational direction in relation to which the situation of the main axis of the body (whole torso) must be made clear. In the weightless state (to be presented fully in Book II) movements of the body as a whole are usually described as revolutions, and paths of one form or another, while movements within the body are described as flexions of the joints or as directional gestures relating to the torso. In normal circumstances the Body key does not apply to steps or to tilts of the whole torso, but affects directional descriptions of the limbs, and of individual movements of the head, chest, shoulder area, and pelvis.

COMPARISON BETWEEN STANDARD AND BODY DIRECTIONS

The following examples illustrate various situations of the body and placements of the limbs notated for purposes of comparison from both the Standard and Body systems of reference. The words "up," "down," etc. placed by the figures refer to the unchanging Standard directions. The Standard key is placed in parentheses as it is not normally written, being automatically understood.

Directions when Standing or Supporting on the Hips

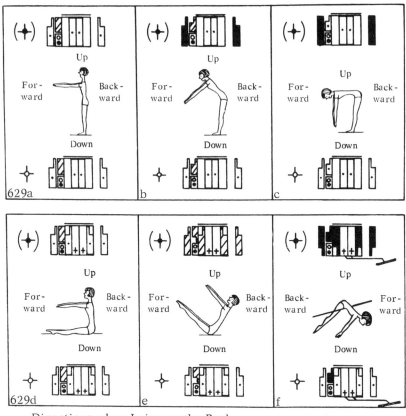

Directions when Lying on the Back

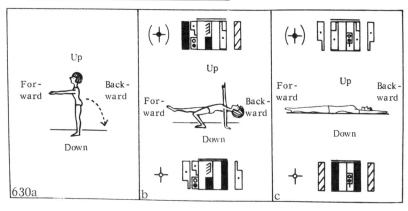

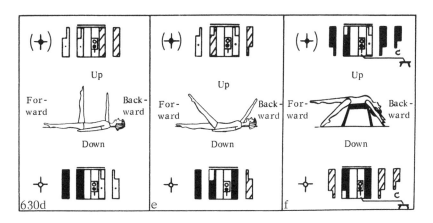

Directions when Lying on the Front

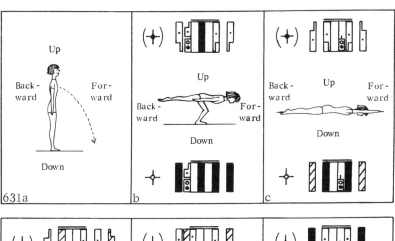

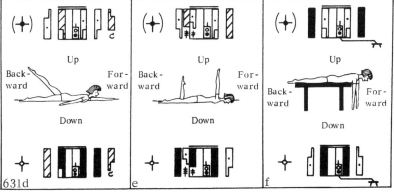

Directions when Lying on the Side

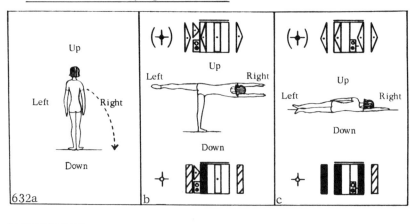

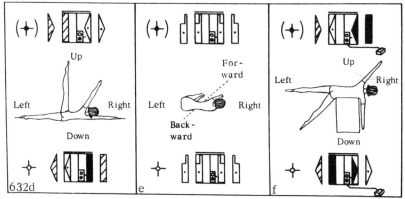

The directions and levels which have been illustrated with the body supported hold true when it is in an unsupported state.

When we lie on the ground our limbs can gesture only in middle or high level. For the limbs to move in low level, we must be supported on a table, chair, or other object allowing them to hang down. Such a situation is depicted in the last example in each of these sets of illustrations.

If the direction forward does not immediately seem clear when the Standard system is in use, the sudden command "Get up and run forward!" will produce the right result. Without having time to think the individual automatically goes in the correct direction. This test works whether one is lying on the front, side, or back.

THE CONSTANT CROSS OF AXES

The cross of axes based on directions in a defined area, called the Constant Cross of Axes, was discussed on pages 106-107. For abbreviation, directions based on this system are called "constant-backward high," "stage-backward high," or "room-backward high," etc. according to the circumstances.

APPLICATION OF THE THREE CROSSES OF AXES

Because the Standard Cross of Axes is the one generally in effect when no key is stated, use of this key will be given last. The Constant Cross of Axes was explored in Chapter 8, page 106. A brief resumé of the use of this system of reference is given here.

USE OF THE CONSTANT CROSS OF AXES KEY

As Front Signs*

The key for the Constant Cross of Axes provides front signs which indicate where in the room the performer is facing. These are placed outside the staff on the left at the start of a score and whenever a change of front has occurred, as in Fig. 633 (a).   633a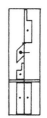

As Destination of Turning

When the destination of a turn is best des-cribed according to where the person or part of the body ends facing, a pin (tack) from the front sign is placed within the turn sign as in (b). Here a tack is used for the destination of a pivot turn and of a turn of the head.   633b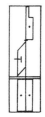

As a Key for Direction of Steps and Gestures

When the direction of movement is to be judged from the room rather than from the Standard system, the Constant Cross key is used (a) within the score as a pre-sign where it modifies a particu-lar step or gesture, or (b) outside where it modifies all directional indications until it is cancelled. In all cases level of steps and gestures is judged in the usual way.

* See Appendix B, note 3.

Within the Columns: The key ⧈ may be used within a column as an accidental in a way comparable to the use of an accidental in music, where it shows a momentary departure from the established key. In such usage either the key sign must be repeated for each symbol or a caret used to avoid key sign repetition. The following examples provide a comparison between instructions given in terms of the Constant Cross and those with a standard description (Standard system of reference).*

Constant Directions

Standard Directions

The arm and head move toward the audience, then toward the back of the stage. A caret instead of a repeated key has been used ☑ for the head.

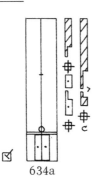

634a

The same as (a) written in the usual way: the key ◆ is understood.

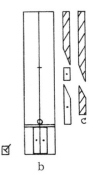

b

When a gesture occurs in a room direction while the body is turning, the effect is the same as if a space hold were written within a direction symbol. (See Fig. 178 (c), page 139.)

Constant Directions

Standard Directions

The arm and steps move toward the back of the room. The arm is rising constantly during the steps and turn.

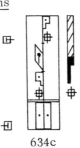

634c

The arm moves toward that direction which is side left at the start of the action and ends up as a side right gesture.

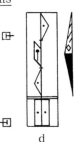

d

Outside the Staff. When a system of reference key is placed outside the staff on the left it is understood to refer to all directional indications until cancelled. Level for steps and gestures is taken from the Standard system as usual.

* See Appendix B, note 31.

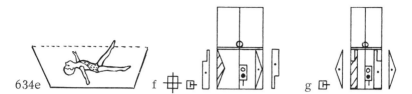

634e

f   g

In Fig. 634 (e) the performer is lying on his back, facing stage right. Fig. (f) describes the direction of his limbs from the Constant Cross of Axes, while (g) is the Standard description.

For Performers with Different Fronts

When several dancers have different fronts, uniformity in the direction of their paths or gestures may best be described in terms of stage direction.

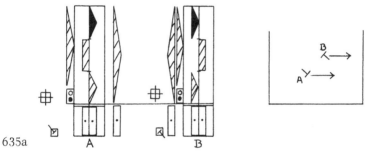

635a   A   B

In Fig. 635 (a) both dancers A and B travel toward the right side of the room on parallel paths, and gesture an arm in this same direction. For A the Standard direction would be right back diagonal, for B left forward diagonal.

Four dancers
on stage each
facing a diffe-
rent direction
repeatedly per-
form a stamping
and hopping pat-
tern while tra-
veling toward
the audience.

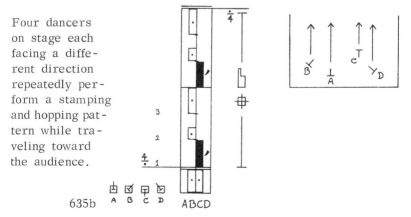

635b   A   B   C   D   ABCD

For Paths Involving Turning

The direction of a path may best be described according to the room direction in which the performer is traveling. This is true of turning on a straight path, or of deviating toward a room direction during repeated turning patterns. Fig. 636 (a) shows a waltz step in place which changes facing direction at the end of each measure and also gradually travels toward the side right room direction.   636a

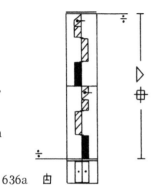

When a performer is revolving on a straight path the direction of the path may best be described in terms of room direction. The usual description for such paths was given on page 195. Figs. 636 (b) and (c) illustrate a walking pattern written both ways.

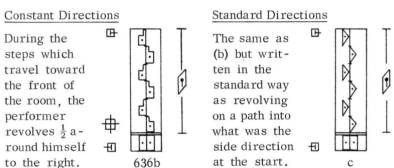

Constant Directions

During the steps which travel toward the front of the room, the performer revolves ½ around himself to the right.   636b

Standard Directions

The same as (b) but written in the standard way as revolving on a path into what was the side direction at the start.   c

For the Axes of Revolutions, Rotations and Circular Paths

Revolutions of the whole body such as occur in acrobatics are only briefly presented in this book. To describe actions according to a Constant Cross axis instead of the understood Body axis (-◇-), the Constant Key is placed within the revolution sign. Circular paths of the whole body or of a limb may also have a Constant axis.

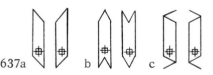

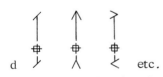

637a

Pivot turns (a), somersaults (b), and cartwheels (c) around the vertical, lateral and sagittal room directions

Paths in space, related to the three types of revolutions occuring around Constant axes

USES OF THE STANDARD CROSS OF AXES KEY

The key for the Standard Cross of Axes needs to be stated only for cancellation of other keys and in modified form when a divided front occurs. Such divided front was described on pages 307-8, and use of keys for a departure from the established rule for describing direction was given on pages 309 and 310. Two additional examples of use of the Stance key are given here.

For Divided Front: Stance Key ◆ *

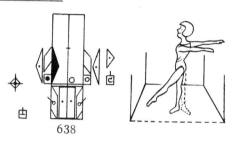

Judged from the established front, the leg gestures and the head looks to the right while the arms gesture left. Degree of rotation for the pelvis and chest is not stated, being left open to the performer. Achieving the spatial directions is obviously more important than relation of arm to shoulder or leg to hip. Below a comparison is made between emphasizing spatial or body relationship in describing direction for gestures.

638

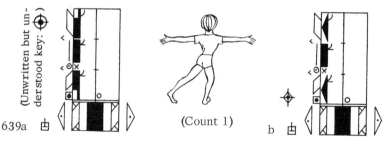

(Unwritten but understood key: ◆)

639a

(Count 1)

b

Because of the established rule of an unwritten but understood Twisted-Part key ◆ , in Fig. 639 (a) emphasis is on the relation of limb to body. On count 1 the leg gestures backward from the hip as the pelvis rotates right. On count 3 the leg gestures forward from the hip as the pelvis rotates left.

Because ability to perform torso rotations varies with each person, spatial accuracy, particularly for unison movement, is best achieved by a spatial description, i.e. use of the Stance key ◆ , as in (b). A change of key within one phrase is not unusual.

* See Appendix B, note 20 (ii) and (iii).

For Axes of Revolutions, Rotations and Circular Paths of Limbs

Revolutions of the whole body or rotations within the body can be specified as being around the vertical line of gravity by placing the Standard Cross of Axes key within the turn sign. Horizontal circular paths of the body as a whole are always understood to be around the Standard vertical axis. The Standard Key is the rule for all circular paths described by limbs. Paths for limbs, introduced on page 331, Fig. 485 (b), will be dealt with fully in Book II Note that for the body as a whole it is not practical to describe somersault or cartwheel revolutions or somersault or cartwheel paths according to a Standard system of reference axis.

 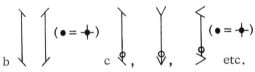

640a	b	c , , etc.
Revolutions (rotations) around the Standard vertical axis	The Standard Cross of Axes is the understood axis ("focal point" for rotations or circling) of horizontal circular paths of the whole body, as in (b), and all gestural paths, as in (c).	

Fig. 640 (d) is the same action as Fig. 459 (h) on page 316 but with the wheeling written as a turn around the Standard vertical axis. In (e) the right arm rapidly performs four backward somersault circles, the understood lateral axis ◁–▷ passing through the shoulder. In (f) the arm performs three cartwheel circles to the right, the sagittal axis ⬦–⬦ being understood. This same kind of circle occurs farther from the body in (g) as a result of the more forward starting position. Fig. (h) shows a circular path without change of front (without rotation) for the head, the vertical axis being understood to pass through the base of the neck.

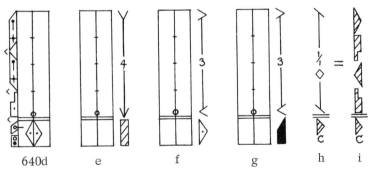

| 640d | e | f | g | h | i |

USE OF THE CROSS OF THE BODY AXES KEY

As Destination for Rotations and Twists of the Limbs

As explained on page 278, the white pin, derived from the key ⟡ for the Cross of the Body Axes, states the destination of a rotation or twist of a limb judged from the normal untwisted state. In Fig. 641 the legs start turned out. The right leg rotates in and out while the head rotates from right to left. (See Fig. 435 (b), page 297.)

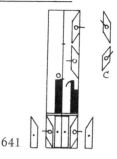

641

As a Key for Gestures

When gestures of the arms, head, etc. accompany a tilt of the whole torso, a description in terms of the build of the body (Body directions) is often desirable.

Within the Columns*

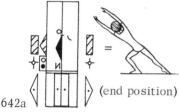

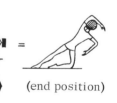

642a   (end position)

b   (end position)

The arms are above the shoulders while the torso is tilted to the left.

The angular positions of the arms are described from the build of the body. (Note use of attached symbols.)

Outside the Staff. When the key is placed outside the staff it refers to all gestures but not to whole torso tilts and supports.

Arm and head directions are described from the Body system of reference. The line of the spine is directed forward high. The head tilts backward from this line; the arms are forward from the chest.

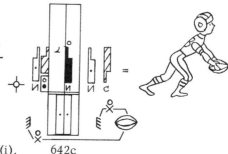

642c

* See Appendix B, note 20 (i).

BODY CROSS OF AXES KEY: DIVIDED FRONT

When the body as a whole is not in the upright situation, it may be desirable to describe direction according to ⤲ , the Body Cross of Axes (Body directions). In such situations the parts of the torso may all have the same front, establishing a Body "Stance", as in Fig. 643 (a) below in which the Body-Stance forward direction is toward the ceiling. When parts of the torso twist a divided front results. The choice of directional description and use of keys for ⤲ are similar to those discussed on pages 307-310 in connection with use of ✦ . Compare Figs. 643 (a-c) with Figs. 449 (a-c).

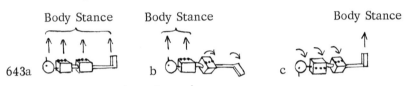

The three keys ◈ , ◉ , ◈ , have their counterparts based on ⤲ . The abbreviated names for these are: Body-Stance key ◈ ; Body-Twisted-Part key ◉ ; and Body-Base-of-Twisted-Part key ◈ . Addition of the term "Body" stipulates that direction and level are taken from the cross of axes in the body. Details on application of these keys will be given in Book II. They are not commonly needed.

It is common, however, for the key ◉ to be used when ✦ is in effect, particularly for movements of the hand when the arm is in motion. The cross of axes is centered in the wrist; the palm is considered the front and the hand in line with the forearm is place high. In a forward hand tilt the palm approaches the forearm; in a backward tilt the back of the hand approaches the forearm, and so on. In Fig. 643 (d) the hand bends toward its own front and back while the arm moves. Because the arm is constantly changing direction and rotating, these hand directions are difficult to describe by other systems of reference.

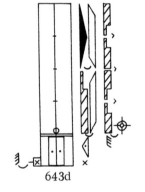

643d

Use of Divided Front Keys Based on ⤲

In the following examples head tilts illustrate use of keys for divided front based on ⤲ . Other descriptions are possible but those given are the ones commonly used in such situations.

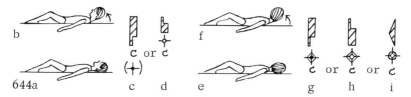

In Fig. 644 (a) the body starts supine. The head is then raised Standard backward high, (c). The performer may prefer to describe this action as a Body-forward-high tilt, (d), judging the direction from ⌖. In (e) the head starts rotated to the right and therefore has a different front from the rest of the body. The head is then raised to Stance backward high, (g), the same Standard direction as in (c). This action can also be described from Body-Stance as in (h), the same direction as (d), or from Body-Twisted-Part, as in (i).

In (j) the chest has twisted $\frac{1}{4}$ right and the head has an additional $\frac{1}{4}$ rotation. The head then lowers toward the right shoulder. Though a Standard Stance descrip-

tion could be used, it is more likely that the performer will think of the action as a forward tilt from ⊕ as in (l) or in relation to the chest, i.e. a side high tilt from the base of the head, as in (m).

Axes of Rotations and Circular Paths for Whole Body and Limbs

A Body Cross of Axes is the understood key for the axes of revolutions of the whole body, for rotations and twists within the body, and for vertical circular paths of the body as a whole; therefore normally no key is written. Horizontal circular paths of the whole body or circular gestures of limbs may be described according to the Body Cross of Axes by placing the key ⌖ in the path sign.

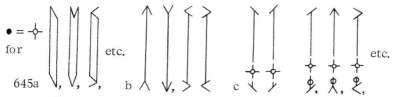

For revolutions and somersault and cartwheel paths of the whole body, a Body key is automatically understood. The key must be stated for horizontal paths and all gestural paths based on ⌖ .

THE FIXED POINTS IN THE ROOM

The fourth system of reference to which movement may relate is based not on a cross of axes but on a system of fixed points on the surface of a defined area such as a room. Whatever the size or shape of the room or stage, it is to the existing corners or walls that the symbols refer. Thus reference to the right front corner will be to that actual corner and not to where it would be if the room were a perfectly shaped cube. Fig. 646 depicts an average shaped room indicating some of the main points. The other points fall into place accordingly.

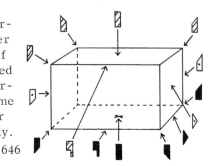

646

INDICATION OF FIXED POINTS

The key for the Fixed Points combines a defined area ☐ with a spot hold ◈ (see page 449), producing the indication ◙ ,* which signifies a spot in a defined area. The spot in question is shown either by a direction symbol or by adding a pin to the key sign.

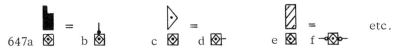

647a ◙   b ◙   c ◙   d ◙┤   e ◙   f ─◈─   etc.

Fig. 648 compares use of the key followed by a direction symbol with use of the modified key sign.

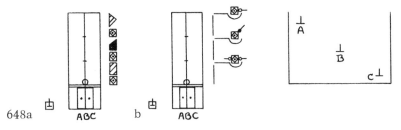

648a   b   ABC   ABC

Performers A, B, and C, who are spread across a room but all facing front, gesture toward the center of the room's ceiling. Each then gestures to the low edge of the right front corner and finally to the high center point of the right wall.

* See Appendix B, note 32.

When placed outside the staff on the left the Fixed Points key states that all directions are judged by the fixed points in the room. Level for gestures is according to the level of these fixed points; steps take their level from the usual supporting level of the body.

A, B, and C, each facing stage left but spread across the stage, all walk toward fixed point center back, while the arms gesture first toward the low center back point, then toward the high center back point.

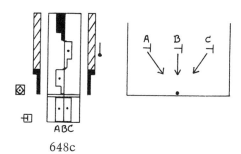

ABC

648c

DIRECTIONAL KEY FOR BALLROOM DANCING

In ballroom dancing the convention is to progress around the room in a counterclockwise direction, moving usually near the outer edge of the floor. (See page 202.) This path is called the "Line of Direction" (L.O.D.). In many ballroom dances there is no need to relate to the walls or corners of the room or to the Constant room directions. Instead performers are aware of their relationship to the Line of Direction, whether they are facing the direction of this line, or have their backs to it, and so on.

Indication of the Line of Direction

A black pin, taken from the pins which describe degrees of turn, placed within an oblong provides the sign for Line of Direction, as in Fig. 649 (a). This sign is placed at the start of a score to indicate how the performer is to relate to his environment.

649a

Front Signs for Line of Direction. Front signs relating to the Line of Direction are similar to those derived from the Constant directions in the room, but a black pin is used instead of a tack.

649b   c   d   e

| Face the L.O.D. | Your back is to the L.O.D. | Face wall, (L side to L.O.D.) | Face center, (R side to L.O.D.) |

Full details on usages in ballroom dancing will be given in Book II.

TABLE OF SYSTEMS OF REFERENCE

	NAME	SIGN	DIRECTION (forward etc.) relates to:	LEVEL (up and down)	APPLICATION of main key
All crosses of axes are centered in the performer	STANDARD CROSS OF AXES		Front of body as a whole (that side or corner of the room which the person faces when in the normal upright untwisted position)	Up and down remain on the Constant Line of Gravity regardless of choice of Front.	Degree of turn — Indication of Line of Direction (as in ballroom dancing)
	Special Keys for Divided Front				Front signs for Line of Direction
	Twisted-Part		For twisting: the front of the free end. For rotating: the front of the individual part.		Understood reference for:
	Stance		Front of the untwisted part (the part which retains the original front).		Horizontal circular paths of the whole body
	Base-of-Twisted-Part		Front of Base (section at point of attachment) of part twisting or rotating		Gestural circular paths — etc.
	BODY CROSS OF AXES		Physical front of body as a whole	Up and down relate to the longitudinal axis of the body as a whole. Entry marked * relates to the longitudinal axis of the base of the part twisting.	Degree of twist from untwisted state — Gestures in relation to the torso
	Special Keys for Divided Front				Movements of extremities during actions of major parts — Weightless state (to be given in Book II)
	Body-Twisted-Part		For twisting: the front of the free end. For rotating: the front of the individual part.		Understood reference for:
	Body-Stance		Front of the untwisted part (the part which retains the original front).		Revolutions, rotations and twists etc.
	*Body-Base-of-Twisted-Part		Front of Base (section at point of attachment) of part twisting or rotating		Circular paths in vertical planes for whole body etc.
	CONSTANT CROSS OF AXES		Constant directions in the room	Line of Gravity	Front signs — Destination of the turn
	THE FIXED POINTS		The physical walls, edges and corners of the room or stage		Addressing — Radial paths for a group — Focal point for group gestures

CANCELLATION OF KEYS

All keys follow the same cancellation rules.

PLACEMENT OUTSIDE THE STAFF

A key placed outside the staff on the left modifies all directional indication within the staff until it is cancelled by another key. A return to the standard description of directional movement is indicated by the Standard key. In Fig. 651 the Constant key stated at the start of the first measure is cancelled on the third measure. The steps which had related to the room directions revert in the third measure to being judged from the front of the performer.

651a

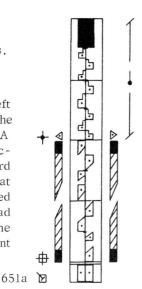

PLACEMENT WITHIN THE STAFF

A key placed within a column before a direction symbol modifies only that symbol. Automatic cancellation is understood. For it to apply to subsequent direction symbols the key must be repeated; carets may be used where their meaning is quite clear. In many cases use of the addition bracket (see page 483) may prove more practical.

651

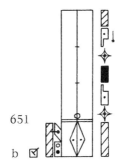

b

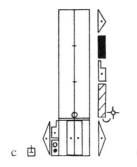

c

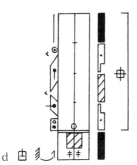

d

Repetition of the key: the arm circle is described according to Stance (the untwisted front).

Adjacent placement: the key, placed next to the symbol it qualifies and tied to it by a small bow, is in effect until cancelled.

Use of the addition bracket: the right arm circle is described according to the room directions.

CHAPTER 26

Variations in Positions, Paths, and Steps

VARIATIONS IN POSITIONS

POSITION SIGNS (RELATIONSHIP PINS)

Pins are used in many connections but always with the same basic idea. They represent in miniature the full range of principal directions. Black pins represent low level, straight pins (tacks) middle level, and white pins high level directions.

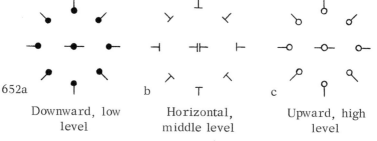

652a	b	c
Downward, low level	Horizontal, middle level	Upward, high level

The signs for below can be written ⃓ or ⊸•, above ⃝ or ⊸o, and center (within, inside) ⯭ or ⊣⊢.

These pins, used for small movements, can be thought of as miniature direction symbols, with the following equations:

$$\text{o—} = ▷ \quad \text{⊢} = ▷ \quad \text{•—} = ▶ \quad ⃝ = ▱ \quad ⊥ = ▯ \quad ⃓ = ▮$$

These pins are used to modify or describe:
1. Positions of the feet
2. Relationship to the center line of the body
3. Relationship of one part of the body to another, to an object, etc.

4. Directions and intermediate directions
5. Degrees of turning, rotating and twisting
6. Deviations: **(a)** from a standard direction or position, **(b)** from the previous situation, **(c)** from the path of the movement.

RELATIONSHIP TO CENTER LINES OF THE BODY

For positions of the feet (page 63) pins placed next to support symbols describe the relation of one foot to the other; they also state the relation of a step or support to the center lines of the body. Use of the center lines of the body in walking (specific "tracks") was introduced with the familiar "tightrope" walking on page 68, Fig. 68. Application of other center line "tracks" will be given in Book II.

In arm positions, such as occur in classical ballet, a pin next to a direction symbol states the relation of the extremity of the arm to the center lines, or, to be more exact, to the center areas of the body.

The Three Center Lines in the Body

The three dimensional directions in the body which form a cross of axes provide three center lines: the vertical (line of gravity), the sagittal (forward-backward), and the lateral (side to side). Reference to the center line for gestures and steps usually denotes the sagittal center line. Occasional reference is made to the lateral center line for steps, though rarely for arm gestures.

Areas Resulting from the Center Lines

For positions of the arms, the extremity of the limb does not fall precisely on the center line itself, but within the area established around each center line. Diagonal center lines are also included, providing diagonal areas.

a - center front area
b - right front diagonal area
c - right side area
d - right back diagonal area
e - center back area
f - left back diagonal area
g - left side area
h - left front diagonal area

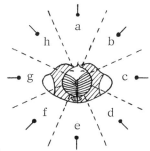

653a

For all positions of the arms, regardless of level, black pins are used following the convention established for positions of the feet. These pins are used similarly to those applicable when the arms are in low level and are separated from one another by the body. The normal situation of the arms in the side areas could be shown with sideward pins, as in Fig. 653 (c) in which the arms are down and rounded, but these are not ordinarily needed.

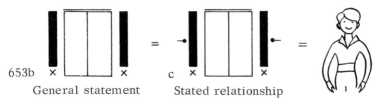

653b   General statement   Stated relationship

Many arm positions are modified by a specific relationship to the center line of the body; a few examples are given below.

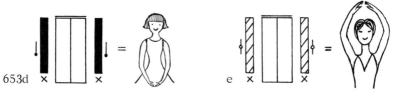

653d   The arms (their extremities) are in the center front area of the body.

653e   The above sign is used for arms exactly overhead.

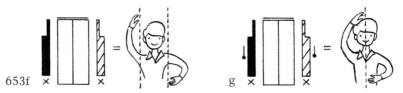

653f   The left arm is forward low of the shoulder, the right arm forward high of the shoulder.

653g   The same as (a) but with the extremities in the center front area.

Correct carriage of the arms (port de bras) in the forward direction in classical ballet: arms are forward, slightly below shoulder level and slightly rounded; elbows are "lifted," (i.e. rotated slightly inward); the extremities of the arms (fingertips) are in the center area (i.e. close to one another).

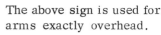
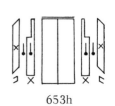

653h

DIRECTION OF RELATIONSHIP OR CONTACT

A relationship indication can be made more precise by placing the appropriate pin next to the active part to state from which direction a contact or relationship occurs.

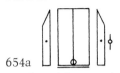

654a

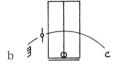

b   c

c

The right arm is above the left.

The left hand touches the head from above.

The right foot touches behind the left knee.

A pin placed in conjunction with an addressing sign is written from the point of view of the active person.

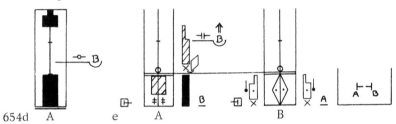

654d   A   e   A   B

A jumps over B.

A's right arm gestures inside the circle formed by B's arms.

Note how in Fig. 654 (e) the floor plan gives a direct visual image of the placement and relationship of the two dancers, even though this relationship has been stated in the movement score. (See Chapter 22, pages 381 and 382.)

INTERMEDIATE DIRECTIONS

For many purposes the principal directions suffice. In any fully detailed description of movement, however, slight variations in the use of direction are needed. In dance, variations in style may rest upon such slight spatial differences.

Two methods of writing intermediate directions are used.

Halfway Point

A dot between two direction symbols signifies a point lying between those two directions; the two symbols are tied together with a small round vertical bow to show that they are one unit in terms of timing and movement.

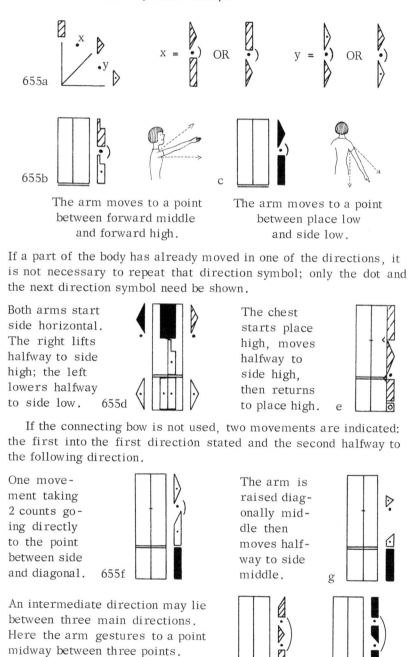

The arm moves to a point between forward middle and forward high.

The arm moves to a point between place low and side low.

If a part of the body has already moved in one of the directions, it is not necessary to repeat that direction symbol; only the dot and the next direction symbol need be shown.

Both arms start side horizontal. The right lifts halfway to side high; the left lowers halfway to side low. 655d

The chest starts place high, moves halfway to side high, then returns to place high. e

If the connecting bow is not used, two movements are indicated: the first into the first direction stated and the second halfway to the following direction.

One movement taking 2 counts going directly to the point between side and diagonal. 655f

The arm is raised diagonally middle then moves halfway to side middle. g

An intermediate direction may lie between three main directions. Here the arm gestures to a point midway between three points. 655h i

Third Way Point

A point one-third of the way toward a neighboring principal direction may be shown by placing the appropriate pin within the direction symbol.

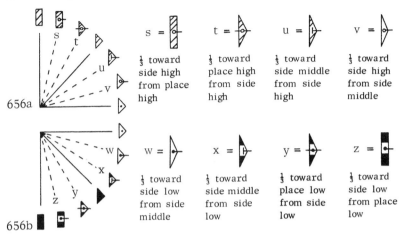

656a

s =	t =	u =	v =
⅓ toward side high from place high	⅓ toward place high from side high	⅓ toward side middle from side high	⅓ toward side high from side middle

656b

w =	x =	y =	z =
⅓ toward side low from side middle	⅓ toward side middle from side low	⅓ toward place low from side low	⅓ toward side low from place low

Note that in high and low level direction symbols a space must be left in the center to allow room for a pin. In middle level symbols a pin replaces the dot. Figs. 656 (c-i) below show variations which occur in classical ballet in positions of the arms.

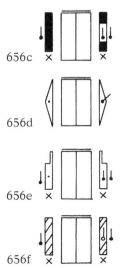

In (c) the left arm is down and rounded with the extremity in the front center area. The right arm is similarly situated but slightly more forward (⅓ toward forward low).

656c

In (d) the left arm is in a strict side horizontal direction, while the right arm is slightly forward and slightly lower (⅓ toward the forward low diagonal direction).

656d

In (e) the left arm is forward horizontal rounded with the extremity in the front area, whereas the right arm, though similarly placed, is lower (⅓ to forward low).

656e

In (f) both arms are up and rounded with the extremity in the front center area, but the right arm is lower (⅓ toward forward high).

656f

In (g) the right arm is raised $\frac{1}{3}$ above shoulder level while the left arm is lowered $\frac{1}{3}$: a slanting line used in a balletic arabesque. 656g

Fig. (h) shows a side high-side low slanting line, the left arm slightly higher, the right arm slightly lower, making a steeper slanting line than the normal side high-side low line. 656h

In (i) the arms are in a forward diagonal open position but slightly closer together and slightly lowered. 656i

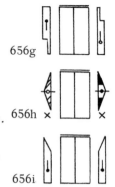

INTERMEDIATE DEGREES OF TURN

Finer distinctions may be needed for the amount of turn performed or the direction faced on stage. To describe less than $\frac{1}{8}$ of a turn, the following methods are used:

657a   b   c

$\frac{1}{16}$ degree from previous situation $\frac{1}{16}$ from the untwisted state   End facing between ⊞ and ⊠

The degree or destination to be indicated lies directly between the two pins written. In turning to the right:

∠ = ∡ = $\frac{3}{16}$ ← = ⟵ = $\frac{5}{16}$ etc.

Intermediate Front Signs

The same method is used to show in-between directions on stage:

658   etc.

INTERMEDIATE POSITIONS OF THE FEET

A double pin is used for positions of the feet to show an in-between relationship. Compare the following with Fig. 60 on page 62.

 659a   b 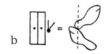   c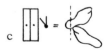

Between 1st and 3rd   Between 3rd and 5th (heel to toe joint)   Between 5th and a crossed 3rd

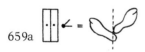

DEVIATIONS

Deviations can be of three kinds:

(1) From the standard direction or position

(2) From the previous situation

(3) From the path of a movement

DEVIATIONS FROM A POSITION

A slight displacement from an established position is shown by a pin. Roughly the displacement can be said to be the distance of an inch to an inch and a half, or three centimeters.

For the Feet

Placement of a foot in a step or a position of the feet may be modified by using a straight pin. It is important to note that a black pin refers to the relation of a foot to the center line of the body (how one foot is placed in relation to the other foot) while a tack indicates a displacement from the stated position. Many subtle variations in positions of the feet which occur in different forms of dance can be shown when the above indications are combined with rotations of the legs.

660a   The feet are together.

b   The feet are slightly apart.

c   The feet are apart in a 2nd position with the right foot slightly ahead and the left foot slightly behind the normal side to side line.

  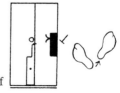

660d The right foot almost closes in front of the left (a slight forward separation).

e The left foot almost closes to the right (a slight left back diagonal separation).

f The right foot touches the floor near the left (a slight right forward diagonal separation).

For the Arms - Satellite Center of the Extremity

Small displacements may occur while the extremity of the limb remains in all other respects in the same main location. In deviations from the normal arm positions, a satellite center is based on the point at which the extremity of the limb is situated.

Satellite centers at the extremity of the head and of the hand

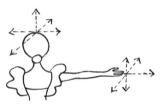

661a

The direction of the displacement is described in relation to this point.

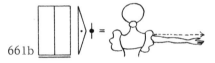

661b

The arm is slightly below the normal side middle point.

c

The arm is slightly to the right of the normal low point.

DEVIATIONS FROM THE PREVIOUS SITUATION

Single Deviational Movement

The arm is raised slightly above side middle, and stays there.

662a

The arm is momentarily raised slightly, returning to the side middle direction.

b

Displacement can be shown to be temporary by using the passing state bow, as in Fig. 662 (b).

Double Deviations

In a vibration or shaking action the movement is between two displacements. The pins may be repeated as many times as necessary, or small repeat signs used. When the action is very fast the vibration sign ⟨ (shaking) should be used. In such cases two pins are enough to show the direction in which the shaking occurs.

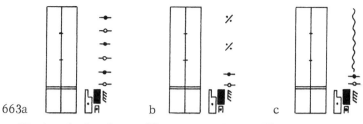

663a Waving the hand up   The same written   The same as often and
      and down 3 times   with repeat signs   as fast as possible

In (a) and (b) the hand will end slightly below the normal point, whereas in (c) the bow produces an automatic cancellation.

Compound Deviations

A typical compound deviation from a given point is a circular pattern requiring at least four pins.

A circle of the right index finger: the bow indicates both the continuity of the individual displacements and the fact that it is a passing deviation. At the end of the bow the finger will return to its normal position. (See page 455 for finger indications.)

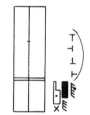

664a

A very small circle of the leg, ending normal

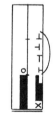

664b

A very small circle of the lower arm

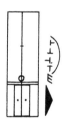

c

DEVIATIONS FROM THE PATH OF A GESTURE

Deviations from a direct path are in the nature of detours, indirect ways of arriving at a stated destination. Through the use of pins many subtle curving paths can easily be described. Each deviation can be likened to an outside influence, which like a magnet pulls the limb off its direct path but is not strong enough to prevent it from continuing on and reaching its destination. Shape Writing, the notating of visual linear patterns (trace forms), will be given in Book II.

Satellite Center for the Line of the Path

A deviation from the path of a gesture is described in relation to the path itself and not to the point of origin or the destination of that path. Each movement path has its own system of directions, much like a satellite center.

The following is a simple example of a direct path which lies in front of the body and hence is easy to view.

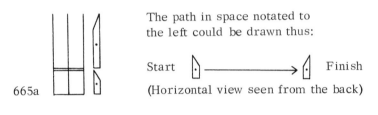

The path in space notated to the left could be drawn thus:

Start ━━━━━━━━━━━━━━━▶ Finish

665a

(Horizontal view seen from the back)

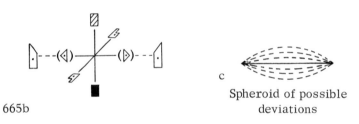

665b

c

Spheroid of possible deviations

In the case of a simple deviation affecting the whole path, the satellite center for the direction of the deviation lies in the middle of the path as illustrated in Fig. 665 (b). From this center a deviation may occur into any direction or level. The directions are local replicas of the Standard system of reference centered in the performer. As the limb approaches the center of the path the influence of the deviation increases, and as it passes the center the influence diminishes; thus a curved line is produced. In certain directions flexion or extension may be necessary for the limb to perform these curved lines.

Simple Deviations

To write a deviation place the appropriate pin (representing the direction of the detour) within a vertical passing state bow.* This bow has time significance and shows when the deviation starts and when it finishes. Note the following variations in timing.

* See Appendix B, note 33.

When one deviation is spread throughout a movement, the zenith of the deviation occurs in the center of the path in question. Thus the zenith occurs in the middle of the time indicated for the deviation.

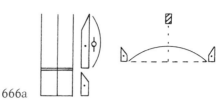

666a

The dotted line represents the direct path.

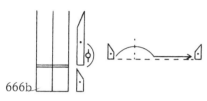

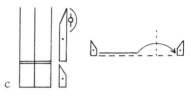

666b

The rising curve occurs during the first half of the path.

c

The rising curve occurs during the second half of the path.

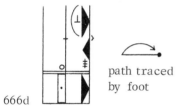

path traced by foot

666d

The lower leg deviates over forward on the way out: a rond de jambe en l'air en dehors in classical ballet.

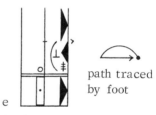

path traced by foot

e

The lower leg deviates over forward on the way in: a rond de jambe en l'air en dedans in classical ballet.

Compound Deviations

Two or more deviations occurring on a single path may easily be indicated by appropriate pins.

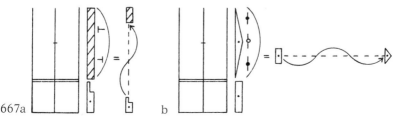

667a

b

VARIATIONS IN PATHS

STRAIGHT PATHS FOR GESTURES

The direct path described by limbs normally produces a slight curve because of the structure of the joints (see page 118). When a straight path for an extremity is required it is indicated by the addition of a small version of the straight path sign I .

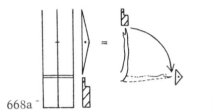

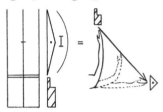

668a

b

The arm remains normally extended, the extremity following a curve.

The arm must flex slightly for the extremity to follow a straight path.

DEVIATION FROM STATED PATH FOR STEPS

A path stated by steps in the support column may deviate toward another direction. To avoid writing in between directions for each step, we show the deviation in a straight path sign placed alongside the steps to be modified. In Fig. 669 (a) the sideward steps veer slightly forward. Such deviation may be described in terms of stage direction (Fig. 635 (b), p.423), as movement toward a stage area (Fig. 258 (f), p.184) or as arriving at a stage area (Fig. 259 (e), p.185).

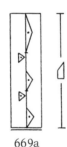

669a

Modification of path in terms of stage area means radial paths when performed by a group. Compare Fig. 669 (b) in which the performers ar-arive at the center front area on stage with Fig. 635 (b) in which they veer toward a stage di- rection (parallel paths).

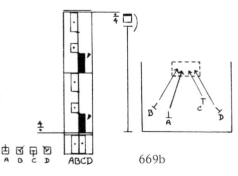

669b

MODIFICATION OF STEPS

GRADUAL CHANGE IN PERFORMANCE OF STEPS

When steps should gradually become shorter, longer, lower, or higher, etc. this change is shown within a path sign placed outside the staff. Placement within a path sign stipulates that the indication refers only to steps.

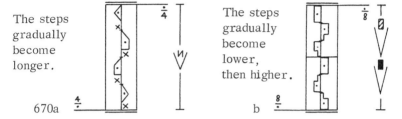

The steps gradually become longer.

670a

The steps gradually become lower, then higher.

b

STEPPING ON THE SAME SPOT

When a touching gesture is followed by a step, it may be desired that the foot should not move before the step, or that if it does lift, the step should be on exactly the same spot. Note the difference between the use of a caret and a staple in this context.

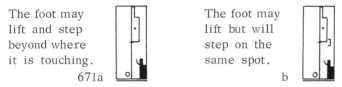

The foot may lift and step beyond where it is touching.

671a

The foot may lift but will step on the same spot.

b

In (b) the staple follows the usage established in Fig. 97 (b), page 86, where it means "on the same spot." The use of the caret in (c) is based on its usage for shift of weight in Fig. 81 (c), page 75, where it has the meaning of "the same," i.e. continuation of the same action.

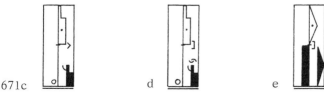

671c

The foot does not lift and so steps on the same place.

d

The foot lifts before stepping on the same place.

e

The step occurs on the place above which the foot had been extended.

OVERCROSSED STEP IN PLACE

When the foot should step in place
but on the other side of the previously
supporting foot, two pins are needed.
The first pin directs a cross in front
or behind and the second pin indicates
the sideward relationship to the other foot. In
Fig. 672 the right foot steps in front and to the left of the left foot.

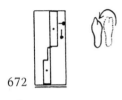

672

RIGID KNEES

Inflexibility (lack of natural pliancy) in a joint is indicated by the hold sign o following the appropriate joint
sign. Fig. 673 shows a stiff-kneed walk. A state of
x or И may be added where appropriate.

673

PARTIAL SUPPORT

A touching leg gesture may take some weight but not be a true
support, or a foot may in stepping become only a partial support.
Such partial support can be shown in three ways: equal division
between support and gesture, a $\frac{1}{3}$ or $\frac{2}{3}$ division between support and gesture, and an unstated degree of weight-bearing for a
gesture.

Half Support, Half Gesture

By writing indications in both support and gesture columns of the same leg, we show an equal
division between these two activities. In Fig.
674 (a) half the weight is held back on the forward
step. This is shown by the presence of a similarly directed gesture for the same leg. Because in
a half support a symbol appears in the support column, it is considered in the category of a step, not a gesture, and so the step
on the left foot which follows is written as being backward of the
half support. (Compare with (b) and (c) below.)

674a

Two-Thirds Support

When the division is mostly support and only
partially gesture, the inclusion bow extends
from the support symbol into the gesture column, indicating the inclusion of gesture quality.

674b

One-Third Support

If only one third of the weight is taken, the leg action is main-ly a gesture; therefore the direction symbol appears in the gesture column. An inclusion bow drawn from the leg gesture symbol into the support column shows inclusion of weight. In Fig. 674 (c) the forward gesture is partially weight-bearing, the inclusion bow indicating the addition of support quality. This action is followed in (c) by a sinking on the left foot, and in (d) by a step in place.

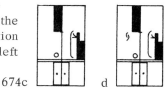

674c   d

Some Degree of Weight-bearing

The angular horizontal bow for support, carry (see page 338) is used for gestures to indicate leaning, (some degree of weight-bear-ing). The bow is swung from the appropriate limb to the support column or away from the staff, the floor being understood. If need be, the floor can be specified by the letter T (for terra) placed in a box.

674e

DISTANCE SIGN

Distance to be traveled can be specified in terms of step lengths by placing the appropriate number in a box. A step length is under-stood to be that of the performer unless otherwise specified. Dis-tance between performers can be stated in terms of step lengths.

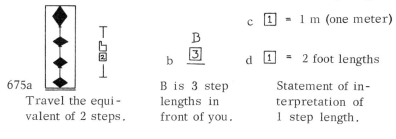

675a

Travel the equi-valent of 2 steps.

b   B is 3 step lengths in front of you.

c $\boxed{1}$ = 1 m (one meter)

d $\boxed{1}$ = 2 foot lengths

Statement of in-terpretation of 1 step length.

RETENTION ON A SPOT

A spatial retention (space hold) can be pinned down to a parti-cular spot, either actual or imaginary. The symbol for such a re-tention, ◈ , called a "spot hold," is a combination of the space hold sign ◇ and the indication for a focal point ● .* A spot hold

* See Appendix B, note 34.

is stronger than a space hold: when using a space hold, a performer can travel around while one part of the body maintains a relation to a room direction, whereas with a spot hold he is tied down
to a particular spot. A body hold requires that a bodily aspect
(contraction, extension, etc. of a joint or section) be maintained.
A space hold requires that a room direction be retained, for which
bodily adjustment is necessary and taken for granted. A spot hold
also demands bodily adjustment which, in the case of touching,
grasping, etc. may include sliding friction.

Retention of an Imaginary Spot

An extremity of the body may be given the instruction to remain
where it is (a spot hold) while the rest of the body turns, lowers,
rises or moves slightly away. Adjustments in the body that must
occur to fulfil the spot hold instruction are the natural result of
this effort and are not written.

During
side-to-
side steps
each hand
remains
on the
same spot. 676a

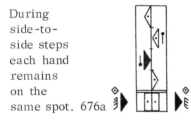

The same as (a),
showing approxi-
mately the change
of arm direction
that must take
place.

b

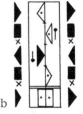

The need to retain an imaginary spot often occurs during pantomimic sequences. In (c) the
top of the head has a spot hold as though someone
has hold of it and will not let go. During the circular walk the body must bend to maintain the
spot hold. For use of a spot hold with the center
of gravity see page 405, Fig. 617.

676c

"Spotting" for Turns

A swift whipping action of the head is usually used in rapid
turning such as pirouettes. The technique of this head action can
be written in detail. Its central activity is to look as long as possible toward a chosen spot, usually the front of the room, keeping
the face to that direction while the rest of the body is turning, and
then at the last minute whipping the head around so that it again
looks at that spot, arriving there before the rest of the body has
completed one revolution. This head action, called "spotting," is
indicated briefly with a face sign followed by the spot hold symbol.

A double pirouette performed with head "spotting." As nothing specific is stated regarding the direction to be spotted, it is taken to be where the body is facing. A room direction, person or object can be stated as the point to be spotted; e.g.   677a

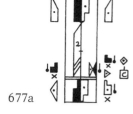

Spot stage right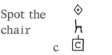

677b

Spot the chair   etc.

c

<u>Undeviating Aim</u>

A gesture may move toward a stated destination (terminal point) despite other actions in the body which ordinarily would detract it from its course. To show this retention of the aim of a gestuie, we place a spot hold sign within the direction symbol.

The arm ges- tures toward a point which at the start is dia- gonally left for- ward low. At the conclusion of the side steps, the point is di- agonally right forward low.   678a

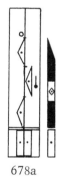

The same idea as (a) perform- ed with a turn. The arm aims at what started as the right back high diagonal point while the body both turns and travels. The arm ends   .

b

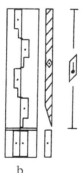

<u>Retention of a Tangible Spot</u>

When an object or the floor is contacted, the point of contact is the spot to be held.

The left foot has a spot hold during the hops on the right foot.

679a

The feet keep on the same spot while the hips slide backward.

b

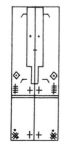

Spot Hold at Point of Relationship

The spot to be held (point of contact) may move in space. Such a spot hold occurs when two dancers holding hands move around, twist, turn, move closer to one another or farther apart without letting go hands. In such instances the spot hold is placed over the contact indication rather than over the sign for the part of the body. A body hold sign o placed above such a relationship indication would mean the state of the hands in grasping must be retained. The spot hold allows sliding friction and adjustment to occur.

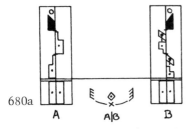

680a

A   A|B   B

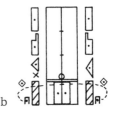

b

A's right hand and B's left hand keep their point of contact in spite of subsequent movement.

The palms remain near one another during the arm movements.

CANCELLATION OF A SPOT HOLD

A spot hold remains in effect for the duration of the action or series of actions in conjunction with which it is used. Where there may be doubt as to how long it should be in effect, the hold sign o can be used immediately after the spot hold sign. The conclusion of this retention is indicated by an angular release sign ⤰ or ⤲.

The forward step on count 4 obviously cancels the previous spot hold for the right foot.

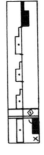

681a

The spot hold for the right hand is cancelled on count 3.

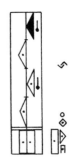

b

CHAPTER 27

Specific Parts of Limbs;
Movements of Hands;
Manner of Performing Gestures

DETAILS OF THE LIMBS

For Motif Writing as well as for Structural Description designation of a limb or a specific part of a limb may be necessary. The smaller the part of the body and the more specific the particular area or point, the more complex the indication. A few of the possible specific indications are given here. The basic logic of the method of indicating limbs, areas, and surfaces is applicable to all parts.

SURFACES OF A LIMB

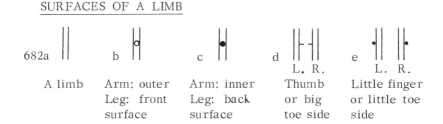

682a	b	c	d	e
			L. R.	L. R.
A limb	Arm: outer Leg: front surface	Arm: inner Leg: back surface	Thumb or big toe side	Little finger or little toe side

Use of a stroke for thumb or big toe side and of a dot for little finger or little toe side provides a clear distinction between these two sides. An in-between surface is shown by combining two signs, as in (f) which shows the part between the upper (outer) and the little finger (or little toe) side.

682f

Specific Limb

The sign for a limb can be combined with the various joint signs, either by being placed above the joint sign (limb above that joint) or by being combined with the joint sign.

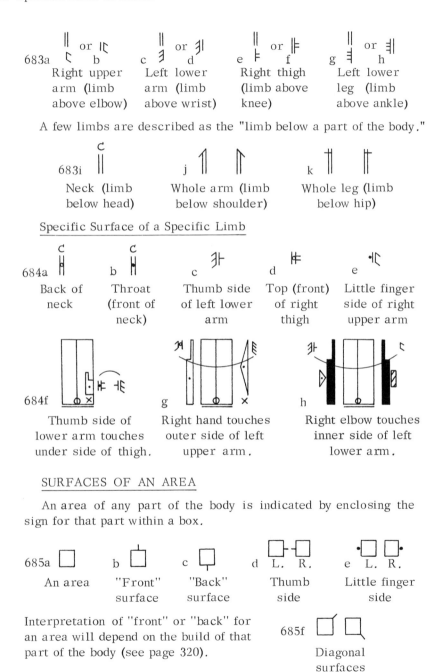

683a Right upper arm (limb above elbow) b

c Left lower arm (limb above wrist) d

e Right thigh (limb above knee) f

g Left lower leg (limb above ankle) h

A few limbs are described as the "limb below a part of the body."

683i Neck (limb below head)

j Whole arm (limb below shoulder)

k Whole leg (limb below hip)

Specific Surface of a Specific Limb

684a Back of neck

b Throat (front of neck)

c Thumb side of left lower arm

d Top (front) of right thigh

e Little finger side of right upper arm

684f Thumb side of lower arm touches under side of thigh.

g Right hand touches outer side of left upper arm.

h Right elbow touches inner side of left lower arm.

SURFACES OF AN AREA

An area of any part of the body is indicated by enclosing the sign for that part within a box.

685a An area

b "Front" surface

c "Back" surface

d L. R. Thumb side

e L. R. Little finger side

Interpretation of "front" or "back" for an area will depend on the build of that part of the body (see page 320).

685f Diagonal surfaces

Surfaces of Area around a Joint

The sign for a particular joint is placed within an area sign to indicate the area around that joint. To this sign is added the indication of front, back, right, left (thumb, little finger side, etc.) as is appropriate.

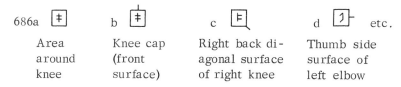

686a   Area around knee

b   Knee cap (front surface)

c   Right back diagonal surface of right knee

d   Thumb side surface of left elbow   etc.

PARTS OF THE HANDS

Specific signs for the hands and feet fall into two categories: those based on Figs. 687 (a) and (b), and those based on the symbol for the area of the hand or foot, shown in (c).

687a   b   c

The signs of (a) and (b) are used more for movement indications and for touching, while symbols based on (c) function mainly to indicate guidances and directions faced.

FINGERS

The general signs for the fingers ⅊ and ⅃ are modified by dots to indicate the specific fingers.*

688a Thumb   b Index   c Middle   d "Ring"   e Little

These signs are placed before a direction symbol to indicate a movement of the specified finger as a whole. Where touching is concerned the signs also express the finger in general, no part being specified; the tip is commonly used, however.

Joints of the Fingers

Additional dots on a finger sign indicate specific joints of that finger. The example given here is of the index finger; the same usage applies to the thumb and other fingers. The base "knuckle"

* See Appendix B, note 35.

456 Specific Parts of Limbs

of the thumb is where it is attached close to the wrist. Thus the
thumb has the same number of joints as the fingers, though it appears to have one less. Finger joints can be likened to the leg
joints; such a comparison is made for clarification.

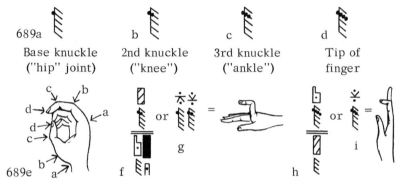

689a   b   c   d

Base knuckle   2nd knuckle   3rd knuckle   Tip of
("hip" joint)   ("knee")   ("ankle")   finger

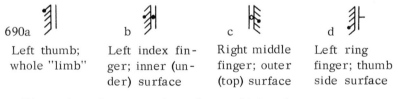

For a touch these signs represent the joint or tip itself; in
movement the segment above that joint is displaced. For example
a movement of the "knee" joint, ("b" in Fig. 689e) will displace
the "thigh" (a-b) in space, as illustrated in (f). This action could
be described as 90° bending movements of first and second joints.
In (h) moving the last segment of the index finger forward could
also be described as bending the last joint forward 90° as in (i).

Specific Surfaces of a Finger

The signs in Fig. 682 are combined with those of Figs. 688 and
689 to indicate any surface of any part.

690a   b   c   d

Left thumb;   Left index fin-   Right middle   Left ring
whole "limb"   ger; inner (un-   finger; outer   finger; thumb
                der) surface   (top) surface   side surface

Diagonal surfaces are shown by combining the
appropriate indications. Fig. (e) states the upper
and outer surfaces of the right index finger.   690e

Specific segments ("limbs") and
surfaces of these segments are
shown by combining the signs in   690f
Fig. 690 with those for a limb and
surfaces of a limb.

Outer (nail) side of last
segment of little finger

AREA SIGNS FOR THE HAND

For hand indications which are needed frequently, the sign for an area ☐ is modified as in Fig. 691 (a) to indicate the area of the whole hand.

691a

691b   c   d   e   f

| Palm side (inner surface) | Back of hand (outer surface) | Thumb side edge | Little fin-ger side edge | Finger-tip edge |

In Structural Description placement of a symbol on the right or left side of the center line indicates right or left hand. When these area signs are used out of context or in Motif Writing the hand indication is added as in (g).

691g

Base of the Hand

The area sign is inverted as in Fig. 692 (a) to show the base of the hand. The "heel" of the hand may be used for touching, pressing, sup-porting, leading, etc. This sign is not synony-mous with the wrist sign, though in certain respects they are close. To this area sign are added the in-dications for surfaces and edges. The "edge" of the base of the hand shown in (f) strictly speaking cannot be touched being within the limb, but it can be point-ed into a direction and has been used as a convention for touching and part leading instead of ↿.

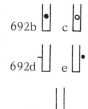

692a

692b   c

692d   e

692f

PARTS OF THE FEET

The same specific indications used to show joints and surfaces of the hands are applied to the feet.

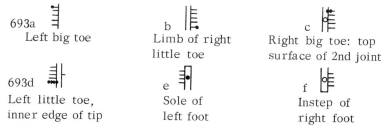

| 693a Left big toe | b Limb of right little toe | c Right big toe: top surface of 2nd joint |
| 693d Left little toe, inner edge of tip | e Sole of left foot | f Instep of right foot |

DETAILS OF BODY AREAS

Specific subdivisions of parts of the body areas can be shown by combining the symbol for that part with the range of pins. A few examples are given here.

SURFACES OF BODY AREAS

The chest sign is given as an example of detailed indication of surfaces of a body area.

Chest in general 694a   Front surface b   Upper front surface c   Lower front surface d

An intermediate point can be shown by combining indications. Fig. (e) states the surface between center back and right diagonal back in the low area of the chest.   694e

HANDS ON HIPS OR WAIST

The term "hands on hips" can be given more than one interpretation. In Labanotation the hip sign + used with a contact sign means touching the break at the top of the leg, the location of which is quite obvious in sitting. (See Fig. 321 (i), page 225.) The instruction "hands on hips" may mean hands on the upper rims of the pelvis (iliac crest), or even at the waist. The following examples illustrate these differences in Labanotation. The hip sign is modified by the addition of a dot to indicate a point slightly above the hip "joint" or slightly below.

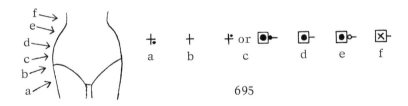

695

The specific meaning of (a) is just below the break at the top of the leg; (b) is the break itself; (d) is the center side part of the pelvis; (e) is the upper rim of the pelvis and (f) is the waist. In general usage the hip sign replaces the specific pelvis sign. When exactness is required the appropriate pelvis sign is used or a key is written at the start of the score, e.g. + = ⬡⊢ or ⊠⊢ = ⬡⊢ .

MOVEMENTS OF THE HAND

The symbol ⟨ represents the hand as a whole and is used whenever a general description is required. For a more specific analysis the hand is divided into its component parts: metacarpus and fingers (phalanges).

MOVEMENTS OF THE HAND AS A WHOLE

The hand is normally held with a slight curve through the palm and fingers. The degree of curve varies with the individual; the indication ⊙ refers to what is normal for the reader.

Two-Dimensional Extension and Contraction

Two-dimensional extension and contraction may occur along the longitudinal line or in the lateral plane of the hand.

Extension - Longitudinal. The hand has two degrees of lengthening or stretching along its longitudinal line.

696a ⟨ = ⟨⟨⟨⟩⟩⟩

Straight (flat)

b

Extra stretched (as long as possible)

It is difficult to show the difference between (a) and (b) in an illustration though in movement the added degree is quite obvious.

Extension - Lateral. Spreading (separating, abducting) is extension on the lateral plane. Two main degrees are used, though the specific six-degree scale is applicable. In spreading most of the action occurs in the fingers, though the palm also contributes to the movement. The fingers need not be extended when spreading, but may be naturally curved.

Slightly spread   Very spread

697a   b

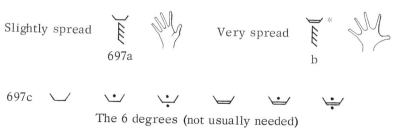

697c

The 6 degrees (not usually needed)

* See Appendix B, note 36.

Contraction - Longitudinal. The hand contracts in a way similar to the whole arm, the knuckles providing a center joint; the difference lies in the presence of additional joints in the fingers which produce a rounded effect. In a complete contraction the pads of the fingers rest on the base of the thumb and palm. The thumb will be outside the fingers, resting against the index finger. The fingertips and base of the wrist retain the original line of direction; there is no movement in the lower arm itself. To get a clear picture, rest the hand palm down on the table and then contract the hand. The table will help keep the line of direction.

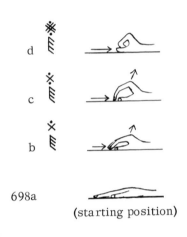

(starting position)

Contraction - Lateral. Closing in (joining, adducting) is contraction on the lateral plane. Two main degrees are used, though the specific six-degree scale can be used when needed. Complete lateral contraction can only be performed with outside help.

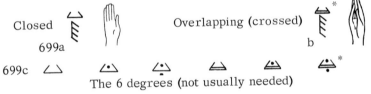

Closed   699a   Overlapping (crossed)   b

699c   The 6 degrees (not usually needed)

Three-Dimensional Extension and Contraction

The hand often extends (opens out, expands) and flexes (closes in, contracts) three-dimensionally, i.e. as though filling or enclosing a sphere rather than moving on a plane or striving for a linear use of space. Such three-dimensional actions, applicable also to the chest and body as a whole, can be defined precisely through the use of the signs И, Λ, ⌣ or Χ, Υ, ⌢. When only a general description is required a general symbol is provided. The straight line — (a shortened version of ⌣ and ⌢) representing the third dimension is added to the basic signs И and Χ producing ⊬, ⊬, and ⋇, ⋇.

* See Appendix B, note 36.

Three-Dimensional Contraction. An ordinary
fist is the result of a three-dimensional contraction. The performer should be aware of closing
in "from all sides." The six degrees of contraction apply, the sixth degree producing a tight fist.

700

Three-Dimensional Extension. The hand commonly extends three-dimensionally in that it combines straightening (stretching) with spreading.
The physical use of three dimensions in performing this action is best felt when starting from a
contracted state. The double sign ⩜ is used for
a general statement; specific degrees may be
given when needed.

701

Curving the Hand

The base of the hand remains where it is while the finger joints
form a curve. The most common direction is forward, toward
the palm. Hyperextension, curving toward the back of the hand,
can be performed to a high degree by some individuals.

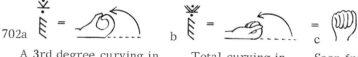

702a

A 3rd degree curving in   Total curving in   Seen from
of the hand (thumb and   (a form of fist)   the front
fingers meeting)

b   c

The six degrees of curving (curling) the hand are:

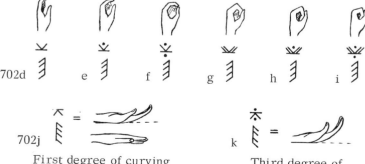

702d   e   f   g   h   i

702j   k

First degree of curving   Third degree of
backward (hyperextension)   curving backward

MOVEMENTS OF THE FINGERS

The fingers are capable of all the actions which can be performed by the hand as a whole. The palm should not be affected by such finger actions. The following examples illustrate some of these possibilities.

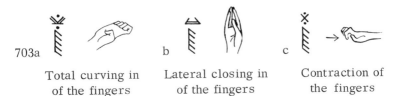

703a

Total curving in
of the fingers

b   Lateral closing in
of the fingers

c   Contraction of
the fingers

MOVEMENTS OF THE PALM

Palm facing was given on page 130. We are concerned here with the various forms of contraction and extension of the center of the hand, the knuckles at the base of the fingers. The palm sign is usually used instead of the sign for these specific knuckles in writing movements of this part.

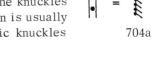

704a

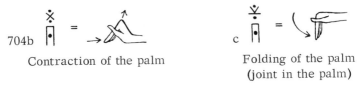

704b

Contraction of the palm

c   Folding of the palm
(joint in the palm)

COMBINED ACTIONS

Every hand and finger action can be written by combining parts of the hand and possibilities in movement. For fields in which movement concentrates specifically on the hands, a special staff is used incorporating columns for the parts of the hand. In general practice when simultaneous actions happen for one part of the hand, the indications are placed side by side, as in Fig. 705 (c), or one after the other and tied together with a bow, as in (b).

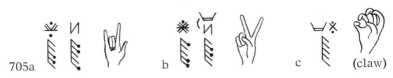

705a   b   c   (claw)

MANNER OF PERFORMING GESTURES

On pages 253-259 we discussed movements which follow a main
action and those which accompany a main action. We now explore
use of parts of the body to lead or guide a movement. The term
"leading" implies initiation of movement by a part of the body,
usually a joint, which moves ahead into the stated direction, the
rest of the limb following. In part leading there is a temporary
break in the normal line of a limb. In a guidance a surface of the
limb faces the direction of the movement, pushing the air, so to
speak, away from the limb's path. Guidances do not usually involve displacement of a part of the limb.

PART LEADING

The sign for a specific part of the body which leads (usually a
joint or part of the hand) is placed within a round vertical bow.

706a   b   c   d

Led by the hand. Led by the elbow Led by the knee Led by the hip

This bow is placed adjacent to the action to be modified.

Fig. (e) shows the right arm being led upward by the wrist: the wrist will be the first
part to move in that direction. Because the indication within this bow is a passing state, at
the end of the movement the arm is back to its
normal state: wrist not flexed, hand merely an
extension of the whole arm. Note that no particular surface of the wrist is specified.

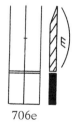

706e

The difference in notation between an inclusion and a part leading must be clearly observed. In a part leading the indication for
the part of the body is surrounded by the round vertical bow. In
an inclusion the vertical bow, rounded only at the ends, is broken
and the specified part of the body placed within the break.

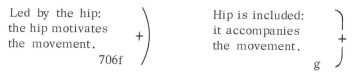

Led by the hip: Hip is included:
the hip motivates   it accompanies
the movement.   the movement.
       706f   g

TIMING OF PART LEADING

An indication written within a round vertical bow is considered a passing state: its influence lasts only as long as the bow. In Fig. 706 (e) the leading action lasted until the end of the arm gesture. Variations in timing can be indicated by the length and placement of the bow.

The arm gesture starts with wrist leading but soon continues as a normal arm movement.   707a

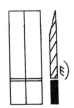

Wrist leading occurs only near the end of the arm gesture.   b

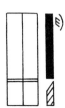

RETENTION OF A LEADING STATE

A particular body position resulting from a part leading may be retained even though the leading action has concluded. The hold sign o placed at the end of the bow shows such a reten- tion which must subsequently be cancelled by ⊙.   708

GUIDANCES

In a guidance there is no displacement within the limb. The adjustment is usually one of rotation so that the stated surface faces in the direction of the movement. A guidance makes the per- former aware of that surface of the body and its importance in the performance of a given action.

The left arm is guided by its outer sur- face, the right arm by its little finger side. 709a

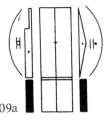

The left arm is guided by its thumb side, the right arm by its inner surface.   b

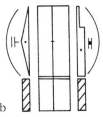

When a guidance symbol is placed within a vertical bow, auto- matic cancellation follows. To retain the state produced either a hold sign must be added or an addition bracket used (see page 483).

SUCCESSIONS, SEQUENTIAL MOVEMENT

A sequential movement is one in which movement flows from one part of the body to another in succession, passing from joint to joint, or from vertebra to vertebra in the case of successions in the spine. Movement of this kind passing through the whole body is called a body wave. When a change of direction occurs, a sequential flow alters the manner of performance. When there is no change of direction for a limb or spine, a sequential flow is often called a ripple. Such ripples and successions are familiar to Oriental dance. Two forms of succession exist: inward and outward.

ANALYSIS OF SEQUENTIAL MOVEMENT

A sequential movement could be written as a series of parts leading, as in Fig. 710. Although this produces the right result, it is a cumbersome way to write the action. Because a succession is a basic manner of performing a movement, special symbols V and Λ are provided.   710

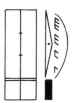

Outward Sequence

The sign V states an outward sequence moving from the center or base of the limb, as the case may be, to the extremity.

With Change of Direction. One part of the limb after another moves in the new direction indicated. This action can be compared to that of laying a scarf on the floor. The part nearest the floor (base) will reach the horizontal first and each succeeding part in turn will assume a horizontal direction.

(Note: the "base" of the scarf has been pinned to the floor to make clear which is the "free end".)

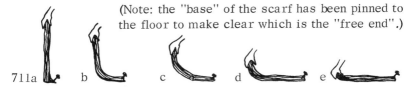

711a   b   c   d   e

An outward sequence occurs when a performer lies down from a sitting position, the sequence taking place in the spine.

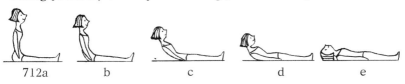

712a   b   c   d   e

Without Change of Direction. The limb as a whole retains its previous direction. A slight displacement must occur to allow the ripple to form and progress. If the limb is extended, there must be a slight drawing in to provide "slack," just as a caterpillar will drawn in its rear end in order to progress forward. A caterpillar is able to progress through a succession (ripple) in the body.

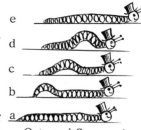

713   Outward Succession (tail to head)

Inward Sequence

The sign Λ represents an inward sequence in which movement commences at the extremity and flows toward the center or base.

With Change of Direction. The extremity is the first part to take the new direction and each neighboring part follows until finally the base of the limb takes the new direction. The following illustration shows a scarf being sequentially lifted off the ground.

714 a   b   c   d   e

An inward sequence occurs when a performer sits up from a lying position, the sequence taking place in the spine.

715a   b   c   d   e

Without Change of Direction. The limb as a whole retains its previous direction, the ripple starts at the extremity and moves inward. For the caterpillar this means starting at the head. Note: when there is no other indication of change, the limb finishes in the position and state in which it started, e.g. if bent at the start, it will finish bent; if extended it will finish extended.

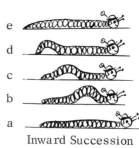

716   Inward Succession (head to tail)

METHOD OF WRITING SEQUENTIAL MOVEMENT

The sign V or Λ is placed as a pre-sign before a direction symbol when the timing of the sequence and change of direction are the same, as in Fig. 717 (a). When placed within a round vertical "passing state" bow, the timing of the action can be shown by the length of the bow to be the same as a change of direction, as in (b), or momentary as in (c) where the sequential action occurs only during the first half of the movement. When there is no change of direction the succession sign is followed by a duration line to indicate timing as in (d).

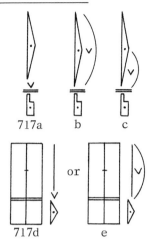

717a   b   c

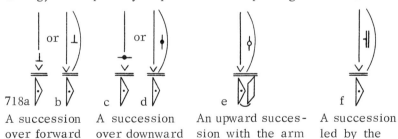

717d   e

SPECIFIC PERFORMANCE OF A SUCCESSION

The manner of performance of a ripple can be varied by the direction in which the slight displacement occurs or by the surface or change of surfaces of the limb guiding a succession. The following examples are understood to be 'for the right arm. The method of writing may use a pin followed by a duration line to show timing, or the pin may be placed within a passing state bow.

718a   b   c   d   e   f

A succession over forward   A succession over downward   An upward succession with the arm rotated outward   A succession led by the thumb side

In (e) there is an unstated inner surface guidance of the arm.

OVERLAPPING SUCCESSIONS

Each of the symbols V and Λ represents one complete succession. It is quite common for a new succession to start before the previous one is finished.

719a The whole arm moves side, then down

b The arm moves side sequentially, then down sequentially.

c A downward sequence starts before the side-ward sequence ends.

Overlapping successions may occur without change of direction. Fig. (d) shows a second ripple starting before the first is concluded. This could also be written with the vertical bow as in (e).

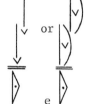

719d   e

BODY WAVES

A body wave is a sequential movement through the whole body, usually an outward sequence, though inward sequences can also occur. To indicate a body wave, we draw a double V sign across the entire staff. Displacement in space during such a wave may be slight or considerable. The appropriate direction symbols are written within the V across the center line. The following examples illustrate first a general indication then more specific statements. If a succession is only in the torso, it should be written as such, either with a pin followed by a duration line to show the timing or with a pin placed in a bow. A body wave performed with a sudden accented start is called an "impulse."

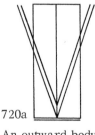

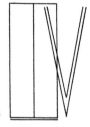

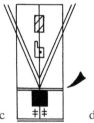

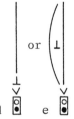

720a An outward body wave; general description

b A body wave on the right side of the body

c An impulse over forward and upward

d   or   e A succession over forward through the torso only

CHAPTER 28

Types of Revolutions;
Dynamics; Miscellaneous

THE THREE BASIC FORMS OF REVOLUTIONS

The body can revolve in three basically different ways. Each form
of revolution is around one of the three-dimensional axes in the
body. In the commonly used terminology they are:

Name: 1. Turning (pivoting)   Axis: Vertical (up-down)

2. Somersaulting   Lateral (side to side)

3. Cartwheeling   Sagittal (forward-backward)

SYMBOLS FOR THE THREE FORMS

Each of the three revolutions has two possible directions.

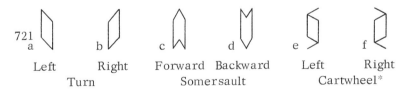

721
a   b   c   d   e   f

Left   Right   Forward Backward   Left   Right

Turn   Somersault   Cartwheel*

Each is based on the Cross of the Body Axes key ✛ .

These actions are analysed on page 470. Since any revolution is
comparable to a wheel around an axis, a wheel is used in the diagrams for clarification.

A brief survey is given here for the immediate needs. Deriva-
tion of the signs and their application and revolutions around diagonal axes will be given in Book II.

* See Appendix B, note 37.

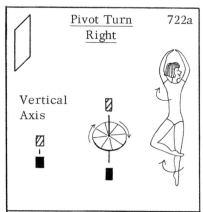

Pivot Turn
Right   722a

Vertical
Axis

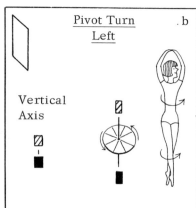

Pivot Turn
Left   . b

Vertical
Axis

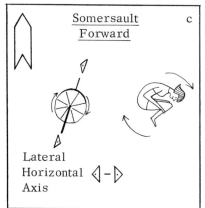

Somersault
Forward   c

Lateral
Horizontal ◁ – ▷
Axis

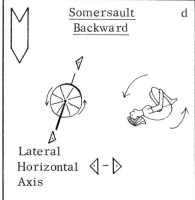

Somersault
Backward   d

Lateral
Horizontal ◁ – ▷
Axis

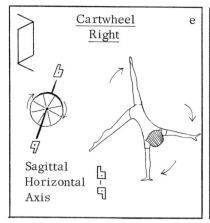

Cartwheel
Right   e

Sagittal
Horizontal
Axis

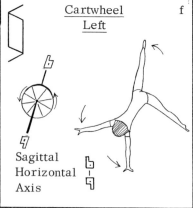

Cartwheel
Left   f

Sagittal
Horizontal
Axis

DEGREES OF REVOLUTION

Because a cartwheel includes within its action a change of front
degrees of cartwheeling are usually shown with black pins.

A full cartwheel   Half a cartwheel
to the right   to the left
          723a   b

In the case of somersaulting there is no change of front; therefore black pins, which express change of front, are not applicable
and fractions are used instead.

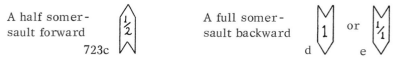

A half somer-   A full somer-
sault forward   sault backward   or
          723c   d   e

Because the number 1 may look like a pin, it may be written 1/1.

REVOLUTIONS WHILE LYING ON THE GROUND

One of the basic modes of traveling is through rolling, that is,
revolving while lying on the ground. In Motif Writing rolling is
first indicated as any revolution which is constantly supporting.
For this the composite sign for any kind of revolution is used.

Any kind of   Any kind of
revolution   rolling
          724a   b

In Structural Description the specific form of revolution is
stated and placement of the sign in the support column of the staff
indicates constant support. A path automatically results. A rotation which does not travel is a specialized movement requiring
rubbing against the floor and written briefly with a spot hold sign.

Log Rolling

When the performer is lying down, ordinary pivot turning
and produces log rolling, the rotation being around the longitudinal axis in the body.

If the path traveled is important the direction and distance can
be indicated outside the staff in a path sign. Though most rolling
produces straight paths, curved paths can also be achieved.

In Fig. 725 (a) the performer starts lying on his back. The one-and-a-half turn to the right produces log rolling, which results in the body traveling toward the right side of the stage and ending lying on the front.

In (b) the performer starts lying on his right side facing upstage. He then rolls over three times, producing a path toward the audience (forward room direction).

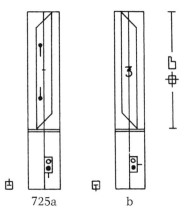

725a   b

Wheeling

In wheeling, an extremity of the body describes a horizontal circular path around a vertical axis. Where no progression is indicated wheeling is around the center of the body, i.e. on the spot, comparable to circling with steps in place. If the axis is at the head, the feet will describe the circular path, and vice versa. Such an action may be written with a circular path sign or described as a revolution around the vertical line of gravity by placing the key ⟶ within a turn sign. An exercise called "Around the Clock" provides a good example of wheeling the whole body on the spot.

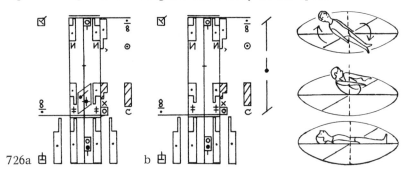

726a   b

In Fig. 726 (a) the performer starts lying on his back, limbs extended, facing the front of the room. On count 1, as the knees draw up to the chest and chest and head lift off the ground, $\frac{1}{8}$ turn is performed. Chest and legs then return to the ground. This is repeated eight times to "go around the clock." In (b) a less analysed, overall description of the wheeling is given.

Somersaulting

In a somersault on the ground the body progresses forward (or backward, as the case may
be) rolling along the ground. In Fig. 727 which
gives a very general description, the body
starts lying on the back, contracted, facing the
audience. The two forward somersaults that follow produce a path traveling toward the audience.

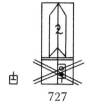

727

REVOLUTIONS IN THE AIR

Simple revolutions in the air - that is, without special leg gestures - are written in the same way as simple turning jumps. Two
straight lines are drawn in the leg gesture column to show that the
body is no longer supported on the feet.

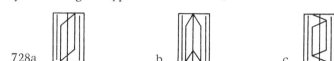

728a   b   c

When leg gestures occur during revolutions on the ground, a
hold sign is placed within the revolution sign to indicate that the
weight remains on the ground.

728d   e   f

In the air   On the ground   On the ground

Somersaulting (Aerial)

In the acrobatic exam-
ples given here no detail
as to exact performance is
shown; knowledge of the
form is taken for granted.
Many such forms make use
of revolving on a straight
path. In a book of instructions, however, notations
on the correct use of timing,
weight and other factors
must be given.

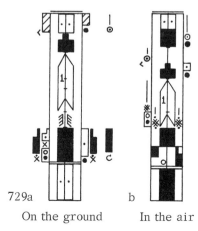

729a   b

On the ground   In the air

Cartwheeling (Aerial)

Note that indications for supports may make it more practical to place revolution signs outside the staff on the right as in Fig. 730 (a).

Parts of the body signs placed within a rotation sign indicate the axis for that revolution, e.g. the head, feet or hands. These will be dealt with in Book II.

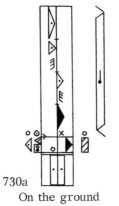

730a

On the ground

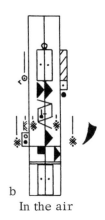

b

In the air

REVOLUTIONS FOR PARTS OF THE BODY

A somersault or a cartwheel type of revolution can occur in certain parts of the body to a limited degree. The body areas which can perform portions of somersault or cartwheel are the head, chest, pelvis and shoulder girdle. Some possibilities are explored here to make such usage clear.

ANALYSIS OF SOMERSAULTING FOR BODY AREAS

In the following illustrations a black dot represents the axis of the movement.

For the Head

The head, pivoting on the Atlas vertebra, can rotate in a somersault manner forward and backward, the axis being an imaginary line passing

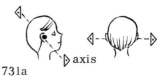

731a

through points near the ears. The head as a whole should remain vertical; no change in basic direction should occur unless written. The neck is not involved. A tilt is illustrated for comparison.

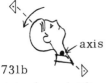

731b

A backward tilt
(involving the neck)

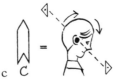

c

Forward somer-
sault rotation

d

Backward somer-
sault rotation

For the Pelvis

Though the pelvis is "captured" between the hip joints and the vertebrae in the waist area, by using each of these joints at once it can rotate around an imaginary lateral axis which passes through the center of the pelvic area. When such rotations are performed there should be no displacement of the upper body; head and chest remain where they are.

732a
Axis

732b

Forward rotation   Backward rotation

Displacement of the rib cage which has the feeling or intention of being a somersault can be so described though the action is not so clearly defined as somersaulting of the pelvis. Such rib cage actions can be seen in certain forms of African dance.

ANALYSIS OF CARTWHEELING FOR BODY AREAS

For the Head

Pivoting on the Atlas vertebra, the head can cartwheel around a sagittal axis located roughly at the nose. In a cartwheel the top of the head is displaced as much in one direction as the chin is in the opposite direction. The head as a whole remains upright,

733a
Axis for Cartwheel

no change of basic direction occurring unless written as an addition. The neck is not involved. A tilt is illustrated for comparison.

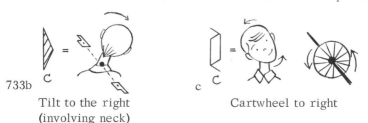

733b

Tilt to the right
(involving neck)   Cartwheel to right

For the Pelvis

The pelvis cartwheels around an imaginary sagittal axis. Many pelvic actions are tilts rather than cartwheels. In a tilt one hip joint is the pivotal point and the upper body is displaced in space. In a cartwheel one hip must be lowered as much as the other is raised; there should be no displacement in the upper body.

734a  b 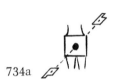 c

Axis for Cartwheeling   Tilt to the left   Cartwheel to left

For the Chest

An imaginary sagittal axis passes through the center of the chest. In a cartwheel the chest as a whole and the head remain vertical, no change of basic direction occurring unless written. The rib cage should move as much as possible as a unit. In contrast, in a tilt the upper body and head are displaced in space.

735a  b 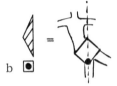 c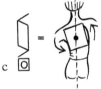

Axis for Cartwheeling   Tilt to the left   Cartwheel to left

DEGREE OF REVOLUTION FOR PARTS OF THE BODY

Because of structural limitations, body areas can perform only fragments of cartwheel and somersault rotations; therefore degrees are expressed in terms of little or much, rather than $\frac{1}{8}$, $\frac{1}{4}$, etc.

736a   b   c

A very slight for-   A great deal of   A slight backward
ward somersault   cartwheel of the   somersault of the
of the head   head to the right   pelvis

DYNAMICS

The study of dynamics is concerned with the action of forces in producing or changing the motion of a body. Aspects of dynamics which may be used for practical or expressive purposes can be described in fine detail in Labanotation. In dance dynamics is the area of study that concentrates on how a movement is performed, the quality or texture. Dynamic description includes use of energy, of the weight of the body, resistance to or giving in to the force of gravity, control or lack of control in movement, difference between muscular or emotional intensity, and so on. For many purposes only a general statement need be made and only a few basic symbols employed to modify the structured time-body-space description. Full details on dynamics will be explored in Book II.

INNATE DYNAMICS

Many patterns of movement contain innate dynamics which are usually performed unconsciously. For example, high steps tend to be lighter, lower steps heavier. The timing of a movement may influence the dynamics. In a movement where the body must cover a great distance in a short time, there will be an inevitable increase in the use of energy. A visible change in dynamics can be seen in jumps performed at too slow or too rapid a tempo. In a swinging motion the body makes use of the force of gravity: the motion speeds up as the path descends and slows down as the path rises. These examples show such changes in timing.

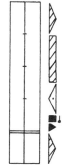 

737a Swing in which the pull of gravity is utilized: there is a natural slowing up as the arm rises.

b This timing requires a controlled lowering of the arm and additional energy to speed up at the end.

In terms of dynamics the effect of musical accompaniment on movement must not be overlooked. The same movement sequence will be performed with different dynamic qualities when danced to different pieces of music. This will be so in spite of the fact that the same tempi and metric structures may be present in each piece.

ACCENTS

An accent is the result of a sudden momentary increase in the use of energy. The additional energy disappears immediately. A distinction is made between a strong and a slight accent. When there is contact between two parts of the body or with an object, a strong accent produces sound, as in a stamp, clap, etc. A slight accent requires a slight use of energy, more than the normal level but not much; it is also a momentary happening which disappears immediately. Only a very slight sound, if any, is heard when a slight accent occurs with contact.

Accent Signs

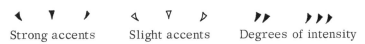

Strong accents   Slight accents   Degrees of intensity

These signs are doubled or even trebled for a greater effect of the same dynamic quality. Placement of the accent sign beside an action indicates when in the timing of that action the accent occurs.

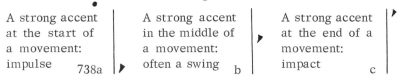

A strong accent at the start of a movement: impulse 738a	A strong accent in the middle of a movement: often a swing b	A strong accent at the end of a movement: impact c

An accent sign is placed so that its point slants toward the movement symbol or part of the body sign to which it applies. A large accent sign placed outside the whole staff on the right indicates that the whole body is affected. A vertical accent sign in the support column during a spring indicates accenting the motion of rising.

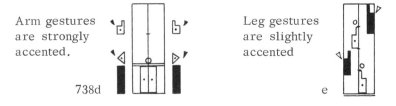

Arm gestures are strongly accented.

738d

Leg gestures are slightly accented

e

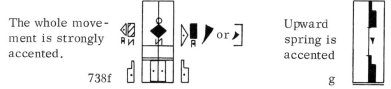

The whole move-
ment is strongly
accented.

Upward
spring is
accented

738f

g

Stamps

An accented contact with the floor produces a stamp. This may be strong or slight and may occur on a support or on a gesture.

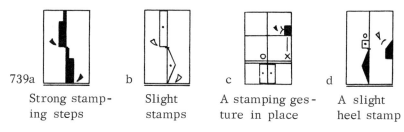

739a

Strong stamp-
ing steps

b

Slight
stamps

c

A stamping ges-
ture in place

d

A slight
heel stamp

By using an addition bracket (see page 483) constant repetition of the accent signs can be eliminated. Within this bracket, which is placed alongside the movement symbols it qualifies, is written the indication to be added to the movement pattern. In (e) both steps and touching gestures are qualified. If only steps are to be qualified, the appropriate indication is placed within a path sign, as in (f). (See pages 161, 179 for such use of a path sign.)

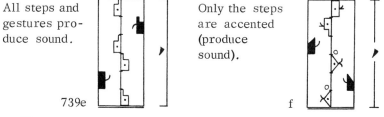

All steps and
gestures pro-
duce sound.

Only the steps
are accented
(produce
sound).

739e

f

Claps

Contact of the hands with a strong accent produces clapping. A general description may be written with the hand sign or with the palm sign. Specific use of the parts of the palm as in Spanish dancing will be given in Book II.

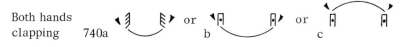

Both hands
clapping   740a   b   c

The bow may be swung downward or upward; its ends state the moment of contact. One hand can be shown to be active by using only one accent sign.

The right hand
claps the left. 740d

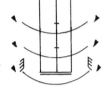

The left hand
claps the right. e

When the bow is swung out into the appropriate column, use of the hand can be understood, the hand symbol need not be written each time.

740f

Contact or Release of Hands after a Clap

If nothing specific is stated, exact performance is left open. The hands may remain together after a clap or may release. When the hands are to remain together, a hold sign is used; when they are to be released, a release sign is used.

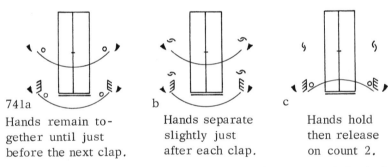

741a Hands remain together until just before the next clap.

b Hands separate slightly just after each clap.

c Hands hold then release on count 2.

Claps may also involve contacts with other parts of the body. Figs. 741 (d-f) may produce sound depending on the clothing worn.

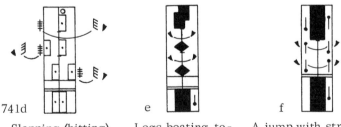

741d Slapping (hitting) foot as in a Schuhplattler

e Legs beating together (clapping) in the air

f A jump with strong leg beats (in ballet an entrechat six, written fully)

Bouncing

Indication of elasticity (resiliency 🗲) gives a general statement of a bouncing action. To be specific we can state whether a bounce results from a foot action or flexion in the legs. Pins can be used to show the direction of bouncing.

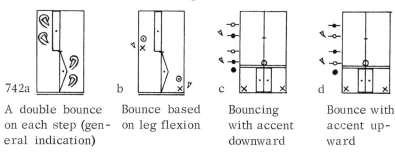

742a A double bounce on each step (general indication)

b Bounce based on leg flexion

c Bouncing with accent downward

d Bounce with accent upward

VIBRATING

A small wavy line is used to indicate vibrating, trembling, or shaking. This is the same indication used in music for tremolo, trill. Such shaking actions can be described in greater detail by adding dynamic signs. An example specifying the space pattern is given on page 443, Fig. 663 (c).

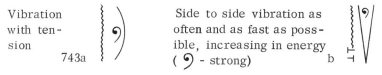

Vibration with tension   743a

Side to side vibration as often and as fast as possible, increasing in energy (🗲 - strong)   b

USE OF ENERGY

A full discussion of the ebb and flow of energy in movement, its use in relation to the force of gravity and other dynamic aspects will be presented fully in Book II following the present intensive international research discussions on this subject. (See Glossary for trial symbols which may be found in experimental scores.)

PASSIVE

A passive movement is one which occurs as the result of another movement. An outer force, such as a partner, may be the initiator, or one part of the body may initiate a movement causing resultant motion in another part; in each case the part of the body which moves passively must allow the movement to occur. This involves an adjustment in the use of energy (dynamics) for that part. Such adjustment can be described in full detail, but the passive indication usually suffices to produce the desired performance.

The solid line representing an action is changed to a dotted line to indicate passivity.

An action (move-	Passive, resul-
ment is initiated)	tant movement
744a	b

The dotted line may be (1) used on its own, (2) placed in connection with a direction symbol when a specific destination is required as in (c-e), or (3) applied to path signs when a path results from some outside action as when a partner causes a performer to travel, turn, etc. as in (f).

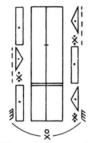

744c   d   e   f

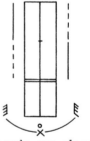 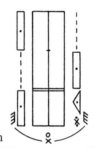 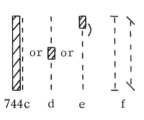

744g

The hands are clasped. The right arm performs an action which causes a movement of the left arm. The roles are then reversed.

h

The same as (g), but a specific direction is stated for the active arm.

i

The same as (g), but a specific direction has been stated for the passive arm as well.

The dotted line may also suggest passivity in movement where there is no actual contact. In (j) the hands do not touch but the relationship of active part to passive part is the same as that in (g). The limb marked as being passive must make its own movement but a different expression results from the suggested influence of the active arm.

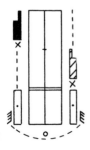

744j

MISCELLANEOUS

ACCELERANDO AND RITARDANDO

It is possible to speed up or slow down a single directional movement. Such change in timing is shown by writing the same symbol twice in different lengths, and binding the two together with a small round vertical bow to show unity of action. The relative proportions of the symbols indicate the relative degree of accelerando or ritardando.

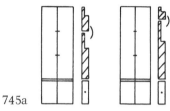
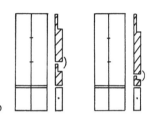

745a — The gesture starts slowly and becomes more rapid.

b — The gesture starts quickly and then gradually peters out.

THE ADDITION BRACKET

Details to be added to stated movement may more conveniently be written alongside rather than within the columns. For this purpose an angular vertical bracket is used.* The indications within it are valid as long as the bracket lasts or as long as the final indication next to which it is placed is valid. For this reason it is sometimes preferable to the vertical passing state bow.

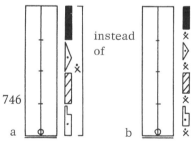
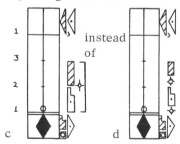

746 a, b — All four directions are to be passed through with the arm 2 degrees flexed.

c, d — The right arm gesture is to be read from the Body System of Reference.

---

* See Appendix B, note 38.

In (a) the bracket makes repetition of X unnecessary. In (c) the addition bracket obviates the need for subsequent cancellation required in (d). See also Figs. 447 e, 488 d, 651 d, 738 f, 739 e.

KEY SIGNATURES

The term "key signature," taken from music, is given to all symbols appearing before the start of a dance score or kinetogram to indicate how subsequent movements are to be interpreted. These keys may refer to the system of reference to be used, a particular way of holding a part of the body or a specific manner of moving. A key may also be an abbreviation stated in the form of an equation: a simple symbol or group of symbols represents a more complex action.

The key signature is placed below the starting position as a separate indication written between double horizontal lines.

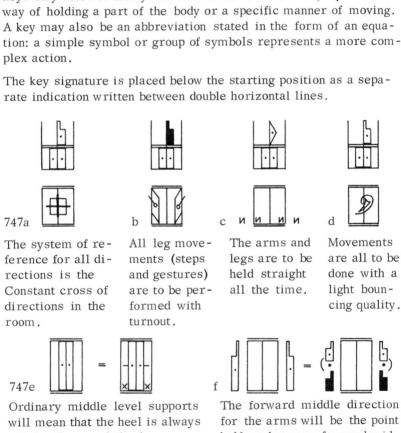

747a   The system of reference for all directions is the Constant cross of directions in the room.

b   All leg movements (steps and gestures) are to be performed with turnout.

c   The arms and legs are to be held straight all the time.

d   Movements are all to be done with a light bouncing quality.

747e   Ordinary middle level supports will mean that the heel is always off the floor and the knees are slightly bent.

f   The forward middle direction for the arms will be the point halfway between forward middle and forward low.

For additional examples see page 202, Fig. 280 and pages 290-1, Figs. 423 and 424.

Alternate Versions

"KIN" represents usage of the Laban system as established by Albrecht Knust.

1. (pp. 39, 44). When horizontal ticks would not show and the beat must be made clear, ticks can be drawn slanted as in Fig. 748 (a). Many European notators do not use tick marks in general practice; others draw faint lines across the three-line staff to contrast with the stronger bar lines, as in Fig. 748 (b).

748a   b

2. (p. 45). Measure numbers may be placed within a diamond below each staff, the number identifying the first measure of that staff.   749

3. (p. 107). Front signs ⊞ are placed at the right of the staff in KIN.

4. (p. 131). A palm-facing indication is not automatically cancelled according to KIN; a return to normal must be stated in each case.

5. (pp. 131, 179, 245). Back to normal is sometimes indicated by the sign ∧ instead of ⊙. The decrease sign expresses a diminution of the previous state.

6. (pp. 159, 171, 325). To achieve a state of × or И the notator may place the indication after a duration line, tying the two signs together with a small bow, as in Fig. 750 (a) which has the same meaning as (b). Until 1969 (c) was interpreted as destination; it now indicates motion.

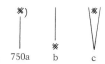

750a   b   c

7. (p. 187). Circular paths to the left are placed on the left of the staff in KIN, all other paths being placed on the right.

8. (p. 211). Indication of timing in achieving a change of touch has been written in KIN with an increase sign, as in Fig. 751 (a).   751a

for   b

9. (p. 219). A sliding support in which weight is held on the ground throughout is written in KIN by placing a hold sign within the support symbol, as in Fig. 752.

752

10. (pp. 269, 305). An understood space hold, i.e. retention of the previously stated Standard direction, is considered in KIN to be the basic rule. Because the appropriate hold sign is always used when needed, in practice this difference in basic understanding causes no problems.

11. (p. 332). Shifting is analyzed in KIN as a small displacement while the part of the body remains in the previously established direction. Appropriate pins are placed next to the appropriate direction symbol. Figs. 753 (a) and (b) are the same.   753a   b

12. (pp. 346, 354). The analogy signs = and ≗ are used for repeats in KIN scores instead of ÷ and ≑ Thus Fig. 754 (a) is used instead of (b), and (c) instead of (d).   754a =   b ÷   c ≗   d ≑

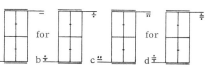

for   for

13. (p. 358). Such indication may also be stated as ⏚ .

Old Versions

Widespread use of the system since the 1954 edition of Labanotation has indicated where for practical purposes simplification and modification were needed. This list of changes also includes pre-1954 items which may be met in old scores.

"KIN" represents usage of the Laban system as established by Albrecht Knust.

1. (p. 21). <u>The Vertical Staff.</u> The advantage of the vertical staff is sometimes questioned. Its historical development best illustrates why a vertical rather than a horizontal staff was finally chosen as being the more practical. Following his first shorthand device based on his known movement patterns, Laban sought to develop a more comprehensive and universally applicable system. His first attempt was based on a series of crosses read horizontally from left to right. Each cross represented the performer as seen from the back, the vertical center line dividing right and left (Fig. 755 (a). On these crosses were placed symbols for movement of the torso and limbs. Supports (steps) were placed at the base, either side of the center line, at S in Fig. (b). Next to these were written gestures of the legs in the air, at G. The line x-x divided the upper part of the body from the lower. At B were written movements of the body, and at A movements of the arms. Only a small amount of movement could be shown on each cross with the result that indications provided more a record of positions with no possibility of showing continuity in motion from one cross to the next. The movement of a left leg gesture on one cross, for example, could not be connected with movement shown on the next cross. The important aspect of the basic flow of movement could not be shown.

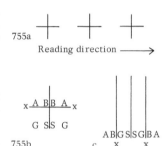

755a   Reading direction ⟶

755b

Laban credited Kurt Jooss with the inspiration to change the line x-x to a vertical line on either side of the center line as in Fig. (c), thus providing spaces for indications of body and arm movements on either side of the support and leg gesture columns. A change in reading direction from horizontal to vertical made it possible to show continuous movement indications for a part of the body without any break in the flow of reading.

Laban also credited Feuillet with the idea of a center line of continuity which is incorporated in the Laban system.

The original staff comprising five lines, which made use of music paper, was reduced to the present-day three-line staff because the extra lines visually detracted from the movement indications.

2. (p. 82). Lifting the weight in an échappé action was formerly analyzed as a minute spring and written with a very small space between support symbols. In KIN no space was left at all, as in Fig. 756 (b).

Old 756a   KIN b   New c

3. (pp. 107, 421). Front signs were originally white pins, as in Fig. 757 (a). (In KIN they were as in (b).)

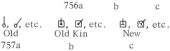

♩, ♩, etc.   ⊟, ⊠, etc.   ⊟, ⊠, etc.
Old   Old Kin   New
757a   b   c

4. (pp. 138, 246). A duration line was used after a space hold sign to indicate how long it lasted. This line is no longer considered necessary though sometimes used in special cases.

758 ◇

5. (p. 139). A round bow was formerly used instead of a caret to indicate continuation of a symbol from the end of one staff to the beginning of the next.

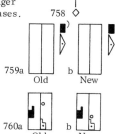

759a Old   b New

6. (p. 141). A hold symbol in the support column was not needed formerly when one leg gesture was stated, the rule having been that one leg gesture presupposed supporting on the other leg. A jump required two leg gestures or none, i.e. a space between support symbols. When a support and a gesture ended simultaneously, a spring into the air was expected to follow.

760a Old   b New

7. (p. 158). The sign for long (stretched) was formerly drawn ⌐.

8. (p. 165). Double stretched ⇄ for an arm or leg gesture used to mean pulling out from the body into the stated direction. Such body participation is now analyzed as an inclusion.

761a Old   b New

9. (p. 175). When the symbols ✕ or И were placed next to quick or slow steps to modify the whole step, a duration line was used. Fig. 762 (a) is now written as (b).

Old   New
762a   b

10. (p. 181). The standard shape for stage plans used to have slanting sides.

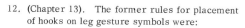

Old   New
763a   b

11. (p. 184). Spiraling in and out were formerly written by placing the symbols ✕ and И, respectively, near the end of a circular path sign, as in Figs. 764 (a) and (c).

764a   b   c   d
Old   New   Old   New

12. (Chapter 13). The former rules for placement of hooks on leg gesture symbols were:

i) (p. 208). The hook modified the whole symbol. Its placement did not have time significance, and therefore it was usually centered to show one single touching action; Fig. 765 (a) is now written as (b).

765a Old   b New

ii) (p. 212). Two different hooks on a symbol did not produce a slide but rather a change from one part of the foot touching to another; (c) is now written as (d).

765c Old   d New

iii) (p. 212). A sliding leg gesture in which a change from one part of the foot to another occurred required two of the same hooks; (e) is now written as (f).

765e Old   f New

iv) (p. 212). Placement of the two hooks for sliding did not have time significance; raising the leg from the floor after a touch or slide required a separate symbol; (g) is now written as (h).

765g Old   h New

Rules for hooks qualifying supports have not changed.

13. (pp. 210, 356). The specific performance sign was formerly encircled.

766a Old   b New

14. (p. 223). Elbow, wrist, and hand signs were formerly drawn with a longer stem.

767a Old   b New

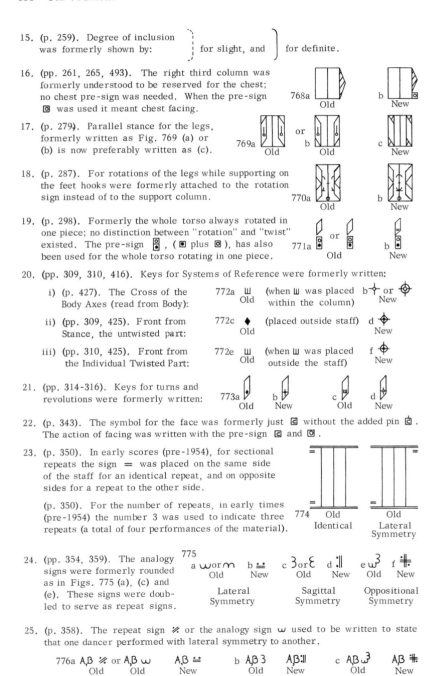

15. (p. 259). Degree of inclusion was formerly shown by: ⌐ for slight, and ⌐ for definite.

16. (pp. 261, 265, 493). The right third column was formerly understood to be reserved for the chest; no chest pre-sign was needed. When the pre-sign ◙ was used it meant chest facing.   768a Old   b New

17. (p. 279). Parallel stance for the legs, formerly written as Fig. 769 (a) or (b) is now preferably written as (c).   769a Old   or b Old   c New

18. (p. 287). For rotations of the legs while supporting on the feet hooks were formerly attached to the rotation sign instead of to the support column.   770a Old   b New

19. (p. 298). Formerly the whole torso always rotated in one piece; no distinction between "rotation" and "twist" existed. The pre-sign ▣, (◙ plus ◙), has also been used for the whole torso rotating in one piece.   771a Old   or b New

20. (pp. 309, 310, 416). Keys for Systems of Reference were formerly written:

    i) (p. 427). The Cross of the Body Axes (read from Body):   772a Old (when ⨇ was placed within the column)   b or New

    ii) (pp. 309, 425). Front from Stance, the untwisted part: 772c ◆ Old (placed outside staff)   d New

    iii) (pp. 310, 425). Front from the Individual Twisted Part: 772e Old (when ⨇ was placed outside the staff)   f New

21. (pp. 314-316). Keys for turns and revolutions were formerly written: 773a Old   b New   c Old   d New

22. (p. 343). The symbol for the face was formerly just ◙ without the added pin ◙. The action of facing was written with the pre-sign ◙ and ◙.

23. (p. 350). In early scores (pre-1954), for sectional repeats the sign ═ was placed on the same side of the staff for an identical repeat, and on opposite sides for a repeat to the other side.

    (p. 350). For the number of repeats, in early times (pre-1954) the number 3 was used to indicate three repeats (a total of four performances of the material).   774   Old Identical   Old Lateral Symmetry

24. (pp. 354, 359). The analogy signs were formerly rounded as in Figs. 775 (a), (c) and (e). These signs were doubled to serve as repeat signs.   775   a worm Old   b New   Lateral Symmetry   c 3 or Ɛ Old   d New   Sagittal Symmetry   e ꞷ³ Old   f New   Oppositional Symmetry

25. (p. 358). The repeat sign ✕ or the analogy sign ꞷ used to be written to state that one dancer performed with lateral symmetry to another.

    776a A,B ✕ or A,B ꞷ   A,B ═   b A,B 3   A,B:‖   c A,B ꞷ³   A,B ⫴
    Old   Old   New   Old   New   Old   New

26. (pp.387,391). Unspecified touching and sliding were formerly shown by use of a short stroke —.

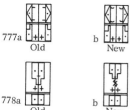

777a Old   b New

27. (p. 391). For distance in supporting on the hips (sitting) the unqualified direction symbol used to mean a comfortable distance from the previous point of support.

778a Old   b New

28. (p. 393). Lying used to be written as supporting on the hips and shoulders. Lying on the front or back was indicated by the appropriate direction symbols.

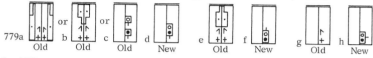

779a Old   b Old   or   c Old   d New   e Old   f New   g Old   h New

29. (p. 399). The center of gravity sign was formerly written ▣.

30. (p. 401). Formerly only the degrees of ✕ and ✳ existed for distance of the center of gravity; now all six degrees are used.

Level of center of gravity in a high kneel used to be described as high; it is now considered to be halfway down on the normal scale toward the point of support. Changing from a high kneel to a low kneel used to be described as center of gravity moving backward middle. Because the center of weight is supported all the time, it is now described as change of level in place. (Backward would be a falling action).

780a Old   b New

780c Old   d New

A high jump was formerly written as the center of gravity traveling a long way up; this is now written with a path sign.

780e Old   f New

In very early scores (pre-1954) the center of gravity at floor level was described as low level, and the point halfway between the floor and normal standing was middle level.

780g Old   h New

31. (p. 422). Direction judged according to the Constant Room directions was formerly indicated by a small box (i.e. the present key without the cross superimposed).

781a Old   b New

32. (p. 430). The sign for the Fixed Points in the Room was formerly ⊠ .

33. (p. 444). Deviations were formerly indicated by tiny direction symbols placed as pre-signs before standard-sized direction symbols indicating the main movement. As a pre-sign, the deviation was included in the time value of the symbol.

782a Old   b New

34. (p. 449). The spot hold sign was formerly drawn ⊠ or ⊗ .

35. (p. 455). Fingers were formerly indicated by dots placed between the strokes of the hand sign ≋ .

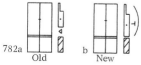

783 Old New   Old New   Old New etc.
     Fingers   Thumb   Little Finger

36. (pp. 459, 460). The double lateral extension
and contraction signs were formerly drawn:

784a b

Old   New

37. (p. 469). The cartwheel sign
was formerly drawn:

785a)) b)   ((c) d

Old   New   Old   New

38. (p. 483). Some indications which are now placed in an
angular addition bracket were formerly placed in a
curved vertical bow.

786a ×) b ×]

Old   New

Appendix C

Orthography and Autography

In Labanotation the symbols have been devised so that differences between them are obvious and their meanings remain clear even when drawn hastily or by a child. Standardization in orthography is based on what is visually practical to facilitate reading. Full details on orthography for finished scores for publication can be obtained from any center using Labanotation, such as the Dance Notation Bureau in New York City.

1. DIRECTION SYMBOLS

i) The length of the "indicator" on direction symbols
is one third to one quarter that of the whole symbol.
In using a notation typewriter flexibility in proportionate length is limited. Side symbols are usually
drawn to a point, but when much elongated are flattened as in (d) so that the symbol fits into a column.

ii) Symbols meeting with slanted sides, as in (e) should
not overlap as in (f). In (g) dotted lines are used between the side symbols to show clearly the space
which indicates the amount of time spent in the air.

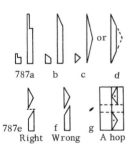

787a b c d or

787e f g A hop
Right Wrong

2. PLACEMENT OF HOOKS

On symbols with slanted edges hooks are placed as
in (a), as though attached to straight edged symbols.
When a hook appears at the end of the symbol it should
terminate where the symbol terminates as in (c).

On slender indicators the hook is placed on a line with
the other hook, as in (e). Fig. (f) is not considered
correct; (g) is acceptable but not preferred.

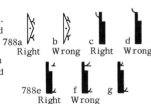

788a b c d
Right Wrong Right Wrong

788e f g
Right Wrong

3. USE OF THE COLUMNS

The following chart illustrates standard placement of symbols on the vertical three-line
staff. Alternate placements are described in the various chapters dealing with specific
parts. When hand and finger indications do not exist, head indications and path signs
are placed closer to the staff. The same is true of measure and count numbers and
front signs.

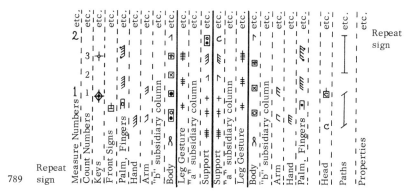

Only the three basic lines of the staff are used in actual practice.

4. EXACT TIMING

A general statement of timing for a movement presupposes a general interpretation. Precision is indicated by the size and placement of the movement symbol, or by the specific performance sign ✳ . The following examples illustrate how the timing of one beat is generally interpreted and how it is made more specific. (See also page 356, Fig. 533.)

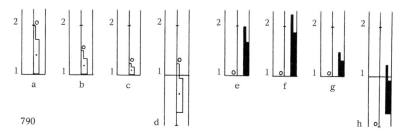

In Figs. 790 (a), (b), and (c) a clap occurring right at the start of beat 1 would come at the moment the foot contacts the ground (start of step). Any preparatory movement prior to this contact is taken for granted. The timing of such a preparatory movement is in proportion to the timing of the following step. In (a) the step on count 1 comfortably takes the duration of the whole of this beat. By count 2 the step is over; there is no more movement. In (b) a swifter step takes only the first half of count 1 so that by the second half of the beat, "&", there is no more movement. Fig. (c) shows an extremely staccato step occurring right on the beat with a minimum of preparation. In (d) a step of the same duration as (a) finishes exactly on count 1, having started comfortably before the beat. If in this example a clap occurred on count 1 ("on the dot") i.e. exactly at the start of the beat, it would coincide with the final centering of weight at the conclusion of the step. Fig. (e) shows a leg gesture occurring on count 1 (i.e. count 1 in general). By count 2 all movement has ceased. In (f) the gesture takes all of count 1 and arrives at its destination only at the very beginning of count 2. In (g) a quicker gesture starts on count 1 and is finished by "&". In (h) the gesture starts ahead of count 1 so that it can finish right on the dot of 1. If the foot hit a drum at the conclusion of the gesture, the sound would come right on 1 (the start of the beat).

Upper Body Movement

A method of analysing and writing torso movements, known as Upper Body Movements, has been in use among Kinetographers since the early days. This usage, explained in this appendix, has its particular advantages, but in general has not been used by Labanotators whose concern has been more with exactness of detail. The analysis and method of writing are given here for all who need it.

A general description of body (torso, trunk) movements is suitable for the type of actions in which the spine, the thorax, and shoulder areas participate in movements of the arms. Such actions can be seen in work activities as well as everyday actions. Many folk and national dances use the torso in this manner, it being a natural and unstudied usage. The term "Upper Body Movements"* has been given to such actions which may also occur without arm movements.

DESCRIPTION OF UPPER BODY MOVEMENT

When caused by an arm movement, resultant participation of the upper body is indicated by an inclusion bow (see pages 253-258). When the same form of upper body movement is required but without an accompanying arm gesture, it is described by the direction symbol which would have been written for the arm had the arm caused it. To understand such usage, the reader must comprehend the special analysis of Upper Body Movements.

ANALYSIS OF UPPER BODY MOVEMENT

The term "Upper Body Movements"* refers to movements which range from involving only the shoulder section of the spine (the upper dorsal vertebrae) to involving the whole of the movable spine including the lumbar region. In all these movements the hip joint is not involved. How much of the spine is used is indicated by the level of the movement symbols and may also depend on the movement context. It is purposely not exactly defined since other means exist for exact description of torso movements.

In the analysis of Upper Body Movements the upper torso may be likened to the letter T in which the stem (spinal column) is flexible but fixed at its base; the crossbar at the top of the T represents the shoulder section (upper thorax area of the spine). This crossbar can tilt or twist or do both at once. One side of the crossbar may initiate the movement causing a resultant movement of the other side, or both may move in unison or in opposition to one another.

791

A special convention keeps movement description simple in the analysis of Upper Body Movements. Direction and level are not described in the usual terms of destination, the point reached, but in terms of motion toward a direction. High level means a slight movement in the stated direction, involving only the upper spine. Middle level indicates a bigger movement, involving the dorsal spine. Low level indicates a still larger movement involving the lumbar vertebrae. It is important that this convention of describing Upper Body Movements from the point of view of motion instead of destination be clearly understood from the start. In writing a starting position, the direction signs in the third column indicate the result of such a motion.

Upper Body Movements may feature one side (of the T) or both at once. For this reason columns on each side of the staff are needed.

* Formerly called "upper part of body" movement.

METHOD OF WRITING

Upper body actions are written with direction symbols placed on either side of the staff in columns just outside the outer staff lines (the third column). Generally no pre-sign is used.* Although one side of the upper body cannot move in isolation without affecting the other side, actions are described as being one-sided when one side is predominant. A feeling of one-sided body actions is a particular feature of this description of torso movement.

792   3|2 1|1 2|3

SINGLE-SIDED UPPER BODY INDICATIONS

Movements led or initiated by one side of the upper body are written in either the right or left third column on the staff, according to which is applicable.

In the Lateral Direction

Inclinations to the right side are written in the right third column, as they are usually initiated by the right side of the upper body. The degree of tilt and increase in involvement of the spine are shown by the level.

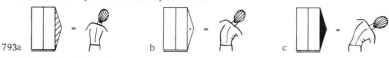

793a   b   c

In the Sagittal Directions

Movements forward or backward with one side produce a twist in addition to a tilt. When a diagonal direction is used this twist is proportionally less.

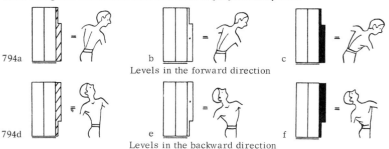

794a   b   c

Levels in the forward direction

794d   e   f

Levels in the backward direction

Involvement of the Head. The head does not actively join in Upper Body Movements, but reacts passively, i.e. is carried along so that there is no stiffness. When a twist occurs the head does not turn.

DOUBLE-SIDED UPPER BODY INDICATIONS

In the Same Direction

When both sides of the upper body move in the same direction no twist occurs. In the sideward direction double-sided indications produce a more definite tilt, both sides being active.

795a

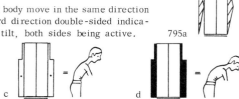

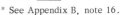

795b   c   d

* See Appendix B, note 16.

In Opposition

When each side is shown to move into an equal and opposite sagittal direction, as in Fig. 796 (a), only a twist occurs, a tilt is cancelled out. A lesser twist is indicated by use of diagonal directions as in (b).   796a

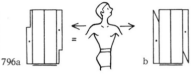

b

ARM MOVEMENTS WITH UPPER BODY INDICATIONS

The arms may move in the same direction as the upper body, or they may move elsewhere. In the former case the Upper Body Movement can be written as an inclusion if the upper body change is a result of the arm movement and not an action on its own. Compare Fig. 797 (b) and (c)

Unison in arm and right-sided Upper Body Movement   797a

On count 2 the right side is predominant, the left arm balancing in the opposite direction.

b

OR

c

The same Upper Body Movement as above, with the arm moving into other directions   797d

The arms are up when the upper spine is twisted, then move diagonally backward when the right side of the upper body moves forward low.

e

SYMBOLS FOR UPPER BODY MOVEMENTS

Because a direction symbol in the third column describes Upper Body Movement, no pre-sign is needed. When Upper Body Movements are described out of context, as in Motif Writing, the pre-sign ⅄ is required. This sign suggests the idea of Upper Body Movements - a free use of the chest with some involvement below the chest. When a one-sided indication is needed, a small stroke is added to identify right or left. Note the following equivalents:

 =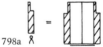

798a ⅄

 b ⅄

c ⅄

CANCELLATIONS

An Upper Body Movement indication is valid until cancelled by:

(a) another Upper Body indication, or (b) a return to normal, or
(c) specific movements of the shoulder girdle, chest, or whole torso.

In Figs. 799 all Upper Body Movements occurring on count 1 are cancelled on count 2.

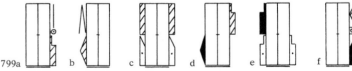

799a   b   c   d   e   f

Figs. 799 (a) to (c) show a return to normal. Fig. (d) shows a left side low tilt cancelled by a right-sided forward high tilt plus twist. In (e) the double-sided forward tilt is changed to a left-sided forward low tilt plus twist. In (f) an Upper Body Movement is cancelled by a chest tilt.

Terminology

a - the name for the second part of a beat of music divided into three (a triplet).

"a" column - additional (subsidiary) column for the legs.

Adequate Curve - equal to the curve stated and expected, sufficient.

Aerial Step - one in which the performer rises into the air, i.e. some form of jumping.

"and" or "&" - the name for the second half of a beat of music.

Attached Symbol - a smaller symbol (representing a minor segment of a limb) attached, i.e. placed immediately adjacent to a standard-sized symbol representing the main segment of that limb. Also called a "parasite" symbol

Augmented Curve - greater than that stated or expected.

Autography - the drawing of symbols, conventions, and standardization pertaining to how symbols are drawn.

Axis - the principal line along which extension or around which a rotation occurs.

"b" column - additional (subsidiary) column for the body and arms.

Bar - a commonly used term for measure in music.

Binary - consisting of two parts. In skips and gallops, the rhythmical arrangement of the three part action into a time division of two equal parts.

Bending - the folding in of a limb toward the center in which the extremity approaches base on a curved line (see analysis on page 318). (See also Folding, Curving.)

Blind Turns - see Non-swivel Turns.

Body Directions - directions described according to the Cross of the Body Axes.

Bound Flow - movement in which the factor of motion itself is restrained, constrained, confined, controlled, held back.

Butterfly - a nickname for the symbols ⋈ and ⋈ or ⋈ .

Center of Gravity - the point about which a body is in equilibrium, balanced.

Central - pertaining to parts of the body at or near the center. For the body as a whole it is the parts of the torso, shoulders, hips. For the hand the wrist is the central part. Movement which is spatially central occurs near the center of the body and may be performed by peripheral parts of the body.

Constant Directions - directions described according to the Constant Cross of Axes.

Contraction - a form of flexion; specifically the drawing in of a limb toward the center in which extremity approaches base on a straight line. (See analysis on page 318.) The term contraction is given its anatomical sense and not, as in certain contemporary dance techniques, specifically applied to a stylized movement of the torso.

Cross of Axes - three lines intersecting at right angles. From the point of intersection each line goes out in two opposite directions into infinity. It is from this central point, called "place," that all directions are judged.

Curling - see Curving.

Curving - the action of bending (folding) in which a multi-segmented part of the body produces a curve (see analysis on page 318). (See also Bending, Folding.)

"da" - the name for the third part of a beat of music divided into three (a triplet).

Dependent Part - a segment of the body attached to a larger or more centrally situated part. (See also Major & Minor Parts.)

Destination - a state or position which is reached by some action.

Deviating Curve - a curve normally lying on a plane (two-dimensional) but which is caused by a turn of the body to pass through a third dimension and become conical.

Deviation - a departure from the main line of a movement or from a standard position.

Diminished Curve - less than that stated or expected.

Distal - that end of a segment of the body which is farthest from the center, or from the point of attachment to the body.

Dynamic - pertaining to power, to physical forces or energy, to forces producing motion.

Dynamics - the action of forces which produce or change motion of a body. In dance dynamics refers to factors which affect the expression, texture or quality of motion.

Effort-Shape - see definition on page 12.

Expansion - three-dimensional extension, enlargement.

Facing - the action of directing a surface of a part of the body toward a person, an object, or a particular spatial point.

Fine - end, last time for a repeat.

Fixed-base Turns - see Non-swivel Turns.

Flexion - the general term for the group of actions to which contracting and bending (folding) belong.

Folding - bending a single joint in which the free end approaches the base on a curved line (see analysis on page 318). (See also Bending, Curving.)

Free End - that end of a limb which is not attached to the body.

Free Flow - movement in which the factor of motion itself is free to follow its natural course, unrestrained, unfettered, uninhibited, uncontrolled, unrestricted.

Friction - the resistance to relative motion between two parts in contact. If the parts are in sliding contact, e.g. the foot and floor in pivot turns, the resistance is called sliding friction. ("Frictionless" turns was a former misnomer for non-swivel.)

Front Signs - signs for the Constant Directions in the room, used to indicate in which room direction (or stage direction) the performer is facing.

Horizontal Curve - a curve lying in a horizontal plane.

Inclusion - participation of one part of the body in an action of a neighboring part.

Jump - specific meaning: the term "a jump" refers to the specific form in which the performer leaves the ground from two feet and lands on two feet.

Jumps - general meaning: aerial steps.

Key - an indication used in dance scores comparable in use to the keys in music notation. The key stated at the start of a score modifies subsequent movement indications. Usually the term "key" refers to a system of reference for directional description.

Key Signature - a statement at the start of a score concerning certain specific usages to be applied throughout the score. These may be abbreviations expressed as an equation. Such statements are also termed pre-score indications.

Kinetography - the transcribing of movement (translation into signs on paper).

Kinetology - the science and study of movement.

Kinetogram - a sequence of movement written in Labanotation (Kinetography Laban).

Labanalysis (Labananalysis) - the analysis of movement based on Laban's investigation and further developed by contributions of specialists in many fields.

Labanotator - one who records movement using the Laban system.

Lateral - lying in or pertaining to the side-to-side plane or directions.

Legato - bound together, a smooth and connected manner of performance.

Major Parts - the central or main parts of the body, e.g. upper arm in relation to lower arm, lower arm in relation to hand. (See also Dependent & Minor Parts.)

Measure - a group of beats in music enclosed by bar lines, e.g. a measure of 3/4 (3 beats of quarter note value grouped together), a measure of 4/4 (4 beats of quarter note value grouped together).

Meter - the time signature of a piece of music or dance, i.e. the division of a composition into measures consisting of a uniform number of regularly recurring beats or time units.

Minor Parts - the extremities of the body, parts farther away from the center, e.g. the hand in relation to the lower arm, the lower arm in relation to the upper arm. (See also Major & Dependent Parts.)

Motif - the idea behind a movement, the concept, the intention of an action, the motivation which causes an action. Also the "germ" or "theme" comparable to a Leitmotif in music.

Motif Writing - see definition on page 11.

Motion - a movement or action, the tendency, intention, or character of which is stated (e.g. rising, advancing, contracting, relaxing, etc.) but for which the terminal state (destination) is left open.

Non-swivel Turns - a turn of the body in which there is no sliding friction of the supporting surface (also known as Fixed-base and Blind turn).

Orthography - art of writing words with the proper letters, according to standard usage, correct spelling.

Parasite - the nickname for a device to simplify writing in which the direction for a minor part of a limb is written as a smaller symbol and attached to a standard sized symbol indicating direction for the major part.

Passive Movement - a change in a part of the body or of the body as a whole produced by an action in another part or by another person, the affected part "allowing" the change to take place.

Peripheral - pertaining to the external boundary or surface of any body. Peripheral parts of the body are the extremities: hands, feet, and head. Spatially peripheral movement is that which occurs far from the center and in which the limbs usually must be extended.

Place (Place Middle) - the zero point, the center from which all directions emanate and from which they are judged and accordingly named. In supporting, place is beneath, at, or above the center of weight.

Point of Attachment - the base of a limb where it is attached to the body, or where a minor part is attached to a major part.

Position - an established and recognized destination.

Pre-score Indication - a statement at the start of a movement score of specific usages which are to be in effect throughout the score. Often these are key signatures.

Pre-sign - a sign placed before the main symbol, e.g. a space measurement sign or a sign for a part of the body placed before a direction symbol.

Pre-staff Indication - any indication placed below a staff, e.g. identification of a person, specific use of columns, or reminder of a previously established position.

Proximal - that end of a segment of the body which is closest to the center of the body.

Resultant Movement - a change for a part of the body or the body as a whole which is caused by an action in another part or by another person. This outside action may be resisted (in contrast to passive where it is "allowed" to happen).

Retention Sign - a sign stating that some aspect of an acquired state is to be retained. While the word "hold" is often used (e.g. hold sign, space hold, spot hold), the term "retention" is more suitable for all uses to which retention signs are put.

Revolution - a progressive motion of a body around a center or axis, a turn or rotation of the body as a whole.

Rolling - traveling by means of revolving (turning over and over) while supporting (lying, etc.) on a surface.

Rotating - the turning as a unit of a segment of the body by means of flexibility in an adjoining segment, e.g. the head rotating through flexibility in the neck. (Compare with Twisting.)

Sagittal - in movement, reference to the forward-backward plane and any plane parallel thereto. Anatomically this term refers to the suture between the parietal bones of the skull, hence the plane of the body in which the above suture lies.

Satellite Center - the center point of a system of directions (cross of axes) centered at an extremity of the body or at the center point of the path of a gesture.

Shifting - displacement (as far as is physically possible) of a part of the body on a straight path. In a shift both upper and lower ends of the area in question move equally in the same direction.

Skew Curve - a space curve (three-dimensional curve) as opposed to a plane curve (two-dimensional curve).

Sliding - traveling by means of moving smoothly across a slippery surface as in skating or skiing.

Spring - term used for jumps when the specific form of aerial step need not or cannot be stated. A spring is the action of rising from the ground, the subsequent landing being taken for granted. (See Jumps, Aerial Steps.)

Stability - the state of being when the body is in balance.

Staccato - separated, disconnected, cut short or apart in performing.

Stance - the support of the body (usually the feet or one foot) which retains the previously established front when a twist occurs in the rest of the body.

Standard Directions - directions described according to the Standard Cross of Axes.

Structural - description of a movement or the notation of a movement in which the elements of timing, space, and the part of the body used are clearly defined.

Style - distinctive or characteristic mode of presentation, construction, or execution of patterns of movement.

Systems of Reference - established distinctions in determining to what a direction symbol refers, i.e. how a stated direction is to be interpreted.

Ternary - consisting of three parts. In skips and gallops, the rhythmical arrangement of the three part action into a time division of three equal parts.

Three-dimensional - the use of more than two directions in movement, movement filling or enclosing an imaginary sphere.

Two-dimensional - movement using two directions at the same time or movement on a plane (describing a two-dimensional surface).

Twisting - a turning of a part of the body in which the free end turns (rotates) farther than the base (the point of attachment to the body, to the floor, or to a person or object). The resulting movement produces a spiral within the part specified. (Compare with Rotating.)

"u" - the name of the fourth part of a beat of music divided into four.

Undeviating Aim - a movement which continues on a beeline toward a specified point regardless of other simultaneous and influencing actions.

Upper Body - term referring not to a specific part of the body but to a use of the upper torso which may involve only a shoulder section (upper dorsal vertebrae), the chest, or the whole of the movable spine down to the lumbar region.

"y" - the name of the second part of a beat of music divided into four.

Glossary of Symbols

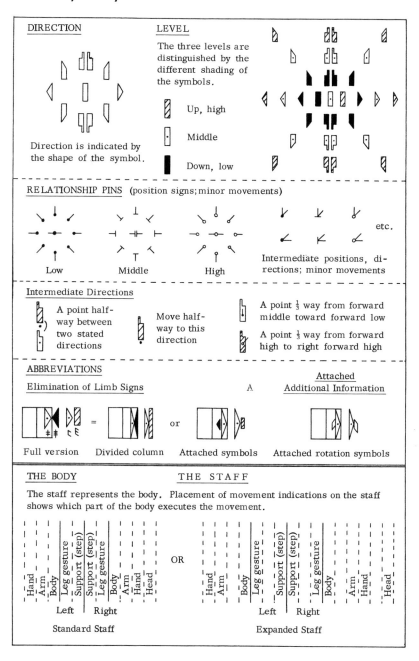

DIRECTION

Direction is indicated by the shape of the symbol.

LEVEL

The three levels are distinguished by the different shading of the symbols.

Up, high

Middle

Down, low

RELATIONSHIP PINS (position signs; minor movements)

Low   Middle   High

etc.

Intermediate positions, directions; minor movements

Intermediate Directions

A point half-way between two stated directions

Move half-way to this direction

A point ⅓ way from forward middle toward forward low

A point ⅓ way from forward high to right forward high

ABBREVIATIONS

Elimination of Limb Signs

A

Attached
Additional Information

= or

Full version   Divided column   Attached symbols   Attached rotation symbols

THE BODY   **THE STAFF**

The staff represents the body. Placement of movement indications on the staff shows which part of the body executes the movement.

OR

Hand | Arm | Body | Leg gesture | Support (step) | Support (step) | Leg gesture | Body | Arm | Hand | Head

Left | Right

Standard Staff

Hand | Arm | Body | Leg gesture | Support (step) | Support (step) | Leg gesture | Body | Arm | Hand | Head

Left | Right

Expanded Staff

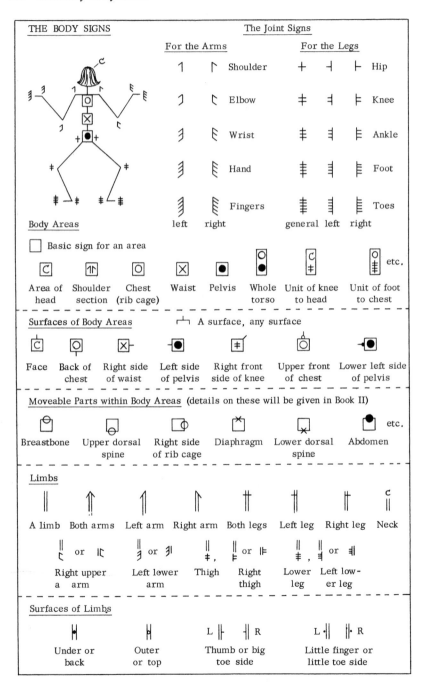

THE BODY SIGNS   The Joint Signs

For the Arms   For the Legs

Shoulder   Hip

Elbow   Knee

Wrist   Ankle

Hand   Foot

Fingers   Toes

left   right   general left right

Body Areas

Basic sign for an area

Area of   Shoulder   Chest   Waist   Pelvis   Whole   Unit of knee   Unit of foot
head   section   (rib cage)   torso   to head   to chest

Surfaces of Body Areas   A surface, any surface

Face   Back of   Right side   Left side   Right front   Upper front   Lower left side
        chest   of waist   of pelvis   side of knee   of chest   of pelvis

Moveable Parts within Body Areas (details on these will be given in Book II)

Breastbone   Upper dorsal   Right side   Diaphragm   Lower dorsal   Abdomen   etc.
             spine   of rib cage   spine

Limbs

A limb   Both arms   Left arm   Right arm   Both legs   Left leg   Right leg   Neck

Right upper   Left lower   Thigh   Right   Lower   Left low-
a   arm   arm   thigh   leg   er leg

Surfaces of Limbs

Under or   Outer   Thumb or big   Little finger or
back   or top   toe side   little toe side

Area, Surfaces and Edges of Hands and Feet

Area of hand or foot	Palm, sole of foot	Back of hand, top of foot	Thumb or big toe edge	Little finger or little toe edge	Tip of fingers, tip of toes

L.⌐ ⌐R.   L.⌐ ⌐R.

Area of base of hand or foot	Under side, sole of heel	Upper side, instep	Thumb or big toe edge	Little finger or little toe edge	Tip of heel

L.⌐ ⌐R.   L.⌐ ⌐R.

Specifying area of foot, left or right	Specifying area of hand, left or right	Specifying area of base of foot	Specifying area of base of hand

Specific Fingers

Thumbs	Index fingers	Middle fingers	Ring fingers	Little fingers

Parts of the Fingers

Right middle finger	Base of knuckle of right middle finger	Middle knuckle of middle finger	Last knuckle of middle finger	Tip of right middle finger

Limb of right middle finger	Base segment	Under side of middle segment	Top, nail side of last segment	etc.

Specific Toes and Parts Thereof

Big toes	2nd toes	etc.	Pad of big toe	Nail of little toe	etc.

Parts Above and Below Joints

Above R elbow	Below L knee	Above R ankle (cou de pied)

Parts of the Head

(Pictorial signs have been used in scores when detailed signs were not known.)

Simple Pictorial signs

Nose	Mouth	Tongue	Ears	Eyes

Detailed Signs (the whole range will be given in Book II)

Top of head	Forehead	Nose	Chin	Throat

Right ear	Left cheek	Mouth	Eyes	Right eyeball

Left ear	Tongue	Teeth	Beard	Right eyebrow	etc.

SIGN FOR UPPER BODY MOVEMENT

Both sides	Right side	Left side

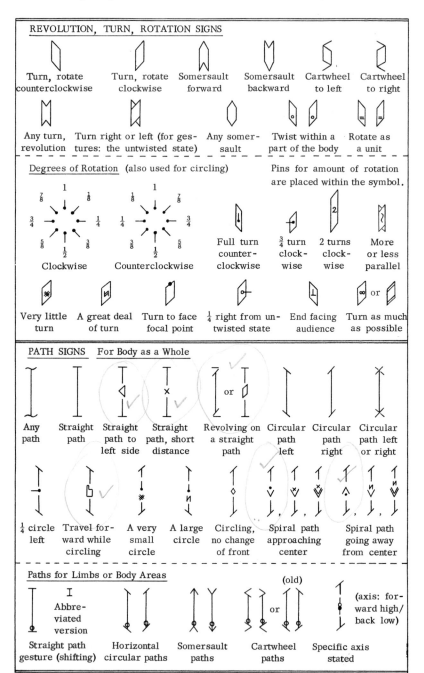

REVOLUTION, TURN, ROTATION SIGNS

Turn, rotate counterclockwise   Turn, rotate clockwise   Somersault forward   Somersault backward   Cartwheel to left   Cartwheel to right

Any turn, revolution   Turn right or left (for gestures: the untwisted state)   Any somersault   Twist within a part of the body   Rotate as a unit

Degrees of Rotation (also used for circling)   Pins for amount of rotation are placed within the symbol.

Clockwise   Counterclockwise

Full turn counterclockwise $\frac{3}{4}$ turn clockwise   2 turns clockwise   More or less parallel

Very little turn   A great deal of turn   Turn to face focal point $\frac{1}{4}$ right from untwisted state   End facing audience   Turn as much as possible

PATH SIGNS   For Body as a Whole

Any path   Straight path   Straight path to left side   Straight path, short distance   Revolving on a straight path   Circular path left   Circular path right   Circular path left or right

$\frac{1}{4}$ circle left   Travel forward while circling   A very small circle   A large circle   Circling, no change of front   Spiral path approaching center   Spiral path going away from center

Paths for Limbs or Body Areas   (old)

Straight path gesture (shifting)   Abbreviated version   Horizontal circular paths   Somersault paths   Cartwheel paths   Specific axis stated   (axis: forward high/ back low)

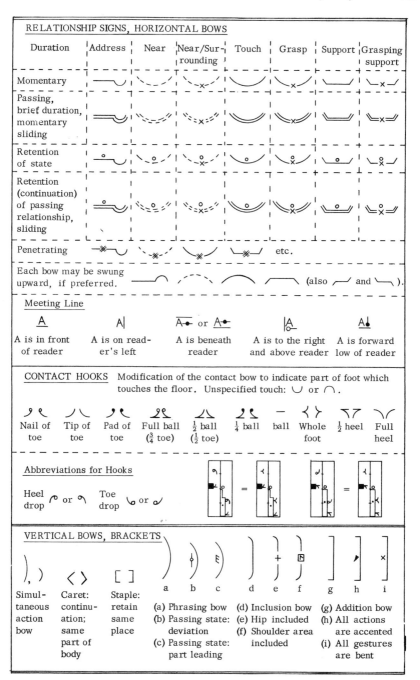

RELATIONSHIP SIGNS, HORIZONTAL BOWS

Duration	Address	Near	Near/Sur-rounding	Touch	Grasp	Support	Grasping support
Momentary							
Passing, brief duration, momentary sliding							
Retention of state							
Retention (continuation) of passing relationship, sliding							
Penetrating					etc.		

Each bow may be swung upward, if preferred.   (also   and   ).

Meeting Line

A   A| A̅• or A• |A   A↓

A is in front   A is on read-   A is beneath   A is to the right   A is forward
 of reader   er's left   reader   and above reader   low of reader

---

CONTACT HOOKS   Modification of the contact bow to indicate part of foot which touches the floor. Unspecified touch: ∪ or ∩.

Nail of | Tip of | Pad of | Full ball | ½ ball | ¼ ball | ball | Whole | ½ heel | Full
toe | toe | toe | ($\frac{3}{4}$ toe) | ($\frac{1}{2}$ toe) | | | foot | | heel

---

Abbreviations for Hooks

Heel drop ⌐ or ⌐   Toe drop ↳ or ↲

=   =

VERTICAL BOWS, BRACKETS

),)   < >   [ ]

a   b   c   d   e   f   g   h   i

Simul-   Caret: Staple:
taneous   continu-   retain
action   ation;   same
bow   same   place
 | part of |
 | body |

(a) Phrasing bow   (d) Inclusion bow   (g) Addition bow
(b) Passing state: (e) Hip included   (h) All actions
   deviation   (f) Shoulder area   are accented
(c) Passing state: included   (i) All gestures
   part leading   are bent

SPACE MEASUREMENT SIGNS Contraction and Extension

Small Distance, Shortened, Contracted   Large Distance, Stretched, Extended

✕ - 1 degree, small (rounded)   ⋀ - 1 degree, long (limb straight)

✕̇ - 2 degrees   ⋀̇ - 2 degrees (limb extra stretched)

✕̣ - 3 degrees (right angle)   ⋀. - 3 degrees

✖ - 4 degrees, very small (bent)   ⋀ - 4 degrees, very long

✖̇ - 5 degrees   ⋀ - 5 degrees

✖̣ - 6 degrees (totally flexed)   ⋀̣ - 6 degrees   ⫽ - 7 degrees

---

Specific Contractions and Extensions	✕	ⱀ	⋀̄	⋀ǀ etc.
	Contract over the front	Contract over the right front	Extend over the back	Extend over the left side

---

Folding (Bending)

⩗ ⩗̇ ⩗̣ ⩘ ⩘̇ ⩘̣   ⩗·   ⩗ ⤙ ⪦ ⤚ ⪧ etc.
1. 2. 3. 4. 5. 6.   F. RFD. R. RBD. B.
The 6 degrees of folding (bending)   Unspecified   The different physical directions
                                       folding   into which folding can occur.

Unfolding

⩑ ⩑̇ ⩑̣ ⩓ ⩓̇ ⩓̣   ⩑·   ⩑ ⤞ ⪤ ⤝ ⪥ etc.
1. 2. 3. 4. 5. 6.   F. RFD. R. RBD. B.
The 6 degrees of unfolding   Unspecified   The different physical directions
                                       unfolding   into which unfolding can occur.

Three-Dimensional Contraction and Extension

✳ , ✴ , ⩑⟋ , ⩑⟋   All degrees are possible: ✳   ✴ etc.

Two-Dimensional Contraction and Extension

Along longitudinal axis: ✕ , ✖ etc.   ⋀ , ⋀ etc.

Along lateral axis: △ △̈ △̣ ⏜ ⏜̈ ⏜̣   ⏝ ⏝̈ ⏝̣ ⏡ ⏡̈ ⏡̣
                     Joining, closing, adducting   Spreading, separating, abducting

---

Reference to Body		Reference to Space	
Placed in a circle, signs refer to body aspects	⊗ Ⓜ	Placed in a diamond, signs refer to spatial aspects	◈ ◈

Space Measurement - Specific Distance

   ⟦3⟧ = 3 step lengths   ⟦6⟧ = 6 step lengths

SUCCESSIONS, SEQUENTIAL DEVELOPMENTS

        ∨   ∧   ⋁   ⋀

An outward sequence,   An inward sequence,   Outward   Inward
     succession   succession   body wave   body wave

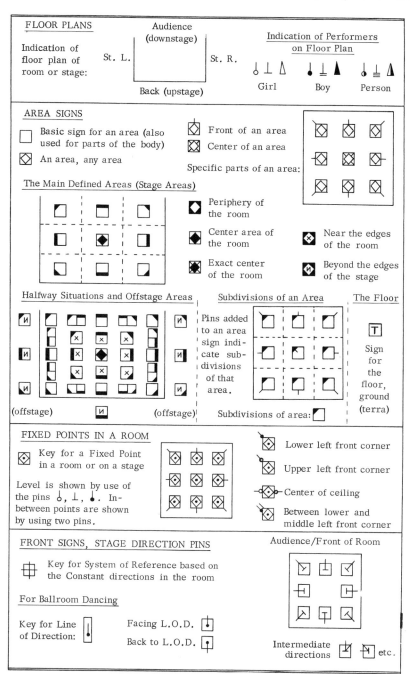

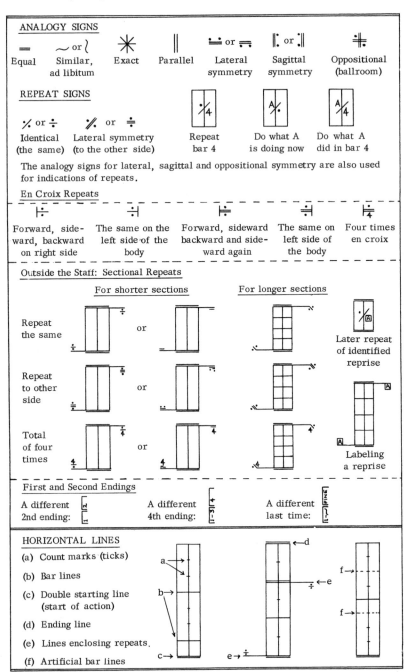

ANALOGY SIGNS

Equal	Similar, ad libitum	Exact	Parallel	Lateral symmetry	Sagittal symmetry	Oppositional (ballroom)

REPEAT SIGNS

Identical (the same)   Lateral symmetry (to the other side)   Repeat bar 4   Do what A is doing now   Do what A did in bar 4

The analogy signs for lateral, sagittal and oppositional symmetry are also used for indications of repeats.

En Croix Repeats

Forward, side-ward, backward on right side   The same on the left side of the body   Forward, sideward backward and side-ward again   The same on left side of the body   Four times en croix

Outside the Staff: Sectional Repeats

For shorter sections   For longer sections

Repeat the same   or   Later repeat of identified reprise

Repeat to other side   or

Total of four times   or   Labeling a reprise

First and Second Endings

A different 2nd ending: A different 4th ending: A different last time:

HORIZONTAL LINES

(a) Count marks (ticks)

(b) Bar lines

(c) Double starting line (start of action)

(d) Ending line

(e) Lines enclosing repeats.

(f) Artificial bar lines

GROUP NOTATION (Note: some indications given here may be met in scores but are not explained in this book. They will be dealt with in Book II.)

Formations: General Group Shapes

Pictorial indication of solid group shapes   Linear formations

Formations, Arrangements

Side by side	One in front of the other	Circle facing in	(pictorial indication)

Any number of people one behind the other, left side to the center, the front person facing the audience, the back person facing upstage, i.e. a semi-circle.

Pre-Staff Signs

A girl   A boy   A couple   Each one   Each girl   Each couple

Use of Numbers

2 — 2nd girl   4 — 4 men   8 — 8 trios   3 — Each 3 girls

6 people side by side facing front 4 step lengths from the front of the stage

5 men in a file one behind the other, each 3 step lengths apart

Plain number = number of person

Encircled number = number of people, couples, etc.

Double encircled number = each set of stated number of performers

Identification of Members of a Group

Person in front, front of group

Center person, center of group

Person on right

Indication of Person Leading

Path led by person in front

Path led by B

Types of Circling for a Group

Individual circling (each on own path)   Wheeling   Shifting the group (circling as a unit around the center)   Whirling: wheeling in which each member covers the same distance on his own track

Canon Staff (placed to the right of the movement staff)

exit
enter
Reverting canon   Synchronized canon   Simultaneous canon

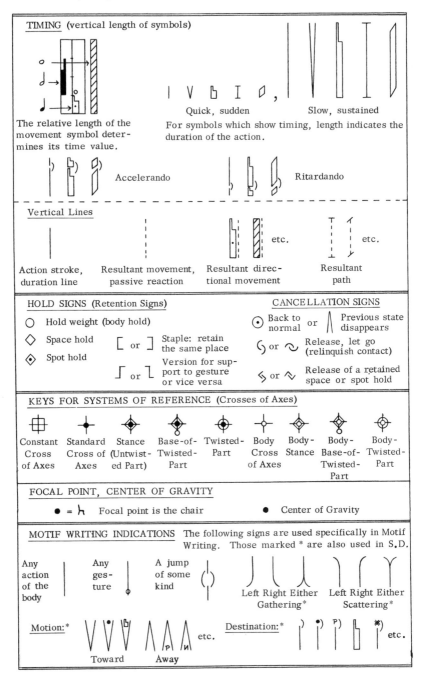

TIMING (vertical length of symbols)

Quick, sudden   Slow, sustained

The relative length of the movement symbol determines its time value.

For symbols which show timing, length indicates the duration of the action.

Accelerando   Ritardando

Vertical Lines

Action stroke,   Resultant movement,   Resultant direc-   Resultant
duration line   passive reaction   tional movement   path

HOLD SIGNS (Retention Signs)   CANCELLATION SIGNS

○   Hold weight (body hold)   Back to   or   Previous state
                                            normal   disappears
◇   Space hold   [or]   Staple: retain
                                  the same place   ⟋ or ⟍   Release, let go
◈   Spot hold   (relinquish contact)
                         ⌐ or ⌐   Version for sup-
                                  port to gesture   ⟋ or ⟍   Release of a retained
                                  or vice versa   space or spot hold

KEYS FOR SYSTEMS OF REFERENCE (Crosses of Axes)

Constant   Standard   Stance   Base-of-   Twisted-   Body   Body-   Body-   Body-
Cross   Cross of   (Untwist- Twisted-   Part   Cross   Stance   Base-of-   Twisted-
of Axes   Axes   ed Part) Part   of Axes   Twisted-   Part
                                                                           Part

FOCAL POINT, CENTER OF GRAVITY

● = ⌐   Focal point is the chair   ●   Center of Gravity

MOTIF WRITING INDICATIONS   The following signs are used specifically in Motif
                            Writing. Those marked * are also used in S.D.

Any   Any   A jump
action   ges-   of some
of the   ture   kind
body   Left Right Either   Left Right Either
                                    Gathering*   Scattering*

Motion:*   etc.   Destination:*   etc.

        Toward   Away

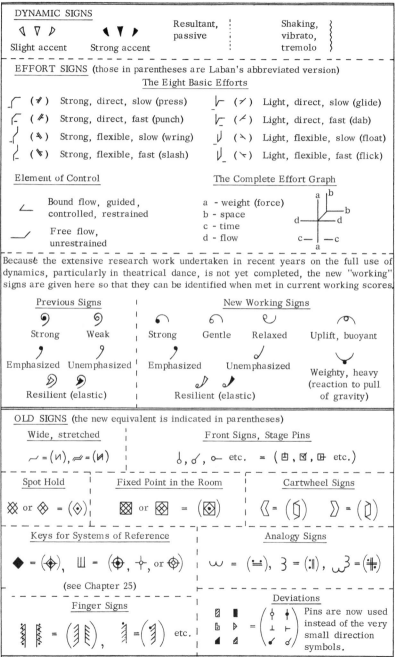

DYNAMIC SIGNS

◁ ▽ ▷   ◀ ▼ ▶   Resultant,   Shaking,
Slight accent   Strong accent   passive   vibrato,
                                                     tremolo

EFFORT SIGNS (those in parentheses are Laban's abbreviated version)

The Eight Basic Efforts

⌐ (⸍) Strong, direct, slow (press)   ⌐ (⸍) Light, direct, slow (glide)
⌐ (⸍) Strong, direct, fast (punch)   ⌐ (⸍) Light, direct, fast (dab)
⌡ (⸜) Strong, flexible, slow (wring)   ⌡ (⸜) Light, flexible, slow (float)
⌡ (⸜) Strong, flexible, fast (slash)   ⌡ (⸜) Light, flexible, fast (flick)

Element of Control   The Complete Effort Graph

∠   Bound flow, guided,   a - weight (force)
    controlled, restrained   b - space
                                 c - time
∕   Free flow,   d - flow
    unrestrained

Because the extensive research work undertaken in recent years on the full use of dynamics, particularly in theatrical dance, is not yet completed, the new "working" signs are given here so that they can be identified when met in current working scores.

Previous Signs   New Working Signs

Strong   Weak   Strong   Gentle   Relaxed   Uplift, buoyant

Emphasized Unemphasized   Emphasized   Unemphasized

Resilient (elastic)   Resilient (elastic)   Weighty, heavy
                                                         (reaction to pull
                                                         of gravity)

OLD SIGNS (the new equivalent is indicated in parentheses)

Wide, stretched   Front Signs, Stage Pins

Spot Hold   Fixed Point in the Room   Cartwheel Signs

Keys for Systems of Reference   Analogy Signs

(see Chapter 25)

Finger Signs   Deviations

                                           Pins are now used
                                           instead of the very
                                           small direction
                                           symbols.

Index

516   Index